Dom Moraes (1938–2004), poet, novelist and columnist, is seen as a foundational figure in Indian English Literature. In 1958, at the age of twenty, he won the prestigious Hawthornden Prize for his first volume of verse, *A Beginning*, going on to publish more than thirty books of prose and poetry. He was awarded the Sahitya Akademi Award for English in 1994. He has won awards for journalism and poetry in England, America, and India. He also wrote a large number of film scripts for BBC and ITV, covering various countries such as India, Israel, Cuba, and Africa.

Also by Dom Moraes

Green is the Grass: Essays on Cricket (1951)

A Beginning: Poems (1957)

Poems (1960)

Gone Away: An Indian Journey (1960)

John Nobody: Poems (1965)

Mrs Gandhi: A Biography (1980)

Absences: Poems (1983)

Collected Poems: 1957–1987 (1987)

Serendip (1990)

My Son's Father: An Autobiography

Out of God's Oven: Travels in a Fractured Land, co-authored with Sarayu Srivatsa (2002)

The Long Strider: How Thomas Coryate Walked from England to India in the Year 1613, co-authored with Sarayu Srivatsa (2003)

A Variety of Absences: The Collected Memoirs of Dom Moraes (2003)

Selected Poems, Ed. Ranjit Hoskote (2012)

NEVER AT HOME
An Autobiography

DOM MORAES

SPEAKING TIGER

SPEAKING TIGER BOOKS LLP
4381/4, Ansari Road, Daryaganj
New Delhi 110002

First published in Viking by Penguin Books India 1992
This edition published in India by Speaking Tiger in paperback 2020

ISBN: 978-93-89231-97-7
eISBN: 978-93-89231-98-4

10 9 8 7 6 5 4 3 2 1

Typeset in Adobe Garamond Pro by Jojy Philip, New Delhi
Printed at Chaman Enterprises, New Delhi

Absorbed with each other's flesh
In the tumbled beds of our youth,
We had conversations with children
Not born, but already named.
Those faculties, now disrupted,
Shed selves, must exist somewhere,
As they did when our summer ended:
Leela-Claire, and the first death.
Mark, cold on a hospital tray
At five months; I was away then
With tribesmen in bronze forests.
We became our children, my wife.
Now, left alone with each other,
As we were in four continents,
At the turn of your classic head,
At your private smile, the beacon
You beckon with, I recall them.
We may travel there once more.
We shall leave at the proper time,
As a couple, without complaint,
With a destination in common,
And some regrets and memories.
We shall leave in ways we believed
Impossible in our youth,
A little tired, but in the end
Not unhappy to have lived.

1

My wife Leela and I returned to India towards the end of 1974. I had not lived in the country for more than twenty years. I was afraid of it for many reasons, one of which was that my mother was still alive in it. The grotesque, insane figure that had dominated my childhood had ridden my nightmares for years. To come back to India and to have, at least occasionally, to confront the reality, was a terrifying prospect. Ironically, I had written a poem about her, at the end of the 1960s, before I knew that I would ever live in any other place except England. It took the form of a letter addressed to her; and this was the second part.

> Your eyes are like mine.
> When I last looked in them
> I saw my whole country,
> A defeated dream
> Hiding itself in prayers,
> A population of corpses,
> Of burnt bodies that cluttered
> The slow, deep rivers, of
> Bodies stowed into earth
> Quickly before they stank
> Or cooked by the sun for vultures
> On a marble tower.
> You pray, you do not notice

The corpses around you.
Sorrow has stopped your eye.
Your dream is desolate.
It calls me every day
But I cannot enter it.
You know I will not return.
Forgive me my trespasses.

I had returned to India, if not precisely to her. Two years after I returned, I committed her to a lunatic asylum, as my father had done before me. In 1976, I felt once more the great hurt and guilt which must have enveloped my father in 1954. My physical nausea at the sight of her, my inability to speak to her, increased my own hatred of myself; but the sorrow she already bore without her at the loss of her husband, through circumstances, and then through his death, must have been augmented by the loss of her only child. My infrequent visits to her usually concluded in my making hasty excuses and rushing out of her cottage at the National Institute of Mental Health and Neurosciences (NIMHANS) at Bangalore. I usually left because I wanted to vomit.

She thought that she was herself a doctor, doing research at NIMHANS. She wrote a number of papers on what she considered to be her research. I remember one in particular in which she linked the Hindu goddess Kali with the Virgin Mary, with whom, like Mrs Gandhi, she appeared to be obsessed. She also said in this essay that Joan of Arc was a direct ancestor of the Nehru family—hence of Mrs Gandhi herself— and of my wife Leela. I should have felt some kind of pity when I read these papers, but I felt only further nausea and horror at these further proofs of her insanity. It was as though I was suffering from acute withdrawal symptoms in an attempt to throw off an addiction.

For whatever I did or said or even wrote during my years after I first left India, the idea of my mother always abraded my mind and was the albatross round my neck, the monkey on my back.

One day at the end of 1989, I was telephoned by a friend from Bangalore. He told me he had been telephoned by the NIMHANS doctors who said that my mother had died that morning. She had been very ill for some days and had been calling for me; but for some reason the doctors had not telephoned me then. They did not dare to do so now. Hence a message at third-hand. 'My car will meet you at the airport,' my friend said.

It met me, but only at dusk, since the only flight I could catch that day landed then. I went to the hospital. Nobody responsible appeared to be present. The only thing the doctor on duty could tell me was that her body was in the morgue, to which he had no key. I could collect it in the morning, he said. It was by now completely dark, but there was a full moon. In silhouette against the sky, some distance from the main offices, I could see her cottage, its windows unlit. A weeping woman, one of her attendants for many years, came and touched my feet, according to Indian custom. It isn't a custom I much like; I pulled her to her feet, and she launched into a monologue in the local language, which I couldn't understand. The doctor said, 'She is asking why you couldn't come sooner, when your mother was begging for you.' I did not reply.

From the dormitories and cells in the grounds of the asylum, I could hear the yelping and manic exclamations of those who had been fellow-patients of my mother, except that they hadn't been so well off. Once, in a forest in Madhya Pradesh, I had heard the same kind of sound from dusk till dawn. A friend, who was with me, said this was due to wolves, which I didn't believe. At any rate they came from creatures of the darkness. My mother had been the favoured child of a rich and Westernized family; she had married a promising young man, out of love, rare in India at that time; she had borne him a son; she had been a pampered socialite, also a good and efficient doctor. Yet she had spent almost twenty years of her life in these environs, listening to these sounds. It occurred to me that I had been rather frightened when I first heard the sounds from the dark forest.

In the morning, when I went to collect her body, I was taken to the mortuary. My mother had by this time been dead more than thirty hours in the Indian heat, and all the air conditioners in the morgue had been out of operation during half this time. The small room was full of an odour. I had last smelt it in Bangladesh and Vietnam. Moreover, her stomach had bloated obscenely. She seemed pregnant once more as she had not been for fifty years. Being in the womb may become obsessive, and colour all one's life. As we took the corpse out of the morgue and to the crematorium, the undertaker's men holding handkerchiefs to their noses, it struck me that all this might represent for me the shedding of an obsession, and some kind of belated rebirth.

As a very young man, I often thought and wrote about death. The death I wrote about was a romantic abstraction, and I knew nothing about its implications in reality. I only collided with these when I saw real death in war, more importantly when I heard of the deaths of friends like James Cameron, and most importantly, of my father. But I think it is only when both your parents are dead, whatever your relationships with them may have been, that the reality, the mystery, and the inevitability of death comes to you fully.

I would never have dreamt that my mother's death would have affected me like this. I had always assumed that it would be a relief to everyone, herself included. But the feeling I now had, of my life having fallen away from me in a gradual but irreversible series of years, made me think of the good days gone, when I had first walked away from my parents into the world beyond, and come to know it, love it, and fear it, all at once.

In 1957, I was studying English Literature at Jesus College in Oxford. That is, I was supposed to be studying it, but my whole intention in life was to write poetry; and it had been so ever since I was fifteen, a boy in Bombay. My father was, in 1957, the Editor of the *Times of India,* the largest and most famous

English language newspaper in the country. My parents spoke no language but English, which had also been the only language of their parents. A huge historical accident had caused this, the colonization of India by the British. In 1953, when I was fifteen, W.H. Auden and Stephen Spender came to Bombay and appeared to like my verse; Spender published it in *Encounter,* of which he was then the Editor. Four years later, as I was strolling down the High in Oxford, Lord David Cecil strolled towards me from the opposite direction. As usual, in summer, he wore a white suit and a straw boater with a New College ribbon fluttering from the brim, almost parallel with his long and kindly nose. I knew him, but not very well. He said, 'A word, dear boy,' and whispered on, 'your first book,' (which I had recently published), 'has won the Hawthornden Prize. Don't tell anyone, will you?'

Then came the announcement, the presentation ceremony in London, the flags, the trumpets, the television appearances, and the offers from newspapers to write for them. Unluckily, I felt I had no ability to write prose, and I didn't want to. My next two years at Oxford were marked by a discovery: how many girls, and indeed women, wanted to sleep with a young poet. I hardly did any study of English Literature at all.

The summer of 1959 brought my examinations, which in some manner I passed. That was a summer of brilliant sunshine, the torpid waters of the Isis covered with punts and canoes in which young women of great beauty always seemed to be lying, their skirts spread out under them like the open and scented calyxes of flowers. The principal of my college, Mr Christie, asked me to his rooms at end of term to say goodbye.

He was a tall and silver-haired scholar, whose blue eyes had surveyed my activities, often very dubiously, throughout my three years. During this period I had developed an affection for him, and he, I think, a concern about me. We sat in his study, his eyes on me, and he offered me his best sherry and his thoughts about my future. 'What will you do?' he inquired. 'You must decide on some kind of career. My dear chap, poetry in itself cannot sustain you. Look at Keats, I urge you. Look at Shelley.'

Had I said I would return to India, his anxieties might have been set at rest; for both he and I knew that if I did, there would be no problem about a career. In those days anyone who was born in India and came back to it from Oxford was assured of one; he could almost choose the one he preferred. But Mr Christie knew, and I knew, that I did not want to go back; and in this one, at least, of my thoughts, he concurred, 'You'd be lost there, dear fellow,' he said, 'lost,' his long, thin fingers tapping on the arm of his chair. 'They wouldn't understand you. Nor, I fear, would you understand them. The other Indian students who have been at this college....' He sighed deeply.

I had made, after the book, the accompanying reviews and the Hawthornden Prize, a small niche in English literary circles, which at the time seemed secure. I had never expected to achieve the ambition of my adolescence in so short a time. Most of my youthful heroes, Eliot, Auden, Spender, Day Lewis, MacNeice, George Barker, were either people I knew, or my friends. To go back to India would be to destroy all this. Also, in 1959, I was in love, though not so much with a particular woman as with my idea of her. I had come a long way from where I started, and I didn't want to recede from this position.

However, there was Mr Christie in his sunlit study, tapping his fingers on the velvet arm of his chair, occasionally sipping sherry, tapping his fingers some more, staring out over the quad, and thinking. 'Journalism would be an honourable profession,' he said, 'if it were not for the people who practise it. I don't mean people like your father, oh no, not at all. But presumably you read the daily papers.... Still, it could be a way to make money. Goodbye, my dear boy. You must come back soon and dine at High Table. The amount of fines we levied on you for your absences without leave over the years have built up to a tidy sum. We've been able to lay in a supply of excellent port.'

I went to London, got a flat, and worried about my inability to write prose. I had enough left of my allowance to enable me to survive for a couple of months. Then, and in the curious way things happen, Mr Christie answered his own question. He telephoned me one afternoon and said, 'My dear fellow, you are well, I trust? You aren't contemplating any drastic step? Tell me, dear boy, don't hesitate. I never thought that you were so lonely and so sad.'

The cause of all this was rather complicated. Before I finally left Oxford, I had made *some* attempts to write prose. One of these pieces was supposed to be a letter written from Rimbaud in Africa to his mother, declaring his detestation for life and his desire for death. I had forgotten it in a drawer, where my scout had found it. Alarmed at its contents, he had passed it on to Mr Christie, who was even more alarmed. The piece had not been addressed to anybody, though supposed to be a letter; Mr Christie believed it to be a *cri de coeur* from me to him. As he said, 'I was extremely puzzled by your frequent references to the Sahara desert, but I take these to be symbolic, dear chap, of your state of mind. After all, you are a poet.'

It took me some time to reassure him; having done so, I considered this telephone call. Mr Christie, a professional academic, might not have been entirely *aufait* with reality, but he was also very intelligent, and in his own way highly sophisticated. If a random piece of my prose could convince him that it meant what it said, perhaps I could, after all, write the stuff. The person I was in love with said, 'But whoever told you that you couldn't?' My writer friends said, 'You *have* been a bloody fool, haven't you? It's all been inside your head. Just get it out, and phone up the editors.'

I did. Those who had already asked me to write for them accepted my ideas. I began to write features and reviews for the Sunday papers. This brought me an income, but it was not a considerable one. Literary agents approached me. I became the client of one of them, and he suggested that I write a travel book. I rang up a friend of mine, a publisher, also a poet, James Michie, and asked him if he was amenable. Over lunch at Bertorelli's in Soho he said, 'If you want to write a travel book, you have to travel somewhere.'

I said, 'Well, I thought, possibly Africa.' James stared at me in amazement.

'Who do you think you are, bloody Hemingway?' he inquired, a bit rudely I thought. 'I can't see you shooting bloody elephants in the desert, or wherever they live. And besides, you know damn-all about Africa, and don't try to tell me you do. India for you, mate.'

It was all right by me; because it would only be a temporary visit. I would not be surrendering myself to the country once more. I did not tell James that I knew little more of India than I did of Africa. Great sums of money rolled my way.

One problem remained, and that was my mother. My father and she had been married almost immediately after my father came back from Oxford and Lincoln's Inn. He had been seven years away from India. A year later I was born. When the Second World War moved from Europe to the East, my father was sent by his employers, the *Times of India,* to the Burma and China fronts. He was the first Indian war correspondent. It was a long absence, and towards the end of it my mother had a nervous breakdown. I was about seven when she went into a kind of fugue syndrome which later turned into manic depression. Immediately before I left for England in 1954, she went into a phase of extreme violence, and had had to be committed to a mental home. Most of my childhood and adolescence had been spent with her. Her alternate waves of violence and depression had swept over me all those years. During this time my father had had to shield me as best he could.

I carried scars from those years which were not only mental but physical. The back of my right hand still bears cigarette burns inflicted by my mother. I did not want to see her. One of the reasons I had travelled seven thousand miles was to obviate the possibility of seeing her. Before I left India, I felt nauseated, and went into a cold sweat every time I saw her. One of my father's closest friends, an Oxford contemporary of his, the diplomat Rashid Ali Baig, once remarked to me, 'I think your father did many extraordinary things in his life, but the most extraordinary was to bring you up relatively sane.'

I arrived in Bombay towards the end of the monsoon. This had always been one of my favourite seasons as an adolescent, but I now found myself looking at it in a different way. It made a mess of the roads, and the city seemed to founder under it. I realized with a certain wonder that I was seeing it as a foreigner; that I was seeing it as a foreign city, though it was less than five years since I had lived there. My encounters with people I had previously known had a certain dreamlike quality: their personalities, familiar before, now seemed seen through a kind of mist. I was treated with some awe, because I had won the Hawthornden. I assumed a posture of arrogance, and secretly felt a little ashamed. The newspapers spoke of the book I had come to write.

Actually, I hadn't planned this book at all; the thought of starting on it slightly terrified me. I didn't know where or how to start: I had never tried anything like this before. In these circumstances, as often in the past, I consulted my father. He said, 'I imagine you want to write this book as an outsider looking in. I couldn't do that myself, about India. The only way I can help is by imagining that *you* are an outsider.' There was a slight double edge to this remark, untypical of him. But then he was entitled to it.

In Delhi I met Jawaharlal Nehru, then nearly seventy. He wore a red rose in his buttonhole, and a white Gandhi cap, under which his features were beautiful and sensitive. When he took the cap off, however, a grotesque element entered his appearance; he then resembled a bald schoolboy. He was probably the most eminent person I had yet met, but my nervousness at the interview wasn't due to this. I had never interviewed anyone before, and he was anything but the ideal interviewee. When asked a question, he allowed a prolonged silence to elapse before he replied, and often, even then, his reply was no more than a monosyllable. But after the interview he summoned me for an informal meeting.

He reminisced about his student days in England. From his tone of voice, they seemed to have been the happiest of his life. 'Had I not been caught up in politics,' he said, 'I would have been a writer.' He had apparently read my poems. 'Why don't you come back to India?' he asked. 'We need people like you here.' I did not feel complimented; indeed, I felt slightly insulted. It was indicative of my attitudes at the time. I said I was a writer in English; what would I do in India? Coming back would be a terrible sacrifice. He looked at me, an awesomely sad look, and said, 'When I came back from England, don't you think *I* made a sacrifice?' I felt very ashamed of myself.

I also interviewed the Dalai Lama, who had fled from Tibet the previous year. He was then only twenty-four, a stalwart young man with rosy cheeks and what seemed a permanent smile. From time to time he laughed heartily. He asked me to describe Oxford, and said that he might send some of his young men there. From his general air, he seemed to want to go there himself. At that time the Khamba tribesmen were still fighting the Chinese in the high valleys of Tibet; when he spoke of their hopeless resistance, he looked not exactly sad, but pensive. Yet I formed the impression that he did not perceive the Tibetan situation to be hopeless; that he felt that an appeal to the outside world might bring assistance and tilt the military situation in favour of the Tibetans. In this he was mistaken, but he did not yet know it.

So he was still full of laughter. His entourage of black-robed senior monks had told me all the forms of protocol I should observe. I was supposed to sit at some distance from him; I was not to touch him; when I left I was not to turn my back on him.

I arrived and, as instructed, presented the Dalai Lama with a silk scarf. He handed it back. So far all was according to protocol. He indicated a sofa and we sat down at opposite ends. As he got more interested in the conversation, he moved towards me, and, each time he wanted to emphasize a point, punched my arm. The interpreter looked horrified; in the doorway a senior monk wagged an angry head. But I didn't see what I could do. I was not touching the Dalai Lama; he was touching me. The interview over, I tried to shuffle backwards to the door. He laughed, took me by the shoulders, turned me round, and sent me on my way with a friendly push.

An Oxford friend, the blind writer Ved Mehta, was then in Delhi. We flew to Kathmandu, and spent a week there. We were on our way to the airport when we received a message. The Nepali poet, L.P. Devkota, was dying of terminal cancer. According to Nepalese tradition, he had been removed from hospital and placed beside the burning ghats. When we arrived, assorted corpses were burning on stone platforms in the polluted river. Devkota was lying in what looked like a stone bus-shelter, some distance off, attended only by his wife.

She had a thermos full of bits of ice, which she pressed, from time to time, into his mouth. He had very fine eyes, but was unimaginably thin, and seemed delirious. He moaned continually. The smoke and smell of the burning corpses rose off the river. Finally he became coherent and asked us to hold his hands. He also asked me to recite my poems to him. I did, from memory, but after a while our taxi driver arrived and said we must leave if we weren't to miss our plane. We flew to Calcutta in absolute silence, and next day the newspapers told us that Devkota had died some hours after our visit. We got drunk that day.

I left Ved in Calcutta, and with a reporter called Ajit Das went to Gangtok, the capital of Sikkim, a very hard trip then. We slept in the only accommodation the town had to offer, an inn patronized by Tibetan muleteers. Then we found our way up the Nathu La Pass to the border of Tibet. We were fired on by a Chinese border patrol, and I saw my first yaks. This was all material; every experience was new material. I returned to Bombay to assemble on paper what I had in my head. I wanted some additional material on the city. It is the centre of the Hindi film industry. I decided to do a bit about that. I was informed that a childhood friend, Leela Naidu, was a well-known actress. So I phoned her up and suggested that we meet. She replied, very coldly, that she would be very busy for an unforeseeable length of time. I was not used to being turned down. I was furious with her. I had no idea that a few years later I would marry her.

Now, thirty years later, everything in *Gone Away,* which emerged from this trip, has faded to sepia in my memory. Of the really memorable people I met, Nehru and Devkota are dead. The Dalai Lama is no longer stalwart or young, and on the few occasions on which we have met, I have been saddened by his loss of laughter. But this book showed me a possible career outside poetry. It was a critical success and it also sold well. It produced some rather undesirable results. I became a TV panellist; the *Evening Standard* published a list of what a person should do to be 'in'. This included having a drink with me. I pretended to be disgusted by all this, but was secretly flattered. I did not know that writers made by publicity are like primeval kings, soon to be sacrificed in order to make way for their successors. Perhaps I didn't want to know. I believed myself to be immortal, in every way I could think of. However, good cometh out of evil. I had made some money from the book, and now had the opportunity to make more. The newspapers had not known I could write prose (neither, of course, had I), and they began to offer me assignments. I spent my lunchtimes in Fleet Street pubs. One afternoon a man ambled over to me. He was thin but wiry; he wore a tropical suit; his face was lined and elegantly expressive, and I recognized it as that of the famous foreign correspondent, James Cameron. 'I liked your book,' he said. 'Have a drink.' At the end of our drink, he asked me to dinner. He then lived in Chelsea with his wife Elizabeth. I arrived, and Elizabeth offered me a whisky. While I drank it, James looked rather impatiently at the time. Then he said, 'They're open.'

He meant the pubs, and promptly took me to one. 'I like pubs,' he said with the husky chuckle typical of him, 'but you shouldn't drink in Fleet Street. You should drink anywhere but in Fleet Street. That has been the ruin of many a good man. I'll show you some excellent pubs.' The result of this was that when we returned to his house for dinner, neither of us was in any condition to eat. His wife was not pleased; and thereafter James and I met frequently, but always in pubs. He had been all over the world, and had seen many wars, but he seldom spoke of his experiences. Everyone, I think, wears a mask, either to impress other people or shield himself from hurt. James' mask was one of perpetual cynicism and irony, though in later years he mellowed very considerably.

One evening I met him by accident in a Chelsea pub. He was very sober. He said, 'I might have a television offer for you. There's a producer who wants to meet you.' He then said, 'My stepson went to Buenos Aires today, to work in a bank. I doubt if I'll see him for the next five years.' We were sitting in an isolated corner of the pub.

After he said this, he was unaccountably silent, and when I looked at him, I saw he was in tears. I attended to my drink. Presently he blew his nose, and said, 'Sorry. I'm behaving like David.' I inquired, puzzled, 'David?' He said, 'David in the Bible. The one who said, "O Absalom, my son, my son!" I did not comment, but thought suddenly of my father.

Some time after *Gone Away* was published, a second volume of my poems appeared. I had been having a sort of platonic affair, and these poems were about it. The book had a decidedly lukewarm reception, and the only good review, at least in London, came from Elizabeth Jennings. At this time the American poet Allen Tate arrived in London. He had been a visiting Fellow of All Souls during my years at Oxford, and though he was forty years older than I was, we had become friends. He also criticized my work with furious acuity. Though often crushed by this criticism, I realized that I had always profited by it.

Allen was a small man with a domelike head, a small moustache, and spectacles. He had the habit of looking over the tops of these when amused, and he was particularly amused by the foolish remarks of the young.

Naturally enough, or so it seemed to me, I immediately started to complain about the way my book had been treated. Allen looked at me over the tops of his spectacles. 'I've read it,' he said. There was a short silence, and then he said, 'The way the poems are written, and what's in them...they're two hundred years out of date. They're kind of unreal.' He had a soft Kentucky accent, which on this occasion acted as an anaesthetic. 'You seem to have created an image of the lady,' he continued, 'which is totally unreal. No living woman could be the way you see her. And the way you seem to see yourself...no living man could be in love like that. Maybe all this other writing is getting to be a bad influence on you.' I attempted to explain my predicament as to a career. 'I don't expect you to starve in a garret,' he said. 'It may sort itself out. Anyway, this is the first bad criticism you've ever had. You'll find it does you good, at least if it makes you think, and I hope it will. Maybe it will.'

He was on a diet, and wiped some kind of pap off his moustache. By this time his remarks seemed to me positively carnivorous. He said, perhaps to soothe my wounds, 'It's very hard to decide what to do to support yourself, if you're a poet. I've been teaching literature and writing books about it, and I've only written one poem in the last ten years.' He then returned to the attack. 'Maybe it's better to write no poetry than write bad poetry.' I said defensively that Elizabeth Jennings had not thought it bad poetry. She, incidentally, had at that time started to write religious verse. Allen looked at me over sardonic spectacles.

'The way your poems present this lady,' he said, 'Elizabeth may have thought you were writing about God.'

Allen returned to America. James phoned me up and suggested that I should meet the television producer he had mentioned earlier. The producer, from Granada, was a tough Australian called Tim Hewat, who had risen rapidly in the *Daily Express* hierarchy before he turned to television. He was now the blue-eyed boy of Sidney Bernstein, who owned Granada. 'Everything I've ever done has been a success,' he said to me, when James and I went to dinner in his flat. 'But this is the biggest thing I've gone into. I want to make a series of four fifty-minute documentaries about India. I may hire you to write them. Now tell me your ideas.' James, during all this, was unusually silent, toying with his drink in a corner. When, in mute appeal, I caught his eye, his expression suggested that I was on my own. I put some thoughts together in haste, and stammered them out, while Hewat fixed me with a glacial glare.

When I had finished, he said, 'Okay. Now go and think it all out and then write me a synopsis.' He saw us to the door. 'And remember,' he told me, 'I don't want any fuck-ups on *this*.' I went home, not in the least happy.

Next day I had a drink with James. I said, first of all, that I had never written a synopsis for a television series. 'Well, you'll soon be writing scripts instead of synopses,' he replied. 'I'll tell you the kind of thing Hewat, bless his Antipodean soul, wants you to write.' He told me. I had other objections. I had tried to distance myself from India, I said, and now, a year after my book on that country, I was being asked to write a television series about it. I didn't want to be typecast. 'Well, at the moment,' James said, 'I should count your blessings. If you do this well, they'll ask you to do more things, outside India. You can hardly blame Hewat for thinking you know something about your own country.' I said, 'But I don't.'

'If you tell Hewat that,' James said, 'the whole thing's over. Go and read some books about India. Remember, Hewat is offering you a lot of money.'

I then told him what Allen Tate had said to me. James raised his eyebrows. 'You have to make the choice,' he said. 'You need the money. It may be a choice between God and Mammon, but at the moment Mammon seems to feel warmly towards you. He may not do that very often in the future, so take advantage of it while he still does.' I went away, read some books, and wrote the synopsis.

About a month later, I found myself in Calcutta. The synopsis had passed muster with Hewat; but it relied heavily on sheer speculation, and the bulk of it was based on hasty reading. I consulted Ajit Das, with whom I had travelled to Sikkim the previous year. Das, a small, bouncy, bespectacled man, corrected the errors I had made about Calcutta, made some very useful suggestions about what should be shot there, and showed me the possible locations. By the time the Granada team arrived, I was ready. I was also fortunate in that the director, Clive Donner, and I became friends almost immediately. Hewat was still to arrive. Das and I showed Clive the various locations.

Hewat blew into Calcutta like a cyclone, sending forth thunder, his brow wreathed in clouds. 'I want action!' he shouted.

Clive said, 'We're ready to shoot tomorrow, if you want us to.' The great wind died; Hewat seemed slightly depressed by the news that all was well. He was one of those people who requires crises to be at their best. From the time we started to shoot, things fell into place. Hewat showed a side of himself that was more than unexpected.

He was slow to make friends, but once he had done so proved surprisingly affectionate; he demonstrated this by not swearing at one, and by sudden thoughtful acts. In the middle of the Calcutta shooting, he arrived at the evening conference followed by porters carrying baskets. Clive and I looked at him in surprise. 'Buying gold, Tim?' I inquired.

'No, Dommie boy,' he said earnestly. 'You two both had colds yesterday. So I bought you some oranges. Vitamin C, you know.' Both Clive and I were touched. Tim was very likeable, when you knew him. The rest of the crew didn't know him and didn't like him.

But the three of us had the responsibility for the films. We discovered in Calcutta that, with a tight schedule, we could not hope to finish on time. Clive and I had already made the acquaintance of Satyajit Ray, a magisterial figure, tall and ruggedly handsome, a shawl draped around his shoulders. He was not, at the time, making a film, and his crew was at a loose end.

'Why don't we hire them?' Clive said one night. 'Make a second unit. We'll speed the thing along. I'll take the first unit south, the second unit can go north.' This seemed a good idea. There were several ancient monuments to be shot in the north, and also the famous social worker, Vinoba Bhave.

'Who's going to take the second fucking unit?' inquired Tim. 'I have to go to London. Ray's top cameraman is sick. We've only got his two assistant cameramen, and they'll never handle this fucker by themselves.' Then both he and Clive looked at me. '*You* take them,' Tim said. 'Clive will show you what to do.'

Vinoba Bhave had been a close follower of Mahatma Gandhi. His idea was one of service to the people, and he was distressed by the number of landless peasants there were in India. He, therefore, started what was called the Bhoodan movement. He and his followers walked all round the country and asked wealthy landowners for gifts of land, which were then distributed to the landless. Most of the people he approached parted with a few acres. The Bhoodan movement was not of the government, but the government was known to look kindly on it. The quality of the land donated, however, was highly suspect. It was fairly natural that the landowners, however much they wanted to please the government, would only hand over their worst, most uncultivable tracts of property. Bhave was regarded in India as saintly; saints were allowed their idiosyncrasies.

I set off from Howrah railway station with Ray's two assistant cameramen. Bhave was supposed to be somewhere in Bihar, nobody was exactly certain where. My companions knew very little English, and I knew no Bengali. Clattering westward towards Patna, the capital of Bihar state, all three of us remained mostly silent: it seemed the wisest policy. At Patna, however, I decided this would not do. I hired an interpreter, which was difficult, since the people in Bihar mainly speak Hindi; and a car. I spoke to a district officer, who pointed out, on a map, the general direction in which Bhave and his entourage were supposed to be walking. Tim had asked me to shoot agricultural scenes and ancient monuments on the way. I thought we should keep these on hold till we had found Bhave.

It took us a bumpy day and a half to do so. During this time I saw more of rural India than I had ever seen before. At every dusty village, we stopped to inquire as to Bhave's whereabouts. In between these brief halts, I rehearsed the questions I would ask him, and also practised on the Nagra tape recorder. Finally we came to the village where he was. He was sitting under a canopy, white-clad and venerable, surrounded by his devotees. A large crowd squatted in the dust, facing the canopy. I went and found someone who was apparently Bhave's secretary, and apprised him of our intentions. He seemed perfectly cooperative.

I ran through my, by now very lengthy, list of questions, while my crew, such as it was, positioned itself. I gave them both precise instructions through the interpreter of how and what they were to shoot. The tape recorder was positioned too. I knelt beside it, to the left of Bhave, and did the namaskar, which he reciprocated. Then I asked my first question. He did not reply. The secretary, kneeling beside me in the dust, constantly whispered, 'It is no use. It is no use asking him thusly.' Extremely irritated, I said, 'Will you stop saying that? Why is it no use?' The secretary rolled his eyes at me. 'Why is it no use?' I repeated.

'Because,' said the secretary, today is his day of silence.'

We had only two days to return to Calcutta, so I left it at that. We cruised back to Patna, shooting what was required along the way, and reached Calcutta at almost exactly the same moment as Clive and the first unit returned from the south. Tim was to meet us in Delhi, and next day we flew there. We were now accompanied by Ray's entire team, including his main cameraman, Subroto Mitra, who, to the mirth of the British cameramen, was nearly blind. This annoyed Clive intensely. 'If he could shoot *Pather Panchali*,' he told one cameraman, 'he's done a hell of a lot more than you will ever do.' On the plane to Delhi, Clive said to me, 'Those two are right bastards.'

Tim met us at the airport, and asked me how I had done in the northern wilderness. 'After you'd gone off to—what's it—Bihar,' he said, 'I was told that the countryside was full of bandits. I was quite worried there, kid, but I knew you'd come through.'

I had always, up to that point, worked alone. I preferred it that way, or so I had thought. But I felt a tremendous exhilaration now, in being a member of a team. Tim, Clive, and I were like officers of a tiny army: the responsibility was ours, and was shared, and we functioned well together, whatever the odds against us. I felt great satisfaction in seeing what I had written being shot, all of us contributing towards an end product which, telephone calls from London assured us, was looking beautiful. Unfortunately, there was trouble in Delhi. We were all, including Ray's people, booked into the same hotel, and we all ate together. Then the British cameramen suddenly declared that they would not eat with the Bengalis, whose table manners disgusted them. They moved to a separate table. Tim shouted at them, Clive coaxed them; but they were adamant.

The Bengalis were hurt, but they tried not to show it. They were perfectly aware of what was happening. Subroto Mitra came and asked me what to do. I found myself in a very strange position. I had spent years trying to become English; Clive and I were from the same culture. The Bengalis and I were not. But neither were the two British cameramen like me. 'If they don't want to eat with us,' Mitra said, 'why do they agree to eat with you?' It seemed to me a very pertinent question, but in a rather cowardly way, I was afraid to face the answer.

The question went unanswered. When we left Ray's people in Delhi, to return to Calcutta, our entire team, with the exception of the two cameramen, gave them presents, and we all swore to write to one another. So we parted friends, but it was, in a sense, a bought friendship, and a way of absolving our consciences. In my case, particularly, what had happened caused me a certain amount of mental confusion. Even before I went to England, I had automatically assumed that I belonged there. This was the first time I had had to confront the issue of whether I really did. My confusion disappeared when we reached Bombay.

For here there was another question to be dealt with, and that was the matter of my mother. She was painfully thin, thinner than Devkota had been, and her grey hair straggled from her bird-frail skull. Had she been someone else, I would not have been repelled by her appearance; but in her case, I was. Throughout my life, from my childhood onward, I had felt this revulsion, for her appearance had many associations for me. But all my life I had also felt a ruinous guilt about this. As far as I could, during this last visit to Bombay I stayed away from her. I doubt if it would have made any difference had I known that I was not to see her again for the better part of a decade.

We came back to London in February. One rather gloomy day, after a morning of watching rushes, Tim asked me to lunch. He was at first rather subdued, I think because he was about to pay me a compliment. Toying with his smoked salmon, he finally remarked, 'You did very well out in India.' I thanked him. He said, 'How would you like to be one of our producers? We have this training programme, we'd put you on it; all you need is a little bit of the programme. I mean, hell, you became a fucking director overnight.'

It had started to rain outside. I said, 'No, Tim, thank you very much.'

He said, 'There's no money in this poetry lark.' I agreed. 'Well, anyway,' he grunted, 'we'll work together again. Even if you're only the scriptwriter.' I thought this rather uncomplimentary, but didn't say so. 'You ought to thank Jimmy Cameron one of these days,' he said. 'We offered these films to him first. He was free, but he wouldn't fucking do it. He insisted we should ask you instead.' This was news to me, and Tim probably saw it in my face. 'You ought to make him your agent,' he said. 'First of all, he forces you on us. Sidney Bernstein says, "The only good thing about this is we get the kid cheap." And what does Jimmy C. say? He says we have to pay you what we'd offer him. We'll need Jimmy in the future, so Sidney had to agree to it.

'As it happens,' Tim finished, 'we struck it lucky with you. But Sidney couldn't understand it, neither did I. I mean, it wasn't as if Jimmy and you were fucking fairies. I'll never understand fuckers like Jimmy,' he said.

The series on India was a great success, despite the fact that Sidney Bernstein insisted on calling it *Mighty and Mystical.* James shrugged away my thanks. 'If that Australian idiot hadn't told you,' he said, 'I would have felt better.' He agreed that I should have turned down the producer idea. 'You're a writer,' he said. 'You're not in bloody show business. Come and have a drink. I'm off to Algeria next week.' I went off too, but only to Scotland, with the poet George Barker, his current wife, and their baby.

George had a Mercedes, which he drove with intense ferocity through the Highlands, his blue eyes shining with a fanatic light. There was a great deal of luggage, and some of it had to be strapped to the back. Distracted by the infant's cries, he strapped it in its carrycot, to the roof. At one point a motorcycle policeman overtook and stopped us. 'Dear heart,' said George, 'I was only doing forty.'

The policeman did not seem to like this form of address. 'Look behind you,' he advised. We all did. One of the suitcases strapped to the back had burst. For miles behind, the heather was strewn with clothes. 'I'll help you collect them,' said the policeman.

'But what's that on the roof?' George said, in all innocence,

'A baby.' The policeman turned crimson, and threatened, unfairly George thought, to report us to the RSPCC. The baby was unstrapped and put into the car. It immediately began to cry. 'The place to which he should have reported us,' George said, 'was the RSPCA.' From this eventful trip I returned to London exhausted.

James came and had a drink with me. 'The Israelis have caught Eichmann, the Nazi war criminal,' he said. 'They're trying him in Jerusalem. Why not cover the trial?'

2

The trial didn't start till April 1961, and I wanted to be in London for the winter. I stopped in Greece on the way to Israel. Here, to my surprise, I found an acquaintance, a girl called Bambi. She had green eyes and long golden hair, and was the daughter of a very rich peer. Many young men had found this combination irresistible, and the London gossip columns were full of Bambi's attempts to run away to Gretna Green with one unsuitable lover after another. Each of these attempts at marriage had been foiled in the nick of time by her father. In the end, he had given her a large sum of money and sent her to Athens. What he hoped to achieve by this was unclear. She had promptly shacked up with an unemployed American actor named Berkeley, and when I went to breakfast in their flat, they offered me fresh pitas and homemade marijuana preserves. Berkeley was quite a pleasant young man, and Bambi charming in her amiable stupidity.

They told me that the beat poet Gregory Corso was now in Athens, another surprise. I had met Corso in Paris and London a few years before, with his friend and mentor, Allen Ginsberg. He had a peculiar lyric talent, quite different from Ginsberg's. In person he was little and faunlike, with black curly hair above a triangular face. Gregory was one of the first beat poets, and one of the best.

I knew several Greek poets, among them Nikos Gatsos, who sat all day, bald, impassive, and almost wholly silent, in a bar-restaurant near Constitution Square. The only time I have seen Gatsos visibly moved was when I mentioned Gregory's name to him. We were speaking in a mixture of broken English and demotic Greek, and he thought Gregory was coming to the bar to meet me. An expression of unalloyed terror came into his face, and he heaved himself, in a mammoth movement, to his feet, clearly determined to leave. Another poet friend, Nanos Valaoritis, had come into conflict with Gregory in Paris. Nanos was a Greek aristocrat, and his comment on Gregory was, 'He is not well-educated. I do not wish to meet him here.'

But Bambi and Berkeley were very fond of Gregory, and when they suggested that we should all drive to the Peloponnese together, I didn't think it a bad idea. Like many young men of his particular kind, Berkeley possessed certain specialized talents. Bambi assured me that he was a fantastic lover, and he himself told me that he was a fantastic driver. Gregory, when I met him, seemed uncharacteristically subdued, which reassured me. I thought perhaps he had changed his ways. I was mistaken.

We started our drive early one day; Athens was scrubbed and whitewashed by the rising sun. Gregory sat beside me in the back of the car with a bottle of Metaxas brandy. He soon became very excitable, and asked Berkeley to stop the car. 'Look at all the flowers in that field,' he said. 'Let us all make it among the lovely flowers.' This was the kind of thing I had feared; but Bambi dampened his enthusiasm with some success, by pouring a bottle of wine over him. We drove on into the hills.

Of that trip, apart from the necessity of keeping Gregory under control, I recall only a few incidents. One was when we decided to picnic in the dark at Olympia. Greek ruins can sometimes be unnerving under a full sun: at midnight, amidst thickets in which owls and small creatures made eerie noises, they were terrifying. Gregory began to tell ghost stories, and Bambi fainted. On another occasion, Berkeley, who was stoned, ill-advisedly parked the car on a beach, where it sank to the hubcaps. With the tide advancing on us, we had to enlist the help of a farmer and his team of donkeys to pull it free. By the time we returned to Athens, I was ready to get back to work.

By this time my circle of friends, or of acquaintances whom I called friends, was large and encompassed many kinds of people. But of them all, only a few could be called serious, either as friends or as people. There was Stephen Spender on one side of my literary fence, and James Cameron on the other. On both sides of the fence, there were people I genuinely liked. As I found out early in life, everyone wears masks, and some people, like the painter Francis Bacon, or in a way James, wore masks of frivolity. But the truly frivolous people were frivolous all the way through; if you dropped a thought into them it would travel all the way down without finding anything to match or impede it. It was frightening to find how many such people were connected with the arts, or existed upon the fringes.

I am not suggesting that I expected to find, in England, the equivalent of the European artistic movement, where everyone was solemn and horribly articulate. But at this point I felt that something was lacking in most of my friendships, because in few of them did I find people with any true awareness of the world, which was, by turns, alarming, funny, and very sad. In a sense I was ready for what I found in Israel. It was then only thirteen years after the country had received independence, and these years had seen two wars. The first, in 1948, had threatened its foundation; the Suez affair of 1956 its existence. Moreover, some of the people who had fought in these two wars had been survivors of Hitler's holocaust in Europe.

On my first day in Tel Aviv I was introduced to a poet called Carmi Tcharni. He wrote under the name of T. Carmi, and had been born in New York, the son of a rabbi. Carmi was a stocky young man with curly dark hair and a prematurely lined, attractive face. He had fought in the 1948 first war of independence, and before that had belonged to the Haganah, which had opposed the British before, the first confrontation with the Arabs. Carmi's American upbringing meant that I could talk with him easily; his commitment to his country and his involvement in the wars made him very representative of Israel. We formed an immediate friendship which has lasted, though now we haven't met for years.

That first day, Carmi asked me to a drink with some friends of his on the beach. These were all writers and painters; one of them, the painter Yosl Bergner, had been born in Poland, had come to Israel by way of Australia. There he had been a contemporary of such people as Sidney Nolan and Arthur Boyd, whom I had met in London. He, like Carmi, spoke English naturally, and I felt an immediate affinity towards him. That night, the entire party migrated from the beach into town, and wound up cruising to and fro between the two artists' cafés on Rehov Dizengoff, in the city centre. It was a riotous night, and I encountered many people whose names I didn't, next day, remember.

However, the general outlines of this party, or gathering, remained clear. I had developed a spontaneous liking for the people I had met. There were no hangers-on among them, as there had been in London, nobody who had been accepted for his vague admiration of the arts, or for his money. All these people were pursuers of a steadfast purpose, in words or paint, stone or music. There was something else about them, which it seemed to me we had in common, which was that many of these were refugees of one kind or another. They had fled here directly from Europe; they had come here from other parts of the world. I could be considered to be in a similar situation in England. Yosl took me to his studio; he showed me his work, he talked about his life.

It was curious how quickly one made real friendships in Israel. It struck me that this might have been because I came from my holiday in Greece, which had been slightly unpleasant through no fault of my companions. But my companions, even Gregory, had no sense of direction whatever. They were incandescent people, the descendants of Waugh's characters, the bright young things of the 1920s, but though they illuminated the air quickly, the flame slipped away through one's fingers and was soon utterly lost.

Yosl's paintings showed a continual climb and development. As a young man he had painted birds, hunched and maleficent figures perched against a backdrop of burnt streets and gutted cities. This was what he had started with, the experience of Europe; but since his arrival in Israel he had begun to paint angels. The angels of the Bible are beyond emotion; they discharge their duties, flap their giant wings, and are gone from consciousness. Yosl's angels were sad angels, angels which looked as though they had no duties to perform and had otherwise lost their way. But in a few of his latest paintings, he had put some colours into their wings.

There were several resemblances between him and Francis Bacon, whom I had known in England. They both drank to excess, and they both had the same aura of living purely in and for the moment: these were their masks. If one talked to Bacon or Bergner person to person, they were perceptive, intelligent, and strangely withdrawn. They were perceptive and intelligent about things far removed from painting; and it was as if they had withdrawn into their real selves. The first few dispatches I sent back to the English and Indian papers which had hired me were much influenced by various remarks Yosl had made to me. He said that both the Jewish situation and the Jewish religion demanded the Eichmann trial. The religion had nothing in common with Christ's interpretation or adaptation of it; it was a religion of vengeance, in which debts of blood had to be repaid. Eichmann was now required to repay.

The second factor was the situation of Israel. I had been driven through the country by a press officer, and it was not difficult to realize how small it was. The pressure of the frontiers on three sides and the sea on the other made me feel claustrophobic. It was obviously much more so for the Israelis, since, from their point of view, enemies lay beyond all the frontiers, and the sea was the last resort. It was necessary for young Israelis to realize that they had to defend themselves. Nearly all of them had. But what irked and depressed them was the knowledge that the Jews of Europe, trapped in the holocaust, had apparently put up no resistance, except in isolated spots like the Warsaw ghetto. 'This trial,' Yosl said, 'is like a history lesson for Israeli children; it will explain the circumstances of the holocaust. I am not sure if I like this or not. Maybe it's good.'

Carmi came with me to Jerusalem, where I had to get my accreditation for the trial. I had not really been brought up as a Christian, though that was what my family nominally was. But I had been to Christian schools. Obviously, I had read the Bible; I had also read T.E. Lawrence and the autobiography of Sir Ronald Storrs. When I went round the country, and visited places like Askalon, Cana, and Lake Tiberias, I felt a curious snatch at my stomach, as when an aeroplane falls away from under one in turbulence. This same feeling came to me in Jerusalem, the only place I had not so far visited. The upward climb into the hills took one past the shattered shells of tanks by the roadside, relics of the 1948 war, left in place as historical monuments: the most recent of all in that city littered with other memorials.

I got my accreditation, my telex card, and a set of earphones. I was the youngest correspondent at the trial, and also an Indian. India was not particularly amiable in its attitude towards Israel, since it had Arab affiliations. I was also a poet. All these factors combined to make people rather sympathetic towards me.

There was another Indian around; Abu Abraham, the cartoonist for the *Observer.* He was working with Patrick O'Donovan, its foreign correspondent, who was a friend of James Cameron's. Abu was slight and bald and smoked a pipe; Patrick was large and florid and, perhaps because of his ancestry, was not only one of the hardest drinkers I have ever known, but a fervent Catholic. He had served in Palestine as a guards officer during the Second

World War, and had been somewhere around when the King David Hotel in Jerusalem was blown up by the Haganah. I met him for the first time on this accreditation trip. Carmi and I spent two days in the city, and Patrick, Abu, and I were introduced to Fink's Bar and the Jerusalem artists. This was a very different atmosphere from Tel Aviv, not only because of the trial.

There were journalists due from all over the world, many of them from Germany. There were also sociologists and historians, Hannah Arendt among them, and writers like Harry Gold from New York. Some Israelis called these writers 'Jewish by profession'. Television and radio crews were coming; the whole city was prepared for this infestation of people from the media. Accommodation was scarce, but Carmi found me a small and very pleasant flat on a gardeny hill, on one slope of which was the bench on which Chaim Bialik, the father of modern Hebrew poetry, used to sit and write.

However, this flat would not be vacant until immediately before the trial, and the trial was still some weeks away. We returned to Tel Aviv, and at a concert I was introduced to the prime minister, 'the Lion of Judah', David Ben Gurion, usually known as B.G. He and Chaim Weizmann had been the founders of Israel, and in a way Ben Gurion was the Nehru of his country. He reminded me somewhat of Kingsley Martin, being short, but with a huge and leonine head. He had piercing blue eyes. He had heard I was the youngest correspondent at the trial, and was very benevolent. I asked him for an interview. 'I give no interviews,' he said, 'until this business is over,' and then smiled and continued, 'now you are accustomed to being the youngest person in each room and nobody will listen to what you say. Isn't that so? But sooner than you think, you will find yourself the oldest person in each room, and still nobody will listen to what you say. That's much worse.' It took me some years to realize the truth of this remark.

Though Carmi and I had become close friends, there was a kind of discrepancy in our relationship. He could read my poetry, but I couldn't read his. During the time immediately before the trial, I stayed with him and his wife in a house they then had. He started one day to translate a poem he had recently written to me, more or less word by word. As I listened, I found myself arranging these words in my mind, to form lines of my own. I then asked him to read it in Hebrew.

He read it several times. I got paper and a pencil, and wrote down lines in English as he read them in Hebrew. It took about two hours, but in the end he was pleased with the translation. We continued to work on these translations over the weeks before the trial, and one day decided that we should try and make a book of them before I left the country, The trial was upon us now; when I went up to Jerusalem, Carmi and his wife came too, to settle me into the flat. Patrick, Abu, and I formed a kind of task force, and met in conference every night, talking about Eichmann and what each of us had read about him. Actually, he was a somewhat obscure figure; he had never been in the top Nazi echelons. He was a bureaucrat who had executed orders, and prisoners, throughout his wartime career. What the trial was supposed to do was point up the magnitude of the Nazi excesses against the Jews through the deeds of this one man. Eichmann had been in almost all the countries where Jews had died in huge numbers, in almost all the camps; a grey and visually unidentifiable headsman, holding sway over life and death.

Some time before the end of the war he escaped, by a circuitous route, to the Argentine. Many other Nazis were thought to have taken the same route, whatever it was. Eichmann did not seem to have been one of those Nazis who took great sums of money with him to help him endure his exile. He worked in Buenos Aires as an electrician, a middle-class man, stoically striving to maintain his family. It is conceivable that, after some fifteen years of doing this, he was looking forward to an uneventful age, perhaps tedious, but almost certainly tranquil, when the Mossad agents fell on him out of a clear sky, drugged him as he came home from work, and brought him to Jerusalem to face what was almost certain death. The trial had taken a long time to come to court, because the Israelis wanted world attention focused on it; also, it was thought, they wanted to interrogate Eichmann on his escape route and who else had followed him on it. He was the biggest fish the Israelis had yet netted. The top Nazis had been hanged at Nuremberg; Mengele, the terrible surgeon of the camps, Bormann, at one time Hitler's secretary, and Eichmann were the three who had escaped; and the Israelis, after years of search, now had Eichmann, At this time he was approximately fifty-five years old.

Coming into court for the first time, all the correspondents were impeded by the immense crowds that surrounded it. This would be the first time Eichmann had been produced in public, and people wanted to see him, for different reasons, most of them morbid. A large number of young men were shouting for his death. Many women were dressed in black; they wanted to see the man who had killed their husbands and children. Placards waved above the heads of the crowd; I couldn't read them. Many people were reported to have fainted, though I did not see this. I was occupied in fighting my way through all these emotional bodies to the entrance. I had an identity card on my shirt, and several women asked me if they could have it. Nobody, rather curiously, attempted to snatch it away, though other correspondents said that it had happened to them. Inside the court, there were minor turbulences, but eventually everyone was in their seats, and was fixing his or her earphones on.

We, the spectators, sat in the well of the court; there were wooden partitions ahead, and then the desks of the lawyers. Facing us from his high seat was the judge; to his right, therefore to our left, was the glass box which was to contain Eichmann. It was like being at some theatrical performance. We, the privileged, with our tickets on our shirts, had our earphones and chairs. Outside, the masses who could not find admittance milled and shouted; we could hear them in the distance. The glass box meant for the main actor was empty, then suddenly it was filled.

Eichmann came in, wearing a grey suit and tie, a white handkerchief peeping from his breast pocket. He looked very ordinary, a thin man, bald and bespectacled. He could not have seen many people in the last few months, and to abruptly be faced by the glittering lights of the court and the television crews, and the serried ranks of the world press, the judge and the lawyers, would have unnerved anyone. Eichmann, however, seemed impassive. Perhaps it was his military training. Voices rumbled Hebrew down the headphones. Then, in the glass box, Eichmann's lips moved, and we all heard his voice for the first time: that flat, careful voice.

During the first few days, perhaps the first fortnight, of the trial, there was a sense of excitement both inside and outside the court. The emotional crowds continued to surge about outside, while inside the initial shock of being in the presence of a real live Nazi took time to wear off. The trouble was that Eichmann was so dull. His shoulders were slightly hunched, his scalp bald, his spectacles rimless, his clothes and face grey. He looked, talked and behaved like a clerk, a natural subordinate used to following orders. My attempts to imagine him in the uniform of a Gestapo Sturmbannführer, the black clothes, the boots, the sinister shoulder-flashes and cap, proved singularly unsuccessful. He continued to look like a clerk.

As the days wore on, he seemed to accustom himself to his unaccustomed role, to realize that he was the most important man in the room, that his was one of the most publicized names in the world; and he felt power for the first time in years, and to some extent began to act accordingly. He scribbled constant notes; sometimes he made objections. He must have been inhibited by the certainty that at the end of all this he would die, that there was no possibility whatever that the Israelis would ever allow him to escape the rope. During these early days the trial proceeded at a funereal pace, much of the time being spent in establishing Eichmann's identity and the various places in which he had been posted during the war. It was really very dull.

During these days, I kept getting demands from London for human interest stories, rather like William Boot in *Scoop*. In fact, every correspondent was looking for one. There was a specimen on our doorstep, and I was lucky enough to find it. Immediately outside the courtroom was a small bar, which also sold rolls and sandwiches, for the convenience of the correspondents. It was attended by a solitary barman called Avram, a sturdy person about fifty years old. Patrick and I used to visit him well before the lunch recess, to avoid the rush, and we became friends. One morning I came out of court without Patrick, and found Avram polishing the bar. His shirtsleeves were rolled up, and clearly imprinted on one arm was the Auschwitz tattoo. When I asked, he said without emotion, 'Yes, I was there. I lost my wife and son there, and my relatives, sixty-two in all.' Part of his work was apparently connected with serving food to Eichmann, whenever the Nazi was in the courthouse during lunchtime. This seemed ironic.

Avram seemed reluctant to say more, but then Patrick arrived, like a great ship in full sail. He carried Avram's defences before him. I watched him at work and learnt much. Patrick drew Avram out till he told us more. 'I would like to poison Eichmann's food,' he said. 'I would like to kill him with my bare hands. But there is a difference, is it not so, between being a Jew and being an Israeli? As a Jew I should like to kill him. As an Israeli, I must protect him till he is tried and sentenced.' Despite the fact that the nature of the sentence was very predictable, this was an interesting statement. Patrick did not want this story; it wasn't, he said, for the *Observer.* He had drawn Avram out solely for my benefit. I filed it for my papers, and received cables of congratulation. The

European press followed it up. I began to feel that I was a real foreign correspondent at last.

There were plenty of people in Israel with the camp tattoos, and I met some of them. It was an extraordinary feeling to meet someone at a party who talked trivialities for a couple of hours, and then, with a chance remark, or deliberately, revealed that he or she had been in the camps. Most people seemed to want to forget about it, and one could hardly blame them. Most had left their dead and parts of themselves behind.

One man, however, not only did not want to forget, but intensely desired to remember. He was a Pole, who would not allow his name to be revealed, but who wrote books under the name of Katzetnik, his Auschwitz number. I read some of these books, which were not exactly novels and not exactly documentary accounts. They had an extremely hysterical tone, and could hardly be said to be well-written. But they filled one with a sort of horror at the events which Katzetnik narrated as having happened; and they had happened. Hysterical the books might be, but the circumstances they came out of were so improbable, so lunatic, as to make any survivor hysterical. I met Katzetnik in a bar during the slack opening scenes of the trial. He drank fruit juice. 'So bad are my nerves,' he told me, 'that if I were to drink, I would actually become mad. Not that I am sure I am sane.' He said he had nightmares about Auschwitz, from which he wrote his books! 'But they are accurate nightmares,' he added, 'document nightmares.'

He was a witness at the trial. Katzetnik, in appearance, was like Eichmann's brother, but also his opposite. He looked clerkly, certainly, but in his manner something lay, partly visible, which suggested absolute dementia; as though, while the clerk Eichmann would never lose control, the clerk Katzetnik might do so at any moment. At the trial he swore his oath and answered the first question with downcast eyes. He was then asked to identify Eichmann. He raised his eyes to the seated, scribbling figure in the box. Then he began to babble in a monotone, again suggestive of Eichmann's monotone, but strangely altered.

'I see them,' he ended, 'the bodies in the snow. I see them… I see them….'

Then he seemed to have an epileptic fit, and had to be helped out of court.

Weeks passed. Some of the correspondents left briefly and went to other assignments, then came back. Others stayed on. These included Patrick, Abu, and myself. It was very exhausting; as the evidence became more terrible in its content, one's tiredness towards dusk increased. We spent two days watching film material which the Germans had taken in the camps. There was also much attention devoted to an episode when Eichmann, in Budapest, found a small boy, a slave labourer, stealing cherries from his orchard. The Sturmbannführer had beaten the child to death, one of the few criminal acts he had physically committed himself. It was horrifying to realize that it seemed to one a minor matter in the context of Eichmann's life.

Clouds of witnesses floated up to testify to this particular incident, and I met one of them after court ended for the day. He had not actually been called to the stand, but was in a very nervous state, constantly blowing his nose and pulling at the corners of his handkerchief. 'Did you see how calm he was, there in his glass box?' he asked. 'He took notes and did not speak. He never spoke when I saw him in Budapest. He always looked calm. How can I tell you what I feel about Eichmann? Among other things, I knew the little boy he killed.'

Crowds still hung about outside the court, but world attention had shifted away from the trial. I was obsessed, however, with a strange need to see it through, and so, apparently, was Patrick. It was very hot in Jerusalem, everything was covered in a fine yellow dust and the courtroom itself was stifling. A certain amount of midsummer madness spread. One day an American company interviewed some of the correspondents, including Patrick and myself. Patrick spoke of his experiences in Palestine in the 1940s 'I was here,' he said, 'when what we then called the terrorists blew up the King David Hotel.' The interviewer did not seem very interested. 'So I have sad memories of this city,' Patrick continued. 'My wife and our five children were killed in the explosion.'

This was utterly untrue, but everybody was awed and shocked. 'God, Mr O'Donovan,' the interviewer said, 'I'm certainly sorry, sir.' Patrick, his eyes full of tears, held up his hand. 'Say nothing,' he said, 'speaking of it upsets me.' Later, he remarked to me, 'They simply shot that because there was nothing else to do. I doubt they'll ever show it. But perhaps we're all getting a little crazy. The court recesses next week. Let's all go up to Galilee and sit by the lake.'

Next week we drove up to Lake Tiberias, stopping on the way to visit a Druse village high up on a mountainside. The Druse, who are a peculiar race with Caucasian antecedents, were surprised by our unannounced arrival, but made us welcome. They were sturdy people with fair complexions and hair, and were mostly Christian. This appealed to Patrick. 'They're very remarkable people,' he said. Abu did a few sketches of the headman, which seemed to please him. They fed us platters of a crumbly white substance, and unidentifiable dried fruit which had been mashed into a porridge. 'Very remarkable people,' Patrick repeated. If their digestions were habituated to what they fed us, they must have been remarkable, for, on the way to Tiberias, our stomachs began to feel the after-effects of our meal, and we reached the lake in very poor shape. Rut Patrick had acquired a lot of Scotch from the British Embassy.

At about midnight, Patrick, Abu, and I retired to our respective bedrooms. Half an hour later Patrick woke me. 'There's a flood,' he said, 'in my bedroom.' I went there with him. He was perfectly correct. We had been warned by the hotel manager about the high water pressure because of the proximity of the lake. The last attack made on Patrick's stomach by the Druse food had sent him to the loo. The effect of the Scotch had caused him to have to steady himself on the flush handle. He had done this for some minutes, and the result was that a kind of geyser of water was rising from the loo, which had itself overflowed. Patrick's floor was under an inch of water, which was rapidly spilling into and down the corridor and starting to trickle down the stairs. I went to try and find someone to switch the water off at the mains, but couldn't. When I returned the water was flowing down the stairs into the lobby. It was four inches deep in the rooms. Abu had been awakened by all the commotion and the fact that his room had been flooded, and was watching Patrick in fascination. Patrick, in spotted pyjamas, was bent above the flooded floor, diligently trying to sweep the water away with a silver-backed hairbrush. Eventually someone came and turned the water off. We had a lot of explaining to do to the management. But, over all these years, that picture of Patrick remains with me, and will always do so. He died about ten years later.

We returned to the heat of the courtroom. Now occasional showers of loose, wild rain fell, to a backdrop of Wagnerian thunder-and-lightning effects. During one such storm, all the electricity suddenly blinked out. There was pandemonium in the courtroom, more so when it flickered back on and we saw that Eichmann was no longer in the glass box. One's first assumption was that his guards had dragged him away; but the guards, guns out, were looking around in bewildered alarm. All this lasted no more than a few seconds; then we saw Eichmann, climbing from under the table, like some great bedraggled bird, adjusting his spectacles. He had obviously thought that an attempt was being made on his life, and sought the nearest shelter. 'Even if you know you're going to die,' someone said later, 'you don't believe it till you're dead.' Nobody knew this better than Eichmann.

In a sense it was like watching the trial of a person already dead. The result was a foregone conclusion. The monumental bulk of evidence that piled up against Eichmann, day after day, in the end seemed irrelevant, almost a bore. In no way could one connect the prisoner in the glass box with all the crimes he had committed. One could not connect him with anything; not with the human processes of eating, sleeping, excreting, even breathing. One could only connect him with the glass box. Even his flat voice, when he spoke in German, seemed unconnected with the speaker. It was equally impossible to feel anything for him. I could not feel pity, because of the evidence, and because of his dehumanization by the glass box; for the same reasons I could not feel anger or hatred. The evidence might have caused those; but the evidence had become unconnected with the man.

Patrick and Abu departed for London. Patrick's fixation on the trial continued, but his editor was sick of it. I went to Tel Aviv and continued my translations of Carmi. The Israeli government then offered me a contract to work with Carmi on translations of other Hebrew poets, from Bialik onward. We accepted. I made intermittent trips to Jerusalem and dropped in at the trial, as one might drop in at a familiar club. There were new faces, but also old ones, as other correspondents came and went. Patrick returned, this time without Abu.

He inquired of me, 'What is a Jew?' I said I couldn't answer that. 'Ah,' he said, 'but Ben Gurion can. He says he won't be interviewed till the trial's over. Presumably that means he's not going to answer questions about Eichmann. But nobody seems to have thought of asking him about anything else. Now this is something he likes to talk about. You and I can ask for an interview. He seems to have a soft spot for you, so he may give it to us. We can always say we were the only ones to interview him while the trial was on.' We applied, and Ben Gurion agreed to give us the interview, not in Jerusalem but in Tel Aviv, and for some reason at six in the morning. We agreed to this, and drove to Tel Aviv the night before. We spent the evening with Carmi and Yehuda Amichai, one of the best poets of our time, a gentle, wise, and thoughtful man, and abstemious in his habits. I had translated several of his poems, with Carmi's help. He left early.

The evening turned to darkness. Towards two in the morning, Patrick said to everyone in a crowded bar, 'I forgive all of you for killing Christ.' They thanked him profusely. At four-thirty we arrived at the Press Club, where we were supposed to be picked up. We were an hour early. Patrick had a bottle of brandy. At five-thirty a bony, bespectacled young press officer arrived, a woman. She looked at us disapprovingly, and asked if we had been drinking. 'The prime minister doesn't like this kind of thing,' she told us. 'Wash your faces.'

She would have done better to advise that we shaved and brushed our teeth. Dawn had commenced its activities in the east, and Patrick and I, seeing each other in this clarity, were rather shocked. We also became conscious, in the clear cool air, of how our breaths smelt. We did our best to repair the damage in the Press Club washroom. A sleepy attendant lent us a razor, but he had no toothpaste.

Ben Gurion was wearing slacks and a pullover, and received us in a study full of books. He looked at us curiously, but made no comment until the interview actually started. Neither Patrick nor I dared speak without holding our hands in front of our mouths, with the result that Ben Gurion couldn't hear us. He courteously moved his chair closer. Something seemed to dawn on him. Then, with a brightening of his blue eyes, he said, 'Why do you not take your hands from your mouths? I would hear you better.' He added mischievously, 'I do not say I approve of drinking, but as a young man I used to drink. Coffee is good to have after you drink. I think we will now take some coffee.'

I had heard that, like Nehru, he had spurts of impatience and irritation, but his recognition and acceptance of our peccadilloes seemed to me indicative of patience. After all, this was the only interview he had yet allowed during the trial. The people who came to interview him might have been expected to turn up smelling of aftershave rather than alcohol. But he took it in his stride; and fortunately Patrick had read a good deal of Jewish history and philosophy. What ensued therefore, turned out to be a discussion with Patrick, which was simultaneously intended as a dissertation to me. He glanced at me often to see if I was receptive.

From time to time he stumped over to his bookshelves, took out a volume, found a relevant passage, and read it aloud, translating as he went. 'The rituals and symbols of the religion,' he said at one point, 'have endured. They held the people together through the Diasporas, through the persecutions and pogroms, through the holocaust. Judaism is not a hermetically sealed religion. It enables Jews to move freely in the world. The Diaspora and the persecutions were important, because they had the simultaneous effect of scattering the people and uniting them. That is how Israel became necessary and practicable.' He illustrated this with references to history and quotations from philosophers. He spoke to me of his youth. 'All young people dream,' he said, 'I made my dreams come true. I and many others, we dreamt a dream of Israel.' The glittering blue eyes had seen many things and places, from the candlelit, cold rooms in Eastern Europe, where the Zionist movement started, to Tel Aviv at the present moment: a Jewish city, in the ancient territory of his people, flowers and palm trees by the window, the summer sun coming up.

Somehow this meeting with Ben Gurion seemed to be a natural end to the trip. I still had to finish the translations commissioned by the government, and with Carmi I did so. All this happened in Tel Aviv, and I only once went back to Jerusalem. This was for Eichmann's final speech in his own defence. He seemed tired, and his voice often faltered, for the first time during the trial. He knew, as everyone else did, that the end was now very near. I was running out of money, and had stopped filing copy to my commissioning newspapers. When I phoned my agent in London, he said that because of currency difficulties it would take weeks to get any money to me. I had enough left to buy myself a ticket home on a cargo boat.

Carmi and I drove to Haifa on the last day. The boat had docked; we went aboard and had a farewell drink. Carmi put his arms round me and hugged me hard. 'Don't be too lonely on the trip,' he said, 'I'm not going to say goodbye. I think we'll meet again very soon.' When the shores of Israel receded, I felt a certain desolation. But then, in Cyprus, Charles and Dorothy Foley came aboard. Charles had been Foreign Editor of the *Daily Express,* and was an old friend of James Cameron's. I think this was the first time he realized that I had a vocation and profession, as poet and writer, whose practitioners were wanderers, and who would meet and recognize one another all over the world.

3

There was a war on in Algeria; I was sent there. It was a bit difficult to settle myself in London after the months in Israel, and, that apart, I had no choice. I had refused Tim Hewat's offer because I felt I would be better off working by and for myself. For the same reason, I had not approached any of the newspapers for a post. This left me free to control my own life, but if it was an advantage it cut both ways. The newspapers had their own staffs, and didn't need to hire outsiders for overseas trips. When one of them offered me the Algeria assignment, I took it, and shortly afterwards found myself in north Africa.

My only previous experience of Arabs had been in Israel. I had gone to visit a Bedouin patriarch called Sheikh Sulaiman, whose encampment of black tents was pitched in the Negev desert, beyond Beersheba. It looked romantic as one approached it; but there was no question of Sheikh Sulaiman's people folding their tents up and silently stealing away. This was in the nature of a permanent encampment, a village of tents. Not only were there hobbled camels around, and an enclosure which contained magnificent Arab horses, but also a sandy parking lot which contained the Sheikh's fleet of American cars.

I was assured, however, that from time to time wanderlust seized the tribe, and that they then drifted off through the desert, regardless of borders, to pitch camp elsewhere, sometimes in a neighbouring Arab country. If this were so, it was possible that the Bedouin did a little harmless espionage for both sides. Sheikh Sulaiman's tent, which, inside, looked somewhat like a suite at the King David, was adorned with photographs of people who had come to visit him, including Eleanor Roosevelt. I asked him if he had any memories of T.E. Lawrence. The interpreter said that he hadn't, but might remember if I could tell him what Lawrence looked like and what he worked at in Palestine.

I told him that Lawrence had been short and fair-haired, had led groups of Bedouins against the Turks, and blown up several troop trains. 'Ah,' said the interpreter, 'the Sheikh says there were many young British officers who looked like that and who did that.' I felt slightly indignant on behalf of Lawrence. Patrick said it was probably only because he had been to my college.

Lawrence had been struck by Bedouin codes of conduct and courtesy, and these were very notable in Sheikh Sulaiman's encampment. Admittedly it was, so to speak, the very latest model. But they roasted a sheep for me, and I was offered the sheep's eye to eat. Afterwards the Israeli press officer I was with said that I had got off easily. 'In the old days,' he told me, 'somebody would have chewed it first, so that you could digest it easily.'

At any rate, Algeria was nothing like this. It was a glaringly white city, full, at the time, of Frenchmen and sullen and inhospitable Algerians in blue denim. I managed to talk to two men who said they were members of the FLN, and also to various French officers. I also went out with the army into a yellow desert of little lumps tussocked with dry grass. Nothing whatever happened for two days and nights, at the end of which we returned to town. But the local peasants treated the soldiers with a sullen indifference, almost with contempt, their flat black eyes lowered as they spoke. The soldiers were aware of this. They were rough in return, pushed the peasants around, sometimes punched or kicked them for no clear reason. Those who say that the French are not colour-conscious ought to have seen them in their last days in Algeria.

It was only in Algiers itself that I saw action. I went into a bar with a *colon* who had some long story to tell me about the destruction of his property. He was a small man with a foxlike face and russet hair, his skin yellow with many suns. He gestured a good deal as he talked, and drank beer in greedy little sips. When we had talked for about an hour, the beer had its normal effect, and he went to the loo, which was towards the front of the bar. As he reached the door, the front of the bar blew up.

I found myself on the floor, with a loud buzzing sound in my head. The ceiling was adorned with shards of broken bottles. When the buzzing stopped I was completely deaf, though I didn't immediately realize it. I got up and saw that while my half of the room was reasonably intact, the other half was a sudden abattoir. Glass, shattered or pulverized, lay amidst blood and bits of bodies, and there were whole and truncated bodies on the floor, like bloodstained bundles of laundry. My deafness began, painfully, to recede, and my mind to clear. I looked for the *colon* with whom I had been in conversation. I identified him by his spotted shirt. He was on the opposite side of the room from where I had last seen him. His glass, half empty, still stood on my table. What was left of the bar smelt of cordite, spilt liquor, and blood, a warm distinctive smell; smoke hung in the air, and the clothes of some of the corpses were burning.

Plastic bomb attacks, I had been told in London, were a hazard in Algiers.

At this time, curious things were happening to my poetry. Four or five years before this, Stephen Spender had warned me about the dangers to a poet who pursued a career connected with another sort of writing, he said, tended to get mixed up with the other, to the detriment of both. No poet should do any thing else in any way involved with literature. There are fallacies in this argument, which show up more clearly now than they did then. Many poets teach literature; many write books about it, or they write novels or edit literary magazines. So long as one can compartmentalize one's activities, I do not see why a poet should not be involved in other kinds of writing.

Indeed, it is hard to see how they can earn a living any other way. Poets, at least now, seem unsuited to work unrelated to literature. Journalism had always been held up to me, not only by Spender, as the one pit into which a poet must not fall. I could not now see why. What my poems had always suffered from was their absence from any kind of reality. The poems in my first book, the one that had been awarded the Hawthornden, had a certain originality about them; nobody else wrote poetry quite like mine. Perhaps, I told myself occasionally, that was because nobody wanted to. But in these poems I had created a world of pure imagination, my own. In my second book I had gone backwards; I created an unreal person, not only for the girl they were about, but for myself. Neither book had anything to do with the world.

But, by now, I had seen something of the world, and of reality. My visits to India, when I had at last experienced the country as I had never done as a child or adolescent; Israel; Algeria; they all added up to a small sum of experiences upon which I could begin to draw. Like many young poets, I sometimes mentioned death in my verse, trying to create a specific effect, which I imagined the word conveyed all by itself. I now knew what death could be like; it could be people starving to death in India, or gassed into extinction at Auschwitz, or blasted to tatters in a bar in Algiers. I therefore felt that I had chosen the right path, or that it had chosen me. Outside my vocation, my own private and ferocious wrestle with words, my public occupation suited my nature. I was curious about people and their behaviour. I liked to travel for some specific purposes, and I wanted to write about it all. The kind of poetry I had so far written was not connected with the kind of person who had written it. Now, increasingly, I tried to write a kind of poetry that was.

Towards the end of that year, 1961, there were rumbles in the English press about what was happening off the western coast of India. They evoked some echoes in me, since Goa, the place in question, had been the home of my forefathers. It had originally consisted of a chain of riparian islands, ruled by different dynasties of Hindu kings before the Muslims came. The Muslims captured much of the territory on the neighbouring mainland, and during the fifteenth century Goa shuttled back and forth between them and the Hindus. Then the Portuguese arrived under Afonso de Albuquerque, drove the Muslims away, and settled down to colonize Goa.

Part of the colonial policy consisted of the proselytization of the inhabitants. The Inquisition came to Goa at about the same time that it started in Europe, and was as poisonous and potent in one continent as it was in the other. A surprisingly large number of Hindus preserved their religion, but many people were converted and given Portuguese names, usually those of their sponsors, who brought them in for baptism, or of the people who stood as godparents to them. This was the way my ancestors acquired the name I now have, and how they acquired a new religion. For a short while, Goa was the greatest trading port in the world, and was called 'Goa Dourada', Golden Goa. Then, for various reasons, which included the internal collapse of Portugal and the dwindling of its fleet, the whole enclave collapsed.

In 1961, Goa had for two centuries been a seedy and decrepit place, whose inhabitants, particularly the Christians, migrated to British India, or even overseas, in search of employment. None was to be found at home. Richard Burton was there in the 1870s, and his book about the place suggests that it was on its last legs. But it went on, rather unsteadily, well into the next century. In 1961, it was the last colonial enclave left in independent India. Nehru described it as 'a pimple on the face of the country'. In November, the Indian forces marched on Goa and took it.

Goa had a Portuguese governor; it had a handful of scruffy soldiers, poorly armed and worse trained, none of whom had ever heard a shot fired in anger. Had they resisted, it would have taken a couple of days to mop them up, but they did not, for obvious reasons, resist. The Indian press hailed the conquest of the enclave as a triumphant feat of arms, but the issue was considerably more complex. The Portuguese had been slothful and slack for more years than anyone could remember. They had arrested and imprisoned a few people who had clamoured for independence, but they had been otiose rather than oppressive. It was reasonably clear that most Goans wanted the Portuguese out, but this was largely because under the Portuguese the area seemed doomed to decay. The Goans in the main did not want to be part of India. What most of them had in mind was an autonomous state free of both Portugal and India. They had their own culture, and their own traditions. They felt that amalgamation with the heterogeneous culture of India would destroy them. Many of their representatives asked Nehru for a plebiscite within Goa.

The Indians moved in without any plebiscite being taken. There were many reasons for this. One was that the idea of an autonomous territory within the country was alien to the whole concept of a republican India. Goa, said the apologists for autonomy, would become a kind of Andorra; but the Indian government did not want an Andorra on its doorstep. Another reason for the sudden movement of troops was that V.K. Krishna Menon, the defence minister of India, and one of Nehru's pets, was at that time in very bad odour. Chinese attacks on Indian patrols and border-posts in 1959, a precursor to full-scale hostilities in 1962, had found the military entirely unprepared, and this had been blamed wholly on him. At one point all three Chiefs of Staff had resigned in protest against his attitude. Krishna Menon was about to stand for election, and a victory in Goa, which was predictable, would raise him in public esteem. So the Indian army went in, and conquered.

All this, at least, was the information I had in London. A number of expatriate Goans in London, including the painter Francis Newton Souza, talked to me about the matter before the Indian invasion, or liberation, or whatever. A newspaper suggested that I should fly to India to cover events, but I refused, for a reason which seemed to me valid. There was a sense in which most of my adult life had been an attempt to escape my mother. She had turned my childhood and adolescence into a macabre kind of purgatory; much of my mind had been affected by it. Of late I had been receiving a steady flow of letters from her, so insane in their content that I had ceased to open them. It was almost as though I feared to be infected by what she said. If I felt guilty about this, I also felt it was one way of preserving myself. But if I went to India, particularly to Goa, which is not far from Bombay, I would inevitably meet her, and this I had come to dread more than anything else.

So I turned down the newspaper offer; but when India went into the enclave, the editor came back to me and asked what I felt about the matter. I wrote a long piece in which I said, among other things, that since Nehru had refused a plebiscite and forced the issue, making the Goans Indians without consulting them, I was ashamed to be an Indian. I was wholly unprepared for the reaction, both in England and in India. The English press supported me wholeheartedly, the Indian press tore me to pieces, an effigy of me was burnt in public in Bombay, and the Indian high commission protested to the newspaper that had published my article. Meanwhile I was carried onward by events. The BBC invited me to appear with Angus Maude, a Conservative MP, in a debate on the *Tonight* programme. The others in the debate were Indian students who had been collected from all over the country.

Maude spoke, and a student spoke. When I spoke, an expression of deep anger and contempt appeared on the faces of the students. I felt a little like Eichmann. One of the students cried shrilly, 'Traitor!' and the others took up the word. It was impossible to say anything much, and that was the end of the 'debate'. My father phoned me from Delhi and said, 'I was speaking to Nehru, and he's very upset. He's thinking of withdrawing your passport. If I were you, I should apply for a British passport at once. Go to X in the Home Office, he'll fix it. If they withdraw your passport here, you'll have to come back, and they may not let you out again.' I laughed, incredulous at all this fuss from my calm father. 'I don't know what you're laughing about,' he snapped over seven thousand miles. 'This is serious, even if you don't think so. If I had time, I'd ask you what possessed you to do all this?'

But it was quite true that I didn't know why there was all this commotion. I tried to analyse my motives, they seemed excellent. I genuinely felt that the Goans should have been offered an option. It was only a few months since I had returned from Israel. Goa, like Israel, seemed to me to have been threatened on three sides, with the sea on the fourth. Moreover, the Indian habit of talking about 'the cultural heritage of the nation', and then attempting to foist it on others, had irritated me for years. There was also a certain lack of sophistication in the reaction to what I had said, not only from the students, but also from the government. I went to my father's friend in Whitehall, and he had my passport processed rapidly. Unfortunately, the newspaper in which everything had started was informed of this, and published a story saying that I had asked for political asylum. This was not exactly the case. I qualified for a British passport, and it so happened that it was issued quickly. But if I had had a subconscious desire to alienate myself from the country of my birth, I couldn't have chosen a better way to do it.

Over the next two years I travelled in Eastern Europe for newspapers, then back to Israel, and later to Cuba, for a television series. I also did some television films in England, including a series on wildlife, of which I was utterly ignorant. I wrote poetry, and I could feel something in it which was trying to emerge, without being conscious of what it was. From time to time, in this period, I felt the surges of pure power, something beyond me, what Lorca called the *duende,* rise in me and take shape on the page. This seems to me the justification for writing verse, the reward for the years of drudgery with language: a sensation one could not, and possibly would not, want to explain to anyone else, a sensation like being weightless, or flying. In past years, when my first two books of verse had come out, I had been so anxious to have enough poems for a book that I had hardly thrown any away. This, at least so far as my second volume was concerned, had been a grave mistake.

I also started writing for the Sunday supplements, which were then fairly new. I was usually commissioned to cover racial riots; I had done the Notting Hill riots, and I was sent to South London and then to Smethwick. All this irritated me slightly. I was being typecast, and it was very annoying when other correspondents on the scene asked me to interpret between Pakistani immigrants and themselves. My attitude towards immigrants was neutral; I did not feel I had anything in common with them. Sometimes I met Abu, with whom I had been in Israel. Abu, a gentle and sensitive man, seemed puzzled by me. He himself—though as the *Observer* cartoonist he was doing well—was already thinking of returning to India, for reasons I could not begin to fathom.

'I feel I'm part of it,' he said, 'and I never intended to stay here anyway. Now that I've proved myself against competition in London, there's not much purpose in staying here.' He had also recently married an attractive young Indian, Sarojini, and they both felt that, when they had children, the children should grow up knowing India. This was all beyond my comprehension. I *felt* English; my attitudes to life were English; whatever sense of humour I had was English; I thought myself accepted in England for whatever I was. It was not that, like a Jew in the Diaspora, I had to disguise my difference. The colour of my skin was not English, but my mind was.

This was why I didn't like covering racial stories. The very facts I discovered underlined my difference, underlined it for emphasis, like Grishkin's eyes. The last race story I went on was in Middlesborough in Yorkshire, an industrial town with a large settlement of Pakistanis, like most northern industrial towns even then, in the early 1960s. There had been an outbreak of violence on a Saturday night, in the ghetto area which the Pakistanis had created for themselves. Unlike most of the racial violence which took place on Saturday nights, this had protracted itself into Sunday. On Monday the London reporters started to arrive in Middlesborough, including me. Chris Brasher, the former Olympic runner, was there, for, I think, the *Observer.* I was there for part of a larger story on the whole British racial situation, for another of the supplements. It says much about the class system, leave alone the racial situation, that on all assignments in England, the representatives of the 'intellectual' papers (we did not like to be called reporters, but correspondents) kept a little apart from the reporters of the popular press. Brasher and I had an interview with the chief constable, who seemed very harassed, and the mayor. 'We don't want the press coming here and blowing this thing out of all proportion,' the chief constable said, and, looking at me, 'particularly those with a vested interest in making trouble.' One point about my not feeling like an immigrant was that I could lose my temper with the English. I did so with the chief constable, who said he had 'not meant his remark in that way'. The mayor said, 'Some of the most respected of our citizens are Pakistanis.' Looking at the ghetto, this became hard to believe.

Like most ghettos in Britain then, it had been a slum to start with, and since the Pakistanis had come in, had deteriorated further. The grey and redbrick houses crumbled, not discreetly, in the rain; some carried great scabs of decay across their frontage, and also chalked or painted scrawls urging the immigrants to go home and telling them what would happen if they didn't. The general decrepitude of the area was now added to by a few shattered windows, mostly of immigrant shops. All the rioting, if it could be called that, was confined to one street, on the corner of which was a pub. Since the Pakistanis, or Muslims, were not supposed to drink, the landlord could not have had much custom since their arrival. He was delighted when the London press decided to make his pub their headquarters.

Half of anybody's life is spent in waiting; waiting for the chance encounter which will change his world, for love, for money, or, as in our case, for something to happen. For three days nothing did. On the night before everyone departed for London, one of the young white men who had taken to frequenting the pub after our arrival came up to me. 'Come outside, mate,' he said to me. I was slightly alarmed; Chris Brasher more so. The young man had long greasy hair and a tattoo on his arm. He had a leather coat on. He seemed mildly surprised at our reaction.

'I heard you say that you hadn't nothing to read,' he told me. 'I gossome books at home. I'll go and gettem if you wantem.' It was very kind. He went off and brought the books back and we bought him a drink and listened to his feelings about the Pakistanis, which were not warm. The 'books' were actually pornographic magazines, with titles like *Knickers and Knockers,* but the intention of the giver was undoubtedly benevolent.

One of the articles I was asked to write by a Sunday supplement was on the fate of old people in Britain. I visited a number of old people's homes, contacted service organizations in various towns, and interviewed so many geriatrics that I feared my mental processes would fail me; they were all so complaining and so confused. But I also made the acquaintance of a very old ex-soldier called William, who had a room in Battersea. William had served in the Boer War, in India, in Afghanistan, and apparently also in Mesopotamia, though he was not clear about this. He was tall and still strongly built, with a white moustache and his own teeth. His face was lined and covered with liver spots, but he had very blue, very clear eyes, which were at the same time knowledgeable and innocent. When I first interviewed him, he was concise in his replies, and also offered me some Guinness. I liked him; I went back to see him with a bottle of whisky. From then on I used to visit him about once a week, always in the afternoon.

We drank together; he talked, but not in a monologue, he was too polite; he asked me about myself. At the beginning he addressed me as 'sir'. This was a clear demonstration of class-consciousness in operation; he could not have failed to notice my colour, and he had been brought up to consider people of that colour inferior, as his reminiscences of India showed; he placed me, class-wise, purely by my accent, by the way I talked. Later on, as our acquaintance grew, he called me 'son'. His little room was fanatically neat. He shopped for his meals every day: eggs, bacon, and bread, and sometimes a chop. When I brought him a bottle of whisky, we had two drinks each out of it; then he capped it with a firm hand. Next time I came, there it would be, untouched since my last visit. His entire life was regulated, uncomplaining, and lonely.

He had no friends; he had no family. 'They all died. It's not so good to live on beyond the folk you knew.' He did his best to keep himself busy. Every morning, when he did his shopping, he bought a copy of the *Mirror*; he possessed no television. Apart from the people he met in shops, he did not speak to anyone except his landlady, the health visitor, and me. But he was full of memories, some of which fascinated me; he was like a soldier out of Kipling. I realized once more what a very good ear Kipling had, and what a great writer he had been, when I heard William talk.

I started to take notes while I did this; it seemed to me that there was a book in him, somewhat on the lines of *Trader Horn*. What he remembered was of value: it was not only of some historical interest, it was also the record of a life. It has often seemed to me that the biography of a perfectly ordinary person could be of great interest. Even if the person has led a very dull life, he has been human; in itself that is of interest. But perhaps this kind of thing is better depicted in novels. William had seen plenty in the course of his life, and done plenty.

I knew him for about six months. Then, one day, his landlady told me that he had developed a cough since my last visit, that it had turned into pneumonia, and he had been removed to a hospital, where he died. It had all happened very quickly. He had been buried by the local council. The landlady and I visited his grave, and left some flowers, in ludicrous tribute. 'I'll miss him,' the landlady said. 'He was a nice old man, wasn't he? Never any trouble, for all that he was so old,' she said, shaking her head. 'Never any trouble.'

Carmi arrived in London. He gave me the shock of my life. Somehow he was the very last person I expected to see, though there was obviously no reason why he should not travel where he liked. Within a very few days, he had adapted himself to London literary life, and fitted in as though he had always been there. This was the life I led when I was not at work in my other world. In that other world there were newspaper offices, editors, James, on occasion Patrick, and the assembled people of the press. James was shy of the literary world, because he had tried it and hadn't liked it. The literary world, or some of it, was contemptuous of my activities outside. Carmi, actually, fitted into both areas. He knew Patrick from Israel, James and he liked each other, and his interests were not solely confined to literature.

London literary life, then, consisted of defined layers, which seldom infiltrated one another. I had started my career, when very young, at what was socially the top. Through Stephen Spender I had met Cyril Connolly, E.M. Forster, T.S. Eliot, and other members of the Establishment. Then there was the *haut Boheme*; and then numbers of writers of varying degrees of success, who often met in pubs to which painters and musicians also came. The pubs I frequented were the Yorkminster and the Coach & Horses in Soho, and the Queen's Elm in Chelsea. Carmi took to these naturally, though they were nothing like the bar-restaurants in Tel Aviv or Haifa. In these establishments one could find, at one time or another, almost every poet in town, and painters such as Francis Bacon and Lucien Freud. The landlords, Gaston Berlemont in the Yorkminster, Norman Ballon in the Coach & Horses, and Sean Tracy in the Queen's Elm, presided over their pubs like nervous trainers, uncertain what the circus tigers in their charge would do next; sometimes the tigers did what the landlord most feared, but most of the time they were on their best behaviour.

Carmi didn't stay very long; he needed to go to Paris for some work. But he made his impact on London while he was there. When he left, he had made many friends, and a few enemies. The enemies were largely due to me. Carmi was as protective of me as the brother I had never had. If anyone quarrelled with me, it became his quarrel. The extreme example concerned a young female novelist with whom I was involved. She was American, and had a flat in London. One day a male friend of hers arrived from New York, and asked to stay with her. She agreed, which complicated my life considerably. Carmi and I, one evening, after a round of the pubs, dropped in at the flat. The young visitor offered us a drink. Carmi said with quite uncharacteristic belligerence, 'Why don't you get out of this flat?' He added, quite calmly, 'If you don't, I'll break your neck. I can, you know. I used to be in the Haganah.' I was alarmed, if touched, by this, and later very grateful. As a consequence of this episode, all relations between the young lady and me were severed, and this possibly rescued me from an undesired emotional entanglement.

In those days I had many casual and friendly affairs; the milieu in which I lived encouraged them. Perhaps because I was so young, many people wanted to order my life. For the same reason, several of my friends wanted to shield me from damage; not only Carmi, but, among others, my first publisher, David Archer. David was a tall, erect, bespectacled man, with sparse grey hair on a mainly bald head, and a slightly Prussian look. He always held a book or newspaper under his left arm, to conceal the fact that it had been stiffened by childhood polio. His grey suit, white shirt, and red tie were the only items of clothing he possessed. He pressed them under his mattress every night and polished his only pair of shoes every day. However, he advised me on my attire, particularly in winter, and also in my choice of female friends. He had done this ever since we first met in 1956, the year before he published my first book.

David was the son of a colonel who came from a landed family in Wiltshire. He had been born in 1907, the same year as my father, and had been at Cambridge when my father was at Oxford. There he had become a Communist. He had travelled to Russia, and had not liked it. This did not stop him from being a Communist, but was the only occasion on which he ever left England. He did social work in the East End for a while after Cambridge, then took some money from a trust and set up a shop, the Parton Bookshop, in a street of that name in Holborn. This sold contemporary literature and Communist pamphlets. It had an art gallery where young painters exhibited, and also served as a meeting place for young poets. David published the first books of three of these poets, one after the other: George Barker, Dylan Thomas, and David Gascoyne.

During the war David moved to Glasgow, started an Art Centre, and published W.S. Graham's first book. Later he returned to London, extracted more money from his father, and started another Parton Bookshop, this one in Greek Street, Soho, opposite the Coach & Horses. The pub, previously undistinguished, became known as a literary pub because of its proximity to the bookshop. It became a rendezvous for writers and painters. David revived the Parton Press imprint (not that it was defunct) and published my first book, and George Barker's *True Confession,* which had been called obscene in the House of Lords some years before after being broadcast.

These six books (five first books and *True Confession*) were the only publications of the Parton Press, but they bankrupted David and through him his father. I once went down to Wiltshire to attempt to get more money from Colonel Archer for the sustenance of the dying bookshop. Ralph Abercrombie, the bookshop manager, was with me. Colonel Archer was a charming old man, quite unlike his son's descriptions of him. He pointed to five hills in the distance. 'Those were part of our property,' he said. 'That one paid for Dylan Thomas' first book, that one for Barker's. Six hills, and each one has paid for a book of poems. Well, I don't read poetry.'

Neither, in fact, did David. He did not read anything but detective stories. But he seemed to possess a faculty for picking out poets. 'You could say they smell right,' he once told me, hastily adding, 'of course I don't mean that any of you smelt, except perhaps Dylan.' This attribute of his may sound comic; but I have always thought it special, and I have never found it in anyone else I have ever met. David had a specialized talent, like a Truffle Hound, and he made use of it. He had no other talent except that of befriending and helping people, and making them his friends. And in the end they failed him. In the days to come, after Colonel Archer died, the bookshop closed, the stock and the Wiltshire property were sold, and there was no money left at all, very few of the people he had helped came forward to help him.

I first met George Barker through David. He would then have been about forty-three, younger than I am now, but seemed immeasurably old and wise. I had read all his poems, and admired them for their power and their virtuosity with language. In fact, as an adolescent in India, I had already read all the poets I now knew. I retained my own reservations about the work of most of them, including George. But in his case, these disappeared as I began to know him. George had perhaps the most mesmeric personality I had ever encountered. He was not a short man, but otherwise he physically resembled Picasso, with burning blue eyes instead of burning black ones. He also, like Picasso, had a need for disciples, and he acquired those he wanted without evident effort, and in a very short while converted them to all his views.

He hated most of the established poets, Auden and Eliot apart, and was contemptuous of their work. Yet, at one time they had—mostly—been his friends. Louis MacNeice and he drank together when they met, and appeared to like each other, but otherwise George met few people of his own generation, preferring younger acolytes. They did not need to be poets; at the time when I was frequently in his company, they included a painter, Tony Kingsmill, and a sportswriter and would-be novelist, Malcolm Winton. All in orbit around George, we befriended one another as well.

If he hated the Establishment, the Establishment hated him. He was a coterie poet, greatly admired by a few, quibbled at by many, because of his 'lack of discipline'. The lack, according to his critics, extended to his life. He had had relationships with many women, and had fathered children on some of them. This tetchiness about the details of people's lives was typical of certain levels of literary society. Those who expressed disapprobation were often by no means sinless themselves; one notably adulterous poet casually said to me of another, 'He divorced his first wife. I won't have him in the house.' George, I think, suffered within himself at this kind of attitude.

He had, in his youth, wanted to be a racing driver, and he still loved to be around cars. He himself had a blue Mercedes, and from time to time he would suddenly say to Kingsmill, Winton, or me that it would be a good idea to get away from London. The destination was decided as we left town, but there were two which were particularly favoured. One was Scotland, the other Shropshire. George had a fantasy about clansmen, monsters in lochs, and Bonnie Prince Charlie; he was also a great admirer of A.E. Housman's poetry. In Scotland we headed for the Highlands;

we once went to Skye, and the Hebrides. One night, on this trip, a fisherman presented me with two lobsters. I put them in the Mercedes, forgetting to tell George. In the morning, when he started the car, one of the lobsters attached itself to his hand. George, with a roar of pain and fury, hurled it into the sea. The other one followed it.

When he had calmed down, he said, 'One Asian in this car is enough. Two crustaceans are too much.' His indiscriminate use of puns, some critics felt, had ruined some of his poetry; but he punned naturally in conversation, and some of his wordplay was brilliant. He taught me much through random talk about writing poetry. He did not, I must add, intend to; he knew that poetry is unteachable, as such; but a certain amount of help can be given by an older poet to a younger one. He often told me that my poetry said nothing, but said it beautifully. A few years earlier I would have been crushed; but now older, perhaps wiser, I knew this myself.

During the Scottish trips, a favourite port of call was Inverness. We stayed by the loch, and speculated on the monster. George was convinced, that it would come if he called it. He conceived it to be a sensitive creature, deeply wounded by the world. 'Like calls to like,' he said, 'across the unanswering sea.' In Shropshire he quoted Housman all the time. Housman had never visited the country, but George didn't care.

Ludlow possessed a small pub on the banks of the river by a stone bridge, where we used to stay. George's wife, Elspeth, who was also a Housman addict, followed her husband in quotations from the poet, but only when we were at this pub. She felt that it must be one of the taverns mentioned by Housman in which the Shropshire lad grew lachrymose with ale while the rain sifted down outside. Indeed, she only quoted from the poetry when it rained.

Myself, I saw no connection between this pub and the Shropshire lad. The landlady grilled homemade sausages and bacon for breakfast, and when we came the bedsheets were always freshly starched, and smelt of lavender.

A round this time the poet James Michie, who was also a publisher, encouraged me to write a novel. I had once written a radio play for Douglas Cleverdon of the BBC *Third Programme,* but had never tried fiction. 'Think if it was made into a film,' James said. Eventually I felt that the only kind of novel I could possibly write was a detective story. I decided to make David Archer the detective, withdrew to a friend's farm in Dorset, and wrote with pain and unsuccess for some weeks. One night a sow farrowed, and I was called in to help. While holding the sow's legs, it struck me that this activity was a far more useful, and even interesting, one than writing a novel. I returned the advance and have not written a word of fiction since.

4

During our trips to Scotland, George and I usually stopped for a couple of days in Edinburgh. Here, at the Abbotsford in Rose Street, we would meet a great number of Scots poets, known or unknown to the English literary world. Norman MacCaig was known to it; he had a great brow, very blue eyes, and a gaunt, tall body, and he wrote in the English language. There were others, like Sydney Goodsir Smith, who composed their verse in Lallans, the Lowland dialect used by Robert Burns. It seemed a bit strange that so many people, including an indisputably very gifted poet, Hugh MacDiarmid wrote verse in Lallans; particularly because I do not recall any prose work in that language. There was an endless dispute between the Scots and the English poets about the feasibility, or, indeed, the value, of Lallans as a literary medium. When we came to Edinburgh, George and I were always out-voted in whatever debate there was about this.

One way in which we were out-voted was by being out-drunk. The Edinburgh poets had a spectacular capacity for liquor; after a night in the Abbotsford the party usually shifted to somebody's flat. There was a morning when I awoke in Goodsir Smith's residence in Dundas Street. My host was seated by my bed, stirring a bowl of steaming pink gruel, loathsome in smell and appearance. 'Get some porridge into yourself,' said Sydney, who, though he wrote in dialect, spoke the Queen's English. 'No Sassenach knows how to hold his drink.' I refused his kindly offer. He read me a number of poems in Lallans, and said, 'Is that not great verse?' I said it undoubtedly was, turned over, and went back to sleep. Next day I regretted this statement, since Sydney was trumpeting news of surrender round every pub in Edinburgh.

I had met Hugh MacDiarmid, or Christopher Grieve, which was his real name, in London; I remembered him once, coming into the Yorkminster pub in Soho, on his way to Moscow; he was a convinced Communist. 'I'm going to persuade the Russians to be generous,' he said. 'I'm going to tell them to withdraw from Hungary.' Grieve was short and stubby in build, with frizzy grey hair and a cantankerous moustache. Though we got on well, we never really talked, until a day in 1970, when some London paper sent me to Scotland to interview him on his eightieth birthday. He was by this time widely called the poet laureate of his country, a title he did not much like.

He lived in Biggar in Lanarkshire, a little way out of Edinburgh. I hired a taxi in Edinburgh to take us there. Leela had recently come into my life; she was enchanted by the spring lambs we saw in the fields by the road. I was less happy; I had rung Grieve before we left, and he asked me to bring two bottles of Bell's Whisky with me, 'to pay for the intrusion on my privacy'. I foresaw a long and difficult interview ahead. The taxi driver, who appeared to be a member of the Kirk, was gloomy too. 'He may be a great poet,' he said, 'but he's an outrageous drunkard.' We got to Biggar.

Grieve received us and the whisky warmly, and, handing Leela over to his red-haired wife, took me into his study, where the taxi driver shortly arrived. 'It's could outside,' he complained. 'Have a wee dram,' Grieve said grudgingly, 'a wee drappie.' The taxi driver seemed discontented. 'Not such a wee yin,' he said, 'the gentleman here brought two bottles.' Grieve poured him half a tumbler, neat, and began to talk to him about the deplorable working conditions of the proletariat. The driver seemed quite satisfied with his own working conditions, but Grieve insisted that he should not be, and told him why.

This was the kind of thing I had foreseen with apprehension in Edinburgh. However, the taxi driver had always had prior opinions about Grieve, and now decided to concentrate on drinking rather than talking. Grieve divided his attention between both activities, which was as well for me and for my interview. He was an extraordinary man. Though he liked to present the image of a drunken bard, he was very intelligent, but he limited the exercise of his own intelligence where it conflicted with his politics.

During our talk, the first serious talk I ever had with him, he became Grieve rather than MacDiarmid. He became the person from whom the poems came, though, meanwhile, the taxi driver passed out and Grieve's wife came frequently and noisily in from the other room demanding when we would be finished. He defended writing in Lallans, because he thought the Scots needed to identify themselves as culturally different from the English. This seemed to me a very lame argument: why didn't the Scots write in Gaelic, if they wanted to be different? Sorley MacLean did, and he was read outside the Hebrides. Why write in a form of English which was not only hard to understand without a glossary, but which gave many bad poets an excuse for trivialities? He replied, 'Most Lallans poets *are* bad. But,' he added after some thought, I'm not, when I write in Lallans.'

He then talked about the *duende* in Lorca: how a poet is taken from outside by some force he cannot identify, lifted, and carried far beyond himself. This, he felt, was the eventual difference between poets and practitioners of verse: this surge of force, which temporarily made a man inhuman. 'That's why all poets are selfish men—because they have known what it is to be made inhuman.' This was a very old postulate, of course, but MacDiarmid's own life was perhaps an example of what he meant. He handed me a copy of his autobiography, every so often naming a page number and asking me to read it to see what he was talking about. Communism, he said, was for him a romantic experience; Communism had been the religion of the first half of the twentieth century, since Christianity and capitalism were both equally dead. But he never explained why he wrote in Lallans except that he said it was the dialect of the people.

I doubted this very much. When the taxi driver eventually had to be aroused, in order to drive us back to Edinburgh, I asked Grieve to read him a poem in Lallans. The taxi driver told Grieve it was 'a fine work', but on the way back grumbled that he hadn't understood what it meant. 'What for does he write that way?' he asked, 'isn't the Queen's English good enough?' And we drove on towards the lighted city.

I visited Ireland, and I met a number of poets in Dublin, but for some reason my encounters with Patrick Kavanagh always took place in London. Kavanagh was supposed to be the greatest poet Ireland had produced since Yeats; but if Yeats' mask, in age, was that of the suave senator, Kavanagh's was that of a Monaghan peasant. Though he was not tall, nor particularly fat, he gave an impression of bulk. He usually wore a cloth cap on his bald head, and thick spectacles. He had small eyes, a large nose, and stubborn lips, in a face rather the same size as that of a camel. He spoke in a thick accent, and once, staring at himself in a mirror above a public house bar, said to me, 'Aren't I the handsomest man you ever saw?'

Kavanagh had been greatly dependent on his mother, and was now somewhat so on his sisters, who ran the Monaghan farm during his absences in Dublin and London. His girlfriend in London was a tough, stocky lady called Kathleen, who mothered and bullied him. Sometimes he would roar at her in a voice not softened by the fact that, as he was constantly reminding one, he only had one lung. The other had been removed following an operation for tuberculosis. At or around the time of the operation, a paper he ran in Dublin, *Kavanagh's Weekly*, had been sued for libel. So had he. In one of the longest cases in Irish legal history, he had been acquitted, but would often bellow, 'They were trying to kill me, I tell you! I say, they were killing me!'

He was the embodiment of the word 'boor', in its more ancient and exact sense; a coarse, unwise farmer with muddy boots and no consideration for other people. But this mask concealed a strangely delicate sensibility, which had produced poems like 'The Great Hunger', and the novels *Tarry Flynn* and *The Green Boy.* Kavanagh's newest poems were also revelations of this sensibility. He suffered, perhaps, from two defects not directly his own fault. One was that he had no technical subtlety whatever in his verse to match the sensibility which produced it. The second, which was partially the cause of the first, was that in Ireland people were either enormously critical or wholly uncritical of his writings. Since he mainly consorted with the latter category, he had never been exposed to any objective criticism.

This, it struck me, was exactly the same thing that happened with English verse in India. The better Irish poets had always had to come to England to be either properly evaluated or properly appreciated, and this was also true of Scots poets. Within their own countries, they found either total hostility or total acceptance. In England, in the 1960s, something was starting which was not unlike what happened when the Roman Empire fell. Artists from the colonies were coming in to the former seat of the empire to be recognized by those who had in a sense created them. The Irish, the Scots, and the Welsh had been present in the English literary scene for some time. Now there were people of Indian or Pakistani descent, like Zulfikar Ghose, Sasthi Brata, and myself; immigrants from the West Indies, like V.S. Naipaul, who was also of Indian origin, Samuel Selvon, George Lamming and several others.

I knew Francis Wyndham, the literary critic, a gentle and whimsical man with an exceptionally developed sense of words; and Colin MacInnes, a tall, crewcut Australian novelist, who was almost obsessively concerned with African students and immigrants. With the best possible intentions, both were concerned with the future of 'coloured' writers in England. They decided that Naipaul and I should be brought together, and attempted to do so at a lunch in the Yorkminster pub in Soho. Gaston Berlemont, the landlord, though he was French, was also a thorough Londoner. Nevertheless, he retained a deep respect for food, and in those days the Yorkminster lunches were excellent, for Gaston also maintained a fine cellar.

Naipaul's first book had been published the year after *A Beginning*. He was, however, a few years older than I was. He was then rather slightly built, and appeared nervous and shy. An intense quality of fastidiousness seemed to pervade him; he disliked being touched. He asked me several questions about India, to which he had, until then, never been. But we really had nothing in common. His work was quite different from any area on which mine touched. At that time he was writing fairly short, rather witty stories and novels about his native Trinidad, but a deep seriousness to be felt in him indicated that this might shortly change. I think both Francis and Colin were aware of this, and this was partly why they encouraged him. But I couldn't help thinking that had we both been English, the feeling that we should meet each other would never have occurred to either of them.

The idea that I was accepted by everybody as what I was had not really worked. Even David Archer, one day near Christmas, in a party full of drunks, murmured to me, 'Hard for you, what? I mean, Indians have finer sensibilities than us, don't they?' It was difficult for me to accept that my English friends saw me as different from themselves in any way; I didn't see them as being different from me. But I became increasingly conscious that this was so. It was so even in those with whom I shared a craft. George Barker called me 'the only Hindu prince among us versifiers', a remark not entirely intended to tease. Of the poets David had published, Barker was the one I knew best. Of the others, Dylan Thomas had died before I reached England. I had met David Gascoyne in Paris, and once he stayed with me in London. He was tall, with a twitchy and sensitive face. Gascoyne had not written much poetry since the 1950s, though he had admittedly started very early. He was sixteen when he published his first book, *Roman Balcony.* He was one of the first British surrealists, and one of the few poets in England influenced by modern French literature. *Man's Life Is This Meat*, the book published by David, appeared when Gascoyne was nineteen. Gascoyne always disowned *Roman Balcony*. He considered his second book to be, in some ways, his first serious work. He had written a quantity of superb, almost visionary, poetry during the war years; afterwards he lived in France, where the flow petered out.

Long after this, when I could not write poetry, I thought of Gascoyne's terminal silence, and felt not only pity, for I could then understand how he must have felt, but awe that he had not let his silence kill him. It was different with the last of my predecessors in Archer's stable, W.S. Graham. Sidney Graham was a Scotsman, but at this time lived in Cornwall. Like George, he had gone on from his first book to be published by T.S. Eliot at Faber. Both the poets had fond memories of Eliot; they had got on very well with him, apparently; Eliot had at one time organized a fund on which George lived. If it was difficult to visualize Eliot close to two men with reputations for eccentric behaviour, it was perfectly possible that they represented a side of him which he, in his daily life, suppressed. I also recollected that Ezra Pound had organized a fund designed to enable Eliot to leave his post in a London bank.

Towards David Archer their attitude was more ambivalent. He had, in a way, discovered them; he had been their benefactor; yet the instinct that had led him to them was not explicable in terms of his actual appreciation of what they did. David had 'smelt them out' through a process that seemed to me a fascinating and insoluble mystery. He had not even read their work when he sensed that 'it might be a good thing to publish it'. He had not made a penny out of these publications; indeed, he had given his own money to the poets. But they somehow could not take him seriously. Gascoyne did; in France, David and his peculiar talent might have become a myth, but in England his achievement was turned into a droll anecdote. I have never understood why nobody has ever written a book about David Archer, his bookshops, his publications, and the varied and fickle friends he made through an amiable and peculiar life.

When there was no money left, and no prospect of finding more from a dead father whose property had all been sold, David, for a while, would not accept the situation. He had always lent, or given, money freely to other people; he now expected them to reciprocate. The fact that the money he had spent and distributed had been his father's, and that few of his friends had rich fathers, did not dawn on him. He developed curious habits. The bank refused him an overdraft; he issued postdated cheques to friends, which he had no funds to meet. So he would borrow more money from another friend to repay the first one, and leave a little over for his own needs. This obviously couldn't continue indefinitely. He started to bounce cheques everywhere, to such an extent that he could no longer enter many of the pubs and restaurants he knew. Then the bank closed his account, he was threatened with eviction from his flat, and it was borne in on all his friends that something had to be done. At that time there was a literary magazine called *X*, edited by the deaf South African poet David Wright and the Irish painter Patrick Swift. After some discussion, we collected a list of a hundred sponsors for a trust fund for David.

Almost everyone in the literary world knew David, either personally or by name. Most people were aware of his predicament. Some weren't; one was Henry Williamson, the novelist, who, many years before me, had won the Hawthornden Prize for *Tarka the Otter.* Williamson was very old, and lived in the country; he was a large, walrus-moustached person, in baggy tweeds on the night I met him. This was in The Queen's Elm, and he was on his way to Victoria station for the trip home. I explained David's situation to him. To my horror, he began to weep noisily. I tried to comfort him; David's situation, I said, was not that abysmal. 'I wasn't crying for him,' said Williamson, 'I am crying for all my friends who died in the First World War.'

But he agreed to become a sponsor; and so did other older writers, like E.M. Forster and L.P. Hartley. Painters agreed: Francis Bacon, Lucien Freud, Frank Auerbach. So did actors like Sir John Gielgud and Dame Sybil Thorndyke; musicians like Malcolm Williamson and Alan Rawsthorne; Oxford dons, Lord David Cecil and Nevill Coghill, who were my friends. It was a distinguished and respectable list. All the former Parton poets signed; the trustees appointed to administer the fund were Stephen Spender, Cecil Day Lewis, and Mary St John Hutchinson. Most of the sponsors answered our requests for patronage by letter; I think it was Paddy Swift, with his ingenious Irish mind, who had the idea of selling these letters to an American university to raise funds. We sent out an appeal to over three thousand people connected with the arts, and nearly all sent money. A very substantial amount was raised and banked for the trust.

What the trustees agreed was that David's rent should be paid, and he should also have an allowance of ten pounds a week. It was planned that we would find David some kind of work that would suit him. If we couldn't, we would keep renewing the appeal for funds whenever the money, ran out. They were good plans, but they didn't work; and the reason they didn't was David himself. He was supposed not to know about the trust fund, but it couldn't be kept from him indefinitely; when he found out, he somewhat embarrassed us by going to people who had already sent us money for the trust and asking them for personal loans which he would repay when the fund was operative.

This was not the total extent of his activities. He also told his creditors, who were many, that they would all be paid by the trustees. They had read the press publicity which had helped us to raise funds, and allowed him, therefore, to run up further bills with them. It was like trying to train a child not to create chaos around the house. By the time the trust was legally opened, the trustees had colossal new bills to pay. David then really went to town. He continued to give money away, or spend it, on other people, as he had always done, and his ten pounds, which was meant to last him a week, usually went in a day. When this happened, he went to one or the other of the trustees, demanding advances on the next week's allowance. Stephen Spender was the editor of *Encounter,* Day Lewis was at Chatto & Windus, Mrs St John Hutchinson was a busy woman. They could not put up with these sudden descents of an impatient person to whom they thought they had already done a service. They all resigned.

This left us in an awkward situation. The trust solicitor, Paul Lamplugh, suggested that all the money that remained should be given to David in a lump sum. It was. Some thousands of pounds dissolved in his hands within days. The idea of finding him work had failed. T.S. Eliot had, very kindly, agreed to be a sponsor of the trust. But T.S. Eliot, whatever the depths of his kindness, couldn't very well employ a poetry editor who knew nothing about poetry, and indeed had never read any, whose favourite reading was detective fiction, and who 'found poets by a sense of smell'.

Nor would any other publisher employ him. I myself thought that one or the other of them would have made him the editor of their crime stories sections, since, at least in that field he had exact and knowledgeable tastes. But I suppose he didn't look as though he fitted into any office. The job we eventually found him was as a salesman of neckties at Selfridge's; but he wasn't very good at that either. So, eventually, we were back where we had been when David had started his crisis. Except that he now felt extreme resentment against those who had tried to help him through the trust fund. Its closure, which had been announced in the papers, had, so he said, destroyed all his credit. Nobody would now accept his cheques, which seemed to me as well, since, though he retained a chequebook, he had no remaining bank account.

If what followed was a tragedy, it was a tragedy of which David was the director. It wasn't as dignified as *King Lear*, but then David—as with his own Parton poets—had never read Shakespeare, and didn't know about this. In the course of a disintegration of personality caused entirely by money, or the lack of it, he had turned from somebody who was in a mad way wise, also often very witty, and usually generous, kind and helpful to other people, into a kind of monster who lived only to borrow money every day from friends who couldn't afford to give it to him. But through being a monster, he was also, in my mind, a kind of latter-day saint, a perfected person.

This taught me many lessons about people, the main one being always to be patient. Other small lessons learnt were never to lose one's temper, however intense the provocation—in my case this was having David demand my last pound off me as rightfully his—because, in a way, you don't know what the person annoying you is like, or what causes him to eventually become annoying. David became, in the end, a cross I bore till I left London in 1968, and I bore his cross thereafter, in whichever part of the world I was (unseen by him, since he had never left England after his brief trip to Russia, 'abroad', in 1928). That was until he died, but that came later.

But there was one thing that the construction of this peculiar and much reported trust fund was like. It was like a great collection of people driven by some political, perhaps even religious objective. The whole business of David, when the trust was founded, was so taken up by every 'important artist' in Britain—though no government body involved itself in it. I had a feeling that, because of it, I had discovered a kind of solidarity amongst people devoted to the same kinds of work, whether they were in words, theatre, music, painting, or the sounds breathed through the nostrils of flutes. During the early days in Paddy Swift's flat, when we were organizing the trust fund, David said to me, 'I don't like the Irish, or Paddy, and David Wright's a colonial anyway. So, by the way, are you, dear boy, and look at it: all of you were foreigners, weren't you? I mean, George says he's Irish, Sidney's Scots, David's a bit like a Frenchman, and Dylan was Welsh. All of you were foreigners, in a way. I don't mean that nastily, dear boy, but there it is.' He himself was utterly English, and he was also English in a particular style: he typified the English eccentric. The really bad days came when nearly all his friends were tired of his importunities and would not help him. He ceased to work; his entire day was occupied in trying to raise small sums of money. Hardly anyone would provide them. He made us all guilty, and a little ashamed. But I think it was perhaps harder for him than it was for all of us.

In 1964, when David's fortunes had reached a point beyond which it was not possible to sink, my translations of Carmi's poetry were published in England and America under the title *The Brass Serpent*. They were not particularly well received, perhaps because they were so very different from anything then being written in English. In 1965, my third book of poems came out; it was called *John Nobody.* Possibly it was better than my first two; it was certainly different, and I was particularly pleased with the title poem, which was longer than usual. It came from a medieval ballad, in which there are the lines,'..'. I would no wight in the world wist who I were. But little John Nobody, that dare not once speak.' These lines strongly appealed to me, but for no specific reason. The John Nobody in my poem—myself—certainly dared speak, the whole poem was him speaking. The original ballad was about social inequities; mine wasn't, but it was not only about myself, it was about the world I breathed.

In 1965 I was twenty-seven; to have published three books of verse meant that I had been pretty prolific, though I didn't feel thus. It seemed to me that I had written less than I should have done. I had wasted my time in liquor and conversations of little importance. Now, when I think of it, I do not think that any conversation can be unimportant. We can perceive people through the conversations they engage in, whatever they may be conversing about; and perceptions of people are perceptions of reality. This reality manifested itself in these new poems. Shortly after they were published, Macmillan in America wrote to me and inquired if they could publish a selection of poems from my three books. I was delighted, of course, and said as much, and the book was scheduled for 1966.

In 1963 I had visited America briefly, or at least I had visited New York, which is a slightly different matter. A magazine commissioned me to do an article on Manhattan; I thought myself lucky. Ved Mehta, an Oxford contemporary and friend, was there, working for the *New Yorker.* I spent time with him; through him I met several people with whom I later formed lasting friendships: they included a West Indian writer, Frank Hercules, who lived in Harlem with his attractive wife Dellora. She was an educationist and teacher. In those days Central Park was a safe place to walk in, but when the Herculeses asked me to lunch with them at their flat, Frank was deeply concerned about my safety. 'Lunch, not dinner,' he said. 'It's safer in the daytime.' I could not understand his anxiety. After all, I was the same colour as many Harlem citizens.

Over lunch—Dellora was an excellent cook—Frank informed me that he was himself not accepted locally, because he came from Trinidad and spoke with an English accent. Neither was Dellora, since, though technically a black American, she had white blood. They had both been mugged in Harlem, but they wanted to live there. 'It would be a sort of betrayal,' Dellora said, 'if we lived any place else.' Frank took me to a neighbourhood bar, where all the drinkers fell into a surly silence when we entered, and stared at us in wordless hostility till we left. I could not understand Harlem; perhaps I could not, then, understand New York, though it seemed to me beautiful.

The great canyons between skyscrapers that lived up to their name were awesome. The very rapid pace of life suited me, somehow; I myself liked to do things quickly. Apart from Frank, I met a number of writers whom I had heard of and read: several of them were Allen Tate's friends. Among them was Robert Lowell, a very gentle and apparently shy person, who had the rare capacity of making me feel that he was really interested in what I did. He had a caring attitude towards an alien and much younger writer, and told me stories about other poets, several of whom were dead. He was particularly affectionate about Delmore Schwartz, whom he greatly admired and who was alive. Schwartz was a poet whom I also admired, he had a delicate and original lyricism and a fascinating mind. Lowell said he could be found in a Greenwich Village bar nearly every evening.

I frequented this establishment until Schwartz turned up. The barman, who was aware of my quest, pointed him out; but I didn't approach him, for two reasons. One was that I knew, by now, how embarrassing it was to have strangers come up to one and introduce themselves as poets; I also did not so much want to talk to him as see him; and also he was aggressively and colossally drunk. 'He's always like that,' said the barman, 'he's got it bad.' The barman knew Schwartz well or so it seemed. 'He doesn't write any more,' he told me, 'he can't write any more. Dylan Thomas used to drink here. It was the same way with him. He didn't write any more, because he couldn't.'

I knew this was an occupational hazard of the trade, but Schwartz saddened me. However, New York had some very cheerful moments. I met Bernard Malamud, who appeared to be very gloomy about something, but did not say what; and, at a party, Anais Nin, who talked incessantly, though people had warned me she wouldn't, and said that Henry Miller 'was really rather a fink'. It was the first time I had heard the word.

America now provided me, in various ways, with quite a lot of income. My agent at the time was James MacGibbon at Curtis Brown. James was tall and loose-limbed, with a face like that of a handsome boxer's, and clothes that were sufficiently well-cut to look casual. He became a friend of mine, and he did his best for me, not only with prose but with poetry. It was he who had engineered the Macmillan offer; he said to me one day, 'Would you like to write an article about a household fixture?' Before I could either express incomprehension or say no, he continued, *House & Garden* are willing to pay one thousand dollars for it.' A thousand dollars, in those days, was real money for an article. I agreed. The magazine apparently wanted known writers to produce an article a piece on something commonly used in a household. They were going, first, to print them, and then to publish them collectively in a book. 'Angus Wilson took table knives,' James said. 'Actually, there's not much choice. You'll have to do light bulbs.' So I did a thousand words about light bulbs, for a thousand dollars. I can't remember what I said.

The *New York Times Sunday Magazine* offered me articles on a regular basis, and these were also fairly profitable. What really made money, however, was the sale of manuscripts. The poet Donald Hall had approached me while I was still at Oxford, on behalf of Buffalo University. They didn't pay me very much, but Texas did. Two buyers came out from the States at the start; later there were British dealers commissioned to buy for the university. I sold my manuscripts for high prices; they didn't only want poetry, but anything I wrote; I could even sell them carbons of my articles. This, in the end, caused the final collapse of the market, at least for me. I did not always have manuscripts to sell, and Texas constantly wanted more.

'Why let all that lovely money go waste?' an older poet inquired. He was on his way to a dealer. 'Look at what I've got.' He showed me a worn and tattered sheaf of drafts for poems. 'I did all that in three days,' he told me. 'Writing all this out is the difficult part. Then you simply bash it about to get the tattered effect. They like the stuff to be old. For that I bake the manuscript in the oven for a bit. That turns it yellow.' I was less honest in those days, or less stodgy, and I tried his methods out, once only. In those days I was writing a 'London Letter' for the *Times of India.* I described the manuscript business in one such piece, and also remarked on the ways in which a convincing manuscript could be produced. I did not think that anyone in the trade would ever read it.

Unfortunately, when selling the carbons of a bundle of articles (which were perfectly genuine) to a dealer, I included this piece. I was not aware that dealers read what they bought. The dealer read the piece, and thereafter my name was mud, not only with him, but with all other dealers, for he promptly told them.

The year 1966 was important to me for several reasons. I was living with a girl who, that March, bore me a son we named Francis. I have written about this in the first volume of my autobiography. At that time, I had hopes that the relationship would turn out well. It did not do so; but, at the time, the fact that I had become a parent made me feel fully adult, and responsible for someone else. At about the time that Francis was born, Macmillan brought out my *Poems 1955–1965* in the USA. This book was very widely reviewed all over the USA; far more widely, Arthur Gregor of Macmillan later told me, than the publishers had ever expected. Most of the reviews, moreover, were good ones.

One that wasn't came from the poet and critic Hayden Carruth, and I still remember the substance of what he said. He remarked on my technical skill, he admitted that some of the poems worked, but he concluded that they were totally without literary value. Here was a young man, he said, who came from India. India was a country with terrible and immediate problems, in which many people suffered deprivation and millions died every year. It was, in fact, unbelievably full of material for poetry. He was perfectly aware that I did not live in India; but why didn't I? There was not a word about the country in the entire corpus of my poetry. This was not quite true, but very nearly so; I admitted it. By choosing to live in the West and not writing about India,

Carruth said, I had thrown away any talent I might possess. It was still not too late; I could return to my proper place.

This review both hurt and infuriated me. I myself knew that people were, in a way, marked out by their place of birth, but I tried to behave as though this was not so. My principle was that everyone was essentially the same, a belief I still adhere to, and that essentially they were only marked by their birthplace if they chose to be. Kipling had lived in India, and had written about it. I lived in England, and had written about it. I didn't see that either of us had betrayed ourselves as writers. After all, were there any real reasons why an Indian *had* to write about India? Its problems were certainly huge and appalling, and quite certainly *somebody* should write about them; but it seemed to me that a foreigner like Kipling might develop a clearer vision than an Indian as to what India was about. There was, at the time, no writer of Indian origin who possessed that clarity of vision except R.K. Narayan. Now there is Naipaul and perhaps Rushdie.

I was in no way qualified to write about India, except as a foreigner. I did not speak any of its languages; I had not travelled very widely in it; from a fairly early age I had resolved to leave it as soon as it became possible. In a way, I feared it. I was a little paranoic about being driven back in its direction. But I could not explain this to someone like Carruth, and I do not think that I could clearly explain it to myself. What I felt about India was not connected with logic.

In the summer of 1966, I had lunch with Charles Wintour, then Editor of the *Evening Standard*. I had always had a good relationship with this paper, and we were, I think, discussing the possibility of my returning to Algeria for some story. In the middle of lunch there was a phone call for Wintour. He returned looking depressed. 'My cricket correspondent has died,' he said, 'he'd been ill for some time.' I said I was sorry; John Clarke had been a good and knowledgeable writer. 'Yes,' said Wintour, 'I'm sorry too. The second Test against the West Indies is next week, and I've nobody to cover it.' If I thought this a faintly callous remark, I could nevertheless understand that Wintour had a problem.

He said, 'I read somewhere that you were very keen on cricket; in fact, that you were a cricket reporter in India when you were thirteen.' This was true. 'If you wanted to cover the rest of the series for us,' Wintour said, 'I'd be glad. But what about this trip of yours?' I said I was much more interested in covering cricket. He looked puzzled, but smiled and said, 'It's a bit of a technical problem. We put out six editions, one after the other, during the day. You'd have to file one piece after another, reporting developments, all day long. Could you handle that?' He sent me off to a county match at the Oval, where Kent was playing Surrey, to try me out. I did not find the work difficult, and accepted Wintour's offer.

In the press box at Lord's, I felt shy and lost. I might be a foreign correspondent, even a war correspondent, but the journalists around me now were a special sort of breed of which I knew little. Among them were cricketers I had idolized in my adolescence: Denis Compton, Keith Miller, Len Hutton, Godfrey Evans, Richie Benaud, Sir Learie Constantine. None of them were likely ever to have heard of me. I didn't expect that Bob Simpson, the Australian captain, who was doing the expert comments for the *Standard*, would have heard of me either. I was surprised by his first remark when he arrived. 'I hear you're a poet,' he said. I shuddered inwardly; this was by no means a remark that sounded approving.

But in the days that followed, my fears vanished. Simpson and I, in the end, got on famously. He was very likeable, a stocky, cheerful young man who was fully aware of his own talent as a player, and exploited it fully; truly a professional in what he did. I think he sensed that I was also a professional, though in a very different field. As time passed, and the Tests went by, at Lord's, at Nottingham, at Leeds, and finally at the Oval, we corrected each other's copy before the boy took it to the phone: he corrected my technical errors, I corrected his spelling mistakes. After play was over we usually had a few drinks together.

Sir Learie Constantine, the former great West Indian all-rounder, also befriended me. A dynamic hitter, a very fast bowler, and a fieldsman so brilliant that he was nicknamed 'Electric Heels', he had become rather slow and portly, and was benevolent with it. 'You don't know what you're capable of till you've done it,' he once told me. 'You know, boy, you think you're settled in life, but one day I think your whole life will turn around. For the better,' he added, 'unless you drink too much.'

5

Shortly before Francis was born, I acquired a house in North London. Though I felt I had become adult and responsible because of his birth, I wasn't really, not in any practical sense. I was totally incapable of dealing with expenditure, and wholly bewildered by bills. Nevertheless, to have a house of one's own also meant one entertained in it. During my coverage of the Test series I had encountered most of the cricketers, including the great Sir Gary Sobers. He had a very successful series; once, on a cold day at Leeds, I watched him put down two large whiskies before he went out to bat. I don't know who said cricketers shouldn't drink; Sobers that day made 174.

But to me the cricketer of most interest was Basil D'Oliveira. D'Oliveira was an aggressive and outstanding right-hand batsman, a right-arm medium pace bowler who could also spin from the off, and a sound fielder. But he had been born into the Cape Coloured community in South Africa, which meant that under apartheid he would never be able to play first-class cricket. His performances in the kind of cricket he was allowed to play in his own country attracted the attention of some English players who coached in South Africa. In 1960 he was offered a contract by a Lancashire league club, and came to England. He did very well in league cricket. In 1965 he started to play county cricket for Worcestershire, was naturalized, and by 1966 played for England.

D'Oliveira came to dinner when he was in London. He was a personable man, handsome and poised, confident in himself after all the hardships he had undergone. The great ambition of his life was to represent England in South Africa. This may have been partly due to the local-boy-makes-good syndrome, but he had a genuine desire to show coloured people in his former country that they had no need to despair. It was possible to be successful in life, even if one had to emigrate to do so. He was friendly with Dennis Brutus, the coloured South African poet and lawyer, who also thought that for D'Oliveira to play in South Africa would be an excellent fillip to black morale.

The England cricketers were due to tour that country at the end of 1968. Basil had done well enough against the West Indies in 1966 for him to feel reasonably sure that he would be selected for this tour. But his desire to confirm his selection beyond doubt motivated him; 'I can't afford to fail next year,' he said.

James Cameron, who also came to dinner, told him, 'Whether or not they select you for the tour, Vorster won't let you in. All my books are banned in South Africa, the government says they're pornographic. They'll find some excuse or other to keep you out.' He was to be proved correct, but we didn't find that out for some years.

In 1967 D'Oliveira did well against the visiting Test teams, as he had hoped. That winter he went to the West Indies as one of the English team. His selection for South Africa hinged to some extent on what he did in the Caribbean. If he were to be selected for the coming tour, there might well be trouble with the South Africans. The full glare of press publicity was turned on him in the West Indies, and uncomfortably conscious of it, he failed. The English press, incidentally, was by no means all in favour of him. During the series against the West Indies, one of my colleagues in the press box, a former Oxford Blue, said to me, 'So you're a friend of D'Oliveira's. You would be. Tell him I know he's sailing under false colours. He says he's thirty-one; but he's much older.

He's too old to play for England, even if he belonged here, which he doesn't, and you don't.' D'Oliveira and I, it seemed, were in the same boat.

In any event, when the 1968 season started, and the Australian cricketers came, D'Oliveira, with the South African tour ahead, continued to lack confidence and form. He did so poorly in county cricket that it was a surprise when he was selected for the first Test against Australia. 'They picked him,' somebody wrote, 'so that he should fail. Then they will have a reason to omit him from the team for South Africa.' D'Oliveira made the highest English score of the match. He was dropped for the next three Tests; but there was so much public protest that he was restored to the team for the fifth and last. In this he made 158, and became a certainty for the tour. Or so everyone thought. When the seventeen players were announced, he was not one of them. A quite incredible uproar followed. At the end of it, the selectors did something else extraordinary. They said that one of the players picked, Cartwright, was unfit, and that D'Oliveira had been selected to replace him, 'as a bowler'.

Shortly after this, the South African prime minister, John Vorster, declared in a speech that any English team which included D'Oliveira would be 'unacceptable' in his country. James' prophecy had been exact, though Vorster hadn't even troubled to invent an excuse. The MCC, then the rulers of English cricket, replied that if this was the case, the tour was off. The 'D'Oliveira Affair', as it came to be called, marked the first stage of the segregation of South Africa from international sport. I went to Worcester after this, to interview D'Oliveira. He invited me and my photographer, David Steen, to breakfast, after which we played tennis-ball cricket in the backyard with his two small sons. One of them, Damian, now plays for Worcestershire.

D'Oliveira's dream had been shattered. He now knew that he would never represent England in South Africa. What he seemed most upset about, however, was that, with the trip cancelled, the other English cricketers would suffer a financial loss because of him. I also inquired into his actual age. 'You know, no proper birth certificates, or any kind of certificates, were issued for coloured people in the 1930s,' he said. 'I've always known my birth *date,* but not the year. I guessed, when I said it was 1934. My mother now tells me it was 1931.' The Oxford Blue had been right; but D'Oliveira's age, it seemed to me, didn't matter, and to raise it was racialist.

I always hesitate before I use this word, it is so encompassingly and so uncritically used as a word of condemnation. In this particular instance, I think I use it correctly. After this I met the black South African singer, Miriam Makeba, and the Zulu actor, Todd Matchekisa, who lived in exile in London. Matchekisa, in particular, became a friend of mine. He once said to me, 'When I first met you, brother, I thought you must be a racialist. In South Africa, the Indians are more racialist than the whites are. That's because they're frightened of their own colour.' I wondered how far the last sentence applied to me. Perhaps what I didn't know was the colour of my mind.

In Israel I had met Lionel Rogosin, a square-set fair-haired man of considerable energy, who had produced two brilliant films. I saw both, and I thought at the time that they would survive in cinematic history. One, *On the Bowery*, was about the lives of the winos and deadbeats in that part of New York. The other, *Come Back Africa*, was about repression in South Africa. Makeba and Matchekisa had helped Lionel and his crew with the film. Lionel came to London to recruit me as the scriptwriter for a new film, which was supposed to be about the horrors of nuclear war.

Many of my friends were members of the Committee for Nuclear Disarmament (CND) or the other organizations trying to ban the bomb. Most of them, in fact, had this in common. I didn't see the viability of saying, 'Ban the Bomb.' The bomb had been invented; it was there, part of our lives. No government would ban it if it knew that another country had it. As slogans go, this one seemed to me foolish. Also to the point, I couldn't see how to handle the subject as a documentary. Lionel's first two films had been very specific, and his material had been there, in front of the camera. Here it was an idea, rather than a physical reality, that we were trying to film; and ideas are usually conveyed by talking heads.

The first talking head Lionel acquired for the purposes of this film was Lord Bertrand Russell. Nobody who was not young in the 1950s can have any idea of how powerful an influence people like him and Kingsley Martin, the editor of the *New Statesman*, were. Russell was slight and wispy, Kingsley Martin somewhat less attenuated; neither was tall, but both had magnificent features, in Russell's case somewhat wizened, and both had impressive heads of white hair. They looked like shamans, or father figures, for the motley tribe of bomb-banners and peace-preachers.

I had ceased to admire Kingsley Martin very much, for purely private reasons. He once came to Oxford to lecture, when I was an undergraduate. We knew each other; I asked him to have a drink with me before his lecture and assembled my friends to meet him. He was aware of his shortness; he balanced on the ledge of my fireplace (it was summer, and nothing burned within), and told us how much he loved Oxford. 'If I hadn't been a great editor,' he said, 'I think I could have been a great teacher.' Some years later, I went to a party thrown by him and Dorothy Woodman in their flat off the Strand; it was attended by many and I left with a raincoat not my own.

Kingsley phoned me the next day, extremely angry; the raincoat happened to belong to his niece. He said that, as a matter of principle, I should personally return it to her, and personally apologize; she lived in a remote suburb, very nearly in Kent. Dorothy Woodman said it was perfectly all right if I posted it; so I did, and the lady apparently received it; but Kingsley went around London saying I had stolen her raincoat.

This was one less idol in my particular shrine; but I had great respect for Lord Russell, which was somewhat increased by the interview I did with him for Lionel's film. He was then very old, nearly ninety, and far from well. Lionel had hired a sort of garage or barn in North London as the studio, and Lord Russell arrived with a nurse-secretary who was supposed to feed him through his nostrils every hour or so. This necessitated constant breaks in the interview, but he stood up to it all like a trooper, and answered the foolish and obvious questions I had to ask with the obvious answers; going through all this hardship, I suppose in the interests of nuclear disarmament. How someone so intelligent thought this possible, I don't know.

His patience snapped at one point. The interview was done, but somebody in the crew suggested an idea. It was put to Russell in a manner that could only be described as clumsy. 'This guy who's been interviewing you,' someone said to Russell, 'is young, he's a poet, he's got everything ahead of him. You're old and sick and dying. Anyone can see that. Why don't *you* interview *him* about the future?' Lord Russell refused.

Fortunately, he bore no hard feelings. I had tea with him at his house in Hasker Street on several occasions. Once, in Battersea Park, while I was wheeling Francis about, I saw him, also being wheeled about by a nurse, and he waved, frowned in a peculiar way at the child in his pushchair, and appeared to see no similarities in their respective states. He was a man of extreme dignity, who had to suffer because of age.

Those protestors against the bomb, who happened to be younger than Russell, had their own areas of privacy. Lionel's next acquisition, after Russell, was a group of intellectuals, some of whom were for, and some against, nuclear disarmament. One of them was an actress who was deeply against it. 'I would give my life,' she said to me before the actual take, 'if I could do something for nuclear disarmament.' What happened during the takes—there were several—was that somebody had so positioned the camera that it was always shooting up her skirt. When the rushes were shown to Lionel, they were also shown to the actress, who insisted that they should all be burned. She was perhaps sincere when she said she would give her life for nuclear disarmament; it was strange that she wasn't willing to give people a look at her knickers, considering that what she was saying at the time was important to her. I suggested to Lionel, after we had gone through all this, that we should scrap what had been done and go to 'filmabilities', which would be actual in Hiroshima and Nagasaki. He heartily agreed, in the sense that he ran out of money and therefore scrapped the film. He was a very gifted film-maker, who I think made no more films.

My feelings about South Africa and the bomb, at the time when all my contemporaries were concerned with those issues, were somewhat ambivalent. That is to say, I disapproved heartily of both; but I didn't see what one could do about South Africa unless one was in South Africa. I didn't see what talking about it, or refusing to consume South African sherry or tinned fruit, was going to do about the South African problem. Nor could I see what talking about banning the bomb could do unless you were in a position to do so, which few people in the world were. James Cameron was a member of the CND, and so forth, but, as he said to me, 'These people only want my name because it's not an unknown name. They grasp that. Otherwise they lack reality.'

I received an invitation from the Food and Agriculture Organization (FAO) to attend a conference of what they called Young World Leaders, which was to take place in Rome. I was flattered to be thought of as a Young World Leader, and I also thought it wouldn't be a bad idea to have a week off in Rome. I went to this conference. Apart from Nigel Calder, who was a scientist, there was nobody at the conference I could relate to. The African delegates were continually out of the hotel in search of whores and Chianti; the Indians did not dare to express such explicit needs; the Americans were very solemn about being Young World Leaders. Calder and I sat through innumerable speeches during which the others talked about how they would 'lend youth' in their various countries.

Calder was more methodical than I; he took down points from their speeches. In the end, the conference was supposed to issue a manifesto, saying what all the Young World Leaders felt. 'What *do* we feel?' I asked Calder. He and I were supposed to compose the manifesto, which was then to be officially read by me under the television cameras of the Italian channels and the United Nations. Before this, the delegates were to visit the Pope, to receive his blessing before they issued their manifesto. I thought the Pope was rather nice to us, but wondered about the manifesto.

Eventually, what it said was that we, the young people of the world, were going to be the guiding elements in its future, and we all intended to see that peace, happiness, and universal welfare reigned everywhere. How we were to achieve this wasn't, so far as I can remember, mentioned. I said all this under the floodlights and cameras, and afterwards I was asked to wait a day after the other delegates had departed. The director of the FAO, who was an Indian, B.R. Sen, then suggested to me that since I seemed to have a flair for writing, and had, he believed, some experience in television, I should write a television film for the FAO, which could be shown all over the world, and which would point out that every country should help other countries to ensure that nobody ever died of starvation.

I was offered a good deal of money for this, which was why I accepted; but I was also totally incapable of believing in what I was supposed to say, and that, I suppose, was why what I wrote was so awful that even the FAO refused to use it. 'What did you think you were doing?' James MacGibbon asked after he had read the scenario I sent Mr Sen. 'If you could write about light bulbs, you ought to be able to write about this stuff.'

I said, 'Light bulbs are necessary, and this isn't.' James agreed. I did not then know who, in the years to come, my employers would be.

In 1967, a neighbour of mine in Islington was a tall, red-haired young painter called Timothy Behrens, who had a pretty wife called Harriet. Tim and I used the same pub, and so did a large person with white hair whose real name was Peter von Bork. His family, during the First World War, had changed its name to Brook. Peter Brook wrote under the pseudonym of Anthony Carson. He produced some extremely funny travel books and novels, though he was personally somewhat sombre. Tim, Peter, and I used to drink together in Islington. One day in June, I heard that another war was likely to break out in the Middle East and that the Israelis had swept over Egyptian airfields and destroyed their warplanes. The first thing that struck me was that I had many friends in Israel.

I telephoned James Cameron, who said, 'Go if you can. I should if I were you. But I don't think there's a single paper which doesn't have someone going already. I've turned down two offers. I'm too old for all this.' Then, in one of the great flights of imagination he was uniquely capable of, he said, 'Try someone unlikely. Try a magazine. Try an unlikely magazine, like *Queen*.' Francis Wyndham was the Literary Editor of *Queen*, which was essentially for women. I rang him; he put me through to the Editor and proprietor, Jocelyn Stevens, who said he thought it a brilliant idea. 'Leave tonight,' he said. Tim, who had been listening to my end of this conversation, said, 'Can I come too? I'll draw pictures.' I suggested this to Stevens.

'Oh, yes,' Stevens said. 'The old concept of an illustrator accompanying the correspondent. Brilliant. Come to the office and pick up your tickets and money, and a car will take you to Heathrow. What did you say the artist's name was?' Peter Brook said, in an annoyed voice, 'If this is going to be a free ride to the Mediterranean, why didn't you think of taking me?' Tim and I rushed off to our respective homes to pack. I was told at the *Queen* office that all flights to Israel had been cancelled, and we would therefore, have to get to Nicosia in Cyprus, and try for onward flights from there.

It was only when we were launched into the sky that I began to have doubts about our mission. This was not so much because I was afraid of what lay ahead as because Tim was worrying me. I had already developed a great respect for anyone who was a professional in what he did; but my respect for Tim was vested in the fact that he was professional as a painter. I had no idea whatever what he would be like as a war correspondent. Some of the English correspondents I had been with in Algeria were almost certain to be in Israel, and I knew in my bones that Tim and they were exact opposites. My journalistic life had for once overflowed into my other life; and I was doubtful about the possible consequences. This feeling became intensified when Tim told me that he had seen part of the bombardment of London as a child, and had loved the colours.

We landed at Nicosia and got to the Ledra Palace, which was full of correspondents, some of whom I knew from the Eichmann trial and from Algeria—also from El Vino in Fleet Street. Everyone was congregated in the lobby, or, in the case of the Europeans, in their rooms, waiting for telephone calls from their head offices or for news of the state of flights to Israel. Two correspondents, dripping wet, came back from Limassol. They had hired a fishing boat to convey them to the Israeli coast. The boatmen had consented to do this for two hundred dollars cash down, circled through foggy seas, and put the passengers ashore on a rocky coast warning them to beware of gunfire. The two correspondents had crept up the beach, and, climbing a hill, had met a massive and rugged man. '*Shalom,*' they said nervously in Hebrew, hoping this apparition was not an Arab. '*Kalispera,*' he replied in a puzzled but friendly fashion, 'good evening.' He was a Cypriot, and the correspondents had been landed within a mile of their departure point.

The correspondents were all warning one another about this kind of thing, except for Tim, who had found the bar, and a very obese, mustachioed Belgian reporter, who wore the clothes Brussels presumably thought suitable for the Middle East: a white shirt, white shorts that displayed his hairy thighs, and a red straw hat which for some extraordinary reason, and through some extraordinary chemical, was fluorescent. 'I am hot,' he said, 'I wish to cool myself.' The swimming pool was down the lawn from the lobby windows, and we could all watch the fluorescent hat moving towards and around it like some rare firefly.

I decided, like most of the others, to get some sleep. I advised Tim, in the bar, to follow our example. 'No, no,' he said, 'I'll stay awake. After all, we've got to get there, haven't we? I'll find a way.'

At roughly four in the morning, I was awoken by the sound of the French windows in my bedroom being shattered from outside, and Tim bursting through. He was followed by a very angry manager demanding money. 'I knocked at your door,' said Tim, 'but you wouldn't wake up. I've just solved the problem. I hired a fishing boat at Limassol, and the fishermen said they'd take us for two hundred dollars, which I've paid them.'

Half an hour later, a plane chartered by an American television station took off, and by means of a rapid deal I was able to get us both on it. We came down through a blackout at Lod airport, and were taken by bus to Tel Aviv at more or less dawn. Since transport seemed slightly difficult, we checked into a hotel; but I was very restless, and managed to fix a friend's car to take me to Jerusalem. I left a message for Tim to follow me, and the addresses necessary, and drove away.

It was cool at dawn, the blue coming up over the old hills as we went into Jerusalem, fighter planes flying overhead on their various missions, the gunfire rumbling from the city, shattered tanks of the 1948 war by the road. Instead of going directly to where the correspondents were to be briefed, I went to Carmi's.

When the car drew up at his garden gate, he was sitting on the lawn with his wife and a new baby son, sorting out groceries from a package. When he saw me his eyes widened, and he ran across the grass to me, arms open, saying, 'You bastard! You fucker!' and the other things men say to each other if they are friends, 'I should have known you'd be here!' and I felt secure, about myself, not about Tim. He arrived shortly after this, and said awkward hellos to Carmi and his family. Carmi was by this time deep in explanations about the beginning of the war. 'I felt so ashamed I was in the reserves,' he said, 'because I'm forty, and so nervous because my elder son, you know Gaddi—but would you believe it, he's eighteen now—he's been called up. Tafni and I went to stock up on groceries when it all started, and you wouldn't believe, there was a man in the queue ahead who wanted 365 packets of toothpaste. I can believe the war will last a year, but how many teeth would he have had?' His arms went round me once more, and he repeated, 'It's good you're here, *Dommeleh!*' I have never felt so much identified with a race as at that moment.

It was at this point that Tim said to me, 'You're very emotional about all this, aren't you? After all, the Arabs are probably nice guys too.' This was not what was uppermost in my mind; what was uppermost was the night-fighting, illuminated by burning tanks, full of the smells of cordite and petrol, and of clothing and bodies on fire. Looking back on it now, I realize how far back in time it was. Wars nowadays are not fought like this. I recollect, vividly, the morning when the Israelis took the Old City. It was a crisp blue day building up into great heat. Coming up into the city I saw a large number of upturned hand-carts which had contained bottles of aerated water in many colours. Shards of broken glass now gleamed from the ground, amidst pools of blue, green, and yellow liquid, like some exotic kind of blood. Further up the hill, by the entry to the Wailing Wall, was a well from which an American television crew, sweating in the sun, was drawing up water. An Arab passer-by called out warnings to them in a form of English they could not follow. There were two dead men in the well.

Generally speaking, however, the Arab civilians did not seem afraid of the Israeli troops, who were probably under orders to behave well. What was historically important about the Six-Day War was not only the amazing pace at which it was fought and brought to a conclusion, but what that conclusion was. The Israelis had taken back the Old City and its religious monuments, including the Wailing Wall; they had also taken back large segments of territory on the West Bank of the Jordan River, and these conquered territories turned out to be more hazardous in the keeping than in the taking. There were symptoms of it on that first day.

I was with an Israeli major, Shlomo, whom I knew from my previous trips. He was stocky and compact and soaked with sweat, and his uniform smelt of this and of smoke. 'Come,' he said, 'come. I will show you the Wall,' as though it was a personal possession. We came up to the rough, ancient, yellow stones of the Wall. Broken bottles of more gaseous and multicoloured liquids were shattered in the cobble-stoned alley up which we came. The area in front of it was filled with troops, and also with the hasidim, the orthodox Jews in their black suits, sidelocks, and hats. 'None of us have touched the Wall,' Shlomo said, 'since 1948.'

The hasidim seemed in a bad temper, for some reason; they turned when they saw me, and began to protest against my presence. Apparently they objected also to the fact that my head was uncovered. Shlomo lost *his* temper; it seemed to be a morning for doing so. 'Look,' he said, 'this is a friend of Israel. Whenever there is trouble, he is here. Look, my head is uncovered. But I fought for the Wall, and he is with me. Did you take part in the fighting?' He refused to cover his own head, or to allow me to cover mine.

It was an embarrassing and ridiculous little scene. But the hasidim had been a national embarrassment for some years. In 1961, on my first visit, ambulances taking invalids up to the hospital on Mount Scopus had been stopped on the Sabbath. Friends of mine, who had been divorced and now wanted to marry other people were forbidden to so, unless they went to Cyprus or somewhere outside the borders of Israel. Certain Jews, who had come from countries where rabbis had not been provably available, were considered to be of a bastard race because their ancestors had not been legally married. The hasidim were even more of an embarrassment, because, in a sense, they represented the values to preserve which so many had died for. In the future, they were to become more powerful in Israel.

After the Wailing Wall, I found Tim, stained with dust and trying to find some beverage stronger than aerated water. I also found Carmi, who put us into a Land Rover with two officers, friends of his, who were going to survey the territories captured on the West Bank overnight. Prior to this, we visited the Church of the Holy Sepulchre, which was itself divided into territories; the Protestants, the Catholics, and the Greek Orthodox Church all held different parts of it and each drew separate harvests of money from visitors. Obviously they all wanted to conciliate the new rulers, and were all conducting thanksgiving services for the Israeli victory; the air was full of the thunder of bells and the blue smoke of incense. The sound and smoke suggested some renewal of hostilities.

We drove out on to the West Bank. Jericho and Bethlehem were among the shabby, dusty towns we came to, festooned with religious monuments and populated by Arabs who did not seem dismayed by the presence among them of the conquerors: young, fit soldiers streaked with dust and sweat and carrying Uzis. Their faces were often mild and innocent; in Bethlehem one of these faces was seen by me in a Catholic church wearing an expression of unsecular awe. He was with a beautiful young girl soldier, who resembled a Madonna. They were holding hands in a rapt manner. '*Yofi*, eh?' the soldier whispered to the girl, 'nice, isn't it?'

For some reason this little event touched me. But, also in Bethlehem, Tim vanished for a while with an Arab urchin. 'He's going to sell me some hash,' he explained to us, 'he says it's first-class stuff.' The Israeli officers with us were not amused. 'To sell it is a crime for us,' one said to me, 'to encourage them by buying it is worse.' Tim didn't see the logic of this. He not only bought a supply, but commenced to light up and smoke it in front of the officers, who were horrified.

On the way back, at dusk, we came to a cemetery under the great walls of the city, the tombstones uprooted and broken. One of the officers, Benno, who in civilian life was a professor of history, remarked, 'That is a Jewish cemetery. The Arabs have broken the tombstones to build their houses.' He said nothing more about the matter, but the shock in his face was manifest. We re-entered the holy city, which had been cleaned up considerably since the morning.

Carmi and Tami were at home, and there were a number of other friends who had all come to celebrate. An impromptu party was decided on; tins and bottles and materials for a barbecue were brought from various people's houses, and a picnic site was selected. By this time it was dark; the war was over, but fighter planes were still flying overhead. The women in our party outnumbered the men; some of them had husbands fighting on various fronts, their whereabouts and welfare unknown; and though this was intended as a celebration, many of the participants were in tears. Carmi shook his head. 'You can't help any of this,' he said. But across the sky a fighter came down to land with a prolonged cry, as of release from pain, and all the lights in the city came on. The blackout was over.

We flew home; everything now seemed rather anti-climactic. I couldn't say that my first experience of working with an artist rather than a photographer had been a success. Tim hadn't really known what all this fighting was for; he knew very little of what Israel was about; and I was surprised when, after our return, he told me that he was himself Jewish. 'I didn't feel Jewish when I was there,' he said. The war hadn't, for him, been a serious affair at all. In fact very few of my 'artistic' friends in London considered our visit to the war as more than an aberration. David Steem, the photographer with whom I usually worked for *Nova,* on a glossy magazine, said to me, 'If only you'd asked me to come.' In many ways, I wished I had. Tim was a fine painter, and, in London, an excellent companion. But I no longer felt that a connection with the arts should necessarily imply a severance from reality.

The time I had spent in Israel—less than a week though it was—had provided me with a connection to the actual world. In future, when on assignment, I always went with a photographer. The photographer represented reality; he always knew as much as I did about our mission, and I could discuss it in detail with him. David Steen, tall and dark and often with an air of abstraction, was the first of many photographers with whom I formed a working partnership. I did a piece for *Nova* every month and he was usually paired with me. Since we were both freelancers, Dennis Hackett, the Editor, did not send us abroad together; but we went on assignments all over England, and these assignments were often difficult.

There was, for example, a time when Christine Keeler came back into the news. She had, of course, been a principal participant in the sex scandal of 1962, which had nearly brought down Harold Macmillan's government. Stephen Ward, the doctor who had been a kind of amateur procurer for his friends, committed suicide, others connected with Miss Keeler went to prison, and eventually she did too. Mandy Rice-Davies, who had been an associate of hers and a friend of Ward's, was at that time married to a nightclub owner in Haifa. I met her briefly during the Six-Day War; she appeared to be a reformed character nursing wounded soldiers.

After the pyrotechnics of 1962, Miss Keeler had submerged once more into the more peculiar strata of London life; but she had now come up with an autobiography which was causing much alarm among those who expected to be mentioned in it. Hackett suggested that I should do a piece on her, and found me a phone number. I tried this a dozen times, but whatever hour of the day or night it was, I was told by the variety of voices which answered that Miss Keeler was asleep. I had almost given up on the story when she phoned me herself; she had a Cockney accent which, even on the telephone, sounded sexual. She said she wanted five hundred pounds to be interviewed. Hackett was not willing to do this at first, but after some thought he consented; maybe it would be worth it. Miss Keeler suggested that we should buy her lunch in a restaurant called Alvaro's in Chelsea the next day.

Alvaro's was said to be one of the most expensive restaurants in London; so expensive and exclusive that, when I telephoned for a table, I was told that no reservations could be made. Only the owner's friends were admitted. 'That can't be true,' David Steen said, 'we'll simply turn up and see what happens.'

The appointment was for one in the afternoon, and next day we arrived at Alvaro's. It was Alvaro himself who met us, not effusively. 'I only give tables to my friends,' he said, 'and my friends are all famous. Christine Keeler, yes, she is my friend, but I do not know if she is your friend. If she comes here, I will give her a table, yes, but until she comes you must wait for her outside, and, yes, you may telephone her.' We followed his advice, and after some difficulties were told by an operator that the phone was dead, because the bill had not been paid. It was by this time about half past one.

We went and stood outside Alvaro's. It was raining, and we were in the position of mendicants at a millionaire's front door. After half an hour or so, two taxis drew up and Christine Keeler and half a dozen other young women, gaily garbed and expensively scented, tumbled out, like a flock of birds of paradise. 'Pay the taxi, will you?' said Miss Keeler, 'I've brought a few friends to lunch.'

No interview was possible. All the girls talked vociferously all the time, and also insisted on drinking pink champagne. The result was that when the bill came, David and I, between us, could not find the money to pay it. Alvaro, when we showed him our press cards, grudgingly consented to take a cheque, on one condition, which was that we should not only pay this bill, but two previous bills which Miss Keeler had not settled. When we had done this, she became more helpful in her attitude.

'Sorry about the interview,' she said. 'But I have to go to Reading this afternoon to see my little son. If you drive me there, you could interview me on the way.' Reading is about forty miles from London, possibly a two-hour drive in the weekend traffic; certainly, if David drove, I would have time to interview Miss Keeler. She had become very chirpy, and there was no difficulty in drawing her out. However, she said she would not sign a release letter till I had paid her the five hundred pounds.

She had dark hair and eyes and a slender figure, but was not beautiful; the main quality about her was difficult to describe accurately, but it could be called a kind of grubbiness. Apart from the amatory activities so graphically described in the world press, she had very briefly been married, and the small boy we were going to visit had been the result. She told me at great length that she cared for nothing in life except this child, that he lived with her parents, and that she sent them all the money she had for his upkeep. She would not say where the money came from.

We arrived at Reading. Though Miss Keeler had said she visited her parents every weekend, she didn't seem to have a clear idea where their house was. We found it at last, through the directions of a passer-by. Miss Keeler said her little boy would dash out to welcome her. That would be a good picture for David, she felt. He got himself ready, and she rang the bell. A middle-aged woman of sour appearance, Miss Keeler's mother, opened the door; she was accompanied by an ill-clad child, Miss Keeler's son. As soon as the child saw his mother, he uttered a cry of terror, and rushed back into the house. This not very cordial reception did not seem to disconcert Miss Keeler. 'He must be tired,' she said, and, to her mother, 'give the boys a drink.'

'A drink of what?' demanded the mother. 'Madam here doesn't send us enough for the kid's milk, and "Give the boys a drink," she says. Well, if you want a drink, there's a pub on the corner and you can have one there. After what she's already done to our good name, I'm not having her bringing men down here from London.' Miss Keeler threw up her hands. 'They've come to interview me,' she said, 'and they're paying me five hundred quid for it.' Her mother didn't look impressed. 'I doubt that we'll ever see a penny,' she said, but grudgingly told us, 'I could make you a cup of tea.'

At this time Edmund Blunden and Robert Lowell were contenders for the professorship of poetry at Oxford. Blunden won. He was an old man, a lyric poet of minor, but definite, talent. Lowell was among the best living poets. It was natural that Blunden's as a choice be criticized, but this was done very brutally, and he was said to have no credentials at all for the post. David and I went to his country house to interview him. Blunden seemed utterly shocked and bewildered by the attacks on him. 'The greatest experience in my life was the First World War,' he said, 'and the most horrible. I go to France every year to look at the old battlefields. I don't want ever to forget them, or all the people who died there. But the attacks now, they're nearly as bad as that was.' He was nearly in tears. His distress affected us.

Driving back, David said, 'We get all sorts, don't we? The Keeler, and then him.' We did get all sorts; it all went down to experience.

6

Nova, which had its offices in Southampton Street, had started out as a women's magazine, a child of the International Publishing Corporation (IPC). The 1960s market was full of women's magazines, and IPC, or Hugh Cudlipp, its boss, decided to make *Nova* different—more sophisticated than the others, more witty. As a result, it proved a failure with most women, but was found to have a large male readership. When I first started to write for *Nova,* the editor, Dennis Hackett, was attempting to switch policies in midstream, to continue with the concept of a women's magazine, but make it more appealing to men.

The fashion pages, for example, used models somewhat bustier than the average; they were sometimes shown in their underwear, holding up the clothes they were about to put on. Occasionally two of them were shown together, both in their underwear, and these photographs had slight lesbian undertones. Hackett wanted other stories which were connected with sex apart from Christine Keeler. At that time *Playboy* had already existed for some while. But two new magazines, supposedly modelled on it, had appeared in Britain: *King,* and *Penthouse*, the latter run by an American called Bob Guccione.

David and I were despatched by Hackett to talk to the editors of these magazines. Ted Simons, of *King*, was not very interesting, but Guccione definitely was. He was large and languid, attired elegantly in a *Playboy* version of casual clothes. A gold chain gleamed against his hairy chest. He lived in a small Kensington flat, attended by a blonde nymphet; this seemed to be his office. It was quite obvious that he knew his way around; he had lived in England a while, as a cartoonist and pin-up photographer, before he was seized by the idea of a magazine which would be a kind of stepsister to *Playboy*; that is, it presented a male image for its readers to aspire to, the image of a suave young man, well-heeled, well-dressed, a successful seducer, and 'with it'. But the female image it presented was less clinical than *Playboy's*, more overtly sexual.

Guccione had carried out a very successful launch campaign; he had sent subscription forms and copies of the first issue to a carefully chosen list of people, including bishops, MPs, and eminent women. None of these, obviously, were likely to read the magazine, except in private; but nearly all of them could be depended on to denounce it in public, and most did. The natural result was that the Post Office confiscated the copies sent by mail; and that the sales of the second issue were remarkable.

I found Guccione a rather attractive personality. He was tough, and streetwise, and knew what he wanted, which was success and money. At the same time he was very open, and had a curious quality of independence about him. We bought him lunch at a nearby trattoria, and several years later, when he was successful and rich, I went to interview him at his newly opened Penthouse Club in London. 'I owe you a lunch,' he said and insisted that I try the club's steak. At our first encounter, he enlightened me, in several respects as to his business. 'A girl's at her best before she's twenty,' he said. 'After that her tits fall. And once you use a girl in a magazine, it's important that you don't use her a second time. The readers want change. In fact it's better if she's never posed nude before. That way, the guys get a feeling they're violating her.'

He also explained how, as a photographer, he had persuaded young women to remove their clothes for the camera. 'Say she's come to be shot in her bra and panties. You have to work on her to take the bra off. Tell her how beautiful she is, how great her tits are. Once the bra comes off, there's no difficulty about the panties. I've known them, after a picture session, to make coffee without putting anything back on, jiggling around all over the place. Basically, babes *like* to pose with no clothes on.'

On the way back to the office, I asked David if he had picked up any instructive tips from the conversation. He grinned, shook his head, and said, 'Why don't you do another story from a different angle, the angle of the girls who take their clothes off?' It was not the first time he had given me an excellent idea *gratis*.

Eventually we decided to construct a huge story, starting with Simons and Guccione and going on through the various aspects of the nude model business. We interviewed several young women who were successful in this field. A few were rather sinister, but most were pleasant girls, rather like receptionists or secretaries, chastely clad: not at all the kind of girl one would think of making a pass at. June Palmer, one of the most successful models in Britain, was one such; she was annoyed with Guccione because he *had* made a pass at her. But after lunch in her flat, she suggested that we might like to take a picture of her in the nude. This was not a sexual suggestion in the least. Her business was having herself photographed in this way; she didn't mind if we did if it helped us.

She also ran, in what seemed an altruistic way, an agency in which she trained nude models. She did not charge them for this, but once a week ran a camera club where people paid to photograph the trainees. Often the club members had no film in their cameras. We attended a session where I met a girl who was in tears about it all. She was learning to pose in the nude in order to support her husband, who was an alcoholic. Another model, attempting to comfort her, said, 'It's not like being a whore, dear,' and the first girl wept even more. June seemed unmoved by all this. 'She's being childish,' June said.

Hackett was immensely pleased by this article. He was a well-travelled Yorkshireman, with strong likes and dislikes. One day he telephoned me and asked me to interview David Frost. 'He's a bastard,' said Dennis, 'take the hatchet to him.' I suggested that I be allowed to make up my own mind. Frost then stood me up five times in a row. I started to agree with Dennis, and when I had seen Frost at script conferences for his current programme, and met him a few times, I saw no reason to revise my opinion. Dennis was delighted by my article, especially when I quoted someone who claimed that he wrote Frost's *ad libs*. He suggested that I come on the *Nova* staff to edit the Arts Section.

In this capacity I shared a large office with Ruth Inglis, who was American and had spent her youth in China, and Tom Hutching a large, bearded, Falstaffian film critic. None of us had any work that occupied us full-time; so we went and came freely, without being tied down by fixed hours. We became friends, and habitually lunched together in one or the other of the pubs around Southampton Street. Ruth, however, had a female instinct for thrift. Dennis Hackett had a bar in his office, she said; why didn't we have one in ours? We used a filing cabinet; we took it in weekly turns to stock it up with liquor, various mixes, and an ice bucket replenished from Dennis' bar. On one occasion—IPC was prone to experiment—a young journalism student, who had won some award or other in his college, was put in charge of the entire office for a week in Dennis' absence. It was thought he would obtain experience from this responsibility. The young man, who was still besprinkled with adolescent acne, came into our office at lunchtime on his first day as Ruth was pouring drinks. He seemed unable to believe his eyes. *'What are you doing?'* he cried. 'Having a drink,' we replied politely, and offered him one. He refused, and said, 'You're all fired.' 'Not at all,' we said as one, 'we resign.' We all walked out, clutching bottles, boxes of paper cups, and the ice bucket. When Dennis returned, it took him nearly an hour to persuade us to be apologized to and come back.

For variety, we lunched outside the office. Tom Hutchinson was not around on an afternoon when two secretaries and I went into a pub on the Strand. This pub was crowded, except where three drunk youths, one of them black, were leaning on the bar. There was a wide, empty space on either side, and I rapidly learnt why. The three of us leant on the unoccupied space of the bar to the left of the three youths and ordered. The barman, who seemed to have had an epileptic fit, shrank away. The three youths turned as one upon us. Two of them began to fondle my female companions. The black youth asked me in a Glaswegian accent if I objected. I said I did. They abandoned the two secretaries, pushed me against the bar, and while the two whites held me, the black one started to beat me up. I had come through Algeria and the Six-Day War unscathed in body, and the idea of physical pain being inflicted on me by another human being had seemed remote. The fists and boots hurt me in the mind rather than the body. While all this was happening, the barman phoned the police. When a single constable burst into the pub, the black seized a bottle from the counter, broke the neck off, and pointed it at him. The policeman leapt efficiently on him, threw him to the floor, and sat on him. Other policemen arrived and seized the two whites.

They were taken out to police cars. While an inspector took my statement, the whites were pushed into one car. The constable who had been threatened with the broken bottle by the black, said, 'I want the darkie to myself.' The black was hustled into another car, accompanied by the aggrieved constable. He was by now sobbing hysterically, and called to nobody in particular, 'I didn't mean it.' The inspector asked me to come to Bow Street later to make another statement. The two secretaries had fled; I had told them to go back to the office. The crowd of other customers remained.

Several of them said, 'Have a drink. You'll need one, after all that.' One said, 'My God, to see you go through all that—we were together at Oxford, remember? It's my shout. To think of an Oxford man being put through all that….' I felt rather fuzzy, but said, 'If you all want to buy me drinks now, why didn't you help me then?'

It was not long after this that a Smithfield butcher, who was then a leader of the nascent National Front, started some kind of racial riot, the details of which I don't remember. I went to interview him for the *Daily Telegraph* (Hackett at that moment didn't want to touch this kind of thing) with an elderly photographer, who seemed, despite his newspaper, to have strong Labour views. The National Front man had not been told of my colour, and upon my arrival seemed rather surprised, but offered us tea and biscuits. He then went on somewhat about the racial bloodbaths that would soon take place, and said that the best advice he could offer me was to leave England before this happened. 'You got our education from us,' he said, 'I can tell by your voice. But you aren't going to take our work from us.' After a while we left.

I wrote the article, and there was a response not only from the butcher but from a number of anonymous members of the National Front. The butcher wrote the *Daily Telegraph* a letter saying that he had been misquoted and my attitude throughout the interview had been hostile, which was to be understood because my colour prevented me from being impartial. The anonymous letters simply said that I had better watch out, since they, the writers, knew where I lived. Some days after the article appeared, the photographer who had come with me met me in Fleet Street, and said, 'Come and have a pint.' I did. He said to me, 'I only wanted to say I'm very sorry. What else is there for me to say?' He added, 'These people are bloody maniacs. Lay off this story.'

Around this time Dennis said, after having read the article and the butcher's response, but not knowing about the other letters I had received, 'Look, this is turning out very interesting. Forget the

Telegraph. Follow it up hard for us.' David and I met in a pub to discuss what we should do. With his long sombre face and hands, he resembled an El Greco saint more than ever. I sketched a plan of action for us, and he listened without comment. I inquired, 'Are you frightened?' I was nervous, otherwise I would never have asked this. He replied, with his unfailing honesty, 'Certainly. But you should be more frightened. So far as these guys are concerned, you're a different species from me.' I said, 'The hell with them.' 'I agree,' David said, 'but you've got Judy and the kid to think of. Live amongst your own people, mate, and that means us, don't bugger off into the wild woods.'

When Hackett said to me one day, 'Why don't you fly across the pond and interview Marshall McLuhan?' I said yes, I'd like to. McLuhan at that time was in vogue; his book, *The Medium Is the Message*, had acquired a wide circle of admirers. Though I wasn't one of them, I thought it would not be a bad idea to be out of London for a while with Judy and Francis. It was arranged that I should fly ahead with Ruth, who was taking her children to Boston on a visit to their grandmother. Judy and Francis were to come out a few days later and meet me in New York. At take-off and landing, Ruth, terrified of a crash, clutched my hand so tightly that on arrival it was actually bleeding.

To my great surprise, I found my father in New York. He was staying at the Plaza, and I moved into a room there. My father was sixty that year; there was much more grey in his hair than there had ever been, and he was more forgetful than before. He also said, once, that he expected to die soon. He seemed to be hastening the process by drinking heavily. I did that too, but while I was not alarmed for myself, I worried about him. I thought myself invulnerable, at that time. My father's talk of death affected me, in part, for selfish reasons. I loved him and did not want to lose him, and I also felt that his death would in some way make me more vulnerable.

In New York I telephoned McLuhan's agent, who told me that the Canadian sage charged heavily for an interview. I was surprised to learn that he had this habit in common with Christine Keeler. When I telephoned Hackett to ask for instructions, he said McLuhan was asking far too much. The agent would not lower the price, so that assignment had to be scrubbed. I resolved to do whatever else I could in America.

The temper of the country was much fiercer than it had been on my previous trip. That summer saw the Detroit riots; servicemen were coming back from Vietnam, mostly disaffected, and the violence had increased in New York. Central Park was now positively dangerous. Frank Hercules once more warned me not to come to Harlem, but this time more strongly. In Washington there were protest marches against the war in Asia. I did interview returned servicemen, young protestors, and sociologists. The nature of the times seemed more clearly reflected in them than in Marshall McLuhan.

Judy and Francis arrived. My father and I met them at the airport. It was night in New York, the skyscrapers lit up like ocean liners in an immense darkness; I looked at the city as Judy, on her first visit, must have seen it, and realized how awesome it could seem. With Francis, one place was the same as another. I had a lunatic desire that his childhood experience should follow mine, that he should travel widely while he was still young and remember it all his life. I forgot, or didn't take into account, the fact that I had been eight years old when my voyages started, and that he was one-and-a-half. He could hardly have been expected to be impressed.

He was, in fact, difficult to move around. New York cab-drivers did not take kindly to small people in push-chairs, and Judy's daytime excursions with women friends were limited by this. I was usually busy all day; by night we hired a babysitter, a prim and elderly lady of German extraction, provided (expensively) by the Plaza. She gave me, perhaps, the best story of my stay, though it was not really a magazine story. She came every night for a week; when we left New York, she wept profusely, and said, 'I can't bear to say goodbye to my darling little girl.' Since she had been changing Francis' nappies for a week, I was more than mildly surprised.

We went to Washington. Here I had a brief and unsatisfactory interview with President Johnson, who merely emitted a few sentences on his determination not to pull out of Vietnam. Several people I had met in Israel were now at the Israeli embassy in Washington and my father knew everyone at the Indian embassy, so we saw a good many diplomats. Both the Israelis and Indians were of the opinion that the US forces would undergo a huge and traumatic defeat in Vietnam. The ghettos of the capital were full of angry black Vietnam veterans who said that many of their friends had been killed in Asia in a war that was not theirs. Washington society floated far above all this; I met some of the wasplike social columnists, and some of the great hostesses at parties where everything appeared to glitter and flash, including the people. Considering the proximity of the ghettos to Georgetown, these were like parties thrown on the eve of a revolution, a revolution of the mind rather than the flesh.

In New York I had met the editors of several magazines, and one of them suggested that I write a series of articles on Mexico. This was immensely appealing to me. In my childhood I had read Prescott's account of the Conquest; the figure of Montezuma interested me deeply. I had also read *The Plumed Serpent* and D.H. Lawrence's other writings on the place. It was a dream of mine to go to Mexico. We went by way of New Orleans, since my father for some reason wanted to visit the city. I had no work there, so it was a kind of holiday, also a temporary farewell to my father, about whose state of health I had become acutely concerned. We ate the famous French Quarter brunches, and patronized a restaurant that served food from round the world, including giraffe and kangaroo. I have forgotten what the place was called, but in view of the present attitudes on conservation, it seems rather improbable that it has survived. On the way to the airport Judy quarrelled with a cab-driver who said that black people were worse than animals. Otherwise it was a pleasant stay. We flew into Mexico City through a thick blanket of smog and polluted air.

I looked at the great volcanoes; I hired a car, and an affable young driver called Vicente took us on the usual tourist treks, as far as Oaxaca. I then formed a great desire to visit Tehuantepec, only because it had acquired an aura of romance in my mind, being mentioned in a Wallace Stevens poem. Vicente was astonished when I expressed my wish. 'There is nothing there,' he said. And there was nothing there, except a rather exciting hurricane, which kept us stranded in the town for two days. Then we went over the border into Guatemala, for a Tehuantepec-like reason: in my childhood I had had a collection of Guatemalan stamps, which depicted a colourful and scenic land. But when we got to Guatemala, there was nothing there either. However, my new-found ability, on the trip, to gratify illogical whims in the matter of travel, proved rather unfortunate. I developed the illusion that I was rich, which took some years to shake off.

Back in London, I started to feel some disquiet. This was not caused by the National Front, but, indirectly, by the work I was now committed to do. The *New York Times Sunday Magazine* had started to commission work from me in England and in Europe; *Nova* remained; and there were assignments from other magazines and newspapers. The point was that it had been two years since my last book of poems, and in that time I had written only three poems that had satisfied me: two, 'The Gardener' and 'Son', concerned the birth of Francis, and one, 'Craxton', was about a geriatric writer with a malevolent manservant. Otherwise I had been wholly barren, despite a number of false starts.

This preyed on my mind, and I was constantly reminded of it, because so many of my friends were poets. They seemed productive, and I was not. If any of them asked me about my work, I found it difficult to reply. Things had never been like this before. I had had breaks in my poetry, but never such a block as this. My whole intention in life had been to write good poetry, but now, not very satisfied with what I had already produced, I was unable to continue. I brooded about this, drank much more than before, and began to botch up assignments. I also had a quarrel with George Barker, a close friend and mentor. It was about some totally unimportant matter, but he never spoke to me or met me after 1967. At about this time I asked to travel to France for some kind of First World War veterans' reunion. It was to take place on the battlefields of that war. I took the ferry to Calais and a train northward, then hired a taxi, and chased the veterans round the battlefields, interviewing them before they got too shakily drunk. Eventually I produced a rather good piece. It was centred on an old man from Stafford, who, in some Norman village, drank in a bar he had last visited in 1916. Fifty-one years ago to the day, he had been briefly buried under the ruins of a house opposite. The house had now been rebuilt, but he knew the site. It was a grey, cold, windy day, and I remembered all that Edmund Blunden had told me, and, out of that lost war, the memories of 'mighty poets in their misery dead'. In London I wrote a poem called 'Beldam', about a dead war poet trying to climb out of his grave and into the modern rain.

A little later, the Turret Press, which operated from a little bookshop in Kensington Church Walk, where Pound used to live, and which was run by the eccentric Bernard Stone, published a pamphlet of the poems I had written in the previous two years. It contained only four poems; nobody reviewed it, but for my peace of mind it was better than nothing.

In 1968 I celebrated, or lamented, my thirtieth birthday. I had produced six books of verse—three single volumes, a pamphlet, the collection in America, and the translations from Carmi—and one book of prose, *Gone Away*, plus the television films, and hundreds of articles and reviews. I could, I suppose, have been considered prolific, but to me it seemed that my life so far had been a series of missed opportunities, of poetry that had not been written through laziness or other preoccupations. I had become increasingly difficult to live with and was drinking more. After 'Beldam', I dried up completely.

At this point I was commissioned by my English and American publishers to write my autobiography. I found at this time that I dreamt much of my embattled childhood, and of my insane mother. It seemed to me that I had escaped from her into the life of poetry I wanted to reach, only to come to another dead end. The book I wrote, *My Son's Father*, was largely concerned with my childhood and my coming to London, and effectively ended when I was twenty-two. I then skipped the eight years which I have described earlier in this book and concluded with an epilogue in which I spoke of myself as a householder and a father: a responsible man. In all truth, I did not feel responsible at all. My own behaviour tended to worry me deeply.

Other things worried me. One Sunday afternoon I was smoking and writing my book when I ran out of cigarettes. I pulled on a coat from an assortment in the hall, and set out for the tobacconist on the corner. The coat was suede and had once been very expensive, but was now torn down one side. I hadn't shaved that Sunday. Halfway down the street a policeman stopped me. I knew most of the policemen in the area, but this one was new. He barked, 'Here, you! Stand against the wall. Let me see your papers.' I was startled, and stood against the wall, and he moved forward to frisk me. As he did this, I found that I was angry. 'What the hell is all this?' I asked. At the sound of my accent, he stopped and looked at me hard. Then he said, 'I'm sorry, sir. I'm really very sorry.' He then stepped out of my way and saluted.

After this I felt even more furious. England was my home. Was I to be treated like an immigrant? Then it occurred to me that I *was* an immigrant, and that I knew very little about how other immigrants lived. I felt suddenly very guilty about this.

A week later, the BBC asked me to do a film in its *One Pair of Eyes* series. Each film centred on a supposedly well-known person looking at an issue which seriously concerned him or her. When the director, Francis Megahy, asked me what my film would be on, I had a subject very much on my mind, and said without hesitation, 'Immigrants.'

Francis Megahy was a wiry, bespectacled young man, somewhat tense, who knew very little about immigrants. Since I didn't either, *we* decided, over a pub lunch, that the film should be not about West Indians, who were quite different from the others, but about Asian immigrants, more particularly Indians and Pakistanis, and my efforts to understand their situation. I suggested that we might also try and include their efforts to understand mine. 'That shouldn't be hard,' Francis said, 'you can talk to them in their language.' He was amazed to be told that I spoke none of the languages of my native subcontinent. 'That's what I mean, that's what the film should be about,' I told Francis, who seemed to realize my idea. James Cameron, later, fell about with laughter as he said to Francis, 'I'd love to see Dom trying to interview a Pakistani wool-washer in Bradford.' As it happened, this was exactly what the film was about.

Tony de Lotbiniere, who was very senior in the BBC, talked to Francis and me about this film, since the topic, as he said, was slightly touchy. Tony was tall, grey-haired, and looked simultaneously like a Guards officer and an elderly film star. 'I *like* India,' he said dreamily to me, 'can't you work out something I can direct there?' This was supposed to be witty, and he followed it with raucous laughter. 'All right,' he said abruptly to Francis about the script, 'get on with it.'

This abruptness, and these loud bursts of laughter, were habits of his with which I was soon to become familiar, but I wasn't acquainted with them then, and they came as a bit of a surprise. Francis and I went up to Bradford to set up parts of the film. Meanwhile, *My Son's Father* appeared in London and New York, and the critics were unanimous in praise, though it cannot be said that many people bought copies. My London publishers threw a launch party, and about a week before it the organizer came to me with a complaint. He said the only women at this party were female authors and the wives of male authors. 'You know what they look like, mostly,' he grumbled, 'there aren't any pretty girls.' Where we were to get pretty girls at a week's notice was beyond me, till I thought of Miss Keeler and her friends, and the people David and I had met with June Palmer. Invitations were sent to some of them, and they accepted.

The result was perhaps predictable. Before the end of the party they had all left, and so had many of the wealthier literary men present, though several weeping wives remained.

Part of the film concerned my own life. In this, I was shown being interviewed on television, and at the launch party. I was filmed talking to friends like Julian Mitchell and Peter Levi on Oxford lawns, going to my local pub, and moving around with Judy and Francis. This section of the film depicted my normal life in London, one that mainly concerned the acceptance of me by British society. The main portion of the film, however, was to be about my meeting immigrants in Bradford, and my attempts to understand their problems. Like most films of this nature, parts of the structure were constructed artificially, but the bulk of it came from genuine events and experiences. Francis and I went back to Bradford, this time accompanied by a BBC crew.

This included an Indian assistant cameraman. There were several ironic things about him. One was that he really disliked and despised the immigrants from the subcontinent, who seemed to him, I think, to lower him personally in the eyes of the crew.

The second was that the crew thought him funny precisely because of these attitudes, and because he made such a fuss about his food. While the rest of us gnawed meat pies or fish and chips or hotel food, he kept inquiring of everyone he met, including immigrants, if there was a French restaurant in Bradford. At that time it was like asking whether such a restaurant existed on the moon. Bradford then *was* a bit like the moon.

It was alien to London; the crew, Londoners all, found it hard to take. There were the dark satanic mills around a core of middle-class architecture; then mile upon mile of sooty, terraced houses and an area which the Pakistanis had already turned into a ghetto, with restaurant signs in Urdu, and groceries which sold spices and vegetables never seen in Bradford before. Here, almost the only people to be seen were Pakistanis. The women were often in purdah. But small children did not seem to exist; apparently they were then maintained by relatives in Pakistan until they were adolescents.

Nearly all the men were employed in factories, washing wool, a very dirty task which most British workers refused to undertake. The unmarried ones shared houses, where uncountable numbers stayed; the exact figures were not disclosed to us for fear of the law. But between ten and a dozen men slept in a room at once, in six-hour shifts, and when they awoke and went to work others took their places. A cauldron of curry simmered in a communal kitchen throughout the day and night; the inhabitants helped themselves whenever they were hungry. At defined hours sirens brayed to call the workers in, and this was the only time when the houses were full of movement and life.

But there were some immigrants who did not work in the mills; and these included our chief contact, Saeed Khan. He had been a lawyer in Pakistan, and quite a successful one. His degree was not recognized in England, so he worked as an interpreter in a Bradford firm of solicitors with a large immigrant clientele. He accepted this demotion humbly, and even seemed grateful to have found employment in a foreign land. He had saved money and lived in a rented house with his wife, whom we interviewed. She seemed happy in her home, which was cluttered with furniture in mauve rexine. She showed us photographs of the spacious house they had left in Pakistan, simply but elegantly furnished with cushions and bolsters on carpeted floors, and servants around.

But she appeared to prefer Bradford to Lahore. She liked, she said, 'gardening, ice cream, and the courtesy of the English neighbours'. The woman next door, she said, hailed her every morning across the garden wall. I had glimpsed this neighbour, an elderly harridan, and was surprised to hear of this. So I went next door to make inquiries. The neighbour said, 'Yeah, I say something to her every day. I say, "Why don't you go back where you came from, you bloody bitch?"' She couldn't bear the smell of Mrs Khan's curries, and had once been enraged when Mrs Khan offered her some. 'What does she think I am?'

I met a bespectacled man who washed wool and wrote Urdu poetry. 'In Pakistan,' he said wistfully, 'I was well known.' He recited to me his ghazals for what seemed hours; it was clear that he seldom had what could be described as a receptive audience. I met a huge man who also washed wool and had been a wrestler by profession. 'In Pakistan,' he said, 'I was well known.' I asked him why he had come to this cold country, away from the wrestling rings of Pakistan. 'I came to wrestle with money,' he said, with a humour wholly unexpected in someone of his profession, 'but I find I only wrestle with wool.' I asked him why he did not wrestle for survival in England. 'Because I only know how to do it the way we do it in Pakistan,' he said. This might also have been an epitaph for Saeed Khan and the poet.

The wrestler had a daughter of fifteen, who had recently arrived from Karachi. She spoke no English, and was not allowed out of the house without female companions. 'Otherwise,' the wrestler said, 'she will become bad. You know what I mean?'

The girl seemed rather resistant to this idea. 'If she disobeys,' the wrestler said, 'I will beat her.'

A quarter of a century after we filmed all this, I met an Indian woman, Zerbanoo Gifford, who had written a book about the successes of Asian ladies in Britain. She assured me that such fathers and daughters no longer existed. The concept that they had ever existed, she said, had been foisted on the British public by irresponsible television programmes. I wondered if one of these could have been ours.

The summer of 1968, at least the end of it, had a curious feel to it, and was full of dreams and premonitions. I was busy with the film and at the *Nova* office, but no poetry came into my head. This complete impotence was something I had never experienced before, this crippledom, this martyrdom. During previous blocks I had never been far from poetry; lines and ideas had trickled to me through the dryness. Now, for some reason, nothing came to me whatever. When I looked at the poems I had already encased in three books, I felt an almost physical revulsion, and I could not face reading the verse of other people. It was a wet summer, but it had been a successful year, and I could not understand my continual depression. My relationship with Judy seemed to have fallen apart, through no fault of hers. Sometimes, when I picked Francis up, and smelt the apples and milk on his breath, I felt secure, otherwise not.

In July, I think, my dream of my gargoyle mother, hair flying, pursuing me with a knife, changed, and I began to dream of Brian Higgins. He was a weird person to dream of, but then my mother was equally so.

At the time when David Wright and Paddy Swift were running *X*, they received a number of letters and poems from a poet from Hull. The writer seemed very unhappy, and wanted to know if there would be any future for him in London. David was tremendously struck by the poems, and so was George Barker, to whom he showed them. He wrote and invited the poet to London, adding that he could not promise him any work. The poet, Brian Higgins, arrived a couple of days, later, announcing his arrival by telegram!

A number of poets waited for him in the Museum pub, but I think all of us were surprised when Paddy Swift ushered him in. Higgins was squat and bulky, ursine in build, with the face of some large rodent. He was partially bald, with curly sideburns, a pallid skin, and thick lips. Someone said that he looked like Dr Johnson. He certainly ate like Johnson, whose table manners Boswell had deplored. When offered a pie, he accepted eagerly, and immediately began to sweat. When the pie appeared, he sweated even more, seized it in both hands, the veins standing out on his forehead, and ate noisily, chumbling it in his mouth. Everyone stood round and watched.

Higgins had a thick Yorkshire accent. In it he began to sing 'Ilkley Moor', and then, lurching from his chair, did a clog dance. The landlord asked us all to leave. At this time I hadn't read Higgins' poems, and found him very funny. When he showed me his work, I was greatly impressed. Oonagh, Paddy Swift's wife, told me, 'He spent his first night in London with us. You'd be surprised how delicate his hands and feet are.' This had some relation to his personality. He wanted to be accepted; he thought one way to endear himself to the London literati was to shout and be the clown, the Yorkshire boor, the butt of many witticisms. He did not like this, but suffered it. His was a very complex personality. More than anyone else I ever met, he needed love.

Higgins had no source of income whatsoever, until David persuaded a publisher to bring out his first book, and then he didn't get very much. He lived, therefore, off his friends. A female novelist used to invite him to dinner once a week. 'I put his food on the table,' she confessed, 'and then go away, because I can't bear to watch him eat.' He provoked physical revulsion in people who did not know him, even when not eating. He knew this, which must have added to his inner grief. It also limited him in his search for love. It was not only love he wanted, but sex. He may have received love from his friends, but no girl would come near him. Higgins didn't help matters by telling anyone who would listen 'how quickly Ah coom'. He told me a story to illustrate this. He had been a teacher at, of all places, Ankara, and on the way back stopped off in Paris, where he went to a whore. They entered a hotel room, and she, naked by the sink, asked him to wash himself. 'And what happened then?' he asked rhetorically.

'I don't know, Hug. I wasn't there.'

'She was naked, right? She was there by the sink, and she beckoned and said, "*Viens*," and Ah knew in French that meant "coom", so Ah came.'

He belched and farted quite a lot. He was not everyone's favourite guest. He had not had any employment since his return from Ankara. It is possible that he could have been found some, but for ideological reasons he refused. 'Property is theft,' he said.

'Ah often quote that.' One day, finding our front door open, he came into an empty house and headed for the kitchen, where a very substantial leg of lamb was in the oven. When Judy and I came back, a gnawed bone was lying on the floor, and there was a note from Higgins, saying simply, 'Thanks for lunch. Back later.'

Once I met him near Paddington station. It was evening, under a luminous but soiled London sky, and he was carrying a packet of fish and chips in one hand. 'Ah'm goan home,' he said. 'Coom along. You can buy some ale.' He was living, or squatting, in an abandoned house which seemed about to fall down. He ate all the fish and chips and drank most of the beer. He seemed rather subdued. Eventually he said, 'You know Ah'm in loov with A. She won't look at me.' I did not say anything. The whole floor—there was no furniture, so we were sitting on it—was strewn with bits of poems scrawled on lined paper. He went on, in an unusually flat voice, 'Ah'm thirty-three and Ah've no family and no home.

And Ah wunnut, never.' Since there was no electricity, all I could see of him was a humped troglodyte shape in the dark. Suddenly I heard a peculiar, whiffling, snuffling sound. It took me a while to realize Higgins was weeping.

A little later he fell sick with some disease which had a long name and was taken to a hospital. 'You could call it,' a doctor told me, 'premature senility of the heart.' I went to see him in a public ward, pale, shrunken, wrapped to the throat in a blanket.

'You'll be better soon, Hug.'

'Na, Dommie. Ah've been a bad boy, and now Ah'm for the high joomp.' And he was. This was the last time we met. Shortly afterwards, he died. His *Collected Poems* were published seven months later, something which would never have happened had he been alive. For some reason, I always felt, even before he died, that I had wronged Higgins in some way. I was, in terms of career, home, and even earning capacity, far ahead of him. I felt I should not be. George Barker had once made a remark that what I felt was perfectly true. 'Dom writes very beautifully and says very little,' he told someone, 'and the Hug has no idea of style and technique, but he says everything.' I thought I owed Higgins something, though I didn't know what.

In any event, during that summer of 1968, he visited my dreams. It was, as I said, a wet summer, and he seemed to emerge out of rain, dripping, weeping. 'Why do you have a house, Dommie?' he seemed to be saying, 'Property is theft.' And, as he went back to wherever he came from, he seemed to raise his hand and say, 'Goodbye.' But next night he returned.

Despite my extreme depression, the film production went on, and presently neared its end. I went to Lord's to watch the Australians play a Test match. Rather surprisingly, the man in charge of the press box recognized me and let me in. Bob Simpson was one of the reasons I had come; I wanted to ask him to dinner. He wasn't in the press box when I arrived. Keith Miller, once a great Australian all-rounder, said he would pass my message on. 'Simmo's a bit sad these days,' he said, 'it's only a few months since he retired, and he wants to be on the field with the boys. I know how he feels, I felt it too when I stopped playing.' It was raining, there was nobody on the field, and Keith and I were drinking beer. He was a tall, very handsome man, with a sculptured head which he turned towards me. 'When you stop doing what you were born to do,' he said, 'it's not good, it's no good at all.'

7

A camel caravan swayed down the road from the airport in clouds of dust. Each beast, goat and serpent in one body, chewed cud; one, annoyed by some minor inconvenience, threw back its head and emitted an atonal yawp. Francis stood up in the back seat of the car and pointed, demanding what these creatures were. Brij, my father's driver, replied, 'Camels, baba.' Francis thought for a while and said, 'Caramels.'

This was exactly how I had imagined a return to India with my small son. I had wanted to bring him to the country from which I came, so that he could see and remember it, as I had done when travelling in various places with my father. I never considered that I had been a very much older child during my travels; even today I am rather disappointed that he remembers nothing about this trip. The original motives for it both turned out to be failures; the other one was an attempt at a reconciliation with Judy, and that, too, was to fail. But I did not know this on that first day of my return to India.

The trip had been on my mind for some months. I thought that once the film was done I should write another book; and my publisher suggested that it be one on the new India after Nehru: Indira Gandhi's India. When I mentioned this to Francis Megahy, he said immediately, 'I've always wanted to go to India. Why don't you write something into the script about your visiting your father? Then maybe I can persuade Tony de Lotbiniere to send me along.

We can shoot a bit there. Actually, it could be quite interesting.' The arrangements were made, and so I was accompanied by two Francises. Mark Tully, the BBC man in Delhi, had hired a local camera crew.

During these days, I clung to the elder Francis somewhat. He was to return to London in a few days, as soon as the shooting was over. It seemed to me that with his departure I would lose contact with the life I knew, and India had started to frighten me. One day, Judy, the two Francises, and I drove to Agra to see the Taj Mahal. It was very hot, and on the way the engine overheated. We stopped in a village for water. The car was immediately surrounded by people who pointed, laughed, tapped on the windows, and made faces at us. Judy and Francis Megahy were rather alarmed, and my small son started to cry. These villagers were alien and incomprehensible even to me. I did not feel that I myself had ever really understood India.

Francis Megahy flew home, and I slowly settled down. My small son played noisy games with the servants' children, for my father had a fairly large garden. His friend, Marilyn Silverstone, an American photographer with the Magnum agency, took Judy round Delhi. I interviewed various people, including Mrs Gandhi, whom I met for the first time, and planned an itinerary with my father. I wanted to go around India, but this would be very expensive with Judy and Francis, and my funds were not unlimited.

The rhythm of life in the house ran to a set pattern. My father was the editor of the *Indian Express,* and in the morning went to his office to work. He returned for lunch, and worked during the afternoon, or rested. He was now sixty-one and there was white in his hair. He had been an influence on me throughout my life, ever since my childhood, when he had been the only bastion of sanity between me and my mentally troubled mother. Now he was delighted to see his grandson, and rather proud of me. I was glad that we were able to make him happy; he had not had a great deal of happiness.

Behind the house, which was fairly large, was a lawn. On this, as evening fell, with blue wood-smoke rising from the squatter encampments in a nearby field, the servants set out comfortable wicker armchairs and tables. Around seven o'clock, my father came down from his study, and at about this time visitors commenced to arrive. They did not come by invitation; every evening, my father held open house for anyone who cared to drop in. It is more than possible that many did so for the liquor, which flowed freely. Otherwise there were visitors from abroad, journalists, politicians, diplomats, and simply friends, of whom my father had many. He was a very quiet man, who became quieter in drink and was by no means gregarious, though these evening courts of his took place every day. I have sometimes thought that people came to him because there was a kind of comfort even in his silence, as I had found in my childhood.

Usually twenty to thirty people came every evening, but sometimes the number was much smaller, and sometimes much larger. The newspaper paid for these soirees, and they were actually useful for it. Amongst the guests there were, almost always, one or two of my father's Editors. The guests being such a mixture, bits of news were always afloat in the air: news from several fields; news of what was happening in Parliament and the Cabinet, the latest stories about Mrs Gandhi and her most recent favourites, news of science, news from abroad, news about yesterday's ambassadorial appointments. My father picked some of this up, and his Editors the rest.

The guests, as I say, came as a rule by choice, and they were aware that they were, in a sense, being used. But they were supplied with liquor and interesting company, and it was a fair exchange. My father sat quietly in their midst, less and less communicative as the evening wore on. The gathering usually broke up at dinnertime. My father didn't often eat dinner. In fact, he didn't eat much lunch; for breakfast he had a glass of orange juice and a soft-boiled egg. John, the bearer, told me with a wink, 'Big Master has the keys to the liquor cabinet.'

'Well, I suppose he would have, wouldn't he?'

'Yes, Little Master,' John said, 'but the liquor cabinet is in his bedroom.'

'So?'

'So, before he leaves for the office, he drinks half a bottle of Scotch. This is why the order for Scotch is so large every month. Marilyn Memsahib doesn't know.'

John himself was hardly in a position to speak. He was responsible for much of the secret consumption of liquor that took place in the house, and, frequently, could hardly stand. He had once, in the past, really disgraced himself at a dinner party, when, leering down the decolletage of a foreign ambassador's beautiful wife, he had allowed a dish of cream souffle to pour down it. This had nearly resulted in the sack, but, as my father said, 'He'd be unemployable anywhere else, so I suppose I must keep him.'

I communicated with John in English, and also with the rest of the house staff, since they were Tamils from the south, who had studied the language at school. Brij, the young driver, was a northerner. He spoke some English, but was more comfortable with Hindi. I drew from deep recesses of memory and remembered enough broken Hindi to be able to converse with him in a mixture of two languages. I was coming back into a culture. For many years I had run my own life in England, but I became aware that the servants expected a great deal from me. I was the Little Master, come back from across the kala pani, the black waters that separated India from the rest of the world. It was for me to take affairs in hand, since the Big Master was not always well. Marilyn Memsahib was not blood kin, however fond of her they might be. Little Master had to handle whatever awkwardnesses Big Master might have, and they were thankful that I was here, with a grandson to make Big Master happy.

The grandson provided light relief in the evenings, scampering about with toy trucks under the feet of the diplomats and Editors. 'What's the matter with Frank?' somebody asked me, 'All he does these days is say "Watch Heffie." Who the hell is Heffie?' I said, 'My son. His grandson.

'Oh,' said my interlocutor. 'Well, I suppose he needs something to amuse him.'

A day or so after this, there was no evening court; my father went to a party. Brij came back from this to where I was sitting with Marilyn, Judy, and the child, and said a great deal to me in Hindi. I understood none of this; Marilyn did. 'He says your father's very drunk at this party,' she told me. 'He says you should go and bring him home. I said *I* would, but Brij says it's none of my business and it's *your* duty.' For the first time in our acquaintance, she sounded rather angry.

I went out to the car as I was. On the way to the party, Brij philosophized. 'You see,' he said, 'Big Master shouldn't go out in the evenings. If he is at home he feels safe. He does not drink too much. When he goes to these parties, I am telling you, Little Master, he drinks too much because he does not feel safe. And who is there to look after him? Now you are here, the responsibility is yours. After all, now that you are here, he will have his son to light his funeral pyre. We are all happy about this.' I wanted to point out that this was a visit, not a re-establishment of residence, but at the time I didn't want to argue. We arrived at an ambassador's house. The flunkey at the door said I wasn't properly dressed, I couldn't come in.

So I sent a message, and waited at the door. I was attired in a crumpled shirt, slacks, and sandals; beyond, in the great room where the party was happening, I could see men in evening dress and attractive, well-dressed women, all of whom seemed to be looking at me. I started to feel very resentful towards my father, perhaps for the first time in my life. Presently an aide brought him out of the crowd, holding him by the elbow, while he lurched alongside. 'Here is your father,' he said, as though making me a present which he himself considered rather contemptible. I took the offered elbow, and got him back to the car. Brij helped settle him in the back seat.

As we drove home, my father said in surprisingly sober tones, 'I think I insulted the American ambassador. I didn't mean to. D'you think I should go back and apologize?'

'No,' I said, 'phone him up tomorrow and apologize. Or simply let it be.'

He said, 'Your mother. She's in Bombay and she knows you're here. If you don't go to Bombay soon and see her, she's going to be terribly upset. I don't want her to be.'

This unexpected turn in the conversation surprised and annoyed me. I said, 'I don't want Heffie to meet her, if she's still mad. It's not fair on him at all.' He replied, 'Sooner or later, if you're all in India, he's going to have to. And you're certainly going to have to. I know you want to avoid it but that's a coward's way.'

I was angry; I said, 'How long is it since *you've* seen her?'

My father replied, 'Several years. That's not the point. She doesn't *want* to see me. The person she wants to see is *you*.' All the claws that had previously held me to India, which, I had thought, I had one by one detached, seemed to rehook themselves into my mind. We got back home. Brij and I undressed my father and put him to bed. He lay there like a child, like my son, his eyes open, in pink-striped pyjamas from Saks Fifth Avenue. But he was not quite asleep. He said, 'My son, your mother…'

I said 'Go to sleep.'

He whispered, 'I'm sad about her all the time. It's gone on all these years.'

'For Christ's sweet sake, go to sleep.'

'That's why I'm like this,' he told me softly, but followed my instructions.

My parents had met while they were at college in Bombay in the late 1920s. His father was an engineer, a successful one, from

Goa, the Portuguese colony situated south of Bombay. As I've said earlier, it was because of the Indian take over of Goa that I had surrendered my Indian passport seven years earlier. My mother was the daughter of a wealthy doctor. The family was East Indian, that is to say, it came from the coast near Bombay. The Goans and East Indians are both Roman Catholic communities, but they have traditionally disliked and disapproved of each other. The engagement proposed between my parents was opposed by both families. However, when my father went off to Oxford, my mother waited for him. His absence lasted seven years, during which time he never returned to India; for, after Oxford, he took silk at Lincoln's Inn. When he eventually came back, they were married. In 1938 I was born.

My father was not very successful as a barrister, but the *Times of India,* the largest paper in the country, hired him as an Assistant Editor. During the Second World War, he became the first Indian war correspondent ever, and was sent to cover the Burma and China fronts. While he was away, my mother, till then a successful doctor and a rather glamorous socialite, began to suffer from depressions. Then she became paranoic and violent. One of the tragedies of my father's life was that the more successful he got, the more disturbed and violent she got. Her life centred around me, and when she realized I was going to Oxford, as my father had once done, the patterns of her madness hardened, and she was confined in a mental home.

This was in 1954. In 1956, by which time I was in England, she was discharged, and began to live with my father in their Bombay flat. Her condition was very unstable. In 1963, when I was in London, I was telephoned from India by Peter Jayasinghe, one of my father's oldest friends. Peter told me that my father had fallen very ill; my mother had sent away the servants, disconnected the telephone, and refused to answer the door. The servants told Peter of my father's state. He had the door broken down.

My father was by this time near death. He was rushed to hospital, where he now was. He had some kind of lung infection, and badly needed a certain medicine, unavailable in India. If I could get it in London, could I fly out a supply? As it happened, the proprietor of the *Indian Express*, Ramnath Goenka, who at this time was my father's employer, anxious to preserve the life of a valuable employee, obtained the medicine in Tokyo, and eventually there was no need for me to send any. My father lived, but was for six months in a hospital. When he came out, the consensus of opinion was that he should not live with my mother. The paper moved its headquarters to Delhi. My father went to live there leaving my mother in the flat with the servants. But she shortly then moved out and started to live in a hotel on Juhu beach, which was built on land rented from her brother. She was there now.

My feelings about this were very ambiguous. It was not a question of out of sight, out of mind. My mother was very much on my mind. I had suffered a good deal from her as a child and adolescent. My father, at work, was not as constantly exposed to her as I was. She had attacked me several times with knives; I had a scar on the back of my hand, where she had stubbed out a cigarette. I remembered wild and violent scenes: my mother, dishevelled, with bulging eyes and maenad hair; the sound of her screams. The only thing which had made me doubtful about a trip back to India was the knowledge that I would have to meet her, and that it would be hard to keep Judy and Francis out of this. But I had to go to Bombay, if I were to write this book; there was no option.

Meanwhile, my father suggested that from Bombay we travel to Goa. I had got into so much trouble over this place that I thought I might as well set eyes on it once. 'You were there, actually, as a small child,' said my father, 'about Heffie's age, so naturally you wouldn't remember it.' This damaged the illusion I still preserved, that my son would remember this trip all his life.

'We also have some property there, I think,' my father said. 'You might go and have a look at it. Who knows, you might find it useful some day, or Heffie might. If,' he added wistfully, 'you ever decide to come back.'

Three weeks after we arrived in India, we found ourselves at Bombay airport, after an internal flight from the capital. Travelling with Francis had been a problem in America the previous year, despite the mechanization and efficiency of the transport systems. It had been less so in Mexico, because people like our driver, Vicente, had been so full of care for children. People had always been ready to help with Francis, to hold him at airports while we struggled with baggage and immigration officials, or to amuse him when we were busy. This was even more so in India. The villagers in Delhi had been a bad start; but I had now started to think that that day, when they surrounded our car, had we unlocked the doors and been friendly, things would have been different. As it was, for the first time in my life, I felt sympathetic towards India.

We were staying with Peter Jayasinghe and his vivacious wife Lily. Peter was originally from Ceylon, Lily was a Parsee. She had been the personal secretary of Mrs Vijayalakshmi Pandit, Nehru's sister. Mrs Pandit was, at various times, the Indian ambassador to the United Nations, the USA, and the USSR, and high commissioner to the UK, so Lily was very well travelled. Peter was the first important publisher in the English language in India. He owned and ran Asia Publishing House, a large concern with branches all over the world, which faltered somewhat after his death, but at this time was prosperous. They had a large flat in Peddar Road, near where my family had lived in my adolescence, and since their children were away there was plenty of room. Lily made us very welcome.

I had decided to get the worst over with as quickly as possible. I telephoned some relatives to inquire about my mother. They assured me that she was as well as could be expected (though none of them had seen her for several months), and urged me to take Francis to see her, since it would calm her down. I consulted Peter and Lily about this. They hadn't seen my mother for years. 'We've both had very bad experiences with her in the past,' Lily said, 'especially that time when your father was ill. But I suppose she has a right to see her grandchild.' Peter thought any such visit would only do Francis harm. They were very old friends; they were already deeply protective of my son.

I could not make up my mind. I was ashamed of myself. I went to visit D.G. Tendulkar, another old friend of the family. Tendulkar was a short, gentle man with white hair, who always wore khadi shorts and shirts. A Communist in his youth, he had studied in Germany in the 1930s and been imprisoned for a while. Afterwards, he lived for some years in Russia. When he returned to India he fell under Gandhi's spell, and had spent much of his life writing a massive, and handsome eight-volume biography of the Mahatma. In earlier years, Tendulkar had shown me a lot about Indian handicrafts and artefacts; he lent me translations of Russian novels and poetry; and he advised me on many of the problems of adolescence. At that time he lived in a slum in Kalbadevi. Nehru, however, had built him a small house in the grounds of the governor's mansion, in token of his services to literature, and he now lived, very proudly, in it, with a huge number of books, peasant textiles, antique bronzes, and tribal artefacts. He was glad to see us.

'Beryl may be mad,' he said, fondling Francis's hair, 'but she would not hurt a small child, particularly her own grandson.' Then, to my dismay, he looked doubtful and added, 'Would she? I have known her for thirty years, but I have not seen her for ten.'

I said it was not that I feared physical, but mental harm to Francis.

'Domski, do not be ridiculous,' Tendulkar said. 'Are you telling me that a child of—what is it?—two, is going to suffer permanent mental damage through meeting his grandmother, whatever her mental state may be? If anything happens which you do not like, you can simply take the child away. Tell Beryl you are passing through Bombay and will be gone the next day. Then, if it is so painful for you, you need not see her again.'

Judy said, with British brevity, 'Why not get on with it?' Prevaricating to the end, I phoned the hotel manager and told him to tell my mother that she would be having visitors. 'She will be very pleased to see you, by God,' he said.

The last time I had seen my mother, in 1961, she had changed in many ways. She had, in 1959, been thin, with a somewhat drawn face; two years later she had become pallid and bloated, like a corpse recently taken from water. She had also developed a habit of laughing hysterically, for several minutes at a time, for no apparent reason. I had the uneasy feeling that there must be a valid cause for this wild laughter, which I was too insensitive to see. In between these bursts of laughter, she would insist on feeding me cake and sweets. She forced them on me; it was an affirmation of possession. I wanted to assert my independence, but when I refused to eat any more, a look of suppressed fury would come over her face. 'If you don't eat this lovely cake,' she would say, a threat in her voice, 'I shall really hate it.' I knew what this implied: hysterics, screaming, perhaps violence; so, however much I resented it, I would eat some more cake. This surfeit of sweetmeats made me feel extremely sick.

I now associated this feeling of nausea with my mother. On the way to Juhu, some miles from the city proper, the nausea came back, wave upon wave of it, so that bile filled my mouth, and I could not speak. At last the car reached Juhu, one of the beaches of my childhood. It had once been a charming and isolated place, with white sand, balloons, food, and so forth.

It was Sunday afternoon, and the beach was packed with people, the sand discoloured underfoot. Mangy camels were hired out for rides, an innovation; their excrement littered the edge of the sea. Somehow all these changes made it worse for me. I broke into a cold sweat as we reached the hotel.

The manager awaited us. He was a swarthy man with a moustache, and nervously affable. He received us in a tin-roofed shack, beyond which a sandy sweep of land led down to the beach. Palm trees rustled above several other shacks set at some distance from one another. I looked at the beach, the camels on the beach, the sea. In other circumstances it would have been a pleasant enough place, but as a hotel it puzzled me.

The manager explained. 'This is not exactly a hotel, sir,' he said, 'it is more of a weekend place. People who want a quiet weekend hire a shack. They bring their families, they swim and relax. We have a restaurant, so they can eat here.' He hesitated, then went on, 'Your mother has been here two years, sir. I allowed that because your respected uncle owns the land. But it is very inconvenient. She comes out of her shack and abuses the weekend visitors. She will not allow anyone to enter it, and so it is never cleaned. It is not healthful for her, sir. Will you not prevail on your beloved uncle to take her somewhere else?' I felt even worse than I had.

He led us under the palm trees, across the sand, to a largish shack thatched with palm leaves. It had a small balcony, with a rickety door on which he knocked. Francis seemed happy, and was studying the beach with interest. I was afraid for him, for all of us. I felt not only sick but dizzy. The door opened; my mother appeared.

She was not a figure of nightmare, except in my mind. She appeared to have shrunk; her small body was now skeletal under a blue housecoat. Her hair was white, and cut very short. Her once beautiful face was wrinkled like that of a sick monkey's. But she looked an inoffensive old lady. She put her arms round me and kissed me, incoherent with happiness. I noticed that she had lost most of her teeth. She greeted Judy in an offhand way, and, to my surprise, and actually relief, ignored Francis completely. She asked us to come inside; a large rat scampered off as we entered.

I detest rats. Scorpions, snakes, the other things many people fear, have no effect on me whatever. But rats, which are much less lethal, disgust me, and I am also rather frightened of them. I entered the shack with some trepidation. It consisted of one large room, partitioned off at the far end for a bathroom, and cluttered with my mother's trunks and suitcases. There was something ineffably sad about this room; it smelt of loneliness and of lost hopes, some of them possibly to do with me. We sat down on metal chairs, and my mother began her usual inconsequential prattle.

My nausea had partly disappeared; I was able to think fairly clearly. Suddenly I felt, as I sometimes had in the past, great sorrow and pity, not so much for my mother as for a world in which there was so much personal loss. Then Judy caught my eye. She nodded upward, and I looked up at the raftered roof. What was on the rafters and in the thatch above was like a scene from a horror film. There were more rats there than I had ever seen together in my life. There were literally dozens; and they were real rats, not mice. They scuttered and clambered about, but made no sound. Some of them were really large, with red and evil eyes. All were mangy.

I went outside the shack and was sick.

I did not tell my mother, as I had intended to, that we were leaving Bombay the next day. This was partly because I feared the scene which would probably ensue. So we had a second encounter. Though I insisted that we sit outside the shack, because the fresh air would benefit Francis, this was as unnerving as the first encounter. We took chairs out under a palm tree, and had barely done so when a large coconut fell from it, narrowly missing my head. This provided my mother with an excellent excuse to take us all back inside. Then she proceeded to force Francis and me to eat huge quantities of cake. Even Francis began to protest. At that my mother attempted to force-feed him, and he started to cry. I suggested that Judy and he take a walk on the beach. They departed.

Shortly after this, my mother, who had seemed unusually withdrawn, began to shake with inexplicable fury. Leaning towards me, she almost snarled, a toothless old vixen, and said, 'You know he's not your son, don't you?' Before I could lose my temper, I heard familiar wails from the beach. I ran down to find Judy with an almost hysterical child in her arms. They were followed by a band of small boys throwing stones. I drove these children away. Judy, herself almost in tears, said she couldn't understand what had happened. 'I met them further down the beach,' she said, 'and said hello, and then they started throwing stones at us.' It seemed to me another instance of the mindless violence that underlies the docile surface of much Indian behaviour.

I said goodbye to my mother, and we drove back to the Jayasinghes' house. I felt relieved and comforted by the thought that this was after all a short trip. We would be returning to England, and I would probably not be compelled to see her again for several years. I did not envisage, at the time, the turn that my life was shortly going to take.

'We must have a little cocktail party for you,' Lily said, 'so that you can meet all your old friends from Bombay.' Frankly, I could not think of many. Since our arrival, I had frequently met Tendulkar. Mickey Chagla and Satish Moolgaokar had been close to me at school, Mickey, now a successful barrister, was out of town on business, and Satish apparently now lived in Canada. Derek Rocha, another school friend, ran a successful department store in Melbourne. Two out of three of the friends of my adolescence now lived outside India, and so did I: three out of four. The Bombay papers had interviewed me fairly extensively, and since then several people had phoned me up to ask if I remembered them. Usually, I didn't; if the name rang the faintest of chimes, I met them, and they often asked me if I could help them to leave

India. Generally speaking, they did not know where they wanted to go or what they wanted to do; the main thing they had in mind was departure.

But Lily greatly altered the course of my future life when she asked, 'Do you remember Leela Naidu? I think your father knew her, and you used to play together as children.' A memory stirred in my mind, and I said, 'Yes, I remember.' During the war, my father and a scientist, Dr Ramiah Naidu, had been on the Brains Trust of All-India Radio. Dr Naidu had been married to a Frenchwoman, and they had a daughter who was six or seven, about my age. Leela used to come to our flat and I to hers. She had had, as I remembered, a somewhat forceful temperament, and had been pleasantly plump.

'She isn't plump now,' said Lily. '*Vogue* said she was one of the ten most beautiful women in the world, and she's quite a well-known film star.' Another memory stirred, which was of trying to contact her while I was writing *Gone Away*, and being unsuccessful. I said, 'Thanks very much, Lily. Do ask her,' and went back to typing. Lily said, 'You ought to remember a few things. She studied in Switzerland when her father was with UNESCO in Paris. She got married when she was about sixteen to a fellow called Oberoi, whose father has a chain of hotels. She had twins I think, but she got divorced and her husband kept them.' I knew that Lily had spent much of her youth briefing Mrs Pandit about her prospective guests, and was grateful to her for doing the same for me.

A couple of days later, Lily said, 'You *do* remember that tonight is the cocktail party? I asked Judy to remind you.' I had known Lily since my adolescence, when she had sometimes gently chided me on my forgetfulness. 'It's not exactly a cocktail party,' she said, 'more like drinks. I don't understand *why* you can't remember *any* of your old friends in Bombay.' Neither could I, I suppose, except that subconsciously, when I started in England, I wanted to put Bombay behind me. That evening, Francis was rushing around the flat roaring, in a sportive mood, Judy attempting to capture him and put him to bed, when the doorbell rang and Leela Naidu arrived, limping, having turned her ankle on a stone outside the front door. She *was* very beautiful, wearing a green-and-white chiffon sari. When Lily seated her beside me on the sofa, and she bent towards me for a light to her cigarette, I also noticed her attire included a transparent white bra, which appeared to be very well filled. I averted my eyes.

At this time the relations between Judy and me were a little difficult. I was either drunk, or, wretched about not feeling the ecstatic release of a made poem, grumpy, or simply detached, as I had been all my life. I had spent my childhood in creating fantasies in my mind, to get away from the incessant lunatic demands from my mother, my adolescence attempting to toughen myself; but now that I considered myself a responsible young man, I could not change my nature. It was not that I drifted away on dreams, but that, as in dealing with my mother years before, I simply took myself away from everything and everyone around me and thought my own thoughts. I wanted to be an ideal father to my son, but I knew that in my present state I couldn't be. Often I was irritated by his constant demands, by the impingement upon my mind of a world of reality. I was irritated by the demands of other people.

I was not 'My Son's Father'. I was not capable of being that. At least, not yet. My thoughts at this time revolved around my loathing for my mother, and my separation from my real work. But, putting these thoughts aside, I took my small family to Goa, the birthplace of my ancestors, and once the cause of my trouble with Pandit Nehru. Before we left, my father phoned Lily up, and she, somewhat bemusedly, said to me, 'He wants you to buy him sausages and fruit. I don't understand, I can get imported sausages here, and surely *he* can in Delhi, and I could probably get late mangoes....'

What my father in fact desired, as he told me when I phoned him back, were the kind of sausages produced in Goa, which he had eaten at his father's house in Bombay. These were brought in by the Portuguese, and are a version of the Spanish chorizo. The fruit he so particularly wanted was something called a jackfruit, for which Goa is famous. My father was a sophisticated man, and I was rather surprised at these atavistic tendencies, but concluded that anything he wanted to actually *eat* might be a worthwhile purchase. We flew in over amazingly green islands, cut through by brown rivers, which rose from a turquoise sea. These confusions and symmetrical clashes of colours continued after we had landed, in emerald paddy fields and a profusion of flowers in the trees. Panjim, the capital, sat by the Mandovi river, which at that time could only be crossed by ferry, and on which butterfly sails fluttered.

We had come more or less unannounced, and on the first night in the Mandovi Hotel by the river of that name, I went, as was my wont, to the bar. It was very crowded, and I shared a table with a man who presently asked me my name. I told him my surname and, puzzled, he said, 'How do you spell it?' I spelt it. I had pronounced it 'Morrayz.' But when I spelt it, my companion cried 'Ah, Moraysh! Yes, man, you come from the village of Santa Cruz, and your father has land there.' I recollected what my father had once told me. 'But,' said my new friend, 'you have a funny voice. You don't sound Goan. What is your first name?' When I told him he said, 'Dom Moraysh? You are the man who tried to save us from the Hindus! Man, you are our hero!' He leapt to his feet and brought the crowded bar to silence by waving his arms and shouting, 'Here is our hero! Here is Dom Moraysh!' I returned very late to our room.

The following day I had a number of visitors. The first was a tall, prematurely bald man with a neat moustache, and the mournful eyes of a violinist, called Chico Fernandes, and with him was a hawk-faced and handsome person called Lucio de Miranda, who was actually a guitar player and a famous singer. Both were also businessmen; both were around my age; both have remained my friends for a quarter of a century. They told me that, under the Portuguese, the Goan economy had sunk to unimaginable depths. This was the reason for the great exodus from the territory during the days of the British. The Portuguese in Goa received no financial help from the home country, all trade had stultified, all businesses had to turn to British India for help. The Goans did not particularly like the Portuguese, but at least the Portuguese had left them alone.

But when the Indians threatened 'liberation', most young Goan businessmen were nervous, on the principle that the devil you know is better than the one you don't. Since the Indians came anyway, the young men hoped that business prospects in Goa might be bettered. But they hadn't been, because the Indians signed contracts with firms based in India, and also because there had been a huge influx of immigrants from neighbouring states, whose arrival had lowered the Goan standard of life. This was not only the complaint of my Christian friends in Goa, but of a Hindu friend, Mohandas Naik, whose family had been grievously persecuted by the Portuguese. 'You may not have known what you were doing when you attacked the "liberation".' One of my newfound friends said, 'But you expressed what all of us were feeling. That's why people want to buy you drinks whenever you go into the hotel bar.'

Goa is a very small place, and the only delay in going around it was the presence of the Zuari and Mandovi rivers, which one had to cross by ferry, and the smaller waterways, to be traversed by canoe. The ferries carried cars, motorcycles and bicycles; priests, students, farmers with produce, women carrying basketfuls of poultry. The canoes across the waterways were propelled by lithe brown fishermen. Everyone was unremittingly friendly and cheerful. A friend from Bombay, a brilliant cartoonist, Mario de

Miranda (through whom I had met his cousin, Lucio, and Chico), sent me to his house in the village of Loutolim, on the far side of the Zuari from Panjim. This was a huge, rambling house built in Portuguese times, with its own ballroom and chapel; it was run by a senile but likeable cook called Pedad who baked a cake for Francis, Though nobody was supposed to know we were there, many people turned up, all bringing liquor. 'One can see how you came to drink so much,' said Judy tartly, 'it would seem to be in the blood.' But Francis was happy, the cook made much of him and provided him with daily delicacies, and I myself felt euphoric.

The reason for this was that I mistakenly felt that I had at last found some kind of identity. The reason I made this mistake was that so many people told me I was a local hero. In a few years, when the trauma of the Indian arrival was finally over, I wasn't. It was a mistake I will never make again. My friends sedulously protected me from visiting my ancestral property. 'Your aunt lives there, no?' said Chico. 'If you go there it will make you sad, no? So don't go there.' But we attended barbecue parties on the beach, with a suckling pig on the coals and Lucio singing *fados* under the stars; and at the end Chico bought sausages and a jackfruit for my father. They both smelt abominable; but with them we flew back to Delhi.

John, in my father's house was amazed. Chico had armed me with five kilos of chorizos, but he didn't know how to cook them. Neither did Judy or Marilyn; nor did I. But my father did. He stood over John and instructed him, and all five kilos vanished in two or three days. 'Chota Sahib,' John marvelled, 'Little Master, I haven't seen Big Master eat like this in years.' The jackfruit, of which an observer in 1330 remarked that they were 'fruits so big that two will be a load for a strong man', went the same way. I remarked to my father that he ought to retire to Goa. To my surprise he said, 'No, I'd prefer London,' a preference which was to have tragic consequences.

Meanwhile I applied for permission to enter Bhutan. I had already got permission to visit Nepal and Sikkim, where we had arranged to stay with the king, the Chogyal, and his American wife Hope Cooke, both of whom were friends of my father's. Marilyn, in fact, had photographed the coronation and marriage of the royal couple a few months before, at a ceremony attended by the world press, because it was supposed to be so romantic: the king of a wild Himalayan country united with an American socialite. But Bhutan remained very difficult, especially for me. Very few people were allowed in, and someone who had openly defied the Indian government over Goa was considered a bad security risk. Bhutan was then an Indian protectorate.

Shortly before we left for Kathmandu, I looked out of the drawing room window into the garden where Francis was playing with John's children. I said, 'I'm glad we brought him here, aren't you? He seems to have been happy all the time.'

'*He* may be,' said Judy, 'but I'm not.'

I asked her why not.

'Because,' she said, 'I feel like a prisoner.' I could not understand her then, but perhaps I do now. She was penned up with Francis all day, while I wandered about, free as the wind, drinking with friends, interviewing people, making her feel she had no place in my life. On that note we set off for the Himalayas.

8

I crouched on a ledge in the cliff, with my small son in my arms. Below us was a sheer drop of about 4,000 feet into the forest. I kept my eyes tightly shut, so that I need not see it. Judy and the guides had vanished behind a waterfall, and were climbing a narrow and slippery goat-path towards the monastery on the mountaintop. I crushed Francis' small body against my chest so that he should not slip away from me and fall all the way down to the forest. The harder I held him, the more upset he became; he squirmed and kicked and cried, making my task more difficult.

I have always had a complex about rats; I also suffer very badly from vertigo. It isn't only that I feel giddy, I actually want to surrender myself to space, and, if I am at a great height, with no barrier between me and what lies below, an irresistible impulse to leap from it possesses me. I should never have agreed to this expedition, but in Thimpu, the capital of Bhutan, which now lay somewhere below me in the forested valley I did not want to see, and desperately wanted to return to, the king's protocol officers had suggested that I observe an impressive feature of the landscape. This was called Tiger's Leap, which was on a mountain. On top of the mountain was a monastery. They suggested we should visit it. I inquired very nervously about the nature of the ascent. 'Oh,' they said, 'a child could climb it.'

Maybe a Bhutanese child, I thought bitterly, as I clutched Francis and crouched on the ledge. We had come from Thimpu by a Land Rover to the foot of a formidable escarpment, climbed halfway up a mountain on ponies, and forded two rivers on the way. The path had then become too steep for the ponies, and we went further up on foot. It was not only a steep path but a narrow one, and my vertigo became so intense that the officer of protocol had to hold my arm. Eventually we had emerged on this ledge. Beyond it an even narrower path led under a waterfall, up to the monastery.

I suggested that we turn back; the protocol officer seemed amazed. Judy wanted to see the monastery. So I remained on the ledge with Francis. They took about an hour to come back. This was the most terrible hour I have had in my time, because for most of it I was in a state of sheer panic. I truly believe that Francis saved my life that day; I felt a powerful pull towards the edge of the cliff, and had I not been responsible for him I might well have leapt off the ledge. But when they came back from the monastery, I recovered, and was in good shape going down.

Ever since then, from time to time, I have had nightmares about my vigil on the ledge. I wake up biting the pillow, clutching the bedsheets, and shaking all over. I remember the battle in my senses between the desire to plunge downward and my emotions towards the little body in my arms, fighting me. When back in Thimpu, I asked Judy what the monastery had been like. She said, 'There was nothing in it.'

This was towards the end of our stay in the Himalayan kingdom.

We arrived in Kathmandu shortly before Christmas. There was nothing there that I had not written about before. The purpose of the visit was twofold. My father and Marilyn were spending Christmas in Nepal, so I thought we would too. I also had a lucrative assignment from London. A newspaper wanted me to see how the English hippies in Kathmandu spent Christmas. The fee would pay for most of our expenses in Nepal. My father and Marilyn were already ensconced in a hotel when we arrived, and had made our bookings for us. Also in the hotel were two reporters, an Indian photographer, Kishor Parekh, and a Malaysian writer, Gerry Delilkhan, who, by coincidence, were on exactly the same mission as I was. They were from something I had never heard of, the *Asia Magazine*, which at that time had its headquarters in Singapore.

Kathmandu had changed a good deal over the decade since I had last been there. The exotic nature of the city had departed: there were luxury hotels, like the one we were staying at, banks, offices, even a casino. The main change was the hippie presence. Ragged white people, with beards and necklaces, paraded the streets; in a decade they would be part of the middle class of their respective countries, but they were now busily breaking away from their parents, an admirable attempt on the whole. Quite a large proportion of them in those days were English. Boris, the Russian refugee, who on my previous visit had run the Royal Hotel, had opened a Tibetan restaurant called the Yak and Yeti; but in the byways in the centre of town were tiny establishments with chalkboards outside advertising the menu. Every menu included eggs and chips, and in fact there were chips with everything. These places were exclusively for the hippies, with whom Delilkhan and Parekh had already, they said, established contact. They generously offered to help me. 'After all, we are colleagues,' they said. I was grateful.

On Christmas Eve we arranged to meet in the hotel bar. It was bitterly cold outside; I dressed in what I thought were sensible clothes, a woollen shirt and trousers, a sweater and anorak. As I sipped my whisky in the bar, two extraordinary figures entered. One wore a fringed buckskin tunic and leggings, the other what seemed to be a Buddhist monk's robes. Both were festooned with bead necklaces and bells, and the one in buckskin had a feather in his hair. I forget which was Parekh and which Delilkhan; I think the Red Indian was Parekh. Seeing me, he cried, 'But how can we take you to see the hippies? You are most unsuitably dressed!'

Delilkhan said, 'We've got other costumes like these. We'll lend you one.'

But I turned down this kind offer though it was repeated several times. Finally, shrugging in despair, my colleagues led me out into the freezing darkness. After a fairly long walk, we found ourselves outside one of the egg-and-chip establishments. 'This is one of their haunts,' said Delilkhan, like Sherlock Holmes on the hunt for Moriarty's men. We went in. The restaurant consisted of a large room furnished with benches and trestle tables. It was filled with smoke, partly from kerosene lamps and incense burners, partly from the hashish which all its occupants were smoking. In the middle of the room was a pathetically small and wilted Christmas tree, the young people round it far from home. A portly Nepalese and his wife served them; apart from the drugs, there were a few bottles of wine strewn around, and a box of Black Magic chocolates.

The hippies were mostly English; there were a few young French people and a couple of Americans. While Delilkhan attempted to talk to some of them and Parekh tried to persuade others to be photographed, I went up to an English boy and told him what I was doing and who I was doing it for. He seemed greatly excited by the name of an English newspaper. 'Hey,' he called, 'this bloke's from the *Telegraph*.' Others came over, and I soon had a circle round me, all of them asking how things were at home.

Even in hot weather, I had been told, hippie attire was not very eccentric. They wore Indian costumes, which was not unreasonable. The ornaments and beads were what made the men unusual in appearance to the Nepalese; the absence of brassieres in the women shocked them a little, especially in summer, under transparent tunics. But it was winter, and they were all enveloped in sweaters and shawls. Had they not been so gaunt and pallid, they would have looked like young climbers in some mountain hut in Europe. Among them, my colleagues stood out like twin peacocks.

'Who are those two clowns you came with?' asked one of the boys. 'They've been snooping around for days trying to find out now much grass we smoke, if we sleep around, stuff like that. And the way they dress, like, it's kind of embarrassing.'

'Journalists,' I said, 'like me.' Laughter ensued. 'Well, why don't they dress like you then?' someone asked. 'This isn't a fucking fancy dress ball.' Then they began to talk about their lives, which seemed to be unremittingly miserable. 'Lots of us aren't here,' a girl said, 'because lots of us are sick. Nearly all of us have had hepatitis.' The Nepalese rented them huts on the outskirts of town at exorbitant prices. 'They told us the Nepalese were very hospitable,' a boy said. 'Well, they aren't. They treat *us* like beggars, but they overcharge us whenever they can, even for food. We know they overcharge us, but there's no way to bargain. We don't speak their language, they don't speak ours. The only things cheap here are grass and hash, but it doesn't seem worthwhile now.' They all, but in particular the girls, seemed homesick at this season. I suggested that some of the girls visit Judy in the hotel. They asked if they would be allowed in. 'If those two can *stay* there, dressed like that,' said another girl, pointing at Delilkhan and Parekh, 'why the fuck can't we visit it?'

My colleagues were looking very disconsolate. I had my story, and was getting more by the minute. It was very obvious that they hadn't got theirs, or at least not what they wanted. Suddenly inspired, I said to one of the boys, 'Poor buggers, you ought to help them out. Why don't you go and answer their questions? You could use your imaginations a bit, you know? Give them a Christmas present.' They immediately obliged. When we left, Delilkhan and Parekh were delighted with themselves. 'You've no idea what I've got,' Delilkhan said. 'The orgies these depraved people have! The amount of drugs they take! What a story! But you're a colleague. I'll share it with you.'

The only reason I didn't share mine with them was that I knew it wasn't what they wanted. Some of the girls came to the hotel to talk to Judy. 'They're all very ill,' she told me later. 'All they wanted to talk about was how London looked when I left it. They wanted to know what films were on. They wanted to know about the fashions. They started to play with Francis, and then one of them started crying.'

Christmas over, celebrated in the hotel with bonfires, crackers, and a Sherpa Santa Claus, we flew up to a place called Pokhara, in the shadow of snow-laden Annapurna, where I had another story. At Pokhara, around this time of year, the British army sent recruiting officers to the Gurkhas of the area. I had hardly got off the tiny plane before the interpreter I had hired in Kathmandu was hustling me uphill to a clearing among the trees. Two British officers were sitting at a wooden table, with files heaped on it, and also a great pile of official forms that kept trying to blow away in the wind off Annapurna. Around them stood a crowd of Gurkhas. The sun in the mountains had had an effect on the officers; their faces and necks were reddened by it, yet they remained cool. They conducted long conversations in Gurkhali, not only with the young recruits, but with their fathers, and even their grandfathers, who had turned up for the occasion. These older men came in their uniforms, with their decorations in their lapels, and in the main they seemed as buoyant and sturdy as Gurkhas are supposed to be. But their descendants seemed a little anaemic, malnourished.

'Why do they take such a long time to recruit one man?' I asked the interpreter. 'Ask the officers, sahib,' he said. 'There is only one hotel, and they are also there.' Later, I did. One of the officers said, 'When they come with their fathers and grandfathers, the old fellows usually have distinguished regimental records, and like to tell us about them. It wouldn't be courteous to stop them. Anyway, it all runs in the family. As to the recruits being a bit skinny, so were their grandfathers, before they came into the army. They got strong on a diet of red meat and other people's blood.'

I knew what he meant, and thought he put it rather well. But behind the small hotel was a Peace Corps camp, and one of their people, who had come to the hotel for water, overheard this conversation. He confronted me later, very agitated. 'Look,' he said, 'we liked you. We knew you were a poet. What kind of poet are you, when you can talk to these butchers in their own language? We don't want to speak to you.'

I felt abashed; but I also felt that one should be able to speak to all sorts of people in their own languages to obtain any knowledge of what the world was like. By the morning of my second day in Pokhara, the British officers, my Peace Corps antagonist, and I, were all drinking beer amicably together in the hotel.

These two stories had to be done, and were; there was nothing much else to do in Nepal. Judy was taken round Kathmandu and the surrounding valley. Marilyn sometimes went with her, otherwise she went with Nepalese friends. I usually stayed behind in the hotel, talking to my father. Though he was an unusually reticent man, he liked, as most elderly people do, to reminisce; he told me a number of stories about Gandhi, Nehru, Jinnah, Mountbatten, and the Burma and China theatres during the Second World War, during which time he had interviewed Chiang Kai-shek. When in China with an Indian cultural delegation in 1953—the rest of them had been singers, dancers, and so forth; Nehru had sent him as a 'spotter'—he had also talked to Mao Zedong, and we spent an interesting afternoon during which he compared one Chinese leader with the other.

I still couldn't produce any poetry. I scribbled bits and pieces down, but I knew that they were uniformly terrible, and my hand seemed to have lost its power to fit pieces together on the page. My personal life was far from satisfactory, partly as a result of this. Something else happened in Kathmandu which caused me immense disquiet. At night, because my father was often in the bar, and because I would probably have visited it anyway, I was there. Judy used to bring Francis, until his bedtime, at which point she would go back to our room with him. Some Nepalese poets, whom I had met on my previous visits, used to come to the bar to drink with me; local journalists used to come to meet my father; we usually occupied the place until midnight, but I was still young enough to recover by the next day.

But on the first night I visited this bar, which was a little like some of the country pubs I knew in England, with a wood fire and hunting prints on the walls, I met an English girl who was researching some aspect of Gurkha history and therefore spending time in Nepal. Anyone who looked less like a researcher could hardly be imagined. She had long dark hair, violet eyes, and delicately structured features; though slim, she was well-breasted, and had long and shapely legs. For very good reasons of my own, I tried not to speak to her. But the bar was a small one, and we were in constant proximity. I wound up in private conversation with her most nights, after Judy had gone upstairs with our son. One evening, she said, 'This bar's awfully boring, isn't it? Always the same people. Why don't you drop in to my cottage for a drink?' She had rented one, not very far away from the hotel.

I said, 'We'd love to, but Judy's busy with the child every night.'

She leant close and said, 'That's exactly what I meant.' Her breath smelt of the violets which were in her eyes. My eyes buried themselves between her violet-scented breasts.

We flew back to Delhi, and then from there to Calcutta and Bagdogra on the borders of West Bengal. At the airport the Chogyal of Sikkim's car awaited us. We were driven up to a certain point in Siliguri, a nearby town, where we transferred to a jeep nearly ten years before I had travelled this way with Ajit Das, bound, with different companions, for Gangtok. On that previous occasion we had travelled by bus, very uncomfortably, and in Gangtok we had stayed in a hotel in the bazaar patronized by wild Tibetan traders who had come in by way of the Chumbi Valley. But, by jeep or bus, the route was the same, and the road no better. Moreover, night was already falling when we left Siliguri. Kichu, the driver, was slight and boyish, and seemed a little nervous, but his hands were steady on the wheel. This was caused by Francis; so far as I understood Kichu, he felt he had greater responsibility because of the child.

As we climbed away from the plains, the wind acquired a keen edge. It became excruciatingly cold. I was on the outside, and the jeep had no doors; when well past midnight we saw the lights of Gangtok ahead, I was chilled to the bone. Kichu came down off the shoulder of a mountain into the little town and took us into the palace area, where I had never been before. He drove us to the doorstep of a large and comfortable guest house. A Eurasian housekeeper, who seemed alert despite the hour, welcomed us. 'For you, madam,' he said to Judy, 'and for our Little Master, soup, sandwiches, and sweet. And for you, sir,' he added, turning courteously my way, 'the whole bar has been freshly stocked. His Highness says you must have the same tastes as your father.'

Next morning the housekeeper was back to supervise breakfast. 'All the menus in the royal household,' he said, 'are personally directed by Her Highness, Her Majesty Miss Hope Cooke.' It was, as I recollect, a large and very American breakfast, with special cereals for Francis. Once it had ended, the housekeeper suddenly produced a file and thrust it upon me. 'I am a true poet, sir,' he said, 'like your good self. Here is the total sum of my poetic work for the last forty years. Keats, sir, Mr John Keats, has been my master in all I do. I too have written an "Ode to Melancholy," and an "Ode to a Grecian Urn." Unfortunately, I have never seen a Grecian urn except in photographs. I have not had the same cultural opportunities as Mr Keats. Kindly read these humble works, sir, and tell me your opinion.' I was saved from the immediate necessity to reply by Hope Cooke herself.

She arrived by car, though the palace was not far away. She was petite, with an elfin face, and was clad in a long flowing Sikkimese robe. The elfin impression was heightened by the fact that she spoke in a continuous husky whisper, with a pronounced Indian accent. The whisper, apparently, was Sikkimese court etiquette for women. Later on, when we knew her somewhat better, Hope would slip out of the palace and walk down to the guest house in a sweater and slacks. Her accent changed with her apparel. When in Western clothes, she spoke in a normal voice, with a well-bred American accent. On this first visit, she was very much the queen of Sikkim.

She whispered inquiries as to our comfort and as to what I wanted to write about in her state. She whispered criticisms, these in really piercing whispers, to the housekeeper as to his arrangements. I wondered what she did when she wanted to call someone from a distance. I soon found out; she used a handbell. She then put us into her car and drove us round to various places where she was running centres for women. At each place people made deep obeisances and whispered at her, and she whispered back. When she dropped us at the guest house she whispered an invitation to lunch. 'My husband was sorry he couldn't meet you this morning,' she said. 'He was meeting the Indian envoy. But he'll be there for lunch.' I had once met the Chogyal at my father's house in Delhi. He had worn Sikkimese robes, not unlike the ones worn by his wife, but simpler, and had given an impression of great, if deliberate, dignity.

Sikkim had once been part of Tibet; the Chogyals were of Tibetan stock. Thondup, the present Chogyal, looked Tibetan: he had a broad, but inexpressive face, and, though not a tall man, seemed bigger than he actually was because of his breadth of body. He spoke softly, though not as softly as Hope. A loud voice is considered bad manners in the Himalayan kingdoms. That first lunch took place in the palace gardens, beside a small menagerie which contained birds, monkeys, and deer. Thondup drank a lot, under Hope's disapproving eye, and visibly relaxed as he drank. He was, as I soon discovered, an alcoholic in quite a big way.

He had some reason to be one. He was the younger son of the previous Chogyal, and his elder brother had been Crown Prince. Thondup became a Buddhist monk. When his brother was killed in an accident, he came to the throne, but, so far as I could gather, did not want to. He was, in his own way, a deeply religious man; paradoxically, it was because of this that he now drank. But he was also proud to be Chogyal, and loved his country. He could not understand why there was opposition to his rule, and thought that it was instigated by the Indians, who hated him.

On my last visit to Gangtok, nine years earlier, I had met a number of young Sikkimese who thought the Chogyal an anachronism. They didn't like the way he lived, and felt that he was ignorant of the problems the poor had. These young men wanted to secede to India. The Indians may not have actually hated Thondup, but they, like the young Sikkimese, disapproved of him. That had been in 1959, but now matters were coming to a head. I did not meet the Sikkimese liberals, or hear their angry mutters. But wherever one went in the town, grafitti on the walls told of popular feeling against the Chogyal's rule.

The peculiarity of this unrest was that the rebels had a deep respect for the office of Chogyal. They wanted the royal line to continue, but they wanted Thondup as a figurehead monarch, which he did not intend to be. His marriage to a foreigner, and the huge and costly wedding, had then caused the rebels to wonder if Thondup should continue as Chogyal at all. They felt that the Crown Prince, still a schoolboy in England, should come back, that Thondup should abdicate, and that the child should take over. Thondup was perfectly aware of all this. He was torn between his country and his wife. People showed Hope all the required courtesies, and she thought she was not only respected but loved. Thondup knew that she wasn't, and, because of her, neither was he. But he loved her, and didn't tell her so. Perhaps he should have done. That day, in the crisp winter sunlight, the white-headed Himalayas distant but around us, their presence felt, Thondup said that he wanted to take us to some ceremonies at a nearby monastery, and to send us to western Sikkim, which was very beautiful and full of monuments. 'We'll send a hamper with you,' Hope whispered, 'and a good cook.' He asked what else he could do for me. This was very kind; I said I wanted to revisit the Nathu La Pass, the frontier between Sikkim and Tibet, where I had been in 1959, and also to get a permit to enter Bhutan. Thondup pondered over this. 'I'll tell you tomorrow,' he said. 'Tomorrow we go to the ceremonies in the monastery.' But that evening he asked us to dinner, and talked of Sikkimese history.

He seemed to know all about it, from the early days of animists and tribal warfare to the Tibetan invasions and the coming of Buddhism. He had a vast collection of taped Tibetan music, which he played; the great conches booming, wind instruments that sounded like the plaintive shrieking of lost ghosts. He played them for hours, and appeared to fall into a deep reverie. I could see how this could happen; I myself felt hypnotized by the immense volumes of sound, and the shrill cadences between and under them. We had dinner very late, and afterwards Thondup read to me from Tibetan parchments, which he then translated. These had to do with his ancestors. It was getting on for dawn when we finally returned to the guest house.

Three hours later we drove to a monastery on a hill outside Gangtok. Thondup and Hope were welcomed by obsequious monks, red-robed and shaven; we were all seated in a small stone pavilion fronted by a courtyard. It drizzled thinly, the snow mountains wore clouds on their shoulders, when, from some invisible source, the same kind of music I had heard the previous night thundered and shrieked forth. With the music came dancers wearing the masks of demons: wooden masks, painted in lurid colours, which maintained a fixed expression of utter malevolence as the dancers capered, stamped, and waved their long sleeves. I had seen Noh plays in London where the masked performers had possessed some of this aura of evil. But here, in its proper place, the dance recalled very high, wind-filled passes where the dead sobbed and shrieked, where great voices called from the peaks, where perhaps the yeti, the man-beast, shambled amongst the demons. The immense loneliness of the Himalayas, and their ability to instil terror into human hearts, were caught up not only in the sound but the dances.

The drizzle turned into heavy rain. The ceremonies abruptly ended, the monks looked very distressed. 'This is not a good omen,' Thondup said. 'In fact, it is a very bad omen.' He himself looked depressed. 'Those ceremonies,' he said, 'were partly to call for my good fortune.' He was silent all the way back to the palace. But there, over a drink, he cheered up slightly. 'Nathu La,' he told me, 'is a high-security area. The Indians don't want to let people up there, especially not people with foreign passports. But Nathu La is also in my country. I have told the Indians that I can send anyone I like there. They cannot stop my guests. So you'll be able to go there tomorrow, in one of our Land Rovers. Then, as to Bhutan, the king isn't only my neighbour, we're related by marriage. If he invites you, the Indians can't stop you. So I've sent him a message. Communications are very bad, but by the time you come back from West Sikkim, in four or five days from now, I'm sure he'll have answered, and I'm sure he'll say yes.'

Thondup suggested that I take Judy and Francis up to the frontier with me, 'so that you will look less of a journalist'. I had my doubts, but the day after the ill-fated ceremonies, we left Gangtok in a Land Rover. The pass is a four-hour drive into the mountains. Last time Das and I had done it in a dilapidated taxi, and it had taken longer. This time progress was brisk and efficient, the Chogyal's flag on the Land Rover saw us through all the checkposts, up through the foothills, into the mountains the taxi had creaked up nine years before. The higher snow mountains came clearly into focus beyond. I recognized the powder-blue water of the Changu lake to the right of the road. On the slopes to the left, exactly as on my first trip, there were huge yaks at pasture, and red flowers that are supposed to be poisonous. I had once written a poem about both. Seeing them again was like reliving the poem, bad though it had been.

Signposts had been visible for the last few miles, obviously put up by the army. Now a couple of military vehicles came down the narrow road, laden with troops. This caused some delay; the Land Rover had to give way, which, considering the available space, was difficult. But a mile or two further on, we came to a military camp. Some of the officers were waiting on the road to welcome us. We transferred to an army jeep, and went on up to the frontier. I was not prepared for what I saw.

Nine years before, there had been nothing at the mouth of the pass except an engraved stone, put up by Nehru, that marked the border. A police inspector and two sleepy constables had sat around it. The Chumbi Valley stretched out beyond them, rocky and tussocked, until it became a forest. We had been ringed around, on the horizon, by the great snow mountains. The atmosphere had the taste of distances and remoteness. Two cairns of stones, topped by prayer-flags, stood near the frontier marker. Tibetans, when they entered the pass, each threw a stone to ward off the mountain spirits. Now there were no cairns, no prayer-flags; almost no valley.

Two encampments, enfiladed by barbed wire, clogged the mouth of Nathu La. These were filled with bunkers and huts, loomed over by sentry towers and radio aerials. The only difference between the two camps was that one was populated by Chinese troops and the other by Indians. The captain who had accompanied us from the base camp took us up to the wire that faced the Chinese. Hindi film music made the thin air hideous. 'That's their loudspeaker,' the captain said. 'They also broadcast propaganda several hours a day. When they're off the air, we take over. It's a matter of courtesy.' Some years later, on the Taiwanese island of Quemoy, I witnessed another example of this peculiar courtesy. The Communists and the Taiwanese, by unwritten agreement, used to shell each other ferociously on alternate Wednesdays.

There was no tension in the air, but Nathu La is 16,000 feet up, and, perhaps because of the altitude, perhaps because of the deafening sound of the loudspeaker, Francis began to cry. As he cried a Chinese officer climbed on to the roof of a bunker and examined us through field-glasses, though we were not very far away. 'A full colonel,' said the captain. 'He must be wondering who the hell you are. We've never yet seen a Chinese baby on their side of the wire. By tonight Peking will know that your son was here.' He was a cheerful young man. 'Perhaps they'll think he's our new secret weapon. There's nothing much more to see,' he added, 'let's go back.'

Actually, there wasn't much more to see. The slope down which I had once scrambled down into the Chumbi Valley was hardly visible, and I could hardly see the valley itself, from which Indian traders fleeing from Shigatse had once approached us on weary mules. But the huge impassive mountains, caked in snow that never melted, still looked down upon the activities beneath. Perhaps yetis watched from their slopes. In these parts, as a Welsh mountaineer once told me, you never knew.

We returned to base camp and lunched in the officers' mess. The officers were mostly young and lonely, and welcomed guests, but lunch took four hours to serve. During this time everyone except Judy and Francis drank rum. It was very cold, but even I thought this unduly bibulous, till it transpired that the cook had spent most of this time preparing a large basket of golden-spun sugar for Francis. It was filled with chocolates and solemnly presented to him by the colonel. When I visited the loo I found the walls plastered with pin-ups from Western magazines. Among these I noticed pictures of two friends I had made while doing my sex magazine article for *Nova*: Eve Eden, otherwise known as Rosa Dolmai, in a black lace bra and panties, and June Palmer, fetchingly nude. When I returned to the plains I wrote them both letters, telling them that they had admirers in distant places, and suggesting that autographed photographs of themselves would be much appreciated in the Nathu La mess. I don't know if they ever sent any. I was never to meet them, or the friendly officers, again. The expedition to Nathu La lasted a very tiring day, and indeed we didn't get back to town until well past midnight. Judy and Francis were exhausted, but at dawn the next day we started off, in the same Land Rover, for western Sikkim. This time Kichu drove us. 'He says he likes driving the baby,' Hope murmured. She had come down from the palace to see us off. She looked very fresh, so did Kichu. But the cook who brought the promised hamper to the Land Rover had bleary eyes, and so, indeed, did the passengers. Judy had had more sleep than I, and so, obviously, had Francis; what with one thing and another, I had had about eight hours' sleep in three days. 'There's a game pie in there,' Hope told me. 'There's cold chicken, tinned pâté, salami, and hard-boiled eggs. That should last you two days, but if it doesn't the cook can always buy stuff in the villages. There's tinned milk and rusks for Francis, too.'

For the first few hours I slept in the Land Rover, which was a considerable feat in itself. When I awoke we were bumping through a forest where wild orchids seemed to flourish everywhere, hanging from the trees and leaping from the tangled grass. The mountains, which throughout these weeks had kept at a reasonable distance, though always visible, now seemed very close, slopes iced with serrated snow. The cook offered me a large slice of game pie and a glass of rum. As I ate, a rapid northern darkness fell. Towards midnight, we reached a house on a hill. Nothing was visible around but huge glimmering shapes, like a dream of icebergs, above dense forest. The cook opened the house, called villagers from where fires smouldered dimly downhill, lit fires and kerosene lamps, and began to kill, pluck, and cook a chicken he had obtained in the last few minutes. 'Cold food no good,' he told me, 'in cold weather.' Kichu fed Francis. We ate; we went to bed on mattresses on the floor. At dawn I awoke, as the fire died in the hearth, and opened the front door.

The cold air rushed into the warm room, into my lungs and my body. It smelt of trees and snow, and woke me up as nothing else could have done. When I raised my eyes I saw the ghostly shapes of midnight solidified; Kanchenjunga, which looked close enough to touch, reared its immense snowcapped head above me; its attendant peaks stood around it. The vastnesses and empty places of the world; I was to see many of them in the future and deal with them in my mind, but this was my first close encounter. I was dumbfounded and electrified; and I saw, on the foothills below the immense mountains, dwarfed by them, monasteries with brightly painted walls. At that hour, the great conches were putting forth their thunder, between monastery and monastery, so that the leaves stirred on the trees, the needles on the conifers, and the valleys beneath received the sound. Behind me Francis began, very irritatingly, to wake up.

Kichu appeared from nowhere, pointed to a painted dome across the valley, and said, 'Today we go there, sahib. Highness say.' The cook appeared too, saying, 'Angrez nashta, sahib? English breakfast?' Villagers appeared with firewood, and he began to boil porridge, fry eggs and bacon, and grill sausages on sticks, all on a smoky wood fire which kept being extinguished by the mountain winds. This image has stayed in my mind for many years. After breakfast we set out for the monastery Kichu had indicated, which was by no means as close as it seemed. Once there, the abbot, who seemed to have expected us, showed us an extensive collection of Buddhist images in stone and jade, ivory and metal; also the tankas, the cloth scrolls on which the Buddhist scriptures were written, ancient, tired, in themselves beautiful.

This went on for two days. I never felt any exhaustion in the mountains, despite my vertigo. Hope had perhaps explained this problem to Kichu. Whenever we were in a high place, he held my arm and interposed his slight body between me and the drop. Judy had a splendid head for heights and scornfully declined help, and the cook usually carried Francis, so that wherever we went we were reasonably safe. Eventually we returned to Gangtok. Judy picked armfuls of wild orchids for Hope, which all died immediately. We came back in the night, and Thondup came over for a drink. 'Your Bhutan thing is all fixed up,' he said, rather tiredly trying to lift a large whisky to his lips, as though the weight of his hand was dragging the glass away. 'I had a message from the king. Kichu will take you in your Land Rover as far as Phuntsoling on his borders. You'll have to go through Indian territory; no matter, they're not going to stop any of my vehicles. But will you stay for a few days more?'

I said we had already stayed for several days, and Hope and he must be very tired of us.

Thondup said, 'My sister died yesterday in Calcutta. They are flying the body here for cremation. I would appreciate it if you stayed. You would be a support.'

I didn't see it, but I said we would stay, and next afternoon it began to snow. The snowflakes weren't like English snowflakes—they were huge, and when the wind whipped them against the picture windows of the guest house, they made a sound like hammer blows; they would partially melt after a few seconds against the pane, then, lifted by the wind, reform, and be sent down a swaying staircase of wind to the valley. The snow was mixed with pellets of hail, and though I had read of howling winds, I had never really heard one howl before. Forced through the funnels of the passes, it made a sound like a hundred melancholy wolves, and when there was a subsidence of wind, the sound died into a hungry whimpering. We had bought silk scarves in the bazaar that morning, to present to the corpse according to Tibetan custom. Towards dusk, Thondup rang us up on the intercom.

He said, 'The coffin can't come, the weather's too bad. So I've decided to give myself a party. I've decided to give it in the guest house. Francis can come and sleep in the palace; there'll be too much noise for him. I've asked a hundred people. Do you mind?' I said no, of course not. He hesitated, then said guiltily, 'I can't bear the idea, you know. My sister in a coffin in Calcutta, and me here.'

He looked unbearably unhappy at the party. He was in grey robes, and looked kingly; but had he had a white beard I would have imagined him to be Lear. The Eurasian housekeeper had mobilized the whole serving staff of the palace, Hope had done her best at short notice. Tibetan cho-cho and momo, aromatic dumplings, kebabs, Indian delicacies, like puffed rice, and American canapés, were circulated, and so was the liquor, extensively, while the wild snow whirled past the windows. At one point Hope whispered to me, 'Can you do something with Thondup? He's insulting all the Indian envoys and officers.... She was his favourite sister.'

Thondup was coming out of a passageway with a glass in his hand, with that regal but forced walk which distinguishes someone who is about to pass out. I said, 'Thondup, are you all right? Why don't you lie down for a bit?' He said, 'Do you think I am drunk?' I said, 'Well, yes, very.' He drew himself up, as if addressing the wind, and said, 'A Chogyal of Sikkim is *never* drunk,' and then silently collapsed. The housekeeper and I put him into a bedroom from which his staff retrieved him. Meanwhile, the housekeeper said to me, 'Sir, have you deigned to read my poems?' I had, in fact, done so. 'Do you think,' he asked, 'that I have dishonoured my master, John Keats?' I said, no, he hadn't. 'What is the difference,' he persisted, 'between me and him?' The aides were trying to get Thondup out of the guest house as unobtrusively as possible. The snow went on outside; the windows shook with wind.

'Well,' I said, 'Keats died very young.' He replied, 'But I have always had a large family to support.' This absurd conversation had started to irritate me.

'Some people need to die young,' I told him, and turned back to the party, and saw Hope's wide, alarmed eyes. I added to the housekeeper, 'I don't mean you.'

9

When I left Thondup standing with Hope at the front door of his palace, he was still fully empowered, in charge of his country. I was grateful to him for many things, not least the sense he had given me of what Sikkim was. The next time I saw him, several years later, in Calcutta, he did not look as he had that last day in Gangtok. His hair had whitened, his shoulders had slumped. He had lost his power to the government of India, and his wife left him as a consequence. Her loss, to make a very bad pun, was a real loss of hope. He had been constructed out of various pieces, like most men. His country and his young wife were two important components, and when they disappeared, the rest of the framework fell apart.

In Calcutta, he asked me up to his suite to have a drink. His hands shook so badly that he could not pour it, but he had someone who assisted him, to whom he was uncharacteristically rude. Some weeks later he attempted to commit suicide, and after that he was discovered to have cancer, was hospitalized, and died. I have seldom been more sorry at the death of a friend; Thondup at the end knew no happiness whatever, and suffered a great deal of pain, both mental and physical. Hope, in New York, wrote a book about her experiences as queen of Sikkim.

But, it was not like that when we left Gangtok on a sunny morning. I had had very little sleep in Sikkim, and snored in the front of the Land Rover beside Kichu. After his experience under Kanchenjunga, he was used to this. As we crossed the Teesta river, it began to rain heavily. We entered India, and veered through the muddy paddy fields of northern Bengal towards the Bhutan border. Shortly after dusk we reached the frontier post of Phuntsoling, and put up at the circuit house there.

In the morning the Bhutanese king's car arrived, and we had to say goodbye to Kichu. I tipped him fairly heavily. At first he refused to accept my money; finally, having done so, he suddenly darted off saying something to the manager of the circuit house. The manager said, 'Sikkim driver saying your honours please to wait.' An hour later Kichu returned, bearing in his arms a package which contained dolls and a toy train. He had bought them in the bazaar out of my tip, and gave them to Francis, saying tearful goodbyes. We climbed into the Bhutanese vehicle and crossed the border. The scenery soon became very dramatic. Jagged mountains rose into the sky, most of them helmeted with brightly painted dzongs, the keeps of dead Bhutanese warlords, part fortress and part monastery. Since the driver could not speak either English or Hindi, I couldn't ask him about them.

We met a turquoise river, improbably clear, so that one could not only see the boulders at the bottom, but the fish that flickered through the water. This accompanied us all the way into Thimpu. In a field outside the capital, I saw archers who might have come out of Sherwood Forest. These people, I was later to learn, formed part of the Bhutanese army, which in those days consisted only of archers with rhinoceros-hide shields. Thimpu itself was a sparse sort of capital. The turquoise river isolated the guest house on its right bank. On the left bank, large and painted, stood the palace. Beyond it was a shanty town and bazaar where common mortals lived. The air was tart and cold, and the mountains rose steeply all around. The guest house manager was Eurasian, fortunately not a poet.

He said, 'I have been ordered to provide you with the best food available. Please sit at table.' There was a dining table in our large room, with a bathroom attached. Neither the flush nor the shower, as I shortly discovered, worked. We had dinner; by now it was dusk. The manager brought in a huge, covered, silver salver. He removed the cover with a flourish; under it were two opened tins of sardines, surrounded by boiled potatoes. The manager smiled happily. 'Special food,' he said.

Later a palace officer appeared, saying that I would have an audience with the king next day. Judy and Francis, he said, would also be permitted to attend. The king was fond of children. 'He is a most lonely fellow,' the officer informed me with a golden grin.

Next day it was brilliant weather. The peaks around looked as though they were covered with serrated cream. We walked over the wooden bridge that spanned the river to the palace. Apart from the bright paint on the exterior, it was like a European castle, with brass studs and massive bolts on the doors. Inside it was sombre in stone. But the apartment in which I was to meet the king was furnished in Western style. We sat down on rexine chairs, and presently Jigme Dorje Wangchuk, the Dragon King of Bhutan, appeared. He was a gaunt man with a benevolent face, in long robes, rather more elaborate than Thondup's. All the guards with us made deep obeisances as he entered. He waved a long hand; minions appeared with sweets and tea, and then we were left alone. I thanked the king for inviting us to Bhutan, though it had been an invitation forced out of him by Thondup. He inclined his head, and smiled at Francis.

The interview proper now started. The Dragon King was very forthcoming. 'You must understand my position,' he said. 'Mine is an innocent country. Mine are an innocent people. They have not been touched by Western culture. Very soon I know they will be. Whether I welcome this or not I do not know. But we are a closed country, as Tibet was; we were once a tributary of Tibet. At least for trade purposes, I will have to open Bhutan. But I am caught between India and China, like our friend Thondup. I do not want to become an Indian colony. But equally so, I do not want my people to turn into Communists. So far our relations with China have been peaceful. Our only confrontations are when our livestock stray over the border and our people go in to bring them back. But, as regards India, we are dependent on them for many things; our trade, our mail, our money, all have to pass through India. We are a landlocked country. But I want to stay independent. Even as a tributary of Tibet, we were always independent, always.'

He spoke good English with an Indian accent. Somewhere in the interview, he suddenly expressed a deep fear of China. It is difficult for people now to understand the almost superstitious terror of China that existed in neighbouring countries in the 1960s. A consciousness had arisen in the Indian subcontinent of the huge land beyond the Himalayas, teeming with millions of warrior ants, and always potentially dangerous. 'If they choose to come,' the Dragon King said, 'who will stop them? My archers cannot stop them. They have already proved in 1962 that the Indians cannot stop them. It is my nightmare.'

Then, perhaps thinking he had said too much, he inquired, 'How is the food at the guest house? I told them to serve you only the best.' We had had sardines and boiled potatoes again for breakfast, but I said, 'Exquisite.' The king smiled. 'I would have asked you to a meal,' he said, 'but I leave for Calcutta in an hour. But stay as long as you like. I hope to see you when I return. In case I do not....' He rang a bell. Servants immediately appeared, laden with shawls and blankets in lamb and yak wool, artefacts in wood and bronze, and a toy bow with arrows. The king said, 'These are for you,' and demonstrated to Francis how he should use the bow; I deplored this, but in silence.

We recrossed the bridge, Judy and I in front, a Bhutanese army officer behind us, Francis enfolded and raised high in his arms, and behind him a train of servants carrying the king's gifts. An astonished figure, small, dark, plump, and bespectacled, rose from the guest house verandah as we approached. I was equally astonished; it was Ajit Das of the UNO agency, with whom I had first travelled to Sikkim.

We hugged each other. 'You old bastard,' I said, 'what are *you* doing here?'

'I might well ask,' he said, 'what are *you* doing here? Especially with a child? Leesten, my friend, have you not yet learnt that these are dangerous parts of the world, where you do not take cheeldren?' His Bengali accent exaggerated itself.

I said, 'Leesten, my friend, I see Bhutanese cheeldren around. Besides, you took me into Sikkim yourself when I was a child.' Das smiled and said, 'Let us have lunch. I have come from Paro, in the next valley, and I am hungry.' We went to the dining table. The Eurasian manager produced his silver, and uncovered it to reveal three, rather than two, opened tins of sardines and a large number of boiled potatoes.

'Do you think,' I asked the manager, 'that we might try some Bhutanese food?'

'No, no, sir,' he replied, 'I have strictest orders to feed you only the best.'

'You don't think sardines and potatoes for every meal get a bit monotonous?'

'I do not understand you, sir.'

'My friend means,' Das said, bouncing about on his chair, 'they will be deefficult to consume if they are produced all the time. I do not myself agree. We Bengalis love feesh. I could eat feesh with appetite always, whatever my circumstances.'

Puzzled, the Eurasian wandered off. 'Hah!' said Das, 'as always, my friend, you are eenqueesitive. You want to know why I am here. Well, they have built an airstrip at Paro, and I have come een on the first plane ever to fly from Calcutta to Bhutan. And what ees more, I have an eenterview with His Highness, who is a close friend of mine, like my brother I would say, for this afternoon. You may have seen heem briefly, but to me he will tell all.'

'You'll be lucky,' I said, 'he's just left for Calcutta.'

Das was always one for drama. He flung the spoon with which he was eating his sardines down on his plate, severely chipping it. 'This feesh has turned to ashes in my mouth!' he proclaimed, as though it was all my fault. 'You mean that eef I had not gone to all thees trouble, I could have seen heem in Calcutta eetself?'

'Well, yes, Ajit.'

'Oh, sheet!' said my friend Das.

Das liked to clown, to emphasize the essentials of his own character till they seemed funny, but he was a good and wise man, an excellent companion, particularly in adversity, as I had found in Sikkim, and the Himalayan kingdoms were his special beat. He was an expert on Bhutan, and he knew the country. He took us up into the mountains, nearly to the Chinese border; he introduced me to some Bhutanese politicians, who had scarcely any knowledge of politics beyond the mountains of their frontiers. He even revealed an acquaintance with Bhutanese food, which is not unlike Tibetan food, and bought some for us in the bazaar, himself staying on sardines and potatoes. He was due to take the return flight from Paro to Calcutta on the day that the disastrous climb to Tiger's Leap was suggested to me by the king's men.

'Eef I were you, my friend,' he told me, 'I should decline. Of course, politely.'

I did not follow his advice, which, as I said, I afterwards deeply regretted.

The day after the Tiger's Leap episode, Judy and I left to catch a plane from Paro. The Dragon King had not yet returned. I left a letter or thanks and a signed copy of my last book, which seemed highly inadequate in view of his gifts and his hospitality. On the way to the new airstrip we passed a village where people were ululating round a well. A coughing little girl had fallen in and seemed in a critical condition. We drove her to the nearest hospital, some thirty miles away, with her father. Judy cradled the dripping child in her lap; Francis sat with me in front, saying,

'What's happened, Daddy?' When we reached the hospital the child was dead. We left the father there, and drove on.

Along the way, I saw that Judy was crying. 'What's the matter?' I asked.

'It's this terrible country,' she said. 'It kills everyone. It's killing me. And you, though you can't help it, you're part of it. You are so utterly impersonal.'

We got back to Bombay, and again imposed ourselves upon the Jayasinghes. They were very kind, but obviously we couldn't stay there forever. I was trying to write my book, but Judy's desire, or need, to return to England was heavy on me. At dawn one day I saw her and Francis off at the Bombay airport. They flew off into a sky beyond the clouds; the pale sun was about to rise; it was April. Somehow I had a terrible feeling of disaster. I thought I would never see them again. As it turned out, this premonition was more or less true. I never saw them again in the way I had seen them before.

Meanwhile, I was very short of money. I had exhausted nearly all the publisher's advance for a book which was causing me endless technical worries; I was drinking far too much; whatever there was in my English bank would have to stay there for Judy and Francis. I still had the hope of finishing the book. I went to Delhi and consulted my father. As usual, he had a good idea; he said, 'Gerson da Cunha is looking for people to write brochures for the tourism ministry. He'll pay for you to go to places you haven't been to. You can use that for the book, and meanwhile you can do the brochures standing on your head.' I went to see Gerson da Cunha, a handsome, square-faced, bespectacled young man. Through him I met John Hinchingbrooke and his very pretty wife, Caroline, who had a small flat in Delhi; John was also trying to pay his way in India by working for the tourist department, but not successfully.

Gerson said, 'Go to Goa.' I had already been to Goa, and such a trip had no value for my book; but I would be, by Indian standards, liberally paid, and I couldn't think of any better place than Goa for a holiday, which I badly needed. I went and did what was required of me, worked on my books, and had a brief affair with a pretty English hippie whom I had met in Kathmandu. She had percolated down from the north, as many of them had done. Thoughts of fidelity were not in my mind; I had known, I realized, since before we came to India, that my relationship with Judy was doomed. I wrote to her often, but there were no answers. Something final had obviously happened.

I came back to Delhi. In the brief paragraphs I had written for the tourist brochure I had compared Goa with Mexico. The tourism ministry said that no place in India should be compared with places that were abroad, and the brochure was turned down. 'Never mind,' said Gerson. 'Go to Rajasthan.' This state is mainly desert, but it also contains splendid and historic monuments: in the cities of Udaipur and Jaipur, familiar to tourists, but also further afield in Jodhpur, Bikaner, Jaisalmer, and Barmer. 'This time,' Gerson said, 'go with an artist,' and he picked one, Mickey Patel, a shy, sensitive young Parsee, at this time engaged to a very beautiful Hindu girl called Sunila. I was grateful for company on my trip. I had no idea what was happening to Judy and Francis; letters, cables, even telephone calls, went unanswered. Friends in London whom I telephoned said that she had sold the house and was buying another. Nobody seemed very anxious to tell me where or how she was, not even her mother.

Caroline Hinchingbrooke, who was a very wise young woman, said to me, 'Look, I think you ought to be prepared for the news that she's left you.' I was prepared, but not willing to accept an obvious fact; moreover, I had had no news whatsoever. I kept writing letters, increasingly desperate in tone; meanwhile I had affairs, all very short-lived. I had previously had no idea how accessible beautiful young Indian women were. I had also had no idea that the word 'poet' is an aphrodisiac to some women, particularly since I no longer considered myself to be one. In

June, Mickey and I took an air-conditioned limousine from Delhi. It was provided by the tourism ministry, was piloted by a lanky and talkative person called Ravi, and was filled with ice boxes, provided by Gerson. He said we would need them. Once we were in Rajasthan, John Hinchingbrooke told me that I might as well forget about the possibilities of hearing from Judy, or anybody else; beyond Jaipur and Udaipur, out in the desert, no communication systems worked. I took this philosophically, but Mickey, deeply in love with Sunila, didn't. All through our trip he kept attempting to telephone her in Delhi. Nearly all these attempts were unsuccessful.

I suppose it was on this trip that I learnt something or the other about India. From the beginning I treated Ravi as I would have done a driver in the West. I talked to him in the car, I offered him cigarettes; Mickey seemed shocked at this; even Ravi appeared to be startled. When we stopped over for the night I would insist that he sat at table with us, drank with us and shared our meal. Ravi, who didn't know much about knives and forks, looked embarrassed. Since I knew very well that he slept in the car, and had a food allowance, there was really no reason why I made these demands on him. For, as I later realized, these were not democratic gestures but demands.

Things came to a head at Udaipur. This was as well, since Udaipur was more or less the last city where modern facilities were available, and we reached it fairly early on our trip. The Maharana here, Bhagwat Singh, Son of the Sun, heir to about fifty other similar titles, was a friend of my father's. He was also a good cricketer, and I liked him for this peculiar reason. He invited Mickey and me to dinner, a magnificent dinner after which Bhagwat introduced us to his special asha. Asha is a drink peculiar to the Rajasthani princes. Its basic ingredients are saffron and raw sugar. It is mellowed, sometimes for many years, in great vats; every so often some item of game is thrown in: a plucked pheasant, or partridge, or a skinned hare. When this game is completely disintegrated, asha is thought to be fit for a king to drink. It is one of the most potent liquors I have ever drunk, and we drank a lot with Bhagwat. But when we left, Ravi and the car were nowhere to be seen, and Bhagwat had to lend us one of his cars for us to get back to our hotel, where we fell deeply asleep.

Next day, awaking with pain and care to face an onward drive, we found the police, and Bhagwat's chamberlain, awaiting us. The chamberlain asked whether it had been on my orders that Ravi had been served a large amount of the royal liquor the previous night. Ravi had said so. The police wanted to know about our car, which had been found in the central square of Udaipur at dawn, filled with vomit, empty bottles, and an unconscious Ravi. It took half the day to sort all this out, and then we had to hire a tourist taxi to take us to Mount Abu, a considerable distance away.

On the road to Mount Abu, Mickey said mildly, 'You know, it's all very well to be democratic, but there's a limit. *You* got Ravi into this state, you know. It's *your* responsibility all this happened. You gave him more liberty than he knew what to do with. I think, really, from now on you should treat him as he expects.'

'Which is what?' I asked, slightly indignant.

'Like a man,' Mickey said. 'But a man who has a certain place in the world, while you have yours. Otherwise—I'm sorry to say it—this kind of thing happens.'

This went against all the training my mind had ever had, but I accepted it.

When we went into the desert, the days blurred and fused together. Gerson had chosen the worst time of year to send us. It was the hottest weather I have ever known. It was so hot that one day the friction of our tyres on the heated tarmac of the road caused all four to explode simultaneously. We were fortunate not to go into the ditch. This was in the middle of the desert road between Jaisalmer and Barmer, and we had seen no other car or lorry all day. It was mid-afternoon. Mickey sat under the only tree in miles, which was dead, and wrote Sunila a letter. I lay down in the shadow of the car. Ravi hired a passing bullock cart to take him to a village five miles off. Here he hoped to obtain some kind of vehicle which could take him to a town where he could buy spare tyres; we only had one.

It took several hours before he returned in a truck with spares and a mechanic. By that time night had fallen, prickly with stars, and it had got to be very cold. Neither Mickey nor I had sweaters. We found some whisky in the car, drank it, and told each other funny stories while we awaited Ravi's return. The trip was full of these mishaps and adventures, and they took my mind off whatever letters had arrived in Delhi, what had happened there, and what might have happened in London.

Back in Delhi, I found a letter. It said, quite simply, that Judy had found someone else, and after years of misery felt happy at last. I debated what I should do, and finally decided that I should finish my book in India. That meant finding a place to stay. The Hinchingbrookes had decided to cut their losses and return to London. Working for tourism in India had been a disappointment to John, and, moreover, Caroline was pregnant with their first child. They said I could take over their rented flat in Nizamuddin. It was small, compact, and ideal for a single person, such as I now was. It was, moreover, simply but comfortably furnished.

I was not so much grieved by what had happened as bewildered. The foundation of my life for the previous six years had been removed from under me. John and Caroline helped me greatly during this period, and so did Mickey and Sunila; I had met her for the first time. Delhi was very hot, though not as hot as the desert, and we used to sit in the small garden that went with the flat under a million stars, waiting for a breath of wind and sipping cold beer. Finally the Hinchingbrookes left, and I moved into the flat with my typewriter, a suitcase, and a manservant called Mani. John, my father's bearer, had found him for me. He was small and dark, with brilliantined hair and a shy moustache, and had a sense of humour. He needed one to deal with me, and fairly often I needed all mine to deal with him.

He had quarters adjacent to the flat, from which he could be summoned by ringing a bell. These were over the kitchen; and whenever I visited the kitchen, which was not often, I found a number of other men in it, chopping and peeling fruit and vegetables under his direction. He told me these were friends who helped him whenever they dropped in. One day, since there was no answer to my ringing, I went up to his quarters. He was out, but I noted that the floor was divided by chalk marks into eight rectangles, and a mattress lay in each of these rectangles. Mani had become a landlord. Seven men shared his quarters with him. He inhabited the largest rectangle, collected rent from his tenants, and also made them do most of his work. This seemed a successful arrangement all round, and I allowed it to continue. What it actually meant was that I had eight servants for the price of one. Sunila pointed out that I was feeding all eight, but I didn't mind. Things ran very smoothly, the flat was spotlessly clean, my laundry was done every day, the food Mani and his cohorts cooked was praised by my friends, and I was able to write in peace. What is more, there was never a sound from Mani's crowded quarters.

In these circumstances, I was able to write without disturbance. But now that our separation was confirmed, Judy started to write frequently, mostly about Francis. But she also said that she would prefer it if I didn't come back to London, since her life would become very inconvenient if I did. This infuriated me: did she feel that I should go into perpetual exile, simply to suit her convenience?

Meanwhile, I had developed two new ideas for television: one of them was for a second *One Pair of Eyes,* about my return to India after so many years, the other a political study of India as it was now. I sent the synopses of both ideas to Tony de Lotbiniere at the BBC, and was surprised to get a long-distance call from him.

'Wonderful ideas, dear boy,' he said. 'I'm going to direct these films myself. I'll be coming to India in October, so we can set it all up before the crew comes.' This was as well, because the book had gone sour on me. I had ideal working conditions, but I could produce nothing that satisfied me. Some television would be a break, and would also bring in money, which I very badly needed. I wrote to my publishers, saying they would have to wait awhile. Then I settled back, also destined to wait. Abu Abraham, once the *Observer* cartoonist, with whom I had travelled in Israel, had moved to Delhi. He was the cartoonist, now, of my father's paper, the *Indian Express,* and I saw him fairly often. He and I knew some of the same people in London; he was a link with England. He said he was happy to have come back to India, but I didn't know if this was wholly true. Indian papers were completely different from English ones. For example, for the editors or writers to travel, even in India, was unheard of. My father was the only one allowed to do so. An English paper could send its people out to Israel, or wherever; an Indian paper was reluctant to send even its editors a hundred miles beyond Delhi. Within Delhi the reporters and photographers usually had to travel by bus. This resulted in some curious stories. Very often a reporter and photographer, anxious to make up their weekly quota of work, would go to the Delhi zoo. Photographs would be taken of some animal or the other, and a largely invented story written about it. Over the weeks, the *Indian Express* carried a great deal of zoological material.

Abu puffed his pipe, and said nothing about these difficulties; but it must have been galling for him to see that his international experience counted for little. The *Indian Express,* like other national papers, did not feature very much international news; the stories were mostly domestic, badly conceived and badly written.

My father made hopeless efforts to train his reporters and correspondents. In terms of circulation, the paper claimed to have the largest in the country; it had editions in half a dozen cities. It sold, to a great extent, because of my father's editorials. I had never had any idea how highly respected he was in India.

My attempts to write poetry were completely futile. The old excitement, the thrill in the blood that produced a poem, the rhythms that had sung themselves in my head, the complete lines that came out of nowhere, none of these visited me any more, nor could they be compelled to do so. I could not put their absence out of my mind. A recurring dream was of myself writing a new poem; I could see the page, and the lines written on it. When I awoke, I sometimes thought this had actually happened, that during the night I had written a poem which would be lying amidst the debris of my desk, but it was never so. Altogether, these were very bad days for me.

Tony arrived as scheduled: tall, lanky, with grey hair and a witty face, chewing cigarillos. I had sketched out a schedule and we followed it, travelling to Calcutta first, then to Hyderabad and Madras, and up through Goa to Bombay. In Madras we met the elder statesman of India, C. Rajagopalachari, who had been the first Governor-General of independent India. He had translated a number of Sanskrit works into Tamil and English, and was a famous scholar as well as a politician. He was then in his eighties, a shrivelled and bespectacled old person in white clothes.

The reasons why I remember this encounter are complex. First of all, he commented on my hair, then very long. 'Do you really wish to look like a woman?' he inquired. Tony, sucking on one of the Burmese cheroots he had acquired since his arrival, said defensively, 'It's quite the fashion now, you know, sir, among young men in England.' Rajagopalachari stared at me pensively and said, 'Do you really wish to ape the fashions of a foreign country?' He added, 'I know all about you. Your father is my friend. Because your mother is unwell, and belongs to this country, you hate it. Why should you hate it? It is only in a metaphorical sense that this country is your mother.' Though Tony did his best to steer things to where we wanted them, that is that he should give us an interview on film, the old man hammered on at me for an hour about returning to live in India. Finally he said, 'I won't give you an interview. I don't like the BBC.' In the hotel bar, Tony said, 'What a horrible old bugger.' I wondered.

We arrived in Bombay. It now seems to me curious that I had not thought of Leela Naidu for some time. Tony said, 'This place is for the first film, the *One Pair of Eyes* bit. You grew up here, right? Right. Now you take me around the places you used to visit as a child, and you roust out some of your childhood friends.' The first part was easy; Tendulkar and the Jayasinghes were easy. 'These are all people much older than you are. Hell's bells,' said Tony, 'even *you* must have known *some* people your own age.' All the school friends I remembered were out of town. Then, on a drive, I saw a film poster with a name on it. 'I know her,' I said, pointing to it, 'she's an actress. She'd probably come over well in the film.'

'Well, why didn't you say so?' asked Tony. He was studying the picture on the poster. 'If I knew someone who looked like that, I wouldn't need to be reminded.'

Mario de Miranda, the cartoonist, had invited us to dinner. I telephoned Leela Naidu and asked her to come too. Mario knew her, and would be delighted, I said truthfully, having asked him. So, that evening, shortly after we arrived at Mario's, she did too. After a while we went out together on to the balcony, which overlooked the harbour. Points of light glittered in the distance, on the dark water, from ships that lay at anchor. It was a warm night, and I felt secluded in it with her. She told me her mother was ill in hospital. I told her what had happened to me since we last met. She didn't say anything. Mario came out of the brightly lit room on to the balcony. He was a handsome man, sturdy and bearded; he said. 'Are you two conspiring to kill Mrs Gandhi? Come inside and meet people.'

Before Leela left to visit her mother in hospital, I made another appointment with her.

I met her several times before we left Bombay for the Punjab. The state was not then a nest of terrorists. It was, in fact, peaceful and prosperous, and full of former immigrants who had come back wealthy from Southall, from Birmingham, from Bradford. Our intention was to tie these returned immigrants in with my return from England, in the *One Pair of Eyes* film, and also to use it in the second, political, film as an example of how an Indian state could become stable. This now seems rather ironic.

Of that visit I remember best a visit we made to a family who owned a huge farm near Jalandhar. Their house was only approachable up a dirt track, and had no electricity. However, they had built it themselves; it looked semi-detached and incongruously lifted out of a terrace in Bradford and set down amidst sun-flushed fields of mustard and wheat. A Jaguar stood outside. 'I wonder how they use it on these roads,' I said.

'What *I* wonder,' said Tony, 'is how they got it up here in the first place.'

The returned immigrants were Sikhs, a couple who had returned from England. They had owned a chain of shops in Southall. The man had discarded his turban and beard, and received us in a three-piece suit. The wife wore Punjabi clothes. Her English was better than her husband's. The four children spoke fluent English with a South London accent. The man's parents, who lived with them, spoke no English at all. In the drawing room, apart from a colour television set, there was a refrigerator, an electric cooker, and a washing machine. The rest of the available space was cluttered with G-plan furniture. Celographs of the Sikh gurus and the Lake District covered the walls.

Tony stared at all this in amazement, a cigarillo gripped firmly between his lips. 'You brought all these electrical appliances from England?' he inquired. 'Yais,' said our host. 'But you have no electricity here?' 'No. At present we are not having.' I asked if they expected to have an electrical connection in the foreseeable future. No,' said the lady of the house. 'We won't have. Not never.

Something is funny about this land, you know? Not possible to bring electrics here. My husband and I, we are keeping these things for show only, you know? So our neighbours are wishing they also are having.'

From Jalandhar we went into Rajasthan; in Udaipur we met my friend Bhagwat Singh, the Maharana. Bhagwat said that there was an interesting ceremony due; his clan chiefs would all be coming to him to pledge fealty; they would do obeisance to him and hand over purses of money. 'The trouble is,' he said, 'I not only have to return all the money each of these fellows gives me, but add some more to it, almost double it in fact. It works out terribly expensive.' He told us the exact date and time of this ceremony. We had picked up similar items of information all through our travels. Interesting events would take place during the eight weeks over which we were shooting. They fitted into one film or the other.

Tony was actually facing a considerable technical problem in having to finish two fifty-minute films within the allotted time frame, especially as they were going to be shot all over a very large country with very poor internal transport.

I had never realized how much work a producer has to do, and was glad that I had not accepted Tim Hewat's offer nearly ten years earlier. Tony had to reschedule the whole original programme, including hotels and cars, and make provisional appointments. Until his secretary, Annie Halliday, came with the crew, he had to do all this alone. I made various fatuous suggestions, in an attempt to be helpful, but Tony's wrath at each new idiocy was such that I soon ceased making these efforts. Instead, I wrote letters to Leela from wherever we were. At last we returned to Delhi. The equipment was shortly to arrive. Tony and I would have to handle it more or less alone, except for hastily hired local help.

On the day that the first consignment was due to arrive, Leela telephoned me from Bombay. She said that she was coming to Delhi to see her twins. She had had them when she was seventeen, from her marriage with Tiki Oberoi, whose father owned the Oberoi hotels. Under the Hindu Marriage Act, her husband had taken the children when they divorced a year later. Several years had gone by since she had last seen Priya and Maya. I knew that she had been severely affected by this. My father said, 'I know Tiki. He's not a bad chap, a bit immature perhaps.' Tiki was actually twenty years older than Leela. 'I'll talk to him if there's any difficulty about her seeing the children,' said my father. 'But it should be okay.'

The first consignment arrived on the day that Leela was due, and Tony and I spent the morning at the airport. The procedures imposed by the Indian customs were maddening, at least to Tony. I did not have to deal with the dozens of unhelpful officials whom he had perforce to encounter. All I had to do was look at dockets and check the cases. But even this was hot work, in the customs sheds, surrounded by people shouting at the top of naturally raucous voices. By the end of this, I was exhausted. Leela's flight was due to arrive that evening. I went home and slept, then drove back to the airport to meet it. She was elegant in a patterned chiffon sari, and seemed a little remote.

At this time, apart from acting in Hindi films, she had her own production company. She made advertising films, and had recently completed one for Air India. She was to see the rough cut of this in Delhi, which was one of the reasons she had come. Of late she hadn't acted very much. Her first film, *Anuradha*, had won the President's Gold Medal; she had also played the female lead in a film in English and Hindi, *The Householder*, made by James Ivory and Ismail Merchant. This had been successfully shown in the West; in the States *Mademoiselle* awarded her a prize for best actress of the year. But after that she had become tired of Indian producers offering her films to which there were no scripts. At the moment she was finishing a film which had taken three years, mainly because the original producer had absconded with all the money. Hindi films were often like that.

That evening we had a drink with Tony. Leela's knowledge

of production in India helped him; he badly needed help. But she maintained a slight aloofness of manner towards me. We went on to my father's house. The evening court was by this time over. My father seemed pleased to see us both. He also seemed to take certain things about our relationship for granted, though, actually, he had no reason for these assumptions. By the time he decided to go to bed, it was very late. 'The servants are asleep,' he said, 'and I can't telephone for a taxi. Why don't you both sleep in the spare room?' The situation had an element of farce. But Leela's eyes met mine, and she nodded slightly. 'I don't know if the sheets have been aired,' said my father.

In the morning, when he came out on to the lawn, Leela was sitting on the damp turf with my head in her lap. 'You shouldn't be out there,' said my father gruffly. 'It's very wet, and you'll both catch chills. Come inside where it's comfortable.' He smiled, and put his arms round us both as we went into the house for breakfast.

'You're a cheery young chappie today,' Tony observed when I arrived at his hotel. He said nothing else. Another morning's work awaited us at the airport. He had got a telex: the crew were to arrive the next day. 'Well, thank God my secretary Annie will be here,' Tony said. 'I was getting a bit sick of not being able to write letters.' We finished work for the day and I went off with Leela. Her twins were with her; this was the first time we had met. I have now known them for over twenty years, but at that time they were only twelve years old. We took them to my father's house. Marilyn, who had returned from a trip that day, showed them her photographs. They seemed interested in photography. But they had surprisingly few interests, for they led limited lives. They were not interested in school, for which, being in India, I didn't blame them. They lived with their father and stepmother in one of the Oberoi hotels; I suspected that their interest in photography had only started because they had met Marilyn. Even then, I could not help feeling concerned about them, not entirely because they were Leela's. There was a lost and pathetic quality about them, a haunted look.

They had a car, in which they eventually went home. We went to see Tony, and, next day, the crew came. The cameraman, Eugene Carr, was of American birth, and had been a childhood friend of Marilyn's; his assistant, David South, was Australian. The rest were English, among them Jeff Appleyard, a short, thick-set Cockney, marvellously cheerful in the most trying circumstances, and emphatically so. All of them had travelled widely for the BBC, and most of them had worked with Tony before. 'It's going to be a rough trip, isn't it?' Annie Halliday, his secretary, said. 'Rougher if the boss throws any of his tantrums.' I had not heard of this aspect of Tony before. 'But I daresay it'll come out all right,' said Annie.

10

The six weeks that followed were long and difficult. Leela flew back to Bombay, the crew and I into Rajasthan. We filmed around the state, where circumstances obligingly followed my rough script. For the first time, however, we started to fight time. It was short anyway, and the days in Rajasthan seemed to become shorter. At one point, to save a day, Tony chartered a small plane to fly us from the desert to the town of Kotah, from which we could drive to Udaipur. It was here that I first experienced what Annie had called Tony's tantrums. We arrived all right, and were met by a small man in an elaborate turban. A jeep had come with the small emissary. Tony looked at him expressionlessly for some moments, 'Is this the only vehicle around?' The small man nodded enthusiastically. 'This is only vehicle I can procure, sahib,' he said. 'No others available now. But,' he added, 'seven–eight people can fit with comfort, sahib.' Then he amended this to, 'Maybe not much comfort.' Tony's voice suddenly rose to a roar. 'And my twenty-two pieces of equipment?' he shouted. *'What about my twenty-two pieces of equipment?'* The little man leapt back like a desert antelope, and eventually stammered, 'Jeep can take you to accommodation, sahib, and I will stay here with equipment. Jeep can come back and forth to bring equipment to accommodation.' 'Where are the cars I ordered?' Tony bellowed. 'Cars come tomorrow, Gene-Carr sahib,' said the man, 'tonight, jeep only.' Tony threw down the remains of his cheroot, stamped on it, and said to Eugene Carr and me, 'You stay here with the stuff. I'll go on with the rest to settle things at this bloody hotel.'

The little man ventured cautiously, 'No need for sahibs to discomfort. *I* stay with your equipment.' Tony clamped another cheroot between his teeth, lit it, and through it spoke. 'This equipment is *valuable*,' he said. 'I'm not leaving it lying around with any Tom, Dick or Hari.' This pun delighted him, and cooled his temper. Cheroot in mouth, he led the others to the jeep, the little man trailing behind. Even his turban looked insulted.

When eventually everything had been brought to 'the accommodation' in a series of trips, Gene and I went in. The place was palatial, and there was Scotch in crystal decanters served by cummerbunded bearers. Tony wanted an early start the next day. He ordered breakfast from the little man. Scotch and more cheroots had made him benevolent. He patted the little man on the turban and said, 'Six a.m., sharp, all right?' The little man seemed about to say something, but didn't.

Next day we were in the dining room at six, but breakfast wasn't. The little man appeared, nervously explaining that the servants had not yet woken up. Anyway, he added, the cars Tony had commandeered hadn't yet arrived. We could surely leave by nine, he said.

Tony turned on him like a wounded leopard. He grabbed him; he shook him. He looked as though he was about to tear the slight body apart. 'What kind of bloody hotel is this?' he thundered. 'What kind of bloody hotel-keeper are you?' He released his prey, and stepped back, glaring down at him. The little man was somewhat dishevelled, but retained his dignity.

'Sahib,' he said, 'this is mistake. I am not bloody hotel-keeper. I am adviser to His Highness, the Maharaja of Kotah. Also this is not bloody hotel. This is palace of His Highness, and you are his bloody guests.'

We left, as previously suggested, at nine o'clock.

On the Rajasthan trip, we all got used to one another. This is something I had found out on other television expeditions. Within a few days, each member of a unit becomes acquainted with the idiosyncrasies, temperaments and habits of the others, and usually accepts them. If he didn't, things would become impossible on a long trip where everyone has to work and live in close proximity. A certain humorous element entered into this mutual tolerance. For example, once, in the desert, we came to a fork in the road. I seemed to remember that the left fork took us to our destination. The whole caravan of Land Rovers followed my directions. After about an hour, the road petered out into trackless sand. From then onward, whenever I told the driver, wherever we were, which road to take, any members of the unit in the same car would say in unison, 'Go the other way!' The same applied to Tony's occasional fits of fury. They were rare, and most of the time he was as charming and witty a companion as one could hope for. At night we sat and worked on the script together, according to what had happened that day and what we expected to happen on the next. Annie took down notes. We made a good team.

We photographed, in Udaipur, the feudal ceremony which Bhagwat had told us about, and before flying back to Bombay, filmed in Chittorgarh. This sequence had to do with the *One Pair of Eyes* film, not the political one, and was connected with the Rajput saint Mirabai. She was the wife of a king, but dedicated her life to the composition and singing of devotional poetry. There is a small stone shrine at Chittorgarh, a Rajput fortress destroyed by the Mughals, where in later life she used to live and sing. This was in the sixteenth century, but at the time of our film, in 1969, another female anchorite lived in this shrine, and sang the hymns of Mirabai. In that place, with the ruins of great buildings—charred by Muslim fire, scarred by Muslim steel—lying around, grass growing over them and trees bursting like fireworks through the ancient walls, the plaintive, desperately sad voice, singing alone in the silence, had a tremendous emotional impact on me.

The sequence we shot was first of her singing in the shrine, then of me walking away followed by the sound of her voice. Chittorgarh is built on top of a hill. When we saw the rushes later, Tony said, 'The way that shot was constructed, it looks as though you're about to trot over the edge of the cliff. Ideally, we should have stopped the singing there. A ten second pause, and then—CRASH!' He roared with mirth through his cheroot.

When I had time to think of my future, which because of the tight schedule I seldom did, I sometimes felt that what Tony said about the Chittorgarh sequence had some relevance to my life. After these films were over, what would I do? If things worked out, and Leela and I were married, where should we go? Back to England? I felt somehow that I should be restarting a career there, rather than carrying one on. I could try America, but that would be even more of a beginning. At the time, I did not see how I could stay in India. The first half of my life had been spent trying to escape it. I realized I would have to think of something quickly, otherwise, as Tony had said, CRASH.

Meanwhile, we returned to Bombay. Leela met us at the airport. I had already asked Tony if she could accompany us through the rest of the filming, and he said, 'Yes. She'll keep you from being your usual sullen self. Besides she can interpret for us, and she knows about production work.' I interviewed the chief of a new party for the political film. Bal Thackeray was a cartoonist who felt that Maharashtra, the state of which Bombay is the capital, should be for the Maharashtrians. Bombay, a port and a commercial centre, contains an extraordinary intermixture of religions and people: the people came from all over the country, and some had originated abroad, like the Parsees, who migrated in the thirteenth century from Iran. However, Thackeray, who started the Shiv Sena in 1965, chose as his prime target the harmless south Indians, whom he said had taken up work that should be done by Maharashtrians. Shiv Sena means 'the army of Shivaji', a Maratha hero of the eighteenth century. It had a petty army of its own, not armed, except with sticks, but prone to violence. Thackeray released it upon the south Indians in 1967. Many small shopkeepers in the suburbs had their establishments burned, and were themselves beaten up. So were city clerks and municipal employees who happened to come from the south.

Thackeray himself, when I interviewed him, was a slight, bespectacled man with curly black hair and a long, impassive face which had a rather sardonic twist to the lips. This was the only evidence that he had ever been a cartoonist. He was passionate about his cause, and invited us to film a rally where he was to address about 100,000 people.

Most of this would take place in darkness, with only the platform illuminated. To get the faces of the crowd, we would have to fix some lights. Jeff Appleyard went off on the morning of the rally to do this. With him went Leela's production assistant, Ghulam Rasool. Jeff later said he had been a great help, and seemed to learn quickly. He had. He had had a long conversation with Jeff, in pidgin English, and afterwards demanded that Leela pay him what an electrician was paid according to the union laws in Britain. Jeff had told him, he said, that this was only fair. East and West had met, and were certainly of one mind in matters of finance. Ghulam Rasool went on (temporary) strike when Leela refused to meet his demands. The rest of the unit thought this hilarious. She didn't; despite that, as we travelled south towards Hyderabad, Jeff and she became great friends, and he used to address her as 'passion-flower'. The team was happy, especially when we finished work in the dehydrated south and flew to Calcutta, where the nights were cool, though the days were humid, sticky, and full of odd smells.

Calcutta is the most horrible city I have ever been to. It is frighteningly overpopulated, mostly by very poor people. It is filthy, and nothing in it works properly, or, at least on the visits I have paid it, nothing has: not telephones, nor electricity, nor the water supply, nor any arrangements. It was here that we first encountered the first hostility we had found in India. The crew went out with Leela to shoot wild, random takes of buildings and parks for atmosphere. It is very difficult to shoot anything in Calcutta without including a certain number of beggars and poor people in the foreground. Not only are they around anyway, but they come to where a camera is, because there is bound to be money there. Passers-by who saw Gene Carr in action stopped and began to protest that the BBC was trying to create a bad image of the city. Crowds started to collect, till Leela decided that it was wisest to stop. This subsequently happened quite often.

The Communists were strong in Calcutta. There were three different kinds of them, the orthodox Communist Party of India, the CPI, still following the Stanlinist line, the Marxists, or CPM, who were left of the CPI, and the Maoist Leninists, the CPI(ML), left of the CPM. To this last party the Naxalites bore some semblance of fealty. The Naxalite movement was a new phenomenon. In the 1960s an uprising of landless peasants had taken place at a place called Naxalbari, in north Bengal. Some landlords had been killed. The uprising was suppressed, rather brutally, by government forces, and very soon the Naxalite movement started. Its leaders were Charu Mazumdar and Kanu Sanyal, at this time underground. Its members were mainly young people, who killed landlords in villages and policemen and rich people in Calcutta. The movement had been successful in its mission of disruption. Many rich people had left Calcutta, and many businesses had closed down their offices in the city. The rural landlords lived in daily terror.

My script included a section about the Naxalites, who were now also active in southern India. We had been unable to find any of them there, but Calcutta was their apiary, and to Calcutta we had come. I went to see the deputy inspector general of police, Ranjit Gupta. Gupta was after the Naxalites harder than anyone else in the force, so much so that after he had announced a huge reward for information on Mazumdar or Sanyal, they had festooned the city with posters which placed an equal price on his head.

Gupta was a small, impish man who seemed always to be laughing, though heaven knew he had little enough to laugh about. He gave me plenty of information about Naxalites and his operations against them, but he also said, 'I know where most of these chaps are, and I'm not going to tell you.' He was otherwise very sympathetic, perhaps because he was also a writer: he wrote novels, short stories, and poetry, as well as occasional pieces for the papers. 'Keep in touch while you're here,' he said. 'Come and have a drink at the Bengal Club.' This was affable enough, but no comfort to someone with a difficult task on his hands. I went back to Tony's room at the hotel.

Tony said, 'We came all the way here to see these bloody Naxalites. If you can't produce them, it will have been a total waste of energy. And I don't think any of us wants to spend more time in this dump than we can help.' I phoned up Gupta and this time literally pleaded with him for a tip. 'Try Presidency College,' he said. 'It's full of them. I may drop in to your hotel tonight for a little drink.'

Leela and I took a production car to the college. It had massive outer walls, covered with quotations from Mao and Ho, in chalk or red paint. Inside it was gardeny, with buildings scattered about, though not many students were visible. I accosted a slim Bengali girl and inquired, feeling utterly foolish, if she knew any Naxalite students.

'Certainly,' she said, pointing across the lawn. 'There's one of their leaders, hiding behind that bush.' I looked at her and she looked back at me in all innocence. 'There,' she repeated, pointing once more. 'That bush. He's hiding from the police.'

Disbelieving, I went to the point indicated. Sitting on the ground behind the bush was a young man of Byronic aspect, swathed in a shawl. At my appearance he leapt to his feet in some alarm. I hastily explained my mission. 'Ah,' he said, 'yes. Our movement needs to be explained to the world. Come with me to the canteen. I am safe on the college premises. Nobody here will betray me.' I felt that if other students offered information as to his whereabouts on the premises as blithely as the girl I had talked to, he could hardly consider this a matter of certainty. But we followed him to the canteen, the walls of which, like the walls of the college itself, were bedaubed with Naxalite slogans. He sat down on a bench, but sprang up once more, saying. 'Oh, God! My piles!' This seemed a very unromantic ailment for a handsome young revolutionary.

Monodeep, for that was his name, may have surmised my thoughts; he promptly explained that he had contracted piles by constantly sitting on cold rocks outside villages, waiting for the moment when he could enter them with his followers and extirpate the landlords. 'We make them ask the people whom they have wronged to pardon them. Then we hack them to pieces,' said Monodeep with some relish, 'and we paint the village walls with the sayings of Mao, written in the landlord's blood.' When I asked him if he would come and meet Tony, he agreed with alacrity. But he said that, since every policeman in the city was looking for him, he would have to lie on the floor of the car till we reached the hotel, and then come in through the servants' entrance and the kitchens, 'Since the cooks are oppressed people and sympathize with the cause.'

All this happened, and when Monodeep was safely established in our room, I picked up the phone to call Tony. There was a knock at the door. I put the receiver down and answered the knock. To my horror, it was Ranjit Gupta. He grinned at me and said, 'I know you have a Naxalite in your room. I just want a word with him. After that I'll leave you alone for half an hour. When I come back, perhaps you'll offer me a drink.'

He entered the room. Monodeep started back in horror, like an actor in a Victorian melodrama. 'Good evening, Monodeep,' Gupta said. 'Sit down, sit down. I was having a drink with your father in the Bengal Club the other day, and he asked if I knew where you were. I shall be glad to tell him that I met you. He wanted you to come home and be a good boy. If I were you, I should do what he wants. Otherwise, next time we meet I shall start being very rough with you, and you won't like that.' Murmuring to Leela, 'Excuse me, Miss Naidu. See you shortly,' he departed. Monodeep sat down, looking very deflated indeed.

However, when Tony arrived, Monodeep said that we were welcome to film Naxalite activities at Presidency College the next day. He would organize a central committee meeting in the canteen, and arrange for other goodies, such as students painting graffiti on walls. I doubted whether there was a square inch of wall in the college which had not been painted on, but he said he would fix all that. When he left, Ranjit Gupta arrived. We had a few pleasant drinks, and he talked to Tony about the situation of Indian television. As he went out, he said to me, 'I shouldn't judge the Naxalites from Monodeep, if I were you. Some of the Presidency College boys are really hardcore. Don't mess around with them. That's not an official warning. Treat it as coming from a friend.'

Next day we all set off for Presidency College, expecting to find Monodeep at the gates. He wasn't there, but about a hundred other young men were. They did not look at all like Monodeep. They were lean, hungry, and unshaven, and they watched in silence as we climbed out of the production cars. 'This doesn't look too good, old boy,' said Tony to me. 'Suppose you and I go across the road and chat them up a bit? Gene can shoot all the stuff on the walls from here.' We began to cross the road towards the Naxalites, rather like two officers strolling away from their men to parley with an entire hostile army. As we approached, a low buzzing sound of fury ran through their ranks.

Tony offered me a slant look. He was leaving it to me. I said, 'Monodeep….'

One of the front rank shouted, 'Do not talk to us of Monodeep,

BBC fascist! He had no permission to tell you to come here. Even now he is under punishment. Go now, and do not come back!' Yells of fury were coming from the crowd of people behind him. 'Well, that's a pretty final brush-off,' Tony said. 'Let's go back, old dear.' When we had recrossed the street, he said to Gene, 'Go on shooting the walls, and take in the chaps at the gate. They're Naxalites, and they look pretty aggressive, don't they?' Gene started to shoot. David South began to work the clapperboard noisily, and capered up and down, with the intention of distracting the crowd. But the Calcutta crowd is far more sophisticated than that. Leela came up and said breathlessly, 'An old man told me that there are a lot of Naxalites coming up the road and we should go.'

'The ones across the road look as though they're going to come at us any second now,' Tony said. 'Yes, I think we ought to go, too. Pack up, boys!' he called, and at that moment we found ourselves surrounded by angry, screaming Naxalites, both those who had come across the road and those who had come down it. David South, flailing around him with the tripod, managed to clear a path for the cars, and as they took off we piled into them. The Naxalites crowded into the road, shouting derisively as we fled.

This was not exactly a failure, since Gene shot enough footage to back up the script, but it was not all we could have wished for. Meanwhile, I had a slightly embarrassing situation on my hands. Leela's previous marriage had been to the son of a man who owned hotels, and the hotel we were staying in was one of them. When we checked in, and I filled in a form that put us in the same room, I felt heavy breath on the back of my neck and found one of her former relatives standing grimly behind me. He asked where she was. I made a vague gesture, and went on filling in the form.

Ever since then, he made life difficult by wanting to speak to Leela. She had so far evaded this, and, when the last morning of our stay came, I felt our troubles were over. However, during the night I developed a high fever. Tony said, 'We'll take some of the equipment with us. Leela'll come with us. Jeff's not needed, so he'll stay and look after you. At noon you go down, get the equipment out of the storeroom, and bring it to the airport. We'll meet you there.' At noon Jeff said solicitously, 'You okay, passion-flower? Let's get down to the lobby then. You sit there while I get busy in the storeroom. You count the pieces as they come past you, nineteen pieces of equipment. Okay?'

I was doing my bit in the lobby when the ex-relative, call him X, appeared. 'Where is Leela?' he demanded. 'I must see her. It is an urgent matter.' Meanwhile I had lost count of the items of equipment being carried past me by the porters. Jeff appeared, hot and sweaty, as I was trying to explain to X that I was busy and Leela would by now be at the airport. Jeff sized up the situation and said, 'Is this bloke getting in your way, then?' I said yes, he was. 'Okay,' grunted Jeff, nodding towards the heap of equipment now lying at the exit door. 'We'd better recount and recheck before we load up. And as for you, poison-flower—' and with this he picked X up and perched him on the reception counter—'not another cheep out of you till my friend and I are finished.'

There were plenty of cheeps from X. He didn't dare to climb off the counter, so, seated on his undignified throne, he shrieked for help. A large number of guests and hotel staff were present, but they didn't help him, being dissolved in laughter. We finished our check and our count, loaded up, and left for the airport.

En route, I said to Jeff, 'You know, that guy's one of the family that owns that hotel.'

'I don't care if he's Aristotle bloody Onassis,' Jeff said. 'Nobody gets in the way of the BBC.' I was touched by his loyalty to the organization he so often loudly criticized.

We flew back to Delhi. From the Indian capital the unit returned to England. Tony said, 'You'll have to come to London in a couple of months for the editing. Annie will call you. See you there, old dear,' kissed Leela, and went off. I closed down my establishment in Delhi and went back to Bombay with Leela. She had suggested that I stay with her parents and her in the large, rambling flat they had near the harbour. Her parents were already old, they had had her late in their lives. Her father had been a nuclear physicist, who studied under Madame Curie in Paris. He ended his career with UNESCO, in the same city. Leela and her mother, who was French, had meanwhile lived in Geneva, where she was educated at the International School. I stayed with them for some weeks. Then Annie called me.

Leela came too; we flew to London in winter. After more than a year away, it had a strange feel to it, like a new city. We checked into a very pleasant hotel of my acquaintance in a cul-de-sac off St James' Street, but within two days Leela found us a flat in west London. Most of my time was spent in the BBC studios with Tony and the editors. Leela also helped with the editing. It was curious to watch scenes one had personally been part of become elements in a shaped film, impersonalized. I had often seen this happen before, but I had never been so intimately involved in any of the other television films I had made as in these two. My entire life had changed in the course of their making.

I also visited Judy and Francis; they were in a new house, also in Islington. He recognized me, to my great pleasure, and I felt a twitch at my heart. But, for his own good, I had resolved not to interfere with his life. Judy and I stayed friends. I saw the book, *My Son's Father*, on sale in the shops, and the title now seemed to me curiously ironic. I wandered the London streets, often without Leela. In the pubs I knew I met people I knew, but none of my friends. They seemed to have disappeared; but I managed to find Ruth Inglis, and we spent a lot of time with her. I also found Julian Mitchell, the novelist and playwright, and James Cameron. Stephen Spender was away in America. I couldn't introduce Leela to the other friends I could not find.

Moreover, other changes had taken place. Hackett was no longer at *Nova,* and there was no place for me there. I didn't really want to work for another magazine. That year assignments were scarce, though I phoned up several editors. Finally I struck lucky with the *New York Times Sunday Magazine*, with which I had worked before. They commissioned me to go to Belfast, write on the situation there, and interview Ian Paisley. I thought it was too dangerous to take Leela, and she was rather hurt by this. I spent a couple of days in Belfast. I talked to the police; I walked down Falls Road, while suspicious soldiers watched me, and talked to people there; I went to the Northern Irish Parliament and talked to Paisley, a massive man with a loud declamatory voice and an unpleasant Belfast accent. After this interview, I was buttonholed by several more liberal MPs, who took me to the bar and got tremendously plastered with me. The northern Irish seemed little different in their drinking habits from their compatriots in the South. I flew back to London the next day, to find Leela rather depressed. I tried to explain to her that it hindered a writer on assignment to take a woman with him. She only said, 'I could take notes for you.' She accompanied me to Scotland on my next assignment, which was to interview Hugh MacDiarmid, and took down notes for me, very efficiently at that.

I had never seen *One Black Englishman*, the film Francis Megahy and I had made in 1968, and the BBC arranged for us to view it. This was on a Sunday, and we asked James Cameron to lunch, and also asked if he would like to watch the film afterwards. During lunch, where there was a lot of wine, James drank a great deal of vodka. We all went to the BBC viewing-room; the film started. Presently there was a sonorous rhythmical noise, which I attributed to a fault in the soundtrack. But Leela pointed to James, who was asleep in his seat. When it was over, and we were going out, I said, 'James, was that a pure act of criticism?' He replied, 'Oh no, my dear chap. I saw the beginning and the end, and they were splendid.' After some thought, he added, 'They're the most important parts of any television film.'

But when the BBC work was over, there was nothing left to do. The assignments I received were few and infrequent, and I did not seem to be able to have the same effect on editors as I had had two years earlier. I had not written the book on India. My temper was short, my drinking deep, and I knew that Leela was miserable. Finally she said, 'I think I'm only being a burden to you here. I'm going to Bombay. If you want me, I'll be there.' I tried to persuade her to change her mind, but she remained firm. One rainy evening I took her to the airport and watched her disappear through the departure gate, a small, lonely figure with a shoulder bag, but ineffably beautiful.

If I could have written poetry then, I would have, but the gift was gone, as I felt, forever. This didn't make me any the less unhappy. What Leela's departure did, however, was to clarify my position. I wanted to be with her, and to be with her I had two courses of action. One was to return to India at once; the other was to try and reconsolidate myself in London, get a steady source of income, and then go and fetch her. There were several reasons why I thought the first course was the better one.

The main one was that Leela was in India. But also, I had started, for the first time in my life, to find London very boring. My literary friends were now around and accessible. It had been an accident that they had all been abroad when I came back. But I didn't want to re-enter those circles now that I no longer seemed able to write poetry. To talk about literature without producing any seemed a hopeless waste of time. And nothing else that interested me happened in London. Compared to India, it was eventless. The events in India, indeed, often life in India, might repel me sometimes, but at least something was always happening. The other question was that of Francis. Once, when Judy had a party on, she asked me to babysit him for the night. I brought him to the empty flat, made him supper, and put him to bed after a little soporific television. All through this, he kept asking, 'Where's Mummy?' It was the first thing he asked when he got up. I felt very depressed, also slightly irritated. 'I'm Daddy, remember?' I said. He replied, 'Yes, but you're not there.' Not there was exactly the way I felt.

This reconfirmed my belief that for me to be in London while he was there would be bad for us both. It would be much better to make a clean cut than for him to see me off and on, which would only puzzle him and frustrate me. And Leela was inaccessible in India; that is to say, I phoned her as often as I could, but she wanted me to come to her. Actually, this was what I also wanted. I assumed an attitude of resolve, put together a package of suggestions for articles on India, and took them to the *New York Times* bureau in London, for despatch to Harvey Shapiro, then Editor of its *Sunday Magazine*.

Shapiro telexed back, accepting the whole package, and I left London for Bombay.

Back in Bombay, I felt imprisoned in the flat where she lived with her parents. They did not understand her world, or the world which I inhabited. As soon as possible, I got us on the road, which once more led to Calcutta and the Naxalites. Shapiro wanted a long story on them and their doings, also on what the police were doing. As soon as we alighted at Dum Dum Airport, I phoned Ranjit Gupta at his headquarters, in Lal Bazaar, and having deposited Leela at the hotel (not the one which contained her ex-relatives), I went there. Gupta was as impish and as full of mysterious chuckles as when I had last seen him, which, after all, hadn't been very long ago.

He said, 'What about that drink at the Bengal Club? You were too busy last time.'

So we went and had not only a drink, but lunch with him in the Bengal Club. This was an establishment left over from the Raj. It had broad verandahs and a large bar and dining room. There were such relics of British times all over India. They must have been necessary for the empire builders; and this one seemed necessary for Gupta, for he melted within its atmosphere.

'I know you never listen to a word I say,' he murmured to me, and smiled at Leela. 'You ought to see that he doesn't get into trouble. These Naxalites are trouble, as I told him some months ago. He still hasn't understood me. But,' he added, this time to me, 'there is a kind of Naxalite broadsheet, which is illegally issued. You might go and see a chap who is connected with it. You should get on with him. He's a good poet.'

Samar Sen *was* a good poet, or had been. He had apparently started out very young, so I had some empathy with him; he had been a Communist since then. I met him in his house, and he not only gave me copies of the magazine he published, but the name of a person from whom I could obtain further, and more extreme, Naxalite publications. Gupta told me that Monodeep had disappeared, so I couldn't contact him. However, I was on the road or on the phone all the time in pursuit of the Naxalites, and established a number of contacts. One of them, a reporter, came to me one night and said, 'The Naxalites have called a bandh for tomorrow.' A bandh is an enforced shutdown of all services, usually caused by a political party. 'So there will be no traffic on the roads,' said my friend, 'and the Naxalites will be very active. But you will be able to travel around in a press car. I have a press car.' I arranged that he should pick me up the next day. I informed Leela, who insisted that she should come too.

This was not a good idea. I told her so, and so did the reporter and his photographer when they came to pick me up the next day. It was no use. The whole car was covered with press stickers, and the reporters drove at about ten miles an hour. The empty streets were full of barricades of bricks, and urchins playing football. These little boys constantly ran across the path of the car, and the reporter drove even more slowly. He had covered Calcutta for a quarter of a century, and knew what to do. 'These are all provocations, you know,' he said. 'If I knock one of the bricks down or bump one of those boys, a hundred people will come from nowhere, the car will be burnt, and God knows what will happen to us.' He, the photographer, and I were very tense, but Leela was in a cheerful mood. She kept waving in queenly fashion to the children playing football. 'Madam, madam, please don't do that,' urged our driver. 'They will imagine you mock them.'

At about this point there were a number of violent explosions to our left, and smoke began to drift up above the rooftops in that direction. A harassed police inspector stopped us. Sweat and rain had collected on his face, and ran down into his moustache. He kept licking the water away, which made him seem even more nervous.

'The Naxalites are throwing bombs from the rooftops,' he panted. 'Get out of this area.' Then he saw Leela and his eyes bulged in disbelief. 'Are you press people mad, bringing a woman with you on a day like this? Get out of this as quickly as you can.'

'We have actually covered most of the city,' said my friend at the wheel. 'Let us return to the hotel.' We did, and found Ranjit Gupta there. 'I have been kept informed of your progress,' Ranjit said, in a not very friendly way. 'Did you have to take Leela with you?' But he came to the bar with the others, and had a quick, and probably needed, drink.

And he continued to help me where he could. He introduced me to the inspector who, under him, had done the most to fight the Naxalites. This officer's room was full of wanted posters, pictures of Naxalites who had been captured, graphs, wall maps with coloured pins in them, and trophies of the chase, such as weapons and literature. A bucket of water stood in a corner. Leela indefatigably inquisitive, delved into it, and brought out a spherical object, swathed in a dripping sackcloth. 'What is it?' she asked innocently. 'It's very heavy.'

'Madam, madam, please put it back,' cried the inspector, leaping to his feet. 'It is an unexploded bomb.'

I now wondered about taking Leela around with me. No other journalist that I knew of worked with a woman in tow. Ranjit usually knew exactly where I was at any given time, and if he did, so must the Naxalites. Since I had been in contact with several of their sympathizers and supporters, closet members of the movement, the activists obviously knew what I was doing. They had so far shown no displeasure, but it was not a predictable situation. I had to go deep into Calcutta, into dingy back alleys, often flooded, in one of which I was confronted by a flotilla of enormous, silently swimming rats; into unlit houses with broken and filthy stairs; into atmospheres which were like those in a horror film. Leela, in these circumstances, became a constant anxiety, and therefore something of a hindrance. I told her so.

She did not like it, but at the very last she turned out to be invaluable as a companion. On the final day of our visit, when we positively couldn't stay on any more, I still hadn't met a Naxalite. At dawn the phone awoke me; a contact I had made said breathlessly, 'I have a wanted activist in my house. Can you come here? I know the police are following you, but you do as I tell you, and you can shake them off.' He gave me some instructions. I postponed our flight till the evening, and set off with Leela. We had to wiggle our way across the city, changing taxis several times, and finally reached my contact's shabby flat. He summoned the Naxalite from an inner bedroom. He was a terrorist, certainly, but not very terrifying; he was scrawny as a weasel in winter, with sunken red eyes, and he held a copy of Mao's *Red Book* in his hands. He promptly told me that I was an imperalist hyena and under no circumstances would he say a word to me, even for the sake of his friends. He turned his back.

I had started to despair, when my contact introduced him to Leela. She told him, which I believe was true, that her father had met Ho Chi Minh in Paris, when the Vietnamese leader was a student there. The Naxalite unfroze. 'I will speak to *you*,' he said, 'but to you only.' This led to an absurd situation. The Naxalite sat on a bed next to Leela; I sat on her other side. I asked questions which she repeated. It was obvious that the questions were emanating from me, but he would not reply till she had voiced them.

Yes, he said, he was an activist. He had been one for a couple of years. He had been inducted into the movement in college, by some friends. He himself was poor, and so were all the people he knew. He believed that the *Red Book* told him everything he needed to know. The enemies of the people were clearly defined in his lexicon: the rich, the police, and the government authorities, not to mention every Western nation. He first went to the villages, but was eventually trained as an urban guerrilla. Six months after he entered the movement, he had killed his first policeman, in a Calcutta bylane.

He was emotionless except when he described this episode. 'I was greatly tormented in my mind,' he said. His mouth twitched. 'For many nights I could not sleep. But all this time I read the book of our leader, Mao, and I realized that my action was necessary for the revolution. Since then I have executed five others, and I have felt nothing.' He was badly wanted by the police; indeed, I had seen a poster offering a large reward for his capture. 'If they catch me,' he said, 'they will kill me.' When we left, he said no goodbyes, but stood up and offered Leela the Communist salute.

We now flew north. Another of my assignments was an article about the Indian princes. The Maharajas had always been mythical figures in the West. They had been pampered in countries where their less-exalted countrymen were made to feel vaguely uncomfortable. They had been the pets of the British. They spent hugely and extravagantly, and not for the benefit of their subjects. Almost all of them were parasites.

They had been made so in a way, by colonialism. Before the arrival of the British, India had been a loosely knit entity of separately ruled states, whose rulers had a responsibility to the people. These states, and rulers, were always making war on one another, which contributed to the disunity of the country as a whole, and made it more vulnerable to invaders. Through many of the invasions, some Indian states would be found on the side of the invaders. When most of the country came under British rule, the princely states were left untouched, nominally ruled by the hereditary Maharaja. But the British would install a resident and an adviser to the ruler, and in effect they ran each princely state. If the ruler was too mad or bad to continue, they replaced him with one of his relatives, handpicked by them. The princes were allies of the British, and few of them ever supported the nationalist movement.

At the time of independence, 1947, the new government wanted, indeed, needed, the states to accede to India, and by a mixture of bullying and wheedling, got nearly all the princely states to do this. The position of the rulers was hopeless. When the Nizam of Hyderabad refused to hand over his state, the Indian army went in and took it. The Maharaja of Kashmir was uncertain whether he should secede to India or to Pakistan: the eventual result, in 1948, was the first war between the two countries. Now Kashmir is a nest of pro-Pakistani terrorists, and has always been one of the hottest trouble spots in India.

However, most of the rulers surrendered their states without resistance. In return, the Indian government, at the insistence of the British, promised that they could keep their titles and their privy purses. Sometimes the privy purses were unimaginably large, and sometimes ludicrously small. But recently, Mrs Gandhi had broken the promises made at independence, and had deprived the princes of their income and their titles. Mixed feelings existed about the probity of her action. Several rulers were standing for

Parliament in the coming elections. Some of them were talking of an appeal to the United Nations. But clearly nothing and nobody could now help the princes. It was this situation that I was to investigate.

So, for the third time in a year, I went into Rajasthan. Literally translated, the name of the state means 'place of the princes'. It was ideal territory for me to hunt in.

11

The solitary singer still performed in Mirabai's shrine at Chittorgarh. I had come to know this land well, and the continuity in it. But, for the Rajput princes I met, who knew it much better, there was no continuity left; great chunks of tradition, ripped from the edifices of their lives by Mrs Gandhi, tumbled around their thrones. They were all willing to talk of their sorrows to anyone who seemed sympathetic. These complaints found their way back to Delhi, and enraged Mrs Gandhi even more. Though the princes were helpless, they did not know it, or, if they did, would not accept it.

Some of them had accepted it. Richard, the son of the Maharaja of Indore, whose mother had been American, started a profitable business. He and his American wife, Sally, had first of all shown philanthropic tendencies, and revived a dying weavers' community around Indore, which they later helped turn into a cooperative. So they were used to hard work; when the privy purses were withdrawn, they went into jewellery design. Sally wrote books about princely cuisine. They were able to earn a good living. A few other princes also worked for their bread and honey, but most didn't. Some were like the Thakore Sahib of Katodia. His privy purse amounted to twenty-five pounds a year, and its withdrawal was relatively unimportant. He had to work anyway, to keep himself. Others worked, for the first time in their lives, in campaigning against Mrs Gandhi. Some sank into a state of bitterness and despair, and decided that it was best to subside even more deeply into inanition.

When Mickey and I were driven around Rajasthan by Ravi, we had once stopped for lunch, as our itinerary advised us, at a Raja's palace. We weren't in the desert proper, but nearly. All round us was a sea of white dust, in which mirages swam; the Raja's palace seemed one of them, for it gave the impression of crumbling apart under our eyes, as in reality it was. In the entrance hall was a block of ice with a blanket spread on it. On the blanket lay a very fat naked man, surrounded by servitors fanning him. This was the Raja. He rose from his chilly couch and welcomed us. But he explained that since his privy purse had vanished from his life, he was unable to offer us anything to eat or drink. We said we had things in the car, and his servants were despatched to fetch it.

That evening, eyeing a squalid rest house kitchen, I suggested that we should open some canned food. 'There is none,' Ravi said. 'That Raja's men took it all.' There had been enough for a minuscule army. 'Well, then, let's have a drink.' Ravi said gloomily, 'There is no drink either. They took all that too. They said it was by your specific orders.'

I had no reason for happy remembrances of the Raja; and, several years later, when I heard that India had exploded its first nuclear bomb in Pokharan, which happened to be his state, I felt little anxiety as to what might have happened to him.

From Rajasthan we went to Delhi, where I was to profile Mrs Gandhi in the framework of the coming elections. One of the main hazards she would face was the question of the princes, which I had already covered fully. Then, twenty years ago, the peasants of India were slow to change their perceptions. I had met a very old woman in the desert who inquired after the health of the empress in Delhi, thinking Mrs Gandhi was a descendant of Queen Victoria. There were not many like this; but the commoners of some princely states, however oppressed and browbeaten they might have been in the past, were true to their salt. They regarded the princes as their natural rulers, and Mrs Gandhi as an upstart. Mrs Gandhi's Congress party feared that the princes would win at least some of the seats they were to contest. Many of them were contesting seats, even the young Nawab of Pataudi, a cricketer who, until two years before this, had been captain of the Indian team.

Delhi was somnolent under dust at the end of its dehydrating summer. I had decided to have a long interview with the prime minister, and frame it within a series of interviews with her friends and enemies. These interviews took place before I saw her at all. Some of them were extremely strange.

Mrs Tarkeshwari Sinha had once been in the Congress, but had gone over to the opposition. She was a bitter antagonist of the prime minister. Her fame in India was not so much due to her politics as to her being 'the glamour girl of Parliament', by which the newspapers meant that she had a reasonably pretty face and was what Indians call 'well-built', that is, she was heavy in the hips and had a noticeable bust. When I went to see her, I was conducted by a servant to her bedroom. She was lying on, rather than in, her bed, wearing a choli, the abbreviation that serves sari-clad women as a blouse, and a petticoat. If one went by Indian convention, this was the equivalent of a British female MP receiving me in her brassiere and panties.

'I have dengue fever,' she told me. 'So I am confined to bed. The doctors tell me it is not infectious. You may sit here beside me.' I hesitated slightly, and she continued, 'It is not infectious, I am telling you! Now listen, I am a great admirer of yours. I have read your book *Gone with the Wind* three times already.' She was referring to *Gone Away.* I had no great desire to be thought of as Margaret Mitchell, but didn't correct her.

At about this point, Leela entered. She had been settling accounts with our taxi driver. Mrs Sinha demanded, 'Who is she?' and as I explained she disappeared under the bedcovers, drawing them tightly up around her chin. 'You did not tell me about her previously,' she said accusingly. Throughout the interview that followed, she emphasized her sufferings with an occasional moan of pain. 'Indira does not like me,' she complained. 'I cannot help it if I am much more beautiful than her. Feroze (Mrs Gandhi's husband, who died in 1960) liked me too much. Once Indira found us talking together in an empty office. We were having only an innocent chit-chat, but since then she hates me too much.'

I visited Morarji Desai, then the leader of the opposition. Desai had once, when he was chief minister of Bombay, a feud with my father. He had threatened to withdraw all government advertising from the *Times of India*, which would have inflicted a serious wound on the paper's economy, if my father did not stop his attacks on the official liquor prohibition policy. My father had won the battle; since then they had been tacitly at truce. Desai, at the time of writing, is still alive at ninety-two. He attributes his longevity to bibulations of his own urine in a diet which otherwise consists of nuts and fruit, and to spinning on the charkha, a handloom much used by Gandhi and his followers, not only to weave cloth, but as a kind of spiritual therapy. When I met him he was spinning, seated on a leopard skin, which did not seem to befit a vegetarian. 'Though I esteem your father,' he said to me, 'I do not wish to speak to you about Mrs Gandhi. That is because I never wish to speak ill of anyone, however immoral they may be.' He then spoke about her for two hours, or rather about her policies, every one of which he assailed. At the end of his polemic, he exclaimed, 'That woman! She is worse than either Hitler or Stalin!'

He continued to speak after the interview was over. 'I consider your father a friend,' he said. 'I do not know how he considers me. But I can see you have a good soul, which has been led astray. I would be glad to instruct you every day in how to spin on the charkha, and on proper diet and exercises which will keep you fit physically and elevate you spiritually, as they have done for me. I am a busy man, but I can spare you twenty minutes a day, at about this time.' I thanked him profusely and said I would phone him.

The strangeness percolated into my talk with Mrs Gandhi. The atmosphere was quite different from the one which had prevailed through our first interview. No tape recorders or press secretaries were in evidence. She talked informally and at leisure, as between friends, of her hopes for the nation. She dwelt a good deal on the menace of communalism, which she thought would emerge in the future, with the strengthening of various fundamentalist parties. Her prophecies have come true, but at that time there wasn't much communal tension in India, and I thought her remarks beside the point.

Towards the end of the interview, she suddenly said that she was glad to hear I wanted my Indian nationality back. This was news to me, but Mrs Gandhi now wore one of her rare and irresistibly charming smiles, and I didn't want to hurt her feelings. To my further astonishment, she insisted on accompanying us to the office of the home minister, K.C. Pant, to whom she put the whole matter (in so far as it existed, for, so far as I was concerned, she had created it). She urged him to assist me. Mr Pant, whom, as an accidental benefit, I interviewed, finally said, 'You know, it is more difficult to become an Indian national than any other kind of national. And the circumstances in which you changed your passport are not conducive to your case. In spite of the PM's interest, I don't think this will be easily done.' I felt great relief.

They ran the Naxalite story in New York, and I received a congratulatory cable. I finished and sent off the Mrs Gandhi profile. We then stayed on in Delhi, where I felt much more material would be available than in Bombay. Towards the end of the year, as the Delhi winter set in, news came of a cyclone that had struck East Pakistan and killed a number of people. The number was first surmised to be 100,000, but rose with each successive estimate. Shapiro telexed me from New York, asking me to fly out and do him a story. It was one of the greatest natural disasters of the century.

East Pakistan existed because of the agreements made at Partition in 1947. The Muslims, with Mohammed Ali Jinnah at their head, wanted the Punjab for Pakistan, and were denied the whole of it. Part of western India was lopped off for the new Muslim state. But there was an area in the east, across the whole breadth of the subcontinent, with a considerable Muslim population, which had also been made part of what Jinnah called 'a truncated and moth-eaten Pakistan.' This area was known as East Pakistan, separated from its component part by thousands of miles of Indian plains, hills, and people.

It was set on the Bay of Bengal, where cyclones are prevalent. October was cyclone time, and the American weather satellite reported one building up east of the bay in remote Asiatic seas. It was headed for the bay, but cyclones are erratic in their behaviour: they fall apart in the ocean, or swerve towards some other shore. This one kept coming. A weather station existed at Cox's Bazaar, in East Pakistan, and it somewhat belatedly reported the imminent arrival of great winds and torrential rains, and called for evacuation of the offshore islands and coastal areas.

Unluckily, the warning not only came a little late, but was ignored by the populace of these places. The previous week, Cox's Bazaar had issued another warning about an approaching cyclone, and that one had fizzled out completely. The people didn't want to vacate their homes a second time for no reason.

Meanwhile, the cyclone built and entered the Bay of Bengal. This is funnel-shaped, and the forces of the great wind were compressed and intensified within the funnel. The wind, accompanied by spears of rain from thick clouds, pushed the sea ahead of it. Waves, which were variously stated by understandably confused witnesses to be anything from twenty to a hundred feet high, burst over the offshore islands, hurling trees, cattle, houses, boats, and people into the raging sea beneath. They then shattered themselves on the mainland, where they swept more villages away. The flood followed the natural course of most floods and receded. That meant that the retreating water swept away most of those who had survived its advance. After the death of the cyclone proper, thousands of corpses were said to be floating in the rivers, into which sharks had come to compete with a native population of crocodiles, and thousands more were lost in the sea. Rescue teams had been sent by various nations.

I flew from Delhi, leaving Leela behind, to Dacca, the East Pakistan capital. The passenger load on the Thai plane that flew me was not weighty; in fact it consisted entirely of foreign correspondents for various papers. Among them was Sidney Schanberg, who was the correspondent of the *New York Times*. He was a quiet, bearded person, a good writer, who later wrote a prize-winning book about his experience in Cambodia. This was made into the film, *The Killing Fields*. Schanberg, however, seemed to have a slight antipathy towards me, and any idea I had of our working together disappeared. It was probably as well; photographers and artists apart, I had usually been on my assignments alone. However, this was a rather formidable assignment.

When we landed at Dacca, at nightfall, there were clouds overhead, and a faint rain fell. Going through immigration, I encountered a plump official, who said, 'You are one of the journalists from Delhi?' I assented, and presented my passport. 'Hah,' he said, 'you are Breetish? Velcum to our beautiful country. I vas thinking you vere Indian. Indians we do not like. Indians are terreeble fellows—Vot you say—like sheet.'

I wondered what Mrs Gandhi or Mr Pant would have said at this point.

A taxi took me to the Intercontinental Hotel, where I was booked. The driver spoke a kind of English. He did not seem much concerned about the cyclone and its effects. 'Too many poor people on coast,' he said. 'What matter they die? You tell me, sir.'

But he seemed very concerned that there were also poor people in Dacca, of which, he emphasized as we neared the hotel, he was one. 'All fault of West Pakistanis, sir,' he said. 'West Pakistanis very bloody people. They care about me? No, they not care.'

The Intercontinental floated, like a huge upended liner in whose portholes lights shone, above the darkened slums of the city. The lobby was full of other correspondents acquiring accreditation cards and government handouts at a desk that had been specially set up. 'An accreditation card is essential,' the receptionist told me when I checked in. 'That desk, you will find people there who will issue such things.' I was very nervous about this, more so when he continued, 'Without such things you can proceed nowhere.'

I had no credentials, apart from Shapiro's telex and a rather imprecise letter from the *New York Times* bureau in Delhi. When I applied for my press card with these, the government man turned me away, saying, 'This data is insufficient, mister.' But a young man who was assisting him followed me as I walked off. 'Sir,' he said, and called me by my name, 'you are the poet, isn't it? I have seen your photo on your books. Please, sir, why you are here? You want to write poetries about cyclone?' At this time I was very easily irritated by people who called me a poet. It reminded me of something I wanted to forget, like a botched but important love affair. However, there was a look about the young man which struck me. Perhaps I had inherited a quality from David Archer: I could see and feel a poet without reading his work. I asked if he wrote poetry. 'Oh, yes,' he said. 'I am writing in Bengali, of course. And all my friends are poets. They will be too pleased to meet you. To think it is taking a cyclone to bring you to us!' We fixed an appointment for the next day. He said, 'How I can serve you?'

I asked about my press card. 'I will fix,' he said. 'I will fix. The government man there is also too much appreciating artists. When I tell him you are artist, he will give.' Within two minutes I had my card, without which I could not have gone anywhere near the disaster area. Grateful and relieved, I asked my new friend to have a drink with me. His forehead wrinkled, and he seemed embarrassed. 'I do not drink,' he said. 'It is not that. I can drink Coke with you, even in the bar. But while the lobby is being okay, inside the hotel I am not liking. There they are eating—how shall I say—*pork*. It is not that I am fervently Muslim, but I do not like it. At tomorrow ten a.m. I come here to pick you up and then take you to the other poets of Dacca. With no fail.'

The bar was packed with correspondents and very young people. I did not know any of the correspondents except Schanberg, who was not present. The young people seemed to be the children of resident diplomats and UN officials. A party of them occupied the table next to mine. A pretty American nymphet said to the boy next to her, 'Jesus, I'm bored. All this rain…and nothing to do.' The boy squeezed her thigh and said, 'Maybe we could get rid of the gang and go for a picnic tomorrow.' She brightened up, allowed his hand free play, then wilted once more, and pushed it away. 'No,' she said. 'All the nice places are way out of town, and Daddy says way out of town it's all full of corpses and stuff.'

Next day the young poet showed up exactly on time, and took me, in a bicycle-rickshaw, through the bazaar to a flat above a sweetmeat shop. The occupant, I was told, was a senior Bengali poet, and he was the mentor of a group of younger men, of whom my new friend was one. The young poets were all university students; the older one was a professor. Though my particular poet had described him as unimaginably ancient, Asif could not have been more than thirty-five. The front-room was filled with unshaven young men, with very Naxalite looks about them, but with manuscripts, rather than AK-47s under their arms. Everyone welcomed me effusively. Asif's wife brought sweets and tea. I was later told that it had been a singular honour to me that she had appeared in male company at all.

Asif made a speech in Bengali, to welcome me. This was translated into English. So were the poems which each person present then ceremonially read. After this I was asked to read my poems. I said I didn't have any with me, and a copy of *Penguin Modern Poets: Vol 2*, much dog-eared, I was gratified to note, was produced and handed over.

I read from it, and then, with the younger men all squatting round, Asif and I—we occupied the only two chairs in the room—entered into a political discussion. It occurred to me that it was perhaps for this that I had been asked here. But, perhaps not. They were all young and very enthusiastic, and they desperately needed to be understood.

'All our poems were in Bengali,' Asif said 'We are Bengali. Our great poet, Rabindranath Tagore, was born in this part of Bengal. But West Pakistan makes no provision for us. There they speak Urdu. It's the national language. How can any of us be recognized?' He touched his cheek. 'See how dark I am. See how dark these boys are. See how small in stature they are. But the West Pakistanis are tall, fair, and also speak a different language. They look down on us as slaves. See the difference between academic facilities, medical facilities, employment facilities, in East and West Pakistan today. See the amount of money from exports they have taken from us and not returned. See how our leader, Mujibur Rahman, has been carried off to prison in West Pakistan. What will you then say? Will you not say, "These fellows are ripe for revolution?" In two weeks there are to be elections. Maybe something will come of them, maybe not. We can only hope.'

And the cyclone? 'Ah, the cyclone, the cyclone,' Asif said. 'That is only one more entry in a long list. How have the West Pakistanis helped us? All the other nations offer assistance, even India, but the West Pakistanis sit still. They hoped perhaps for a bigger cyclone, which would wipe us all out.' Everyone present laughed bitterly.

If this represented fairly widespread opinion in the country, perhaps India would help. At least, I mentioned this possibility, which was received with more bitter mirth.

'You are not a Hindu nor an Indian,' Asif said, 'so we can speak frankly to you. All of us hate the West Pakistanis, yes, but to tell you the truth, we hate the Hindus even more.'

I heard repetitions of all this throughout my stay in East Pakistan. When I returned to Delhi, I passed on my impressions to Mrs Gandhi, who received them with a sceptical smile. But, meanwhile, I was in Dacca, and had no way of getting to the cyclone-ravaged areas. The other correspondents had expense accounts, and were able to hire land and river transport; this wasn't possible in my case. Asif and his disciples, to whom I confided this problem, solved it. At about three a.m. the next morning, Asif telephoned me. 'We have organized transport to Patuakhali,' he said. 'That is one of the worst-hit places. Hussein will be outside the Intercontinental in a rickshaw in fifteen minutes. Please meet him there.'

Hussein, my original contact, met me in the darkness outside the hotel. As we were pedalled towards the airport, he said, 'There is a government amphibian plane taking off for Patuakhali in about one hour. One of us has a relative who is fixing it. There is a West Pakistani military officer flying also. He will look after you. But this aircraft is going only to pick up a West Pakistani minister who went there to observe. It will bring him back here, but you it will not bring. You must be returning by yourself.' I thanked him and sent his friends my thanks; and couldn't have managed otherwise.

At the airport, Hussein took me to the amphibian. I seemed to be expected by the pilot and a young army captain, both of whom were travelling with me. We took off in darkness, flying south; then the broken egg yolk of the sun spilled colour into the land to our left. The engines throbbed and thundered steadily, preventing speech.

As sunlight, yellow and sticky, spread across the horizon, details of the landscape beneath us appeared. We were flying low, and could see a green, flat delta, snaked over by rivers and copiously blotched with brown patches of water. 'Here the flood has receded,' the captain yelled in my ear. 'Further on you will see…' Further on there was little to be seen: the green of the paddy fields was hardly visible through all the floodwater that cloaked it. We were now following a broad river, and coming down. 'Patuakhali.'

The amphibian roared down towards the turgid water. I saw a jetty ahead, people on it, a motor launch moored to it; then another motor launch, advancing directly down our landing path. The pilot swore in Urdu and the amphibian swung to the right, narrowly missing both the oncoming launch and the steep bank beyond. We veered up into the sky and came back, crashing into the brown river nose first, in a blinding cloud of spray, and then settling on the water. We sat quite still and breathed deeply. 'That was quite close,' said the pilot at length, and the captain said, 'You know, the river is full of crocodiles.'

From the jetty the motor launch chugged across the water towards us. It contained, apart from a two-man crew, a vast quantity of luggage. This belonged to the West Pakistani minister, a fat, friendly person, who was at the jetty when the launch took me back. 'Come and see me in Dacca,' said the minister. 'I have plenty to tell the foreign press about the role I have played in solving the problems here. Yes, I have been here, observing the situation, for the last day and night. Ah, but you are looking at my luggage? You think it is too much?' He laughed deprecatingly. 'Only small comforts.'

The commissioner in charge of Patuakhali, a haggard man with a moustache, took me back to his office. 'You have no idea what it was like,' he said, showing me a map. 'After the cyclone came, it was not possible to move from here. All communications were cut off. We could not reach anywhere. This is a tidal river, you know, and the corpses started to come up with the tide. Also the crocodiles and the sharks. Yes, there are sharks as well. I could only guess at the extent of what had happened. When finally I arranged to get to the river mouth, all my guesses were wrong. The damage was much more than I had expected. When I saw how much it was, I was horrified. Every day there are fresh reports of more dead and missing. How many have been killed I do not know. But a British force has come from Singapore to help in rescue operations. They are also dropping supplies on the offshore islands, and burying the dead.'

The British had put up camp inland from the commissioner's office. I wandered through tents to what had been a school. Colonel Bailey, the commanding officer, had made himself reasonably comfortable in a classroom, and offered me some Tiger beer. He told me about what he and his men were doing; he did not seem discommoded by the circumstances. The air was hot and almost palpably wet, clouds of mosquitoes and midges hung in it, and it smelt mildly of putrefaction. After we had talked for a while, I left the colonel in his improvised office. Later, I flew by helicopter over the river and the offshore islands. Heavy clouds filled the sky, the sea was rough and choppy, a deep umber from the earth it had washed off the islands and the mainland. Boats rode unsteadily on this mobile mass of clogged liquid, looking for survivors and corpses. The islands were desolations of mud and water, and no houses remained. It was like an artist's rendition of a wet hell.

I returned to Patuakhali and the commissioner. I had interviewed some of the survivors on the island, and they had told me their versions of what had happened: very incoherent impressions, of huge waves and a wind, and a sudden wilderness of water. The noise was what some of them remembered most; it was so deafening, they said, that it became impossible to think or react. Nearly all of them had lost relatives, particularly small children.

The commissioner said sadly, 'There are more reported casualties since morning. Many more.'

'I have to get back to Dacca. Is there any way?'

'You are lucky,' he said, nervously fingering his moustache. 'The boat service has restarted today. The boat will be very crowded, and it will be difficult... But there is a government cabin, sufficient for two people. There is a doctor who will be going back to Dacca, but so far he is the only cabin passenger. Maybe you can go with him.'

At nightfall he took me to the jetty. The boat was a large motorized ferry. The decks were packed solid with people—men, women, and children, all with curious, terrified expressions. They were all very still. Getting through them to the minuscule cabin under the prow was very difficult and took a long time. My fellow-passenger was already there, a stout person with baggage and bedding, and a tired look on his plump face.

I had no luggage whatsoever, except a half-bottle of Scotch, a present from the helicopter pilot who had taken me up specifically against orders. It was very kind of him, though I had given him a hundred dollars to risk me as an unauthorized passenger. I thought the Scotch might come in handy, especially after I met the captain. He told the doctor that all the depths of the river had changed, and new shoals had been created; also that it was now cluttered with trees and corpses. 'It will not be easy,' he said, 'to reach Dacca.' Eventually, however, the engines started and the vessel throbbed slowly upstream.

'The captain also informed me,' the doctor said, 'that there are only two latrines on this ship. Since it is full to beyond capacity, I am thinking that they will be much used, possibly by people with infectious diseases. Cholera has broken out; I have treated many cases since the cyclone. So...' He opened an attache case and took a phial of pills from it. 'Take two,' he said. 'You will not need to have excretions till we reach. As for urinations, those can be done through the window.' I took the pills gratefully, and washed them down with a sip of whisky. The doctor looked at me sharply.

'You are not permitted to drink liquor in East Pakistan. From where you have got that?' I told him that it was courtesy of the British army, and that I had a British passport. 'Ah,' he sighed. 'Then it is all right. You will allow me a small peg? I am a West Pakistani, and I have been treating cyclone victims for some days.' I gladly gave him a drink, in one of two plastic tumblers that he fished out of his luggage. He did not drink any more; but the small dose of liquor loosened him up sufficiently for him to describe his cyclone experiences to me. All this made very good material.

He was going back to Lahore, he told me. This was the end of his posting in East Pakistan, and he was pleased, 'Because the people here are very inferior, and my wife and other family members are in Lahore.' He showed me photographs of them. He produced packets of food and shared them with me. He was really a very kind man.

Our vessel moved steadily and very slowly on through the darkness, a thick darkness which concealed the shore and the sky. Through the porthole we could see a few yards into it, where the ship's lights fell. Scummed and foamy water spread slowly away from the bows; unidentifiable debris was pushed away by it, into the darkness beyond.

Blown rain filled the cabin. It was impossible to keep the porthole open, and the tiny space available soon became very stuffy. The doctor tried to open the door. Something was wedged against it, but he pushed harder till it moved. When we stepped outside the obstruction proved to be a young woman lying on the floor with an infant in her arms. She had a beautiful face, though it was blotched, drawn, and unwashed; her hair hung in matted strands down her back. 'She should not be here,' the doctor said. He looked at her closely. 'She should certainly not be here. I think she has cholera. I am *sure* she has cholera.' He began to shout at the young woman, and pulled her to her feet. She stumbled off down the passageway. We went back into the cabin. The doctor shut and bolted the door.

'Couldn't you have done something for her? Given her some pills or something?'

'What I could have given her? She is bound to die soon. And I am telling you, my good friend...' his face was ungenial now, perhaps because of hidden guilt '...It would not have helped anyone. These East Pakistanis live like dogs, and they die like dogs.'

Sheikh Mujibur Rahman, the East Pakistani leader, was released before the elections, and flown home to Dacca. That day there was such revelry in the streets as I had never seen before. Not only was the entire population of the city out, but people had come in from rural areas: they all seemed to be banging drums, clashing tambourines, or blowing whistles. Balloons in many colours were released and floated above the streets down which Mujib passed in a cavalcade of Land Rovers and cars. From a distance, he appeared as deliriously happy as his people, laughing and waving at them as he went by.

The elections were quiet; they now formed part of my story. It seemed to me that the cyclone should act, in my article, as a kind of symbol of the political situation in East Pakistan. I talked constantly to Asif, Hussein, and the others. They introduced me to friends of theirs who were not poets, but economists, sociologists, and religious men. All these people were unanimous in their feeling that East Pakistan was unbelievably downtrodden, and that something would explode there very soon. But all of them said with equal fervour that they would never accept Indian help, because they hated Hindus. They looked upon India as a Hindu country, as Pakistan was Muslim.

Eventually my friends and I said goodbye, and I flew back to Delhi. I had left them my address there, and I had their continual help, and I think they felt I was a friend, and sympathetic to them. But, when the election results were declared, things began to happen very quickly. Mujibur's Awamis had been swept in by a mass vote from all over East Pakistan. General Yahya Khan, the military dictator of the time, was alarmed by what he regarded as a threat. He had Mujib rearrested and taken off to the west once more. Then he sent his army into East Pakistan, not thinking that it would be resisted.

It might not have been, had the soldiers not immediately begun to commit atrocities. Men were killed and women raped, and thousands fled across the Indian border for shelter. Mrs Gandhi observed this. Guerrilla bands, the Mukti Bahini and the Mukti Fauj, were formed in the countryside; a young guerrilla, 'Tiger' Siddiqui, became famous for his exploits. Mrs Gandhi also observed this, and sent the Indian army in. It routed the Pakistanis, and drove them into Dacca. The Indian commander sent an 'old boy' sort of message to his Pakistani counterpart, Niazi. They had been contemporaries at Sandhurst. It said, laconically, 'My dear Abdullah, the game is up. Surrender and I'll look after you.' Abdullah, or General Niazi, who had been fondly nicknamed 'the Butcher', surrendered. Mujib came back, and East Pakistan announced that it had broken ties with West Pakistan. It was now a sovereign state, Bangladesh.

But the new country had lost thousands of people during its war. Among the many atrocities the West Pakistanis committed was one that became part of the history of Bangladesh. Yahya Khan deeply distrusted intellectuals. When his troops first occupied Dacca, the commanders were told that such people were to be rooted out. Many of the professors and student leaders of the university were arrested, and, on a chilly dawn, collected together beside a mass grave on the city's outskirts, and shot. Their corpses were then thrown into the waiting trench, and buried in the muddy earth. The West Pakistanis assumed that they would soon be forgotten.

They were not forgotten. I am one of those who have not forgotten. I never heard from any of my friends in Dacca again. I am fairly certain that most of them died in the massacre, though I have not been to the city since. I do not clearly remember their features now, only their voices talking of poetry and the future of their country. They were young and full of hope. I hate to imagine, though I do often imagine, what thoughts flickered through their minds as they stood by their common grave, knowing that their youth was over and their hopes also, with the dawn rising slowly on their deaths.

We had several friends in Delhi. One of the more remarkable ones was Major Hari Ahluwalia, who was about my age. Hari had become interested in the high places of the world while still at school. He started to climb mountains when still very young, and, in 1965, he went with an Indian team to Everest. Here, with a companion, he reached the summit. They were the first two from India to do so. Hari was much lauded for this success. A few months later another war started between India and Pakistan. A sniper's bullet hit him in the neck, and he had to be hospitalized for months.

When he recovered, the doctors said that he would never be able to climb again. He would, in fact, have to spend most of his life in a wheelchair. He was sent to England for further treatment, and learnt to walk, at least to some extent, on crutches. He started to write a book about his experiences, *Higher than Everest*, and I helped him a little with it. It was at this time that we commenced to be friends. He lived with his parents, and Leela and I often visited him there. From the waist upward he looked incredibly fit, happy, boyish. From the waist downward, when he sat in his wheelchair, he was swathed in a blanket. But he was full of plans for further books, for films, for television programmes, all connected with mountaineering. He was also trying to set up schemes that would help climbers in India, and create funds for them.

Despite all these projects, and his work with the ministry of defence, where a post had been created for him, I sensed in him a great loneliness and sense of loss. Someone who had been an athlete all his life could hardly be expected to accept the fact that he was incurably handicapped. Curiously, Hari was closer to me than any of our other friends in Delhi because of this. I felt as if I were crippled, because I couldn't write poetry.

I thought my frustration and pain somewhat similar to Hari's. It was not only that which drew me to him, but the idea that he had been to places that few others had been. I was also struck by his retention of the spirit of adventure. Shortly after we first met, he eloped with a very pretty girl, against the wishes of her parents, and married her.

He had her against his loneliness, as I had Leela against mine.

My assignments for New York were almost finished, and I had started to worry. I had now been away from London, apart from my brief visit there in the summer of 1970, for more than two years. The likelihood of my getting profitable assignments or employment there diminished as time passed. I didn't see many prospects in America. Shapiro might like my articles, but he certainly didn't want to employ me. I also had a fixed aversion to the idea of staying in India. This was fairly irrational; life on the subcontinent was certainly more interesting than it would be in Europe, perhaps even in America. But I felt that I had spent a vast amount of energy to make a reputation outside India, in places where it was far harder to earn one, and that all this would go to waste if I submitted once more to what Nirad Chaudhuri had called 'The Continent of Circe'. The loss of any gift I had ever had for writing poetry, also, for some reason, gave me an urge to travel and to experience much more than I had ever done so far. There was no obvious connection.

But, as someone pointed out to me years later, the same thing happened to Rimbaud. He lost, or deliberately ceased to use, the ability to write poetry. Opinions on this are divided. I am not attempting to compare myself to Rimbaud, but it is true that, once he no longer wrote poetry, he developed a desperate desire to travel, and to become financially stable. I had developed both, though my loss wasn't as considerable as his.

It would be very interesting, someday, if a qualified person were to set out to analyse what 'writer's block' is. Most writers I know have suffered from it, particularly novelists. None of them are really able to understand why it happens. It may be something to do with the brain circuits. Allen Tate, as he once told me, had a block very similar to mine; his block, like mine, was only for poetry. Both Tate and I wrote quite a lot of prose while we endured our sterility, and there was no trouble with that. I have since wondered if my block was not concerned with my working in so many other different fields while it lasted. But I have some reason now to think that theory untrue.

However, at the time, my block felt permanent. This didn't make me any the more easy to live with. After East Pakistan, I was bored with life, and wanted adventure. I had been filling the pages of the *New York Times Sunday Magazine* for some months, and Shapiro thought it was time he had a long gap between my contributions. I could understand this, from my own slight experience as an editor. I could write articles on India for the English magazines, but they paid much less than the Americans, and would be more reluctant to sponsor my expenses. Writing for the Indian press seemed to me, then, out of the question, because of the laughable rates I knew to be current. It was suggested to me later, that had I demanded special rates, Indian magazines might have paid them.

But I didn't demand special rates; I stumbled on with my private unhappiness. Leela complained that I didn't share my worries with her. It was obvious, she said, that I had some, but since I wouldn't tell her what they were, she felt helpless. But it had been endemic in me, since childhood, to keep whatever I felt inside me, not to allow it to seep in to other people's lives. This, I thought, had been one of the reasons why poetry emerged from me instead. Now, despite my block, the same habit persisted. It may even have been that I felt that the return of whatever gift I had was dependent on my keeping my troubles to myself. The gift did not return, and my troubles did not decrease.

As often in the past, I consulted my father. He said, 'I can't help you in any of this. You should know yourself what the possibilities are in England. I can inquire at the US embassy about how to get professorships in America—so could you, actually. As for India, I agree that you wouldn't get very much money here in the present situation. Anyway, you say you don't want to stay here.' He sounded a little hurt. Some days later he phoned me and asked, 'Have you ever been to Hong Kong? I don't think we went there when you were a child.' I replied, 'No, I haven't been there.' My father said, 'Do you remember a man called R.V. Pandit? He came to see me the other day, and he was looking for you. He's gone back to Bombay now, but I think you should go there and talk to him. He says he has a job for you in Hong Kong. He says that it's very well-paid, and the sum he mentioned isn't unreasonable. He also says you'd have to travel a great deal in Asia.'

12

I remembered R.V. Pandit. He was one of those people whom one sometimes sees featured in the *Reader's Digest* under some such title as 'The Most Unforgettable Man I Have Met'. I had first encountered him in 1959, when I came back to India to write *Gone Away.* He was slightly built, young, bespectacled, with a certain shyness about him. His most extraordinary attributes were his eyes, a pale, opaque green behind the lenses of his spectacles, with a perceptive look in them always. He was very intense, but could produce a charming, boyish smile and an unexpectedly high-pitched laugh.

What he did was mysterious, but he seemed to have a finger in many pies. Among other things, he occasionally helped my father, to whom he was a personal assistant, at least some of the time. My father asked him to assist me in Bombay, since I was not now familiar with the city. It had changed greatly during my three years abroad. Pandit and I became friends. His initials didn't seem to stand for anything. In fact, he was very secretive about them. He was simply called Pandit. He seemed to prefer it.

The whole city was his beat. Everyone knew him, and he had some mysterious friends. Once I had a colossal crapula after a party, and happened to meet him. I told him about it. 'What shall we do?' he asked. I replied that in London I would go to a pub and have a drink, and that would cure me. But in Bombay, with its prohibition laws, this was not possible. 'You only want to drink, hah?' said Pandit. 'Come with me.' He led me to the biggest and most expensive hotel in the city, and took me upstairs. Then he produced a key from his pocket, opened the door of a suite, and ushered me in. A well-furnished bar occupied a corner of the drawing-room; he pointed to it. 'Help yourself,' he said, and I did. After a while someone turned the key in the suite's door, and came in. This person was a young Indonesian. 'Oh, it's you, Pandit,' he said. We were introduced. His name was Adrian Zecha, and he was a famous businessman in the Far East, though I didn't know this then. He seemed pleased that I was drinking his liquor, even if uninvited.

Afterwards, Pandit said, 'I have business dealings with him.' He did not elaborate.

These 'business dealings' sounded the more remarkable because Pandit was very poor. He lived in a small room above a Chinese restaurant in Colaba, and told me that he had lived in worse places. Otherwise, the aura of mystery that had commenced to collect around him deepened, at least in my mind.

I used to lecture in some of the city colleges, and at one lecture I noticed an African student sitting in an otherwise empty row. The rest of the hall was packed. None of the other students spoke to him.

Afterwards he came up to me. I asked him out for a cup of tea. Over it he told me bitterly that, though he had been a student in Bombay for two years, he was shunned by his Indian peers. No girl would dream of going out with him, and it was difficult to find lodgings. People in the street shouted 'Hubshee!' at him: the equivalent of 'nigger!' He could not wait to return to Kenya. The few other African students in town, his only friends, shared his desire to go home, because they had shared his experience. I was horrified. I asked, 'Have you *no* Indian friends at all?'

He said, 'Only one. He is called R.V. Pandit. Every Saturday he invites us all to tea in his room. He is the only one I can talk to.' It turned out to be true, though Pandit seemed shy to admit it. 'Poor fellows,' he said. 'In situations like these, I feel ashamed of my country.' I attended one of these teas. Pandit proved to be an excellent host. But, when I said the Africans must be very grateful, he blushed a bit.

'You know something?' he eventually said. 'Very few Africans, as yet, come abroad for their education. These boys are the sons of chiefs. Many of them will go from here to England and America for further studies. When they finish, they will go home. As more and more African nations become independent, they will have more and more power in their own countries. When I go there on business, they will remember me.'

All this was absolutely inexplicable. There were cases in India of poor men who had become rich. But these men had been ungentle and unscrupulous; Pandit was their opposite.

I remembered him when I returned to London, but was surprised when he telephoned me one day and said he was in town. I met him several times. He had put on weight, and looked somehow accustomed to money. He didn't, however, have very much. This, he explained, was because of the Indian controls on foreign exchange.

Once, towards the end of his stay, we were walking down Piccadilly, towards a pub, when it came on to rain. I had no raincoat. Pandit insisted that I should take his, a gesture in the tradition of Walter Raleigh. I was deeply touched. In the pub, we sat at a table and he said, 'Are you worried about something?'

I said I was. I do not usually confide in people, but I told him that I was very broke and had some bills to pay before my next cheque was expected. 'How much do you need?' he asked. I said I didn't want him to lend me money. 'Not me,' he said. 'I can't. But how much do you need?' I told him, 'About fifty pounds.' He nodded and said, 'Come with me.'

I was much reminded of the occassion in Bombay when he had found me a drink in the desert. We went into an office where a burly man with a moustache sat behind a desk. 'This is Gordon

Landsborough,' Pandit said. 'He is a publisher. Gordon, he needs fifty pounds. Give it to him.' Landsborough was unruffled by this peremptory demand. He called his secretary, and she shortly brought in fifty pounds. It was the first time in my life that I had ever obtained hard cash from a publisher on request. But Pandit was completely unsurprised. 'Good,' he said, 'Thanks, hah, Gordon. Now I think we can leave.'

According to my father, Pandit had now really become wealthy. He owned the magazine *Imprint* in India. He also owned a publishing house, and the most expensive bookshop in Bombay. He owned Indian restaurants in Monte Carlo and Nice. He lived in Hong Kong. When he came to Bombay, he had a permanent suite reserved for him at the hotel where Adrian Zecha had once stayed. I met him there. He was, as he had always been, dressed in a suit, but this one was of a more expensive material and cut than in the past. The drawing room was strewn with papers, files, and magazines, and Pandit seemed to belong to it, to belong to a world of high finance and business transactions to which I was a complete stranger.

He explained his proposition to me rapidly, though not very concisely. He had, at some point in the last decade, started to work for the *Asia Magazine*, which then had offices in Singapore. It had been the brainchild of a Singapore Chinese, a multimillionaire called Norman Soong. He thought it up at about the time that the Sunday supplements were starting up in Britain. There were English papers all over Asia: none of them had Sunday supplements. Soong felt that a magazine could be published, its contents of general Asian interest, and inserted as a supplement into one paper in each Asian country, if the paper paid for it. The logistics were tremendous, but Soong and Adrian Zecha worked them out. At present, the *Asia Magazine*, now based in Hong Kong, had a readership of about six million. It went to eleven Asian countries, and had a board which comprised the heads of three of the papers it supplied, and also Rupert Murdoch. I told Pandit about meeting Gerry Delilkhan and Kishor Parekh in Kathmandu.

'Bah!' he said. 'They are no longer employed by me. The magazine was running at a loss. I promised the board I would show a profit within two years. For this purpose I am employing three good men. One is Tom Dozier, who was the Latin-American Editor for *Time/Life* for twenty years. He's very senior. He will be the Managing Editor. There will be two Associate Editors. One will be John Gale, from the *London Observer*. The other will be you. You understand?' He paused, breathless, though he had not yet had the sequence of heart attacks that were later to make him more frenetic in his behaviour.

'Who else is there?' I inquired. Pandit said, 'When I became the publisher, there were fifty or sixty people, all over Asia. Completely useless people. I sacked them all.'

I said in amazement and slight shock, 'All?'

'Well, nearly all,' said Pandit.

It wasn't quite as drastic as he had implied. He had kept on the secretarial staff, and the people in the art department. The accounts people also remained unchanged. Three of the former photographers remained in place, Henry Mok in Hong Kong, Takeshi Takahara in Tokyo, and Dick Baldovino in Manila. He had also hired an Indian photographer, Ashvin Gatha, who was to be Hong Kong-based, and three young writers, who would also be in the Hong Kong office. 'They will take the load off your shoulders,' Pandit said. 'But first, since they know nothing, you will have to train them.'

'Is there any backlog left by the previous staff? I mean, have we got enough material to run a few issues still?'

'No,' said Pandit. 'Adrian Zecha has started a newspaper and a magazine. All these useless people went to him, and before they went they took all their material from the files. I am telling you, for the last few months I have run this magazine alone.'

The job looked harder and harder, the more I heard of it. But it also seemed a challenge; it could be exactly what I was looking for, since it entailed both a reasonable salary and constant travel; and I had no options. Next day I signed the contract, and Pandit flew back to Hong Kong, saying he would call me in a couple of weeks. Tickets would be sent for Leela and myself. 'But you had better get married,' said Pandit, 'because in Hong Kong they are very strict about these things.' So we did.

While we waited for the tickets, my Mrs Gandhi article was published in New York, and caused quite a storm in India. Her party, without asking me, used quotes from it as election propaganda. At about the same time, my father, who had become an opponent of the lady, wrote a piece in his paper, attacking her. The Congress used quotes from this alongside quotes from me, saying that I represented the young and liberal, while my father represented the old and hidebound. My father thought this very funny. But no doubt, whatever existed about the outcome of these elections, Mrs Gandhi had become the heroine of the new Bangladesh, and simultaneously of the Indian public.

What I myself felt about India, and its prime minister, was rather complicated. I had come to like Mrs Gandhi as a person. She seemed to be touchingly vulnerable, though, also, as comes with this chink in one's armour, remittingly bitchy to those who sought to penetrate it. Her policies seemed to me very sensible in the main. The princes, for example, might have been conceivable as an unrewarding but unavoidable expense in 1947 or 1948; in 1970 they were a terrible and unnecessary burden on the national exchequer. Political promises, as Mrs Gandhi well knew, are seldom kept. The Balkanization, or the trend towards Balkanization, in the Indian states, was something she foresaw and feared. She was to see it start to happen, though not in the way she foresaw.

The whole of Bombay was festooned with election posters, most of them with the prime minister beaming out of them, some, but only a few, fortunately, containing the quotes from my article and my father's. As often before, I felt claustrophobic in the country of my birth. The tickets arrived and I booked on the first possible flight out of India. We initially flew to New Delhi, because my father had made the most curious and wasteful decision of his entire life. He hadn't lived in England for something like forty years. He had now decided to go and live there. Marilyn would accompany him, as would their five Tibetan dogs. The staff had all been pensioned off, except for a young bearer and cook named Sauri. He was to go to London as well, and run the house which the newspaper had rented in Bayswater.

I thought this one of the worst ideas I had ever heard, and had come to Delhi to try and dissuade my father from pursuing it. I had had no idea that his preparations for departure had got as far as they obviously had, for the house was stripped of furniture, which was being shipped ahead, and, in two days time, he, Marilyn, Sauri, and the dogs were due to leave. My father and I sat on kitchen chairs in the drawing room, which, emptied of furniture and pictures, seemed oppressively large, and I attempted to reason with him.

It was over thirty-five years, I said, since he had last lived in London. He had visited it often enough since then, but he should have been able to see how unimaginably changed it was. The friends of his youth had dropped away, some were dead. But here, in India, he had plenty of friends. When he wrote editorials, the government took note of them. He was successful in India; he was powerful. Why should he give all this up and retire to a country which was now unknown to him, and in which he would be only marginally known?

He listened and, childlike, agreed with everything I said; but his handsome head, grown grey at the temples, was lowered like an obdurate bull's, and he repeated, several times, 'It's too late. I can't change my mind now.' It struck me when I heard this, that, somewhere during his preparations to leave, he *had* changed his mind, but had been too proud, or foolish, to say so. As a result of this, circumstances were moving him in a direction which he no longer wanted to take. He was right; it was now too late.

'Your mother,' he said, 'doesn't know I'm going. It would hurt her unnecessarily if she knew. I've arranged to send letters from London to be posted from Delhi. You must write to her too. You know how...attached she is to you. Don't forget.' He took us to the airport. The customs and immigration people, on seeing him, ushered us through to the plane. It was the last demonstration of power that I ever saw from my father.

Hong Kong island came up with the dawn, the mainland mountains behind it. I had never been this way before, and these mountains looked as though they had come out of a painted scroll. At the airport we were met by an Indian, Raj Gupta, who ran the Far East Trade Press, which Pandit owned and which put out trade magazines. He drove us through the Kowloon streets, packed with Chinese faces and the signs of bars and restaurants, and put us in the Hyatt. 'Tom Dozier has already come with his wife,' Gupta said. 'Tonight Pandit is throwing a party for him and for you.' I looked forward to this: I was eager for this new challenge in a new part of the world, and wanted badly to meet the people with whom I was to work. Leela and I spent most of the day asleep. At dusk, following Gupta's directions, we took a ferry across the harbour to Victoria, which is what the British authorities called the island, though nobody else did. The ride took twenty minutes.

I was often to take the ferry in the next two years. But the first impact was special. The island, a great hump across dark, flustered water, gleamed as with fallen stars, from the peak down to the illuminations of Wanchai: a turtle risen from the sea, spotted and streaked with phosphorescent weeds. We took a taxi to Pandit's flat. It was large and comfortable, and full of happily drunk people—Pandit's employees, Pandit's friends.

Two of them were Tom and Florence Dozier. Tom, who was to be my chief, was a lean, bespectacled man from the American south. He was in his middle years, and had had a great deal of experience with *Time/Life*. He spoke in a quiet drawl, interspersed with Santa Clauslike chuckles, ho-ho-hos, but in a very low key. He had been reading my autobiography. 'The office is a real mess,' he said, 'Pandit's been running it with three kids and Ted Gowing. Gowing's on loan from the Far East Trade Press, but he's a new arrival too. John Gale's coming in a couple of days, but Gowing's on loan to us till we settle.' He introduced me to Gowing's wife Jenny, a small, pretty, but slightly careworn blonde. They had a small baby, she said, and she was awfully worried about its health in a very foreign country. 'Of course,' she said, 'there's one consolation, it belongs to Britain.' At this moment her husband came up. He was lanky and blue-chinned, with a pleasant but rather undisciplined face, and was very drunk. 'I have been dancing with your wife,' he said. 'She has fantastic knockers.' I could see why Jenny looked careworn.

After the party was over, Pandit asked us to stay on. He looked rather careworn himself. I said so. 'I am worried,' he said. 'Did you see Ted Gowing tonight? He was *drunk*, I tell you. *Drunk*. And Dozier and you drink very heavily. It means that all three of you are alcoholics. My God! I have hired three alcoholics!' I interposed the stupidly defensive remark that neither Dozier nor I had been drunk, but he did not seem to hear, and continued, 'Do you know John Gale?' Not personally, I replied, but he was a good writer. 'Yes,' said Pandit with a sigh that seemed born of despair. 'He has written books. He has written an autobiography called, *Clean Young Englishman*. Have you read it?'

'No.'

'In it,' said Pandit, in a kind of wail, 'he confesses that he spent some time as a patient in a lunatic asylum. I do not know. It seems I have hired three alcoholics and a certified madman. What will the board say? What will Rupert Murdoch say? I do not know.'

Next day I turned up at the office. Leela went to an estate agent to find us a flat. The office was on the tenth floor of a building in Queen's Road, the main traffic artery of the island. The crowded street was alive with noise and people, rickshaws, cars, buses, trams, lorries. But the office was soundproof, a glass-encased haven, and very spacious. Chinese secretaries sat at tidy desks, the equipment was professional, and Pandit, Dozier, and Gowing were there. I was allotted a room, and introduced to the rest of the staff. The three juniors were present. Jim Burke was a young American who had served in Vietnam. His father, also Jim Burke, had been an excellent photographer with *Life*, and had died falling off a Himalayan peak. Tom Dozier and I had known the elder Burke and his widow, Josephine. We, therefore, had an avuncular interest in Jim.

Erika Petigura was a tall, shy girl whose father was Indian. Her mother was Chinese, and Erika spoke Cantonese fluently. The third recruit was a Hong Kong Chinese named Peter Ling, who was thin, bespectacled, and inarticulate. Tom Dozier said, 'We're supposed to train these kids. You take Peter I'll take Erika, and John Gale can have young Jim.' We began to talk, to organize ourselves. Pandit, looking on, seemed to have overcome his fears of the previous night, and could even be said to look happy.

The following day John Gale arrived, and with him Pandit's fears returned. Shortly before Gale's plane was due, he came to my room and asked me to accompany him to the airport, 'because,' he said, 'porters are hard to find at Kai Tak, and someone must carry his luggage.' Greatly affronted, I suggested he take Ted Gowing, who was younger and fitter than I was. He did. When Ted came back to the office, he was laughing uncontrollably.

'I've never seen anything like it,' he said. 'On the way to the airport Pandit told me that he thought Tom, you, and I were all alcoholics. I must say I was a bit annoyed. Then he said that Gale had admitted in some book or other that he was a certified lunatic. He seemed a bit upset. He got more upset when Gale came off the plane with a carton of champagne under each arm. He turned pale. He said, "This one is so desperate for alcohol that he carries it with him on the plane! I tell you, Gowing, this is too much! Now I find that I have employed four alcoholics, and one of them is also a madman!"'

Gale, a large, flushed, robust man with a hearty manner, was much puzzled by all the fuss. 'I've been finishing a book on Africa,' he told us, 'and the night I left we had a party at home. When I left the house for Heathrow I thought the simplest thing was to put my notes and manuscripts in two empty champagne cartons. I carried them with me for safety. What's the matter with Pandit? He seemed frightfully upset. I don't understand him.'

'I don't think he understands any of us,' said Tom Dozier drily.

It was hard work at the office. The sacked staff had left nothing behind, no material we could use, not even photographs. The size of the magazine, between the time they had left and the time we arrived, had shrunk from forty-eight pages to sixteen. Desperate for material, Pandit had sent Jim Burke and the Indian photographer, Ashvin Gatha, who also took along his fiancee, Flora, to Malaysia. They had now come back. Gatha who had curly black hair down to his shoulders and dressed in designer denims and spectacular shirts, had not got on with Jim, a conservative in everything, but particularly in the matter of dress. Nor had the presence of Flora helped. All these factors had contributed to a futile trip.

Because of the pressures at the office—John Gale and I were sent on desperate trips round the island to write what were essentially fillers—I was unable to help Leela very much in her search for a flat. Eventually she found one, at Babington Row in the mid-levels. It was a beautiful flat, and suited us admirably. The drawback was the landlady. She accepted us when we telephoned, but, upon discovering our Indian origins, said very politely that she had forgotten that the flat was already taken.

It had always surprised me that those in India who speak of Sino-Indian friendship—the first was Nehru, whose heart broke when the Chinese betrayed him—have not studied contemporary Chinese opinion very closely. The Hong Kong Chinese, like their compatriots on the mainland, hated all *gwailo*s, or foreigners, but especially the Indians. They hated everything about them, and they had some reason to. In the early days of colonization, the British had brought Sikhs from India to man their police force. They had often treated the Chinese population brutally, and this had not been forgotten. There is a Hindi word, which, by its nature, is constantly on the lips of most Indians. It is acchha, the equivalent of okay. The Chinese called all Indians *ahchah*s. In Cantonese, I am told, the term means 'Respected Dog'. It was often in use.

Leela, once she has an idea, tends to cling to it tenaciously. She had set her heart on the Babington Row flat. She came to the office and suggested that I ring up Derek Davies, the Editor of the influential *Far Eastern Economic Review*. Davies had spent years in Hong Kong, and knew everyone. We had met him at a party, and he had been very friendly. He now said, on hearing the landlady's name, 'She's a very, very rich woman. And she's a friend of Sir John Cowperthwaite's. He's the financial secretary. I'll phone John and see what he can do.' Half an hour later, with Leela still in my office, the landlady phoned up. She had had no idea, she said, that we really wanted to live in her humble flat. She had not thought it would meet our high requirements. Now that we were kind enough to say it did, we could certainly have it. More than that, my wife had inquired about a flat for John Gale, and the one above us was also vacant. If the Gales deigned to take it, they could. I phoned up Derek Davies to thank him.

'Oh, a pleasure,' he said. 'All that she told you after Cowperthwaite rang her was said to save face. You'll find out a great deal here, if you stay with your friend Pandit, about losing face and saving it. It's very important. Also, by the way, I told

Cowperthwaite to tell your landlady that neither of you is really Indian. Leela's half French and you are a British national.'

If K.C. Pant had been right, which he probably was, in saying that it was more difficult to acquire an Indian nationality than any other, I wondered what he would have thought about this, or, for that matter, what Mrs Gandhi would have thought. In any event, Leela began to organize the first flat we had ever lived in by ourselves together.

This was to be the first of many. She designed heavy cane furniture, had it made to order and upholstered, hung up paintings, unrolled carpets brought from India, and finally hired a maidservant. Ah Mui was slight and young, with a calm pale face and impassive sloe eyes. She was with us all the time we were in Hong Kong. She said she didn't mind Indians, but expressed some hesitation about cooking curries. She moved into the flat at about the same time we did. She and Leela instituted a regime. All my life, up to this point, I had lived in a slightly disorderly manner. The only home of my own I had had was in the two years Judy and I lived in Islington. That was now over, and this had started not unpleasantly.

At the office, John Gale refused absolutely to try and train anyone. This meant that I took charge not only of Peter Ling but of Jim Burke. As we scoured the Hong Kong landscape for fillers, I suggested to Jim that he keep an eye open for unusual stories. I had to explain what I meant by this. In a day or two he came back with one which suited me perfectly. This was about two topless waitresses who worked in a Wanchai club of his acquaintance. These two had been abandoned by their husbands—both were English—and supported themselves with their bosoms. But between them they had eight children, who lived with them in a flat they shared. I sent Jim after them to finish the story.

He presented it to me. The first three-quarters of it was an accurate, even rather witty, account of the dual lives led by the two women, as topless waitresses and fond mothers. But in the final bit Jim's innate conservatism took over. I couldn't imagine where he got it from; neither of his parents had suffered from this attitude. In his concluding paragraphs he unexpectedly turned on the hapless waitresses, called them women of low morals, and said they were unfit to be in charge of children. All that he had previously stated seemed to contradict this entirely. I chided him gently about this, and cut it.

I had intended to run two colour photographs with the article. One was to show the two ladies topless. The other was to show them fully dressed, plying their offspring with breakfast. Jim's fit of morality lasted long enough for him to tell the arts department, purely of his own accord, to airbrush the nipples out of the topless picture. A black wash was put over the two pairs of breasts, but, being transparent, lent a singularly suggestive air to the photograph. The *Manila Times* telexed us saying that the Philippines was a Catholic country. The Singapore *Straits Times* said that Lee Kuan Yew, the prime minister, had personally expressed his displeasure at the immorality of it all. Pandit blamed it on me. Jim failed to see that he had made a mistake.

In the meantime, Tom, the two Johns, and I produced our first issue. It was packed with fillers, but our own. We took great pride in it. The system was that the material was laid out and set in Hong Kong; every Saturday afternoon, two weeks before the actual publication date, we flew the sheets out from Kai Tak to Tokyo. Here it was printed and flown out to the eleven newspapers which took us. This first issue was pasted up and ready to leave on our first Saturday. An hour was left before the Tokyo flight took off. The messenger was waiting for us to hand the sheets over before he took the helicopter to Kai Tak. Pandit came in as we were about to do so. 'Let me see,' he said.

We unsealed and unwrapped the parcel. The lead piece was by me, about the relationship between mainland China and Hong Kong. It contained the sentence, 'Every day 20,000 head of cattle pass over the Shum Chun bridge into the crown colony.' The sentence stays in my memory because Pandit, upon seeing it, screamed, 'Grammar! Grammar!'

We looked at him, wholly mystified. Seizing a blue pencil, he began to correct the paste-up. 'I thought your grammar was good,' he shouted. 'I will not have grammatical errors in my magazine! You say, "20,000 head of cattle." How can 20,000 cattle only have one head? It is heads—heads—heads!' The first thing we had to do was to convince him of his mistake. The second was to have a recorrection of the correction printed and repasted. Finally we were able to send the messenger to Kai Tak. He managed to put our package on the Tokyo flight. 'Are there going to be lots of bits like this?' John Gale asked innocently, when it was all over. Tom opened the office bottle, silent.

Meanwhile, I continued with the education of Peter Ling. I sent him out on a few small stories, but the results dissatisfied me. 'I don't think any of these stories interested you,' I told Peter.

'Sir,' he said, pale and stern, 'they do not. They were frivolous.'

'Just as an exercise,' I said, 'write on something that does interest you, what?'

'Sir,' he replied, 'I suggest that I write on my piles. I have been suffering from them since I was fourteen. Only last month I had an operation. This is of great interest to me. Also, some of the readers may have piles and be interested.' I was too taken aback to argue. In due course he brought me a seven thousand-word essay on his piles, their genesis, their symptoms, and eventually on the operation which cured them.

'I can't do anything more with him,' I told Tom. 'So what do we do now?'

Fortunately, Peter resigned shortly afterwards, saying his work wasn't properly appreciated.

Work at the office became progressively less peaceful. This was due partly to Pandit's intrusions into the editorial domain, and partly because we were short of material. John Gale and I were prepared to fly out to parts of Asia where we could find some. But Pandit decided instead to send John Gowing to Indonesia with Ashvin Gatha, who again took Flora with him. I instructed John to keep closely in touch with the office—by telex, by cable, or, in an emergency, by telephone. The first cable I had, after some days, read UPBRICK SHITTEST GOWING. I showed it to Tom and the other John. Tom threw up his hands and chuckled. John earnestly set himself to solving the problem.

'Did you have a code system with him?' he inquired. 'Like in the secret service?' I shook my head. John said, 'If we were frightened in the war, we used to say we were shitting bricks. Perhaps he's shitting bricks because he's frightened.' After his suggestion we gave up. I sent a cable to the only address we had, saying CLARIFY.

We got an immediate reply, ASHVIN MARRYING FLORA SEND CONGRATULATIONS. This time Tom sent a cable, a very irate one. A week later, we received a third message, NOW IN BANKOK, it said, WEATHER FINE ASHVIN VERY ILL. Thailand and Indonesia are on opposite sides of Asia, but at least we had an address. We cabled it, saying COME BACK IMMEDIATELY. The reply was NOT YET. I despatched one of the photographers, Henry Mok, to Bangkok to retrieve our roving correspondents. He telephoned me from Thailand, and said in his customary bleak voice, 'Boss, they will not come.' The next request from Gowing was for more money. Pandit refused to send any. Ashvin Gatha then apparently flew to London with Flora, as yet unwed and John Gowing came back with a grimacing Henry.

This whole expedition had chewed several thousand dollars out of the travel budget, and taken three valuable weeks. Gowing's explanations were rather vague; in any event he was now returning to the Far East Trade Press. Meanwhile John Gale and I had a more serious matter to discuss with him—his wife Jenny.

John Gale was still without his family, since his wife was busy renting out their house in Hampstead. Leela, he and I one night took Jenny out to dinner. We were having a reasonably successful evening when Jenny suddenly turned pale and knocked a bottle of wine into John's lap. 'Do you see the man at the corner table,' she asked, 'the man with a beard?' John, somewhat aggrieved, said, 'You've ruined my only pair of trousers. And that was a perfectly good bottle of wine.' The man in the corner, paying no attention to us, spooned soup into his beard. But Jenny was, trembling all over, her eyes wide.

'That man,' she said vehemently, 'killed my brother. He's come here to kill me.'

What do you mean,' said John, incredulous, 'he killed your brother?'

'He killed my brother with a silenced pistol,' she said, 'in a telephone booth in Seattle.'

John, being practical, inquired, 'Why?'

'Because he had a vendetta against my family,' said Jenny. 'You see, in the strictest confidence, my father is the head of MI 5. That man killed my brother, and now he's come after me.' She sounded entirely convinced of this. Finally we took her home.

We thought it might have been the drinks at dinner. Next day Leela went to visit her. Not only did she seem still in terror of the bearded stranger, but she offered Leela more information about her father, who had a wooden leg and lived in a country mansion, looked after by turbaned Indian menservants. After a long debate, John and I agreed that Gowing might be unaware of Jenny's state of mind, and resolved to tell him as gently as possible. The Savoy bar occupied the basement of our office building, and we took Gowing there and plied him with many gratefully accepted drinks before we broke the news.

He listened as we told him what Jenny had said about her troubles in life. His lean face assumed a worried expression. 'That's bad news,' he said. Deeply sympathetic, we waved to the waiter, who fetched another round.

Gowing said, 'Yes, that's bad news, all right. That man killed Jenny's brother with a silenced pistol in a telephone booth in

Seattle. Two weeks later he nearly did me in a hotel room in Wigan. I wish my father-in-law were here. He could handle this. He's the head of MI 5, you know.' John and I looked closely at him, then looked away.

Tom said, in slight despair, 'Don't tell Pandit about this. He already thinks John's off his rocker.' Until he came to Hong Kong, Tom had lived comfortably with Florence in a large flat in London, bought with the money he had received on retirement from *Time/Life*. He had, he told us, been peacefully writing his memoirs, interrupted very occasionally of an evening by his friend Sir Neville Cardus, the music critic and cricket writer. They would drink and listen to music together, though Cardus was never able to convert Tom to cricket. 'I don't understand it,' Tom would say, shaking his wise head. 'But I'm an Anglophile.' The one thing that put him off England was cricket.

Though I had been associated with magazines before this, I suddenly saw that on *Gemini* and *Nova*, I had been a neophyte. I had got my material together, in each case, and sent it off to the art department, leaving the rest to it. 'There are only three of us on this,' Tom said conspiratorially to John and me as we sat in his office in the evenings over our editorial bottle. 'Apart from Erika, we can write off the young entries. You'll both have to learn it all from the bottom.' John, having stated firmly, and with many great roars of laughter, that he had been in the business for two decades, and had never yet subbed a page, was let off this unrewarding duty.

But Tom Dozier taught me a lot about putting magazines together, particularly in terms of seeing to it that the words and pictures looked good on the pages. 'Look at the way it all sprawls out and spills over,' he would say, flicking a disparaging hand towards the copies of the *Asia Magazine* produced by our predecesors. 'Ours has to *look* like a good magazine as well as be one. I'm running a tight ship here.' (Chuckle, chuckle.) 'I'm thinking here, also, that John and you and I are the only three people in the place who know English. So if John won't, it's up to you and me and maybe Erika to sub it all.' But we took burdens gladly, with the possible exception of Pandit.

Pandit was one of the puzzles of life. I liked him very much, I was even fond of him, but he seemed a completely different man from the one I had met in Bombay a decade before. He had then been relatively simple, but was now complex, a bundle of sensitivities, chips that he mentally computerized borne heavily on his shoulder. He still had flashes of almost overwhelming generosity and kindness, but he always seemed to think that he knew best, about almost everything, which is a dangerous thing in a man. 'What's his first name?' John once asked me. 'He says call him Pandit, but then I sound like some kind of Hindu devotee.' Tom was puzzled too, which made three of us. 'He says he's interested in backing a Hindu political party in India.' Tom said, 'But I've also seen him praying in church on Sunday.' Tom and Florence were both devout Roman Catholics.

Some of the problems were resolved when, quite early on in our editorships, an ecumenical council was held in Hong Kong. One of the prelates who attended it was the Cardinal of Bombay, Valerian Gracias, who had been a great friend of my father's when they were both young. Since then, despite my father's views on religion, they had remained on amicable terms. At his and my mother's insistence, my father had had me christened, baptized, and confirmed in the Catholic faith by him. Though perfectly aware I wasn't a believer, he was by way of being a friend of mine. He liked good Scotch.

When he came from India, we threw a party for him, to which I invited Pandit and my colleagues. Tom Dozier was delighted, Pandit unaccountably shy. I also ordered a large supply of good whisky. The Cardinal arrived in full regalia. After dinner, replete with food and drink, he allowed his eye to stray around the company. Presently it fell on Pandit, and he said, 'Who is this again?' I introduced them afresh. 'But I knew I recognized him,' said the Cardinal. 'His name is not Pandit. His name is Tommy Rodrigues, and, when I had my first parish in Bassein, he was a little barefoot boy who used to bring me bunches of bananas from his parents. Eh, Tommy? In those days your parents could not afford to buy you shoes, my son!'

Pandit was not only slightly embarrassed, but rather pleased. Indeed, he admitted, he was the very Tommy Rodrigues whom the Cardinal so fondly remembered. The mystery of his past had been cleared up, and he seemed relieved. For the rest of the party he conversed in whispers with the Cardinal, who, as a parting shot, blessed him with holy water. A couple of days later, John said to me in the Savoy, 'He was awfully chuffed, Pandit, wasn't he, to be blessed by the Cardinal? Afterwards he explained the whole thing to me. His family were high-caste Brahmins; that's why he calls himself Pandit. When the Portuguese occupied Bassein, wherever that is, they threw beefsteaks into the family well to pollute it. So the family lost its caste and became Catholics. That's why he's called Thomas Rodrigues. I'd have thought the Portuguese would have had more sense, wouldn't you, than to waste perfectly good beefsteaks by throwing them down wells? But there it is. Do you think,' asked John with a huge smile, 'now that all is known, he'd mind if I called him Tommy?'

John was sent to Macau, the Portuguese island near Hong Kong. In those days it was reached by aerofoil, and its main attractions, apart from the decaying relics of the Iberian conquest, were casinos. John visited some of these, drank a lot of Mateus Rose, which he said had not travelled well, and came back glowing. '*Anywhere's* much nicer than Hong Kong, don't you think?' he asked us. 'At least Macau isn't full of bloody Brits.'

It was my turn next. 'Go to Singapore and Malaysia,' Tom said. 'Pandit tells me our biggest circulation is there, with the

Straits Times. When you're back John can fly off to Thailand. I must say, I envy you two. Pandit says I'm too old to travel.'

Pandit was very well informed on Asia. He gave me addresses and phone numbers all over Malaysia. 'Visit Malacca,' he said. 'Visit Penang. Make yourself familiar with Malaysia.' Excitement rose within me; it was the start of what would clearly be a regimen of hard travel. I thought I would take Leela; this assignment would not be dangerous, or even very trying. Henry Mok was the photographer assigned to me. 'Boss, you don't know all these places,' he said, 'but I know, I know. You're all right with Henry.' His wife said, 'Please remind Henry to bring some durian fruit back. I like that very much.' This simple request was to cause more trouble than any other of our various missions on this trip.

13

I had been to Singapore and Malaya before, with my father, in 1950. Singapore had now become an island republic, separate from the new state of Malaysia on the mainland. Under Lee Kuan Yew, it had prospered and become puritanical. Lee had been educated in England; his tiny country was dull and safe, like some garden suburb near London, except that the vegetation was tropical. There was censorship, though nobody seemed to mind. Anyone with long hair, on arrival at the airport, was forcibly shorn before being allowed to leave. Anyone who dropped a cigarette in the street was heavily fined. Singapore has an area of 228 square miles, so the enforcement of law wasn't difficult. As a desirable corollary to this, it had, unlike other Asian countries, a successful birth-control programme. Lee, the Cromwell of Asia, presided over all this.

Henry Mok knew Singapore well. He led me to Bugis Street, where transvestites plied a profitable trade with sailors and peccant businessmen; I wrote a story on it. He took me to the death houses of the Chinese. The older generation wanted to be buried in the soil of their homeland, even though, in some cases, they had never been there. This was arranged. I wrote a story on them; I remember the fumes of incense in these small, closed rooms, where stacks of paper money waited to be interred with the dead, and elaborate coffins were made. Upstairs, in many of these places, the dying lay, their coffins and the paper money ready to receive them beneath. I also interviewed a magician, a musician, and a banker.

Soon after this first trip, there was a crackdown on Bugis Street and the death houses. In a very short span of time, the face of Singapore was changed, though you could still eat chilli crab in the beach restaurants, or satay on the street. The city became laundered, aseptic, unAsian. I was recommended to Fatty's restaurant in Albert Street, which was named after its Chinese owner. If you talked to Fatty nicely, he could make the best Szechuan food in town, and he was also an information post for journalists. He knew all kinds of things of which Lee Kuan Yew was probably ignorant.

I flew my articles back to Tom, who was waiting anxiously for copy, and went on to Kuala Lumpur. The city moved at a much slower pace than Singapore. It was green and leafy and, when we got there, very wet. Since the magazine was so short of material, I picked stories up as and when I could. We went to Malacca by bus. It was a very pleasant drive through a landscape of paddy fields, rubber trees, and houses on stilts, but Leela developed stomach trouble on the road, and, when we reached Malacca, I had to call a doctor. He advised rest. While she rested, Henry and I used to eat in small Chinese cafés, where the food was rudimentary but appetizing. Throughout my later travels in Asia, when Leela wasn't with me, I habitually ate in such places. I had no idea what a good breakfast could be made of fishball soup laced with chilli sauce.

In Penang, I covered a crocodile farm, amongst other things. One could smell this establishment miles up the road: the stagnant, musty odour of live crocodiles, and the stench of hides being cured. We looked at the breeding pens and tanneries, and visited the fenced compounds where the creatures were kept. In one of them was a huge bull crocodile, armoured all over, with yellow eyes. When we entered the compound, to take photographs, it stirred, snorted, and charged. It came at high speed, and it was fortunate that the gate was immediately behind us. My acquaintance with reptiles widened considerably on this trip. Penang had a famous Buddhist temple, whose mascot was a two-headed viper. It lived in a small enclosure at the entrance. The head priest insisted that I took it in my hands. Snakes feel cold and dry, rather pleasant; but, as I held it, the priest told me it had recently bitten a man ('he was evil') to death.

I had picked up a dozen stories in a couple of weeks, and returned to Hong Kong, to enable John to take off for Thailand. This shuttle service continued as long as John was there. When I returned from a trip, he instantly took off, and vice versa.

Our next expedition, to the Philippines, took me into unknown territory. Manila was very depressing, and I never found it otherwise on later trips: it was muddy, with decrepit slum areas, and most of it seemed to be in decay. It consisted, actually, of several cities; one locked with another to form an unimpressive whole. I picked up a number of small stories before going into the bigger ones. Among them was an interview with an old American musician, Whitey Smith, who ran a restaurant. He had lived in Shanghai for much of his life before the Second World War, and had been a bandleader there. He had known Chiang Kai-shek and Madame Chiang; he had been very successful in his profession. But he had had to flee before the Japanese takeover, and had been in hiding in the Philippines during the war. The walls of his restaurant were papered with photographs of his Shanghai days.

All over Asia, I was to discover, there were such people: leftovers from a departed day, who had had times of splendour, and had watched them fade. Many of them were expatriates of one kind or another. They had spent long periods in Asia and decided to retire and die there. Usually they had no desire whatsoever to return to their former countries. They had been absorbed into Asia, though curiously, few of them spoke the languages of their adopted countries. This seemed a relic of their pasts, where 'going native' was considered a stigma; despite this, many of them had Asian wives and Eurasian children. I suppose they are now all dead. But, at that time, they were alive, and not only had, but were, stories.

After Whitey Smith, I interviewed General Carlos P. Romulo, who was then foreign secretary. He was nearly seventy, a small, attractively wrinkled man, with the Aztec look many of the Filipinos possess. Romulo came of a poor family, but had risen to become an eminent writer and editor before the Second World War. Afterwards he became the chief Philippine delegate to the United Nations. During the war, however, though not built like a soldier, he was one, and was with General MacArthur when the Americans retreated from the islands. He also returned with MacArthur after the Japanese had been overthrown. He could, many people thought, have made an excellent President; but he was said to be too gentle.

Romulo had many memories, which I was happy to listen to. He invited us to lunch, and, as we scrutinized the menu, said, chuckling happily, 'Eat me.' A speciality of the Hilton grill-room was Steak Romulo. He also presented me with a barong-tagalog, the lacy dress shirt worn in the Philippines and I wore it to parties for years. Our friendship was maintained until I ceased to visit Manila. I greatly valued it, for the little general was a most remarkable person.

I then interviewed the President, Ferdinand Marcos. He received me in his office at Malacanang Palace, a huge and ornate repository of bad paintings, with broad staircases and endless corridors. Marcos had recently been re-elected to the presidency. It was the first time a President of the Philippines had been re-elected. He seemed popular with the people, and so did his wife, Imelda. At this first encounter, Leela came with me to take notes. Marcos wore a white barong and black trousers, and stood erect as a soldier to shake hands. He was not unhandsome, but there was a slight hardness in his mouth and eyes.

I was impressed by him. I knew little about the Philippines then. I listened as he talked of his wartime exploits, for which he said he had received twenty-seven medals from the USA and his own country. He had led a guerrilla band in the mountains, and, he told me, had personally captured the Japanese general, Yamashita. He also expatiated, as most national leaders do in the midst of a collapsing economy, on his great hopes for the future. The interview lasted for more than an hour. When it was over, he introduced us to his wife. Imelda Marcos was a handsome, rather heavily built woman with small, black, acquisitive eyes. She wore the terno, the formal dress of Filipinos, and was very effusive. She invited us to sail round the islands in the presidential yacht, or, if we had no time, fly over them in the presidential helicopter. I was, then, also impressed by her. She was said to have started several programmes for the beautification of Manila (which sorely needed this), and financed some archaeological excavations. A corps of women in blue dresses, the Blue Ladies, run by her, did social work in the islands.

I paid several visits to the Philippines. The next one was made without Leela, and it was after disastrous floods had followed a cyclone. At this time, I met Chino Roces, the proprietor of the *Manila Times*, one of our magazine's biggest shareholders. Chino, who was nicknamed so because he looked Chinese, was an old man, but very tough and drily witty. His splendidly forceful wife, Pacita, was a great support to him. They were to become friends of ours, and, in later crises in the Philippines, their help was invaluable.

Chino was the first person I met who expressed an open and heartfelt dislike of the Marcoses, particularly of Imelda. 'He is corrupt and stupid,' he said, 'but she is corrupt and clever.' He implied that the flood damage could have been checked if proper plans had been made, and if so much money which could have been used to implement them had not been salted away for personal profit by the President or Imelda. At a party in his house, I met Senator Benigno Aquino. He expressed the same views as Chino, but in a more elaborate way. 'Very soon,' he said, 'the country will find out that it is run by a criminal, and then let Marcos beware!' He was later, after an emergency was declared by Marcos, imprisoned in the same military camp as Chino. Later still, he was shot dead at the Manila airport by gunmen proved to have been hired by Marcos. His widow, Corazon, whom I also met at Chino's party, later became the President of the Philippines, a difficult post to occupy.

It wasn't only Chino and Aquino who thought Marcos and his wife were monsters. I took a helicopter out over the flooded areas, and landed in some of them. The people I met were angry and bitter about the Marcos government. It had promised that measures would be taken against cyclones and rising rivers, common enough occurrences in this part of the world, and had done nothing. Even the action taken for relief of the affected population had proved inadequate. In Manila, I had a long talk with Romulo. He possessed the great virtue of loyalty, and said nothing against Marcos or Imelda, but he was visibly sad and disappointed with the news I brought back from the flooded areas. 'If I were a younger man,' he said, 'I might have stood for President last time.'

An interesting story floating about in Manila concerned Marcos' love life. One function of Imelda's Blue Ladies was to keep an eye on the President. He had a roving eye, and apparently used the Hilton for his liaisons. They had once nearly cornered him in the hotel. He escaped, but the Blue Ladies bugged his suite. A record was available in Manila, allegedly taken from a tape, of the President singing Tagalog love songs to a young American woman. She had taken the lead part in a pornographic film.

I listened to the record, but couldn't say who the singer was. A popular recreation in the Philippines is gossip, the more scandalous the better. But even allowing for this, it seemed disgraceful as well as funny that a head of state should provide reasons to be mentioned in this way. I saw Marcos again, and this time asked him some fairly direct questions, which he evaded. Later, Kit

Tatad, the press secretary, asked me what I had discussed with the President. 'He is not too happy with you now, you know,' Kit said. He could not have been any more happy with the article I subsequently published in the magazine.

Leela had by this time taken a post as a producer and director for Hong Kong television. Romulo came to Hong Kong for some meeting or the other, and his birthday happened to take place during his visit. He agreed to allow her to interview him live. She, with her Chinese crew, came to his suite, where I was already ensconced.

The Hilton had baked him a huge cake, in the form of a Filipino *nipa* hut. This stood on a table in the corner, and dominated the room. As the crew packed up, one of the sound cables managed to entwine itself round the cake. The great edifice of chocolate fell to the floor and exploded, sending glutinous brown gobbets of itself all over the carpet, furniture, and walls. There was a short, tense silence. Then, Romulo, managing a smile, said, 'I had better tell someone to clear all this away.' When Leela and the crew had left, he commenced to chuckle. 'What a pity,' he said. 'It was such a splendid cake.'

I went back to the Philippines after Marcos' first emergency had ended. I applied to Kit Tatad for an interview with Marcos. After the cake incident in the Hong Kong, Romulo, either because of the catharsis of his loss or the fact that he was not at the time in Manila, had speculated to me about the future of his country, which he didn't think looked too good under Marcos. I had some more questions for the President. During my first few days in Manila, I met Chino and Pacita Roces, Aquino, and a few other people. Kit Tatad phoned and said, 'The boss knows who your friends are. He's given you an appointment for tomorrow; but it's at five-thirty a.m.' I inquired if the boss was awake at this time. 'Oh, he is,' said Kit spryly. 'So am I. But are *you*?'

Malacanang is an excessively dismal place, or was when I last saw it. It was raining outside, not heavily, but with the slow persistent drizzle of northern Europe. Kit met me and seated me in the anteroom of Marcos' office. 'I'll let you know when he's ready,' he said. I waited from five-thirty till dawn broke, and then continued to wait.

At roughly eleven, Romulo passed by, on his way to another meeting. I told him what had happened. He said, 'Come and have merienda.' This is the Filipino equivalent of elevenses, and can be a rather heavy meal, but I hadn't had breakfast. While I was stuffing down highly spiced chicken and rice cakes in another anteroom, he said, 'Go.' I looked at him in surprise. He said, 'Don't you see the President is trying to make a fool of you? You may wait all day without seeing him. If you do see him, it will be for five minutes. Cut your losses. Go. Remember, I am not responsible for what the President does.'

So I left the ornate and oppressive Spanish palace, and haven't been back since.

Our photographer in the Philippines, Dick Baldovino, accompanied me on a trip to Australia. This was supposed to be a sales tour. The Australian government was to sponsor our trip. We, in return, were to publish a supplement that ran with the magazine. My mission had two aspects. One was to fill the supplement with articles on various aspects of the country. The other was to obtain advertising to make the supplement worthwhile. In Asia, I was used to people who had already heard of the magazine. They helped its itinerant correspondents, and there was no trouble about advertisements.

Pandit had said that we were well-known in Australia, but this, like some of the other statements he had made in the past, proved to be an exaggeration. Nobody I met in Australia had ever heard of us. With John Havre, our man in the continent, and Baldovino, who was appallingly cheerful always, I trudged through butter factories, car factories, diamond mines, kangaroo farms, and so forth, all over the continent. By the time we had more or less finished the tour, we were in Sydney, with hardly an advertisement to our name.

John Havre said, 'I'm giving a lunch party for New South Wales business people. I'm going to leave hundreds of copies of the magazine around, and you're going to make a speech about the investment potential in Asia.' I replied that I knew nothing about this. 'You're a writer,' said Havre, a very pleasant man who was at that moment in despair. 'Just make it up.'

It occurred to me that Bob Simpson lived in Sydney. The lunch was on our last day, and, when I phoned him, he said he wasn't free for dinner. 'But I can come to this lunch of yours,' he said. 'After that we can go to the Cricketers' Club for a few drinks.' The pre-lunch drinks went very badly, and the businessmen assembled didn't pick up a single copy of the magazine. Neither did they display any interest in me.

Bob then turned up. The businessmen, until then engrossed in their own drinks and conversations, looked up as he came over to me. Their expressions showed disbelief, as though they had suddenly seen God. One by one they came over to where Bob and I were talking and asked for his autograph: 'My kids would like it.' Bob had not played Test cricket for four years; this seemed to show how indestructible legends are. Afterwards, some of the autograph hunters approached John Havre and inquired whether the magazine Editor was really a friend of Bob Simpson's. When John confirmed this, they all booked advertisement space in the supplement. We got more ads that afternoon than on the rest of the long trip.

I also took time off to meet Australian poets and writers, like Douglas Stewart and Geoffrey Lehmann. Why I did this I could not have said; for some years now I had told myself, like Rimbaud, that I 'was finished with all that rubbish'. But I enjoyed their company and talk. I realized that I had not met a poet for four years, except for Cirilo Bautista in the Philippines. I realized also that I had not been near Western civilization for some time:

one could hardly call Hong Kong and Singapore exemplars. I had rarely seen people in a hurry, going purposefully towards fixed appointments and tasks at fixed hours. This purpose, this movement towards objectives, did not really exist in Asia.

Japan was different, but only in some ways. Traffic roared down the Tokyo streets; the policemen who attempted to control it wore masks against the polluted air. Everything ran to time; arrangements were scrupulously made, and there was a work ethic. But this work ethic was barbarically overdone; to most Japanese men, their company was all. Their attitude towards their antlike labours was like that of workers in a totalitarian state, though the companies did not coerce them. Takeshi Takahara, our Japanese photographer, had this attitude, which set him apart from the rest of the photographic team. He was willing to carry on with his assignments night and day, while I wasn't.

The equality of women was an idea that seemed not yet to have reached Japan. Though I met politicians and visited many factories, I never saw a woman in a position of power. Takahara, and indeed other Japanese whom we met, treated me with deep respect, unflattering because it was so formalized. At lunch Takahara would order for me from menus written in Japanese, leaving Leela to fend for herself. When I asked him to help her, he would do so, but his manner was calculated to indicate that he was simply obeying orders. The best days we had in Japan were at a ryokan, a Japanese inn, in Kyoto. We occupied a suite, with tatami mats on the floor, and subtly lacquered furniture; there were painted scrolls on the walls, and the window opened on to a small private garden. In the garden was a stonewalled pool, inhabited by a solitary turtle. The turtle's movements seemed almost preplanned. At certain hours, when the sun was up, it perched on an artificial island in the pool, allowing light to flash on its wet carapace. At dusk and before dawn it stirred the water with its flippers, causing a pleasant sound of splashes.

Hiroshima had become a tourist centre, but even the name had associations. I interviewed a number of officials, and was told about the deformed children who were born yearly, and the adults still suffering from radiation effects. I met several of these people, and visited the hospital where radiation cases were kept: 'kept' not 'treated', because, as a doctor told me, 'What medicine can we give except morphine?' It seemed curious to me that the city contained one of Japan's more celebrated fish restaurants, and that a little way off across the sea was an island much visited by tourists, with remnants of a monastery on it. Here children laughed and played, and Leela bought a fisherman's straw hat. Life continued. Over the Peace Museum, white doves flew.

My monthly peregrinations took me to Taiwan, also with Takahara. Leela was fascinated by the great museums, stocked with what the Kuomintang had brought from the mainland when they fled from the Communists. 'This is China, the real China,' a high Taiwanese official told me. 'The mainland is not China.' Most people in the government seemed to believe this, or at least they said they did. 'This is a democracy,' one of them told me, 'American style.' But in Taiwan, more than anywhere else in Asia, I was sometimes aware that I was being watched. Since all my doings were innocuous, I didn't mind.

At that time, Taiwan was the centre for pirated books. New books from all over the world, "but particularly from America, were on sale in Taipei, the capital. Some of them appeared in the bookstores before they were officially published. 'It's highly organized,' an American friend told me. 'They have agents in America who get hold of the page proofs and fly them over. They're turned into books very quickly and cheaply. They're half the price of the official edition.' The bookshops of Taiwan were full of new English and American novels, biographies, volumes on science: every kind of book, in fact, except books of poetry. I had a great time there, spending my expense money at such a rate that

I was broke by the time we left. I wasn't the only one. Followers of modem literature from all over Asia, and sometimes further afield, used to fly to Taiwan to buy books. The piracy trade was an admirable method of building up the tourism industry.

I also applied for permission to visit the offshore islands of Quemoy and Matsu, part of Taiwan, lying in the shadow of the mainland. I was granted permission for Quemoy, and flew there in a military plane with an army captain to escort us. Takahara was with me. The government was unwilling to allow Leela, since it might be dangerous.

We came in to Quemoy low over wind-tossed water, to avoid the mainland radar, landed badly, and lost a wheel. This wasn't good for one's nerves; we spent the rest of the day examining the fortifications of the island, many of which were subterranean. As night fell, we were all fed an elaborate Taiwanese meal, and sent to a small bedroom which we were to share. The colonel who had hosted the meal provided each of us with a bottle of a clear, watery liquor. 'Mao Tai,' said Takahara knowledgeably. 'Strong like hell.' The captain from Taipei smacked his lips. 'Maybe we will need this,' he said.

He also informed us that there were specified days each week when the Taiwanese bombarded the mainland. The batteries on the mainland would bombard the island on other days. It was a strange, formal etiquette, said the captain. Almost as soon as he finished speaking, the bombardment from the mainland started. Shells whistled through the sky and loud crumps shook the room as they exploded. 'This is a bunker,' the captain explained, 'not to worry.' But runnels of sweat had appeared on his forehead, and he opened his bottle of Mao Tai. 'I said we would need this,' he said, presently, as the explosions came nearer, Takahara and I also resorted to our bottles. It really was very strong stuff, and it did not take very long for all three of us to fall asleep.

I only visited South Korea once. In Seoul I looked in vain for a politician, once interviewed by Patrick O'Donovan, called Lee

Bum Suk. Seoul was a pleasant city, and the people were very friendly. The information minister summoned me. He said that the government would be honoured if I toured the country at its expense. There was no political or military situation worth writing about, so I cast my scruples aside and agreed. The minister summoned a slim, pale, bespectacled young man. 'This,' said the minister in a disgusted voice, 'is Shim-II. He will go with you.' He opened a drawer in his desk, took out large wads of won, and handed them to Shim-II. 'These are for your expenses on the trip.' I said, 'I have my own expenses. A guide, a car, and an itinerary are all I need.' 'Do not be foolish,' the minister said. 'You keep your expenses, and tell your office you have spent them. Everyone needs money, not so?'

On this trip, for some reason I cannot remember, I had no photographer. Takahara was supposed to fly in from Tokyo later, and shoot whatever I had covered. Shim-II and I, therefore, were alone in the government car, except for the driver, who only spoke Korean. On the first day, Shim-II said to me in careful English, 'Please, sir, I have a request to make. It is a very embarrassing request.' He went on to explain that he was very poorly paid and had recently married. His wife was expecting a baby. He couldn't manage on his salary; he couldn't afford a flat; his wife and he lived with his in-laws. He had heard me say to the minister that I had expense money of my own, and wanted to spend it on this trip. 'So,' he concluded, 'will you spend your expense money as you wanted? That is, if you pay for your own expenses, much of what the minister entrusted to me will remain unspent. If I can keep it, it would solve my problems.'

He was too nervous to be dishonest. Besides that, to do what he suggested would do more than salve my conscience: I would be able to do him a good turn. The money I was about to surrender to him was, it was true, the government's. But the government had expressly asked me to spend it as I liked. I told Shim-II as much, and he seemed not only relieved but delighted, smiling rather tearfully at me. 'I was very much afraid, sir,' he said, 'that you would think badly of me after I had made my request.'

We then continued amicably with our tour. We went as far south as Pusan. As we approached the town, I saw an airfield to our left. To our right was the sea, over which a plane was coming in to land. The driver stopped. The plane landed on the road in front of us and continued bumpily into the airfield. Shim-II and the driver seemed unmoved. 'That is what the pilots always do,' Shim-II said. 'The car drivers know this.'

We had a very busy itinerary, and, when not on the road, I spent ten to twelve hours a day working. It was a very satisfactory trip; I developed an intense love of kimchi, the pickled cabbage which every Korean household makes, and the barebecued bulgogi. We visited a village called Yamdong, which was supposed to be as Korean villages were centuries ago. It was a discovery of Shim-II's, and unvisited by tourists. The people, as elsewhere, were kind and hospitable. The wooden houses were heated by ondols, from under the floor. The old men, with wispy moustaches and felt tophats, sat outside in the courtyards, where they played a form of chess. The old women were making kimchi in gigantic clay vessels. The village was mainly populated by elderly people, but there was a symmetry to their lives that was absent in Seoul, which aspired to be American.

We returned to the capital. Shim-II continued to be attached to me by the ministry. He took me to the university, where I interviewed several professors. Korean history is curious and complicated, so is the evolution of its written language. I visited the potteries beyond Seoul, which are part of the country's history. I went to the demilitarized zone between North and South Korea. At Panmunjom, bored American soldiers patrolled the walls, and spent their spare time in the bar. I talked to many of them. They agreed that Korean women were better upholstered than other Asian females, and prettier. I had a drink with a sergeant who was about to marry one. But the grey, bleak walls of the buildings and bunkers did not match the landscape around them. Dead wars had left many scars on the face of Asia. Beyond Panmunjom were the gaunt hills of another country.

Shim-II, like many other South Koreans, had relatives on the far side of the DMZ. Though he was a quiet boy, I knew, from our conversations, a great deal about his life. In Seoul, when we ate together, he would save titbits from the table, put them into a plastic container he always carried, and take them home to his pregnant wife. Towards the end of my stay, he developed what I considered a peculiar habit. He kept asking me what size Leela's bust was. I confessed I did not know. Shim-II then produced a set of photographs of nude Korean ladies, and inquired which one, in terms of bust size, was closest to my wife. It seemed important to him, so I pointed to a picture. He made a careful note on the back, and went off home. When I drove to the airport, a few days later, he came with me, a bulky package in his hands. 'Don't open it,' he said, 'until you meet your wife.' The package, when opened in Hong Kong, proved to contain one of the long, elaborate dresses worn by rich Korean ladies. It was in dark blue silk. A Korean friend to whom I showed it said it must have cost a lot.

'From what I can gather,' he said, 'this boy saved money on your expenses. Then you and he became friends. He may have felt guilty about making you spend money. So he spent the money he had saved on this robe.

'Koreans,' he added, 'have a sense of honour.'

The sort of work I was doing had its advantages. The Korean trip was an example of this. On every trip I made, I usually spent a great deal of my time talking to local people, and I came to see the country through them. Each trip was accounted for in terms of the articles I came back with. So I had to provide fillers as well as lead stories. Fillers had not only to take up space, but be interesting. The ones I wrote were often concerned with the food and costumes of a country, about colourful characters in its present and past, or places off the beaten track. I usually covered a country fairly thoroughly on my first visit, and, on subsequent trips, I was helped by the information I already possessed in the process of acquiring more. The result was that, after a series of visits to a country, I had picked up a large amount of knowledge about it, often about obscure aspects of the place. This knowledge, though by necessity ragged and incomplete, was something I was quite proud of. It came in useful later.

On my visit to Korea, the Korean minister of information had thrown a party for me in Seoul, in a kisaeng house. The kisaengs are the Korean equivalent of the geishas, as expensive and as respectable. Good kisaengs will not sleep with visitors, or at least they didn't then. Like the geishas, they played music, sang, and encouraged guests to eat and drink. The minister had not asked Shim-II to his party, which I thought a bit hard, but Shim-II said, 'How could I expect to be invited? It costs $2,000 a head!' The minister had, however, invited about a dozen cronies. When I reflected that the government would pay for them, the sleight-of-hand Shim-II and I had practised with the expenses seemed minuscule.

The dinner progressed through about thirty courses of Korean delicacies, including, at the end, Polo mints. The kisaengs giggled, fed the guests, and kept their cups filled. Some of them were furtively pawed, but they pushed intrusive hands away with no change of expression. Shim-II was shocked when I told him. 'A few years ago this would never have happened. The kisaengs are respectable women. You cannot dishonour them.' To judge from the behaviour of the minister's guests, this was a matter of opinion.

Japan and Korea both showed the American influence. The three countries had been bloodily and umbilically attached to one another by war. In peacetime, Japan and Korea had, to some extent, liberated themselves from the American influence, though it showed up in the Ginza bars and in Seoul and in attitudes towards life. The kisaengs were treated in an unKorean way by the minister's guests. Shim-II defined this as 'an *American* way'. But, behind all the surface changes in the lives of Japanese and Koreans, the traditional culture remained. This was hard to uproot in countries which had, for centuries, isolated themselves by choice from the rest of the world. So it had only partly been uprooted.

It was quite a different story, I found out, in Vietnam.

John Gale had been to Vietnam before I first went there. He hadn't liked it very much, and had not had time to travel to the war. When Pandit suggested I fly to Saigon, a friend, Terry Khoo, was in the office. He was posted in Saigon by the American Broadcasting Company (ABC), with whom he was a top cameraman. He had been there for a decade. He knew everything about the place and the war that was to be known. Terry laughed a good deal, but, behind his conviviality, much inner tension was visible. He had twice been captured by the Viet Cong and escaped. He was unwilling to talk about those parts of his life. Singapore was his birthplace, and he was very willing to talk about that, recalling past pleasures on its beaches. He told me to look him up in Saigon before I went to the front. 'For a new boy in Vietnam,' he said, 'a friend is necessary. You won't get anywhere there otherwise.'

I arrived at Tan Son Nhut, the Saigon airport, around noon a few days later. My first impressions of Vietnam were unfavourable. A loose, wild rain was falling; the runway had turned into a river. The airport was full of American soldiers and marines. Jeeps and military planes stood around bleakly in the downpour. Barbed wire surrounded the buildings, that were painted in camouflaged colours. There was an atmosphere of dinginess and sorrow about Tan Son Nhut; and when I got into the city this atmosphere strengthened.

I had been to Saigon before, in 1950. My father had then been on an investigative tour of South-east Asia, sent on it by Nehru. At that time Vietnam was known as French Indo-China; the Viet

Minh, named after Ho Chi Minh, were fighting the colonials. Then, as I remembered, the streets of Saigon had been full of French troops, including some from the Foreign Legion. One heard French spoken everywhere. But the war had never been far away. I was sitting in a restaurant with my father when a bomb exploded in the street outside; we were showered with shards of glass from the windows. Later, we went to Hanoi, now, in 1972, the capital of North Vietnam. I saw ruined sentry posts at regular intervals on the road to Haiphong. The Viet Minh, like their successors, the VC, were guerrilla fighters. They lay submerged in the flooded rice fields, breathing through bamboo tubes, till the sentries on the towers were off guard, or a convoy passed. Then they emerged from the water, and their guns breathed out death. That was the first war I was ever conscious of. I had been eleven. This was the first time I had been to the country for slightly more than twenty years.

I was booked into the Caravelle; from my room I called Terry Khoo. 'Go and get your accreditation card,' he said. 'I'll pick you up for dinner.' I went, as he had directed me, to a street photographer and collected six instant passport photographs, then walked over to MACV, the military headquarters, and filled in various forms. The building had obviously once looked rather imposing; now, like the rest of the city, it was shabby. But I was told to come back for my accreditation card the next day. I went and had a drink in the garden bar of a hotel. It was crowded with American civilians, and souvenir sellers hung around, some of them, I was later told, drug pushers. A gaunt Frenchman at the next table looked at the book I was reading, which was by Celine, and said, 'You are a correspondent?' I told him. 'Few correspondents read Celine,' he replied.

He exuded an air of faint corruption, as though the atmosphere of the city had rubbed off on him. 'You permit?' he inquired, coming over to my table as he spoke. I had wanted to be left in peace. He told me that he had come to Indo-China shortly after the Second World War, and had become successful in business. He had stayed on after his retirement. He liked it here, he said.

After a while, when he had talked his life to death, he said, 'I like it here. You know why? Because the Vietnamese have no money? And there is the war.' These seemed peculiar reasons for a businessman to like a country. 'So,' he hissed, 'many people flee to Saigon from the countryside, because their villages are destroyed. Here they have no money. They will do anything for money. Young girls, young boys. *Anything*.' He opened his briefcase and showed me some black-and-white photographs, which demonstrated what he meant by 'anything'. Beads of moisture now shone on his forehead and lips. 'One has to be very careful,' he continued. 'They are quite capable of stabbing one. But, as long as one is careful, ah—what delirious pleasure!' We were speaking in French, in which such a phrase does not sound as ridiculous as it might in other languages.

'Come to my house,' he said. 'I have a collection there. Young girls, yes, and boys.'

I got up and walked away, leaving him to pay the bill. That night, when Terry and his assistant Tony Hirashiki came to pick me up, I told them about this small encounter. 'There are plenty of perverts here,' Terry said, stroking his intelligent little beard. 'There always have been. You must realize that this country's been at war for many years. The Japanese, the French, the Americans. Where there's a war, these chaps crop up. You can satisfy any taste you have when people are homeless and foodless.' I was subsequently to meet many people who bore some resemblance to the elderly Frenchman.

Over a Vietnamese dinner, we talked of the war, or, at least, Terry and Tony Hirashiki did, and I, a novice, listened. 'Look,' said Terry, 'I've booked you on a flight to Danang day after tomorrow. The 197th Infantry is up there, making some sweeps in the valleys. You attach yourself to it; you'll get some stories for Pandit.

Then I suggest you go up into the central highlands. You'll find the montagnards there, very interesting people, tribesmen. They scout and fight for the Americans. As a result, they're better off than they ever were before. You should get to Kontum and Pleiku.'

He pointed at my shirt, which was white. 'Never wear white in the field. It makes you a target. Always wear a coloured shirt.' He stroked his beard and ordered more rice wine. I was deeply involved in this conversation, not only because it had to do with my future welfare, but because a part of me had withdrawn and become a watcher. So many of my conversations in the past had been with other people over a drink, but then we had been talking of literature, an abstract reality. This conversation reflected a concrete reality which I was soon to face. The literary chatter of the past seemed ludicrous in this sober context. Tony Hirashiki said, 'If you get cut off and run into the VC, shout *"Bao chi"* as loud as you can, and put your arms up. *"Bao chi"* means press. If they hear you, they probably won't shoot. I'm saying *probably*.'

'What if they don't hear me? Or if I say it with the wrong accent?'

'Then,' laughed Terry, 'I'll be sending Leela flowers.' He had met her in Hong Kong, and assured her that reporting in Vietnam was as safe as driving a car. 'If anything happens, I'll phone you,' he told her. 'Otherwise I won't. No news is good news.' I did not know, when we dined in Saigon, that Terry had plans. The day after I left for Danang, he phoned Leela in Hong Kong. She was at the television station, waiting to go into the studio, when the operator told her that Mr Khoo from Saigon was on the line. She took the call, and Terry said, 'I'm very sorry to tell you—' and then paused. Leela waited, rather nervous, till he continued, '—that your husband is alive and well.' This particular brand of black humour was common to all those who had spent some years in Vietnam. What made this story so pathetic, and significant, was what was later to happen to Terry. But none of us at the table knew it then, and we laughed together.

Dinner over, we turned into the street outside. Huge rats scuttled away at our footfalls. A mob of urchins followed them. 'That's another thing,' Terry said. 'Never go out at night in this city alone. Those kids are starved, and they'll attack you, even in well-lit streets. They're desperate, and a gang of them can pull down a grown man—even a trained soldier, if he's drunk or stoned.' He was suddenly solicitous. 'Buy some boots. They'll be better than shoes up north.' He gave me the address of a shop.

I went to bed that night and dreamt of Leela, huge rats, and malevolent children, and was awakened towards dawn by echoing explosions from round the city's perimeters.

Next day I acquired my accreditation card. It was raining, and I took shelter in the Caravelle bar. Examining my card, I found that I had been appointed a colonel in the American armed forces. 'That's so they'll treat you according to your rank, if they capture you,' said another correspondent. 'Silly. With the VC, the higher your rank, the worse it is for you.'

14

What I remember about Vietnam is not so much the action I saw as the dreariness of it all. It had been a beautiful country, but it had also been depopulated and deforested; scabbed with napalm, stained with cordite, it lived on in a new incarnation, goddess of boredom and of war. The American troops knew that every Vietnamese, however subservient or cooperative he or she might seem, hated them at heart. The troops at safe bases were bored; the troops in the field were afraid. They were fighting an almost invisible enemy, not something they had been trained for; the people they were fighting were in their own country and had a cause. The Americans had none. The oppressive heat of summer, the torrential rains, the mosquitoes and flies, debilitated them as much as the VC or the North Vietnamese Army. Many American soldiers became drug users.

This was not strange. The soldiers in the field only saw the underbellies of the cities, the brothels, the bars, the drug peddlers. Some, particularly the blacks, drafted from the ghettoes, were familiar with the atmosphere of amorality and actual evil that they entered into when they came into a city. Some were not; these were the college boys, the Archies of the army. But they threw away their memories of milk shakes and rose-petal girls and plunged into their private abysses in Vietnam.

I once visited an army hospital for drug addicts. It was

surrounded by barbed wire emplacements and sentry posts. A sympathetic, but harassed, doctor told me it was to keep the Vietnamese drug sellers away. 'If they get up close,' he said, 'the patients throw whatever valuables they have to them, and they throw back packets of heroin.' The camp consisted of a number of concrete edifices apparently put up at random. Behind the main offices was a cell block. From it rose cries and ululations of pain. 'They're coming off without medical help,' the doctor said. 'We don't have heroin substitutes, like methadone. So it has to be that way.' He did not seem to like the idea at all.

Inside the cells were the addicts. Some were curled up on their camp beds, occasionally moaning. Others expressed their physical and mental suffering more loudly. A big black with red and teary eyes rattled the bars of his cell. 'Lemme out of heah,' he shouted, 'lemme out,' sometimes in tones of rage and panic, sometimes in supplication. The final degradation was to be on display to visitors, as if in a zoo. The cell block smelt like a zoo. 'We keep them in here for five days,' the doctor said. 'Then they go into therapy classes. Then they go back to their units and usually start up again. The ones who come here are usually gone cases. It's not the right treatment, but…'

As his voice trailed away, he clenched his fist and slammed it intc the concrete wall. The big black was doing exactly the same thing at the same moment. 'Oh Jesus,' said the doctor, as though to himself, 'I wish I was back stateside!'

The therapy centre, in which a few dazed-looking young soldiers sat at a trestle table reading, was decorated with drawings and paintings done by the patients. All of them were done in angry colours, and some depicted grotesque shapes, which bore no relation to reality. 'We give them a choice of colours,' the doctor said. 'All of them pick red and black; and sometimes yellow, for the sun. They weren't painted by normal people. Wouldn't you say that? I think, sometimes, I should make a collection of them and ship them back stateside, maybe have an exhibition. If people saw what was in these men's heads, I think they'd all realize that this war has to stop.'

In one army camp I stayed in, I encountered a man called Sergeant Blue. He was fat, with crewcut white hair and the face of a boxer, and had postponed his retirement too long. He seemed to be in charge of the PX, the military kitchen. A great affability pervaded all his dealings with correspondents; I have seldom met anyone with a more intense desire for publicity. This was curious in itself; for the things he did needed to be discreetly veiled rather than bruited abroad. He bartered food and cigarettes from the PX to the Vietnamese, who often paid him in uncut precious stones. He showed them to me. Sergeant Blue had been in Vietnam for some time, but had successfully evaded combat duty for most of it. He had shares in a bar in Saigon and another in Danang. 'They're really cat houses, you know what I mean? I'll give you the addresses. Go and tell them you know me, and it'll all be on the house.' He had other intricate dealings with the Saigon underworld. Since these were the only aspects of his life he didn't want bared to public scrutiny, they were probably really sinister. I strongly suspected that the addicts in the camp were supplied by him. Photographs, which he frequently produced from his wallet, offered me views of a California-style ranch house he had built in Hawaii, and a blue-haired wife. 'We don't have kids,' he told me. 'What's the sense of bringing kids up in a world that is evil and corrupt? Me and my wife agreed on that from the start.'

In the course of my peregrinations through Vietnam, I met a number of senior army officers. Most of them seemed oblivious of what the men under them suffered. They themselves usually lived well, and drank hard. The middle class of the army was sometimes admirable, but I discovered a few replicas of Sergeant Blue. As for the other ranks, few of them were happy. Each had the riddle of Vietnam to solve, and few were capable of it. The blacks were particularly embittered. I witnessed the sweep of a valley by an infantry company, when they were sent in ahead of the white troops. One black soldier talked to me before the sweep started. 'You know Harlem?' he asked. 'Well, I'm goin' to be way out in that fuckin' valley ahead of whitey today, and I guess I'm not goin' to see Harlem no more.' I do not know what happened to him, but there were several black casualties that day.

The colour differences between the troops were emphasized not so much by the whites as by the blacks themselves. Even Sergeant Blue, who didn't seem to dislike blacks, said, in tones of wonder, 'They're so fucking *unfriendly!*' This was an opinion shared by many white soldiers I talked to. *'They* make you conscious of colour prejudice,' one said. All this had to do with something that had happened in America, rather than anything that had happened in Vietnam. Other correspondents disagreed with me, and said I must have met the wrong people. But the blacks were more apt to communicate with me than with my colleagues, because of my colour. They tended to unburden themselves to me.

On one occasion, I had to take military transport to Saigon from Danang. The airport was packed with soldiers, more than a thousand of them, sitting or lying on the floor of the big hall, or standing up, looking very tired. I got a serial number from the desk, and found a place on the floor, back to the wall, between a black corporal and a white one. The white corporal asked me what my number was. When I told him, he said, 'Christ. You're gonna be here for the next twenty-four hours.' As it turned out, it was nearer to thirty-six.

The white soldier turned away to his companions. The black one slouched loosely on the floor on the other side of me, and appeared to be isleep. Presently he stirred, fumbled in his haversack, and produced a bottle of whisky. He drank from it, then wiped the neck on his sleeve and wordlessly offered it to me. I thanked him and accepted. The bottle passed back and forth between us, in utter silence. After about an hour the loudspeaker called a new list of numbers, one of which was his. He rose, but before walking out to the transport plane, said his first words. 'In Vietnam,' he said, 'you gotta learn to wait.' He gave me the remnants of the whisky, said, 'luck,' and went.

All these troops were going on R-and-R, to Bangkok mostly; some were going home. The long hours I spent in the departure hall are now a blur in my memory, but at some point I found myself sitting in a circle of soldiers who had come out of the combat zone the week before. One was very young, and had a small puppy in his haversack. The others, who had a strangely paternal attitude towards the boy, urged him to get rid of it.

'It's no use, kid,' said one. 'It's no fucking *use.* They won't let you take that dog stateside. They'll take it away and kill it. C'mon, kid, carry it out and dump it somewheres. C'mon, kid, dump it.' The boy said, 'Where would I dump it? It's mine.' He told me, 'I found it in a village, nobody to take care of it. These fucking gooks don't understand fucking animals. Wouldn't you say I oughta keep it? It *depends* on me.'

I said that I knew nothing about the American army's attitude towards pets, but it would seem best to leave the pup behind. He looked stricken. His comrades said, 'Listen to what the man says. Leave it behind.' The boy put his hand on the puppy's back. He said defiantly, 'Fuck leave it behind. I got two dogs at home. He'll be company for them. He's gonna have a good life. He's gonna be a fucking American dog.'

But they persisted. Finally another transport came noisily in, and the numbers were called. My companions were lucky; they rose to leave, shrugging their heavy equipment on. As they went out on the tarmac, one of them took the puppy from the boy's haversack and put it gently down. Two others seized the boy's arms and marched him towards the plane. He kept looking back. The puppy scuttered uncertainly after him, then stopped and began to wail, the small noise drowned by the thunder of engines and the shouts of men. In the distance the boy, propelled by his friends to the boarding ramp, ceased to look back. Occasionally, in the hours that followed, I caught glimpses of the puppy, disconsolately scurrying this way and that across the airfield, in the persistent rain.

In Hong Kong, the atmosphere was troubled. Tom Dozier had a row with Pandit and resigned. John Gale told me that, with the end of his contract approaching, he intended to return to London. 'Those were an interesting two years,' he said. 'But this is a bit of a backwater really, isn't it? I mean, for one's career, and shit like that?' He bellowed with laughter. John and I had not had much contact with each other after the first weeks of settling down, though the Gales—his wife and children had come out too—lived immediately above us. This was because we alternated our travel. But I had grown to like John very much. His apparent buoyancy, his loud conversation and laughter, were masks. Everyone needs to wear a mask, and John's concealed an extremely delicate sensibility, and an ability to be hurt.

In his place came John Koffend. He was American, and had recently published a book called *Letter to My Wife*, which was written when they were about to be divorced. John was a slim, elegant man with curly white hair and an amiably equine face, deeply lined. Since his divorce, he had settled in Samoa, which he talked of with affection. He intended to spend two years in Hong Kong, then return to his beachcomber's life. The departures of the Doziers and the Gales had a sharp effect on me. I was grateful to Pandit for offering me the opportunity to work in Asia; but Pandit was not an easy man to work with. The euphoria that had pervaded the first days in Hong Kong had completely disappeared. My trips had become routine, and now lacked the excitement of discovery. Also, what John had said about Hong Kong stayed in my mind. It was, in fact, a backwater. Journalists usually came over from England, America, and, in particular, Australia, because they could find no employment in their own countries. There were, of course, exceptions, like the old China hands: Richard Hughes of the *Sunday Times*, large, rubicund, and white-haired, usually to be found in the Press Club bar, and Frank Robertson of the *Daily Telegraph*. I first met Frank on a train which was taking the press up to the Shum Chun border with China. We were supposed to meet the American table tennis players who had breached the bamboo curtain and played in Peking. This opened the way for Nixon himself to play what was later to be called 'ping-pong diplomacy'.

The ping-pong players turned out, predictably, to be wordless. But on the way back, Robertson and I fell into conversation. He had been in Hong Kong for much of his life, and, like Hughes, had known mainland China well. He had a house on the Peak. His wife was a painter. They had a loyal Chinese couple, who had served them for years, to look after them and the house. Robertson had paid for the education of the couple's son. He was happy in Hong Kong; but the *Telegraph* now wanted to close down its bureau, and the Robertsons had been posted back to London. Frank dreaded this more than death.

'It will be like death,' he said. 'There'll be nothing for me there. I don't *know* anything about England. That bloody weather and the rest of the desk boys thinking of me as a has-been...that'll be all.' He therefore wanted to come into the *Asia Magazine*, which would at least enable him to stay on in the colony. I spoke to Tom, who spoke to Pandit. It was over this issue that Tom eventually resigned. As for Frank, the day of departure came closer, and it became clear to him that he had to leave.

There was one final wound fate had in store for him. When the Robertsons boarded their ship, their faithful Chinese servants, who had unaccountably disappeared for the last couple of days, reappeared with a lawyer. They said that Frank could not leave Hong Kong without settling a large sum of money on them. We had a farewell drink with the Robertsons in their cabin, and Frank broke down and wept. It wasn't the whisky that did it, but he was heartsick over the betrayal.

Ah Mui was a perfect combination of servant and friend. I had got her younger brother, Benny, a position as an office boy at the magazine. Their mother and Leela exchanged presents. We never had any problems with Ah Mui; but it was not that aspect of the Robertsons' departure that worried me. I had a letter from Frank: he said that he neither understood nor liked the Britain he had returned to, and his worst fears had been confirmed as to his position in the office. He *was* looked upon as a has-been. He was given no work that interested him. He was lonely. It struck me that unless I amended my own situation soon, I might face the same problems as he did.

Meanwhile, Pandit sent me to the one place in South-east Asia I had not covered for the magazine. Indonesia was further off from Hong Kong than any other South-east Asian country, and since Ted Gowing's expensive fiasco there, nobody had visited it. I took the photographer Frank Fischbeck with me. Fischbeck had lived in Hong Kong for years. He was a good, tough professional; *Life* had sent him into China in the wake of the table tennis players, and he had taken the first photographs of China by a Westerner for many years. His appointment for this trip, however, caused great wrath among the staff photographers, who sent me a memo and threatened to resign. I passed this on to Pandit, who had seldom so far accepted suggestions from any of his editors.

Indonesia, like several other countries on my beat, held some memories. It was one of the places I had visited in childhood with my parents. When we landed at Jakarta, I was horrified to discover that it was Ramazan, the period when all Muslims fast. It would not be possible to interview President Suharto, or indeed anyone, until it was over. I hired a young man who had a connection with a local paper, to get us small stories. I particularly remember one of these, which had to do with the oldest taxi in

Asia. It was a 1902 Lincoln, and its driver was much older than his vehicle, which he had acquired in 1907. He still plied for hire in it. The morning we visited him and the taxi, both had been polished and spruced up for the camera, but the vehicle bore the unmistakable marks of extreme decrepitude. All the seats in the car had been removed, and cane chairs substituted for them. A burst and stained mattress served as the roof. The driver pointed to it and said with difficulty (for he had no teeth) that we would never guess how many babies had been born on the mattress as he drove their mothers to the hospital. *Dozens,* he told us. Bits of the machine were tied on to the body with string, and the tyres were worn smooth. Fischbeck dealt the bonnet a sharp rap with his fist, and, in a slow and synchronized movement, all the four mudguards fell off.

When we left, Fischbeck said ruminatively, 'D'you think, if I'd given the driver a tap, his arms and legs would have fallen off?' He specialized in black humour. He was South African, an athletic Aryan with golden hair and pale blue eyes. He had gone from South Africa to England, and finally wound up in Hong Kong. Apart from his photography, he had an import-export business, and a shop high up on the Peak. As a photographer he was excellent, if not imaginative, and he was absolutely fearless, as I was later to find out.

We had both become rather frustrated with the days of inanition, but there was a large press corps in Jakarta, and they were very helpful. Frank Hawkins, of the Associated Press, one day said, 'Instead of farting around here, why don't you try and get to Buru?' Then he explained what Buru was; I had at first thought he was talking of some influential politician.

In 1965, seven years before our visit, General Suharto came to power following a military coup. Sukarno, whom my father had interviewed (and I had briefly met in 1949), was ousted. A round-up was made of all those suspected of Communist affinities and sympathies. They had been docketed as A-, B-, and C-class prisoners. The A-class had usually been incarcerated in Java, and the Cs executed. The Bs, however, had been despatched to prison camps hastily set up on remote islands, where they had been kept ever since without trial or any hope of it. 'Pramudya Ananta Toer, who's supposed to be the greatest living Indonesian writer,' Hawkins said, 'is supposed to be there, and so are a lot of other intellectuals. Suprapto, who used to be the Attorney General, is supposed to be there too. But nobody really knows. There's been nothing heard from them.'

Buru, like the other prison camps, was under a commandant. The commandant changed every so often, since this was a post of extreme hardship, and a new one would be on his way to Buru in the next few days. The Indonesians, who had previously refused to allow any members of the press on the island, had now agreed that six correspondents could travel with the new commandant. They had flatly refused the *Tass* man, and made the price for the round trip so high that most newspapers and agencies, including AP, would not consider it. 'It's not only the prices,' Hawkins explained, 'but the amount of bribery involved.'

It was a very big story. The cost would be immense, but there were two arguments which would predispose Pandit towards paying it. One was that so many other people had said it was too expensive for them. He might very well accept the cost, because the *Asia Magazine* would then prove it could spend more on a story than its Western counterparts. The other argument was that I had been awarded the Citation for Excellence by the Overseas Press Club of America for my *New York Times* pieces on India. Pandit had been much impressed by this, and the suggestion that I—and therefore the magazine—might win some further award for this kind of story would weigh heavily with him.

But something else Hawkins had said was on my mind, and, before telephoning Pandit, I took Fischbeck into my confidence and we sat down together with a map of Indonesia.

In my childhood I had possessed a book in which there were coloured sketches of primitive tribes. The picture which had most impressed me was one of a New Guinea aboriginal, with his face painted for war in red, white, and yellow stripes, and the brilliant feathers of murdered birds of paradise sprouting from his kinky hair. He had an axe in one hand, and a long spear in the other. Not much was known about him, the book said. I looked at the picture often, and intensely wanted to know move about him.

Hawkins had told me, 'Most people don't know that half of New Guinea is Indonesian. They took West Irian from the Dutch a while after the rest of the country. West Irian's not that far from Ambon. You have to fly to Ambon to reach Buru. You'll come back to Ambon from Buru, and then from Ambon to Port Biak, which is towards Australia. From there, pal, you fly to Djayapura, which is the only town in West Irian. After that, it's up to you. It's only a trip of about 15,000 miles altogether. Maybe 300 miles inland from Djayapura, you'll find the cannibals. The Yali and Dani tribes are still in the Grand Valley of the Baliem.' He laughed. He had been there.

Hence the poring over maps in the Hotel Indonesia. I was very close to the coloured picture of my childhood, I could almost recall how the page that contained it smelt, and I was determined to reach New Guinea. Ambon, I saw, lay on the Banda Sea, with Buru, or Boroe, as the map had it, slightly to the west. South-east from Ambon was New Guinea, and a little beyond it Australia. No established airline flew to these parts of the world from anywhere; my information about precise distances, modes of transport and prices, would have to depend on the Indonesian authorities. Ramazan was now almost over, and I was able to get hold of the proper people for information.

Next day I called Pandit. When I told him, rather nervously, what the distances involved, the time factor, and, last of all, what the costs were his scream down the line was audible to Fischbeck, who was lolling in a chair cleaning his cameras. 'These are the biggest stories the magazine has ever handled,' I said. 'I'll bet my life on them,' Pandit didn't seem as convinced as I was. 'It's a huge sum,' he said, and, then, to my immense surprise, added, 'Pledge your faith as a journalist that these stories are worth it, and I will consent.' To require such pledges in this way seemed preposterous. However, I said, 'Yes, yes, I pledge my faith.' Pandit replied, 'And Fischbeck, does he too pledge his faith?' Frank put down his cameras. He ambled over to the phone and said, 'Yeah, Pandit, I heard all that. You talk loudly, don't you? Well, anyway, I'll do my best, and I think Dom will too.' This seemed to satisfy Pandit. 'You are good men,' he said, not meaning our moral characters, 'and I will trust you.' Shortly after this, alone in my room, I received a call from him, saying, 'Control Fischbeck's spending. He is extravagant. But I trust you.' An hour later, Frank called me to say, 'I've had a call from the great panjandrum, telling me to control your spending. He says you're very extravagant, but he trusts me.' I said that was splendid.

Next day the money arrived, and, by means of bribery, in part, and also by paying the vast sums the Indonesian government required, we arranged our trip. A couple of days later we met our travelling companions at the military airport. Errol Holmes of Australian broadcasting, and Pieter Schumaker, a Dutch freelancer, were coming to Buru too. Errol was a quiet, cleanshaven man; Schumaker was tall, gaunt, and bearded, but also calm in manner, with a dry sense of humour. We made ourselves known to each other on a grim, warm dawn. Then the commandant and his henchmen arrived, and we all got into a tiny transport and flew off to the south-west, the rising sun behind us. It was a long flight. I decided to acquaint myself with the commandant, who was squat and porcine, and Schumaker acted as a kind of interpreter. His Dutch, obviously, was fluent, but his Indonesian wasn't. The commandant's Indonesian was fine, but his Dutch flawed.

However, we accomplished a small coup of our own. Schumaker had some gin, we had some whisky. Each of us made the commandant an offering, which he accepted. He drank a mixture of the two, and, towards the middle of the flight, fell fast asleep while vowing that we would have a free hand on Buru. 'He von't say that vhen he vakes up,' Schumaker said wryly. 'He vill have vun hell of a hangover.' Still, it was a start.

The other officers had been drinking, playing dice or cards, or snoring. Beneath us lay a turquoise sea, the water so clear that one could see the coral reefs and rocks below, and even the lazy flicker of large fish as they moved through their element. We were flying low, but suddenly came out of cloud over Ambon. The whale-backed hills under us were thickly forested, and mist seemed to steam up from them, as from some prehistoric swamp. This proved to be cloud, and we landed at a primitive airstrip, where jeeps waited. Ambon, Schumaker said, was famous for a fort left by the Dutch, but we saw only trees, flowering vines, and streams, till the jeeps reached a camp.

There were some barracks, in which we all slept. It rained heavily. Schumaker, Fischbeck, and I sat in the balcony, drinking whisky. Errol had wisely retired. The officers were further up the balcony still playing their endless card game, and also drinking. Presently, one of them staggered up to us, carrying a quarter-full bottle of schnapps, with a small discoloured object bobbing about in the remnants of the liquor. Without saying a word, he seized our bottle of whisky, filled his bottle from it, and staggered off. Schumaker held Frank back: he had wanted to remonstrate.

'Remember, ve must live vith these fellows,' he said. 'They are mad, bad men. Buru is very near, also.' He laughed heartily. 'Ve don't vant to find ourselves locked up in it. Vot vould happen to our stories?' I was curious about the officer's bottle.

'There was something in it,' I told Schumaker.

'Ah, yes, I saw,' Schumaker said. 'It is a human baby foetus. They mix it into the liquor they drink, to give them virility.'

Early next day, the jeeps took us to the harbour, where a kind of landing craft was anchored. The whole of Ambon was drenched, the trees and vines dripped, the muddy streams were in spate. But a huge sun came up, and the earth started to steam. The landing craft set off under a cloudless sky, over smooth seas. Presently we saw a great hump of land, with hairy forests on its flanks, ahead of us. 'They say Buru is larger than Bali,' Errol said. The landing craft put in at a pier where there was a reception committee, waiting for the new commandant. We left the sea behind us and walked some distance through the forest to an assembly of small buildings: the main command post on Buru. Soldiers stood simply to attention in a central square. A tattered Indonesian flag hung, slack in its tethers, overhead. While the commandant inspected the guard of honour, we were taken to a room for coffee, rice, and a briefing in English.

The English, as spoken by the officer who briefed us, left great gaps of information open, but we understood that there were fourteen camps on the island, and some ten thousand B-class prisoners distributed among them. 'Some may be dead now,' the officer said. 'Check up later. Dese men no escape. In sea, many big fish. How to escape?' He answered himself, 'Is better be dead.' We could extricate no further concrete information from him, except in regard to our programme. There were no roads inland. But the commandant would be walking round the island, inspecting some of the camps. We were to accompany him. I asked about the writer Pramudya. 'He here,' said the briefing officer. 'He in Camp 14, on top of mountain.' He pointed to the hump in the distant centre of the island. I realized that it was an extinct volcano. 'Camp 14 for very bad men. Very dangerous men. Very hard camp.' The officer picked up a cane and struck the desk in front of him several times. This was what happened to the prisoners in Camp 14. 'Leave soon,' he said. 'You want wash face, you want shit?'

The officials in Jakarta had gone to great pains to tell us how beautiful Buru was, how happy the prisoners were, and, how soon, after they had been cured of Communism, they would be released. The camp officers didn't seem to know exactly who we were. But, since we had come with the commandant, they felt that we needed to be told what he was being told: that is, how firm, even brutal, they were in their treatment of their prisoners, and how sternly they enforced discipline. Later someone asked all of us who had been on Buru about this. Did we not think, they asked, that the soldiers we met had exaggerated their own brutality, because they thought that that was what we wanted to hear, and thought we would commend them to the commandant for it? That may be so, but, from all that I saw or heard on the island, they can only have exaggerated their brutality a little.

We started from the main camp on foot, the commandant in front with the officers. We trailed along behind him and a number of soldiers followed us. Gravelled footpaths had been laid down between the fields where prisoners were at labour. They wore grimy vests and trousers, and some the big conical straw hats of Indonesian peasants. The guards had received no clear orders about us; we were able to go over to some of the men and try and talk to them. Most couldn't speak English, but we struck lucky with a thin person called Barzuki Effendi. He not only spoke English but was a film director. One of his films, he said, had won an award at Cannes. 'You are only able to eat what you grow yourself,' he said. 'That is very hard on the older men.' He was digging up potatoes. 'It is hard on everyone,' he said. 'Hardest on the small boys.' We had not heard of any small boys on Buru, and we asked for further information.

Barzuki said, 'They arrested many people when there were protest rallies in Jakarta and other towns. Small boys used to run after the marchers, and they were arrested with the rest. Some were sent here. They must have been five or six years old then. Now they will be seven years older. Many prisoners and guards use them for sex. They are mostly illiterate. Their parents must think they are dead, since they cannot write letters. But even we, who can write, we don't know if the letters are delivered. We receive no replies. It is, you know...agony. After a while you get resigned. At first they used to beat us. Not so much now. Yes, Pramudya is here. But he is up on the mountain, far from this place.'

We began to see the boys of whom Barzuki had spoken. They were now in early adolescence, pitifully thin, and, like everyone else, sun-stained and sad. We could not talk to them. Pieter tried out his Indonesian without much success. Several of the prisoners we met had eye diseases, and sores, both the result of inadequate diets.

A thatched construction stood off the road. It was an infirmary. Inside there were camp cots, on one of which a patient lay. He had malaria, the attendant said, when we asked through our briefing officer. There was no doctor, but he was being given quinine. That seemed to be all that was available. 'Malaria very bad,' the officer said. 'Very much malaria.' It struck me that the patient looked rather plump for a prisoner. When I asked, the attendant's reply was translated. The man was not a prisoner, but a camp guard. This place was not for prisoners. They were treated in their own camps.

'Some prisoners is doctors,' said the officer helpfully. '*Real* doctors.'

The sun was high. Sweat flowed down our faces and bodies. Clouds of midges and flies collected round our heads, and when brushed away returned within seconds. The prisoners in the fields were similarly affected, but one assumed, as Errol said, they were used to it. I talked to the commandant about Pramudya. Were we going to Camp 14? The briefing officer translated. We weren't going to Camp 14. It was a very hard climb to the camp. But the commandant would send orders ahead, for Pramudya to be brought down from the mountain, and with him Dr Suprapto, the former Attorney General.

A runner set off ahead of us, and we laboured on. Overhead the sky filmed over with clouds, which shortly melted into cascades of rain. The prisoners continued to work and we to walk. Late in the afternoon the rain stopped, and we were shrouded in wet heat. At roughly the same moment Schumaker and I said to each other, 'I am going to fall down and die,' we reached a thatched hut with a glutinous brown river oozing past it. There was dense tropical forest all around, exuding strange scents and the cries of monkeys and parakeets. Inside the hut there was a field kitchen, which dispensed rice, curried chicken and fish, and fresh coconut water. The decapitated coconut shells, thrown from the hut by the officers, heaped themselves up outside.

At about the time we finished this bizarre meal, that a clanking of chains announced that Pramudya and Suprapto had arrived. They were fettered and escorted by armed guards. It seemed a bit excessive; both were slightly built and small; both were dressed in good clothes that did not fit them, and Pramudya also wore spectacles and a black cap without a peak. They were taken into an adjacent tent. 'Dey come down mountain,' said the briefing officer happily, 'specially you to see.' We entered the tent, which was immediately surrounded by guards and soldiers. The commandant came in with us, and sat down on a chair, squinting at his prize prisoners.

He then said a number of things in Indonesian, which were meant to be orders. When he had finished, I said to the briefing officer, 'Mr Fischbeck wants to take pictures of all of you.' Meanwhile Errol set up the tape recorders all of us carried, and Pieter said urgently to the prisoners, 'Do you speak English?' They nodded. This was a prearranged plan. The commandant, after a long period in which he got his muddied boots cleaned and polished, went off with all the other officers to be photographed. The guards followed them, hoping to be included in the picture. We said to Pramudya and Suprapto, 'If you have any messages for your family, or anyone else in Jakarta, speak now.' They began to speak, in Javanese, after giving me the addresses of the people they were speaking to.

They were by then, a little relaxed. Frank was prolonging the photographic session outside as much as was humanly possible. Pramudya said, 'We are not well-treated here. We cannot eat anything, except rice, which we do not grow with our own labour. Dr Suprapto and I...are not used to this, but we have managed. The other prisoners have been kind.' Suprapto said, in punctilious, slow English, which for seven years he had had no occasion to use, ' It is the lack of knowledge of our families.... We write letters, we receive no answers.... We do not know if the letters have ever been sent. If I could speak to my wife, I would say remarry.... I have said this on your tape. We shall never leave this island alive.' Pramudya said, 'They used to beat us, now they don't. It is that we are dehumanized. I no longer feel like a man. And I am a writer. My whole life is writing. And here I have no materials to write. I want to write my memoirs.'

Frank could not continue his delaying operation indefinitely. The commandant came back into the tent, followed by the briefing officer and a variety of lieutenants and captains. 'You no miss something,' asked the briefing officer, 'because I not here?' We said we hadn't. But, I added, to the commandant, 'Why don't you allow Mr Pramudya writing materials?' The commandant quizzed the briefing officer, who said to us, 'He can have enough paper, many paper.' He then guffawed heartily, and translated to the commandant, who slapped his thigh and roared with mirth. 'As many paper he wants, he can have, but pens is dangerous weapon! Paper he can have, but no pens!' All the officers and soldiers in the tent were falling about. Frank suggested to the commandant that the sun was coming back. The officers and he should pose for more photographs.

They all went out. Errol, Pieter, and I thrust our spare notebooks and ballpoints into Pramudya's hands. His pockets weren't large enough to hold them. He clutched them to his breast. The briefing officer came back and issued orders. The soldiers began to fasten the chains back on the prisoners. The briefing officer said, 'You come now.' We followed him to the riverside. Looking back, I saw Pramudya and Suprapto being led away in chains. A number of guards surrounded them. Pramudya's long fingers were spread as though he was trying to protect a bird. The guards were busy breaking ballpoints in their hands and stamping notebooks into the mud. 'We know,' said the briefing officer, 'we *know*. Tonight you give me tapes. *All* tapes. Good, okay; is okay.'

We evaded that by supplying the commandant with a good deal of liquor instead. Then we returned to Ambon. We were now coming, for some reason, from the other side of Buru, which involved a long trip by night, during which a great storm exploded over us. The vessel was a troop transport, carrying the former garrison of Buru back by slow stages to Jakarta. The soldiers lay on the unprotected deck, lashed by rain from above, while tall waves burst on the poop and washed back over them. Since we were amongst them, we didn't waste our pity. The storm subsided before dawn, and I stood damply by the rail, looking down across the clear turquoise water to heavily forested islands. Flying fish raced the ship across the water.

Schumaker and Holmes went back from Ambon. Frank and I waited for the flight that would take us to Port Biak; from there another flight would take us to Djayapura, the only town in West Irian. Both of us had the tense satisfaction that follows the completion of a good story. It was not the same as that pleasure that follows the completion of a good poem, but I told myself firmly, that was part of my past. Behind my new mask, my new identity as an adventurous press correspondent, I was content to hide.

The two days we had to wait at Ambon were worthwhile, in the sense that they enabled us both to rest. Frank suffered from migraine, and he had it in Ambon; it seemed a good idea, in a way, since the attacks only recurred at intervals, and it might be as well to get them over with before the New Guinea trip.

Meanwhile, with a young Ambonese guide, we went round the place, so far as was possible. There were Dutch ruins there and inscribed tombstones one came on suddenly amidst ferns and ragged wildflowers. Streams fell unexpectedly down stone slopes; the forest presided over everything. We stayed at a small guest house, which seemed to be the only place available apart from the barracks. The Ambonese guide took me into the small town nearby. In the market, remembering the various things Frank Hawkins had told me in Jakarta, I bought steel knives and axes, presents for the Stone Age people we were shortly to meet, and I also laid in a stock of whisky, which Hawkins said would be appreciated by everyone.

It was usually sunny until the afternoon; then came the warm rain, and in its aftermath the whole island steamed as the heat came slowly back. I have not met many people in my life who have been to Ambon, and unless they find oil or minerals there, I cannot see many tourists visiting it. Therefore I drank it in, like stagnant wine, till the time came for our departure, on a very shaky little plane headed out over the Pacific.

It started, as I remember, late at night, and we reached Port Biak before dawn. This was not as heavily forested as Ambon, but the weather was the same. It was either very hot or very wet. Quite near the minuscule hotel was a cave full of the skeletons of Japanese killed during the Second World War. These troops had made their last stand in the cave. Buru and Biak had both oppressed me, like Vietnam; Ambon had been a two-day break, but I had no idea of what lay ahead in West Irian. I also missed Leela, and was unable to phone her, as I did from most places. In fact, since we left Jakarta, neither Frank nor I had had any contact with the outside world. I cabled Leela and the office from Biak, not very hopeful about the messages ever getting to their destinations.

15

As we waited at the airstrip for the plane that would take us to Djayapura, a thunderstorm broke. The plane, nevertheless, bucketed down through the deluge, and to our surprise was far from empty. It disgorged a large number of elderly white men, who came dripping into the concrete shack which constituted the terminal. They were Americans who had been stationed on Biak during the Second World War. 'I see the weather hasn't changed since 1944,' said the group leader. 'This is the first time we've been back and we're gonna make a party of it. You boys live here?' The question seemed, from what we had seen of Biak, almost an aspersion on one's character. We denied that we were residents of the place. 'Anyway,' said our new friend, 'have a drink with us.'

Cases of beer and hard liquor were carried in from the plane. We were the only passengers now, and the pilot seemed unwilling to forego the proposed party. One of the veterans complained that there was no ice. 'Shit,' said the leader, 'did we have any ice back in 1944?' They launched into separate stories about what Biak had been like: the flies and mosquitoes, the heat and unpredictable rain, the fighting, the cave in which the Japanese made their last stand. They inquired anxiously if the bones were still there. We said yes, and a lot of burnt-out US Army vehicles as well. They emitted whoops of delight. They were like characters from Norman Mailer's *The Naked and the Dead*, only thirty years older. The party went on till well past dark.

Nobody was expecting us in Djayapura, and after midnight it came on to rain. So we were agreeable when the pilot proposed that we fly at dawn. We had slight headaches when we landed at our destination on a muggy morning. Djayapura had a dishevelled look, as though some gigantic god had flicked a finger at a few white houses and they had landed in a small, random cluster by the sullen sea. There was a neat square populated by flowering trees (Djayapura had been founded by the Dutch, under the name of Hollandia), and a church. The church, Frank Hawkins had said in Jakarta, would be very important to us, since the priests knew all about the territory and ran mission stations where we could stay in the interior.

We checked in at the only rest house there was, primitive but with nets over the beds, to keep out insects and rats. Then we went to register with the army commander. I showed him the permits we had for the interior. He was fat and sweaty, like the commandant of Buru, and he shook his head over them. 'If you can get into the Baliem Valley, you can go there,' he said. 'We cannot help you, eh?' Also, he said, we would need a military escort. 'But I cannot spare mens, and my mens are too afraid of the natives there. Very bad mens, those natives. They are eating other mens. So....' With some difficulty he found two forms, which stated in Indonesian and Dutch that neither the Indonesian government nor the army were responsible for our safety, that we indemnified them from all claims of relatives or friends in case any harm came to us, and that we were undertaking our trip on our own responsibility and of our own free will. The commander stamped the passes with a flourish, and then asked for a fee. This was rather large, and was not mentioned in the documents we had signed. 'If you meet soldiers, you show these,' the commander said, 'and soldiers will help if they can.' But, he added, sucking his moustache, 'I think you not meet soldiers, and, if you meet, I think they not help.' We went to the church.

Here we received a different welcome. The church and the community house beyond were neat and scrupulously whitewashed. The Dutch priests offered us coffee and cake. The librarian brought out books on West Irian, and offered to lend them to us. One of them was *Gardens of War* by Michael Rockefeller. 'He went,' said the librarian, 'to the Baliem Valley, but it was not there he was killed. He was killed on the Sepik river in the south.' The tone in which he said this was far from heartening.

The other priests were less gloomy in their outlook. They said that the Dani tribe in the Baliem were cannibals. As we would learn from Rockefeller's book, they practised a ritual form of warfare, conducted between the clans, and afterwards ate each other's dead. 'The valley was only discovered in 1938,' said the head of the community. 'It is not yet thirty-five years that the first outsiders went there. So they are still wild. They have killed a few outsiders, but not many. Normally they are very gentle people.

'But,' he added, 'they like not the Indonesians. The Indonesian soldiers are afraid of them, and, because they are afraid, they treat the Dani people badly. So the Dani, they like not the Indonesians.' He seemed pleased at this thought; he chuckled, and offered us cigars. Outside the window of the refectory where we sat were trim vegetable plots and civilized flowerbeds. It was different from our rest house, to which we returned after having done our work. Frank went off to the airstrip, where the priests had a Cessna four-seater plane which they hired out. It could take us into the Baliem Valley, at least as far as Wamena, an Indonesian military outpost in the mouth of it. From then on we would have to walk to Giwika, the nearest mission station. A Father Jules Camps was *in situ* there: he spoke the tribal dialect, and would be able to help us.

While Frank was away, I read about the place we were due to visit. The Grand Valley of the Baliem, to give it its proper name, had, for many years, been unknown to the Dutch settlers. It was locked in by a high mountain range, which no colonist had ventured to cross. In 1938, an American flyer, Richard Archbold, had spotted it from his plane, but had not landed. Towards the middle of the war, a US army plane had crashed there. The survivors were fetched out across the mountains by the Dutch. That had been the first time outsiders had entered the valley. After the war, missionaries had been sent in. Some of them had been killed and eaten by the Dani. 'Particularly,' one of the Catholic community at Djayapura told me, 'the Protestants.' But Father Camps had endured fourteen years at Giwika, uneaten.

Frank returned to say that the Cessna would fly us to Wamena in two days time. Later the pilot, a young American called Chris, turned up for a drink. He was trying to log up flying time to become a master pilot. West Irian seemed a peculiar place to choose for this exercise. It was certainly a long way from Denver, Colorado, where Chris had been born. 'But it's fun,' he said. 'I fly to Wamena once a week, taking supplies and mail. It's a fun trip.' He was *very* young. 'The mountains are pretty big out there,' Chris said, 'and I have to fly through them blind. There's no radar on the bird, you see.'

At dawn, in the distance, we saw the mountains ahead. Chris was at the controls, Frank beside him; I was in the back, beside a monumental black lady in a printed cotton frock. All the Irianese in Djayapura wore European clothes, which sat badly on their bodies; they seemed a different shape from Europeans. Very black, they looked more like Australian aborigines than Africans, but, unlike the aborigines, seemed cheerful people.

At the spectacle of the mountains, the large lady began to tremble gelatinously. Chris started to whistle. Mist enveloped the flanks of the mountains, and low cloud covered the summits. 'There've been a coupla crashes in the last year,' Chris said. 'Strap yourselves well in.'

We plunged into the clouds and mist. The Cessna shook violently, but Chris seemed perfectly confident. Perhaps he wasn't entirely so; he kept on whistling. At one point the mist rifted, and through the window I saw a piece of mountainside, wet trees and black rocks, perhaps twenty feet beyond our starboard wing-tip.

Then the mist resealed itself, and we rattled onward through it, and suddenly burst out into sunshine, with a great valley beneath us. At the mouth of it we could see a few tents and buildings, their corrugated iron roofs flashing under the sun. 'Wamena,' Chris said.

Wamena looked pathetic. The valley behind it sprawled out to the horizon, speckled here and there by trees. Low hills, rocky and enveloped in grass, rippled together a little way beyond Wamena, then turned into open grassland. There was no sign of human habitation beyond the military camp, nor any token of life whatsoever. We landed.

All round us were Indonesian officers. A priest had come from the Wamena mission, looking incongruous in his white cassock; particularly so because, beyond him and the officers, were a large number of aborigines. The bodies of the men were bedaubed with a greyish mixture of earth and ash, and some had feathers in their hair. They were naked except for long penis sheaths held on by twine tied round their waists. There were not many women, but those present were hideous, their bodies smeared with the same substance as the men's, their breasts pendulous and black-nippled, their faces simian. They wore minute loincloths. Long carrying nets hung from their heads, swathing them like a kind of cape. 'These are the wild guys from the bush,' Chris said. 'All Dani. The Indonesians make them leave their weapons outside the settlement. Otherwise they'd be carrying spears and axes.'

They had come simply to watch the plane land. Until very recently, Chris said, they had followed the cargo cult; they had thought that the winged things from the sky were gods of a sort, and endeavoured to please them with offerings of grass, fruit, and water. The officials and the priest had come to collect their supplies of mail. The priest, who was Dutch, came up to us, and said, 'I a radio had from the fathers in Djayapura. They me have told to bring two mission boys for guide and porter. Please with me come.' We followed him to a small house. Tribes people followed us, staring. Our mountainous fellow-passenger came too; she was apparently a housekeeper for the Wamena mission.

At the house, the priest offered us coffee and fruit and told us a little about the Dani. 'You have their peculiar colour seen? On themselves they put the fat of pigs, yes, the cold to keep out; and above they put the ash of fire, and some yellow mud.' They had come to the weekly market, and the priest took us to it. It was situated inside a low structure with a tin roof and no walls. The Dani brought in produce, which the women carried in their nets. This consisted mostly of yams and some fruit. Two piglets, trussed with twine, squealed on the earth underfoot. They were covered in long, coarse black hair. The Dani traded these comestibles for iron and steel implements, needles, cooking utensils in clay. Their language was guttural and slow, and they seemed at ease.

The nearest thing to an insurrection to take place in the valley had occurred recently, the priest told us. The government had been shocked to its Islamic core by the nakedness of the Dani, and revolted by their odour, largely due to pig fat, though, admittedly, they never bathed. It had launched Operasi Koteka, which meant 'Operation Penis Sheath'. The garrison at Wamena had been ordered to seize every male Dani who came to market and forcibly bathe him then burn his penis sheath and recompense him with a pair of shorts and a cake of soap. Unfortunately, the Dani had not taken well to this. They had disappeared into the hinterland, so that the small population of Wamena was bereft of fresh food for weeks. Eventually, the camp commander had sent two very reluctant soldiers out to tell the Dani that Operasi Koteka had been abandoned. After this, things had proceeded as before. The soldiers in Wamena looked much more nervous than the Dani. Government officers in Djayapura were remunerated at a high rate because it was supposed to be a post of extreme hardship, like Buru. If that were so, I wondered how much the government officers and troops at Wamena got as compensation money.

While we sat in the verandah of the priest's house, two black mission boys appeared, in shirts and shorts. 'They are good boys,' the friendly priest said. 'From Ambon. The big one, English he speak. The other, not so.' The big one reminded me vaguely of a blacker version of someone I had seen. Frank felt this too and pinpointed the feeling. 'He looks like Cassius Clay,' he said. 'I'm going to call him Cassius.' Perhaps logically, I called his companion Brutus. They piled themselves high with our baggage, and we set out for Giwika. A sort of footpath took us through grass that rose above our heads, dripping with recent rain. The trail was very muddy, but the sun beat down with a dry rasping heat. At first we met a few Dani, coming in to Wamena to market. They were mostly men, carrying fifteen-foot bamboo spears and axes with heads of black stone. We had been advised to shout *'Ey, narak,'* whenever we encountered a tribesman. That meant, 'I see you, man,' and, if he responded in the same fashion, friendly relations were established. One wasn't usually supposed to speak to women, but, if one deigned to do so, the correct address was *'Ey, nara!'* She was to nod in answer.

I shouted, '*Ey, narak*!' to the tribesmen we passed, and established friendly relations so much so that one of them turned back to accompany us for about three hours in the mosquito-ridden heat, finally pointing towards a distant mountain and saying something which Cassius translated as being, 'It is three days walk to Kurulu.'

Sometimes I have nightmares about this walk. We went, at times, through dripping forest; at times, through the high grasslands, like ants in a tunnel. Sometimes we climbed shaly hills, sometimes we came to rivers. This nightmare became intermixed with those I had of my hour with my small son on the slopes of Tiger's Leap. The bridges of the rivers usually consisted of a single bamboo pole. This solitary support connected two banks of the river; each end was wedged between unsteady rocks. Cassius and Brutus ran surefootedly across these terrifying bridges, though they carried heavy loads. I had seen similar bridges in the Philippines and in remote parts of Malaysia and Thailand, but had not been required to cross them. Those, I remembered, had had hand ropes to assist one's traverse. But the Baliem bridges were slippery with the rain. that fell at a prescribed hour every day. They had no hand ropes. Even Frank went over with difficulty, straddling the pole and pulling himself along with his hands. I couldn't do this.

My vertigo forbade it. There were, sometimes, short drops under the single pole which was the bridge, and the turbulent river below, rushing scummily over rocks. But usually the drop was in the nature of three or four hundred feet, and, if I looked down, I was lost. So I straddled the pole with Cassius holding me from behind and Brutus pulling from the front, until we had negotiated the abyss; once I remember the flutter in my heart, as, having come over one such bridge, Cassius said, 'Thirty minutes, more river.'

But at length we trudged up a hill, my boots bursting, and beneath us was a white mission house with a white church and a school-house beside it. The Dani came up to us when they saw us. They helped us downhill, or at least they helped me. Cassius and Brutus seemed in rude health, but even Frank was tired. The solicitude of the Dani made me feel grateful; but there were other aspects of them which we had met in the grasslands.

At mid-afternoon one day, we heard the sound of drumming and chanting through the total, underwater silence. Loud whistles shrieked in between the noise of the drums and chants. Cassius and Brutus dropped their considerable loads and rolled their eyes. 'Bad men, sir!' Cassius said. 'Very bad men, sir! They kill us, sir!' And he and his companion departed into the high grass. Frank and I now found ourselves in the classic, if stereotyped, and somewhat ridiculous, situation of explorers whose porters have deserted them.

Frank picked up his equipment from the black earth and said, 'We might as well go and see what's happening.' This, again, was a classic and ridiculous situation. But there was nothing left to do but that. We didn't know when, and if, Cassius and Brutus would come back, and, alone amidst miles of grass higher than our heads, there seemed no option but to seek the nearest source of human activity, such as that from which the drumming and chanting, and the prolonged and eerie whistles, came. We walked towards it.

A clearing opened before us. It contained about a dozen Dani warriors, with feathers in their hair, their faces painted in red, white, and black stripes. They flourished long spears and stone axes as they danced. It was not exactly a dance: each holding the hips of the man in front, they shuffled in a circle round and round a primitive firepit, covered in leaves, from which blue smoke idly rose. On a little stump beyond this slowly turning wheel of black bodies sat the drummers and a man with a whistle, and also a small, wizened, nearly naked woman, her toothless mouth open in pleasure.

We were concealed by the high grass. Frank got a camera out and began to take pictures. He moved further forward, and suddenly the dancing and sound all stopped. The empty plains spread out around us for miles, wholly silent. Into the great silence the click of the camera exploded like a gunshot. The warriors turned towards the source of the sound, and saw us. They emitted loud yells and ran towards us, long spears poised.

About two yards away, they suddenly pulled up, snorting and panting like hard-ridden horses. The gleaming drops of sweat on their bodies, and the sharp points of their spears, seemed magnified by my eyes. The warriors loped back to their starting point, then turned and charged us again. This time they stopped a few yards away.

We said, *'Ey, narak.'* Nobody had told us the plural of the phrase, but it seemed to serve. They gathered round us, laughing and talking. We could not follow what they were saying; but then Cassius and Brutus crawled out of the grass on the far side of the clearing. They came up, rather fearfully. Whether they were afraid of our wrath or the warriors', it was hard to say. Cassius, however, began to interpret for us.

The Dani were apparently inviting us to lunch with them off whatever was baking in the firepit. Speculation as to what it might be was futile. We took the safest course of action and told them, through Cassius, that our religion forbade us to eat anything that was not tinned. We fished some tinned ham out of a case. Frank also took out some of the steel knives we had bought. These went down very well. So, indeed, did the ham, for on being offered some, they wolfed it all down with little cries of appreciation. We attempted to explain, through Cassius, what we were doing. Frank took some pictures of them, while they talked excitedly. Pointing west, they said, 'Kurulu!'

This was not the first time we had heard the word, but Cassius did not know what it meant. It might be a place, he suggested. Frank said, 'Perhaps it's a god.'

After our encounter in the bush, it was a relief to find the Danis at the mission so friendly, though they were as scantily clad as the wild ones. Cassius told us what they were saying. Father Camps had gone to some nearby village on his motorcycle, but would be back by nightfall. Meanwhile, they gave us water, and showed us into the small house where the priest lived. The front room was full of books; a Cona coffee-maker stood on a table, with a tin of coffee beside it, and several cups. We slumped down in Father Camps' chairs and sipped coffee made by someone who said he was the cook. We equipped ourselves with old magazines from a pile on the floor. Cassius and Brutus disappeared with the mission boys to the rear of the house.

A rustle at the door, and an old man came in. One supposed that he was old because his frizzy hair was streaked with white, and his features bore the sour lines of experience. He wore the penis sheath, and a white bib made of minute seashells. He carried a stone axe. He looked at us and said, *'Ey, narak,'* and we replied as required. Then, seating himself on a chair, his stone axe across his knees like a parson's umbrella, he leant forward and began to study us intently with yellow, feral eyes. This inspection was unnerving, but presently he stopped, and with a sophisticated smile, poured himself a cup of coffee. Picking up a magazine on the way, he went back to his chair. Whenever one of us took a sip of coffee, he did the same. Whenever we turned a page, he followed suit. We had the opportunity to observe that he had lost several fingertips on either hand, also that he was holding the magazine upside down.

At last he broke a silence which had become oppressive. He said something, rose, and went to one of the bookshelves. He selected a blue volume, slowly turned the pages, and finally emitted a satisfied grunt. A tipless finger on the page he wanted, he showed us a picture of himself, younger, but little different from what he looked like now. The caption said, 'The great Dani chief: "The Wise White Heron", Kurulu.'

Father Camps returned on his motorcycle. It must have been a very strong one to traverse the Baliem Valley, as it apparently often did. Father Camps was a strong man: short, bespectacled and squat, with a Roman head. His English was not perfect, but he was a great deal more comprehensible than our other interpreters so far. Kurulu was still there when he arrived. It was getting dark and very cold outside. Though in a valley, we were high above several others. The chief was now with several warriors, who had come not only to satisfy their curiosity about us, but to get out of the cold. Father Camps eyed them without favour, and said, 'That man, with feathers in his hair, is a big thief. You must not leave your possessions about when he is here.' He shouted orders to the cook. 'Chicken for supper,' he said. 'I breed them. It makes a change to eat chicken.'

What he usually ate, like the Dani, was yams, varied by tinned food. He got eggs (sometimes) from the chickens. The Dani delicacy was pork from the huge, hairy pigs, rather like wild boar, which we had seen all the way down the valley. 'But I don't like pork,' said Father Camps sadly. A Dani's wealth was counted by the number of his pigs. They were only killed on special occasions. 'Murders over pig thefts are common,' said Camps. 'Less so for wife thefts. Pigs are more valuable. If a man runs away with your wife, it is a good thing, because the compensation is paid in pigs. It's only if the man won't pay you that you kill him.' He shooed the Dani out into the rain that had started. We gave him two bottles of whisky, which were rapturously received, and each of us had a very small drink before the cook brought in the chicken, stewed with yams.

Next day we crossed the mission compound to the tiny schoolhouse, which was also a chapel. The students were few, and female, and they were clad in white or pink frocks, supplied by Father Camps. None of them was more than about eight years old. 'In a few months,' said Father Camps ruefully, 'they will stop coming to school and go to work in the fields.' He taught them catechism, though they were not converts. 'I have been fourteen years here,' Camps said. 'In all that time I have only made one convert. He died.' He shook his head over the children, and said, 'If they do not go to the fields, they will be—how you say—affianced. Not in terms of the church, but affianced.'

What seemed to me admirable about Camps was that he was resigned to the fact that he would never achieve what he had been sent here for. He would never convert the Danis, and was more intelligent than to try and do so. But he had done something more valuable. He had acted as a liaison officer, a bridge, between the Dani and the total impact of civilization. He also acted as a block to the Indonesian idea of an enforced culture. An unknown man in a hardly known valley, he was playing the role history had assigned to him. It didn't matter to Father Camps if he was forgotten in the future. He had a flock, even though it wasn't the kind of flock his church would have hoped for. With his one convert dead, his mission boys still animists, the girl children at the school ready at any moment to shed their frocks and bed some ardent young warrior under a convenient tree, he was undismayed. He probably understood the Dani better than they understood themselves. And, the Dani probably understood him.

Staying with Camps was an experience to be remembered. Before dawn the air was bitterly cold and laden with mist. The Dani were out, however, in the compound of the mission station. They wrapped their arms round themselves, to keep warm. White plumes rose from their mouths. The ground, then, was silver with dew; by a slight exercise of the imagination, it could be turned in the mind's eye to a snowscape in which the naked black figures with their penis sheaths seemed surrealist. The Dani traded with the Yali tribe in the next valley; they swapped salt for feathers and seashells. The source of the salt was a brine pool on top of a stony hill.

We climbed this hill early one day, in the wake of a number of old women with banana tree-trunks in their carrying nets. The women were witchlike, grotesques from medieval art: some were almost hairless, their monkey faces deeply wrinkled and seamed, and few of them had many teeth. Their pendulous udders flapped like empty bladders as they moved up the slope to the brine pool. My feet should have hardened through all the walking I had done in the recent past, but they had suddenly started to bleed. Halfway up the hill I found my boots were full of blood. Frank went on and a young Dani warrior stayed with me. I took my boots off, and my sticky socks.

The blisters oozed pus and blood. The Dani clicked his tongue in real sympathy, and shook his head slowly in commiseration. Camps had given me some antiseptic cream from his small dispensary, and I anointed the blisters. The young warrior, in the meantime, scrambled off down the hillside and returned with a long tubular piece of grass. He squatted down some distance away and began to blow into it; a soothing music, like that of a flute, floated out into the cool and sunlit air. I put my socks and boots on, and continued the climb. He ran ahead of me, his large feet sure of themselves on the slippery stones; with trills of the grass flute he encouraged me to climb. When we reached the top, we found Frank busy. He had plenty of material.

The brine pool was not very large, but it was very dirty, and insects hovered over its scummed surface. The witch-faced women crouched around it, chewing on the banana trunks, which they held to their mouths with clawlike hands, like lemurs. Once a section of trunk had been thoroughly chewed in mainly toothless mouths, it was immersed in the pool. It had been made porous, so as to absorb the saltwater. When the trunks had soaked up as much moisture as they could contain, they were fished out and spread to dry in the sun. The salt crystals that were left after this were scraped off and carried in pots down to Kurulu's village beside the mission station; they were damp and yellowish, and, like no other salt I have ever encountered, exuded a definite and unpleasant smell.

One day a messenger brought Camps the news that a chief had died of malaria in a village some distance away, and his funeral was scheduled for the afternoon. Camps seemed unmoved by this, but he gave us guides and we set off for the village. To my horror, it lay across more of the one-bamboo bridges. Frank had accustomed himself to them, but I never did: I always had to be manoeuvred across by two men, feeling very undignified. Dignity, in these circumstances, was dispensable with. Eventually, we reached the village.

It lay in a cup between hills, and was surrounded by a high bamboo palisade with spyholes hacked into it. Smoke rose from the village centre, and also ululations of grief and the throb of drums. We scrambled down a slope and took up positions outside the palisade, by the spyholes. Camps had told us not to disturb the mourners. But we had a good view from where we were. Beehive huts stood behind a front courtyard in which two firepits had been dug. It was from these that the smoke came. The dead man had been strapped to a chair made of banana trunks, and sat facing them. Facing him, across the pits, were the women of the village, wailing and crying out incoherently. Behind the corpse stood the warriors. From time to time, without any apparent order, one or the other of them would gash his arm with a stone knife. Across the country, long files of people were approaching the village from different directions, some carrying young pigs trussed for slaughter. One of our guides nudged me, and pointed up the slope we had descended. About a dozen warriors were coming down it, carrying axes and long spears. In Dani country, one was never really frightened. But I felt that each new situation was delicate, and should be handled with care: that it would take very little to ignite whatever sullen fire lurked in the blood of the Dani.

The newcomers arrived and encircled us, looking very unfriendly. We shouted, *'Ey, narak,'* and presented them with the last of the steel knives. The oldest of them, grinning, flung his arms around me, leaving indelible stains of soot and pig fat on my clothes, and led his companions away to the entrance. One of them turned and made gestures that seemed to mean that we should stay where we were and not follow. After this, though I think everyone in the village was aware of us, we were left alone.

The ceremony proceeded in slow stages. The wails of the women were prevented from becoming monotonous by the accompanying screams of the piglets, who seemed to have a foreknowledge of their fate. Presently, it fell upon them. The warriors drew stone knives, advanced upon the screaming, kicking animals, and sawed their throats open. The New Guinea pigs are hairy, with a tough outer integument. The killing process therefore took a long while, and the noise made by the dying beasts was fantastic. When each one had been bloodily slaughtered and eviscerated, the carcass was dumped in a firepit. The pits consisted, so far as we could see, of layers of flat stones, earth, and banana leaves, between which the dead pigs were packed. The smell of smoke in the air changed to a smell of baking pork.

Darkness had nearly fallen. The guides insisted that we go back. Later, Camps said, 'The boys were correct. It was good that you left. Some things they do not even allow me to see, though, for fourteen years, I have been their friend. For instance, I know that when all the pigs are cooked, they will have a feast. But as to the disposal of the dead man….' He shrugged his shoulders, and continued with his dinner.

Camps was constantly in touch, by radio, with Wamena and even Djayapura. For some time the weather had been cloudy and wet. Continual thunder sounded in the mountains, and rain fell in occasional fierce squalls. We had planned an expedition into the next valley, where the Yali were, but one morning Camps returned from the radio set to say, 'A typhoon is coming. I thought so, because of the thunder and rain, but now the radio confirms. We will not be much affected, but it will rain very much. We should tell Chris to fly here and take you out.'

After some discussion, we did this. The Dani smoothed out a rough airstrip from the remnants of an old one. At dawn one day the Cessna dropped out of the sky, with rain and wind behind it, and pulled up a few feet from the end of the improvised runway. Chris turned it round and took us back to Djayapura. Rain and wind shook the Cessna all the way, but he seemed calm, though he whistled as we flew through the misted mountains. Before we left, Kurulu presented me with his stone axe. Its fierce black head was wedged into a bamboo handle, fastened safely with twine. 'He says to tell you,' Camps said with disapproval, 'that he has killed 150 men, some with this axe, and afterwards eaten them. This I hesitate to believe.' Kurulu only grinned.

Many things remained to be seen: not only the valley of the Yali, but caves which Kurulu had told us of, high up in the mountains. These held ancestral bones, and the spirits of tribal ancestors. Father Camps averred that the bones were of canine origin, but dogs were rare in the Baliem, and we wondered. I had also wanted to talk to some women. 'No use,' Camps told me. 'They are not intelligent women, and very loose in their habits. Seven wives have already run away from Kurulu. Of course, he has others.'

We returned to Jakarta. Our exposure to the Dani had been brief, but our entry into their world, and our exit, seemed to enclose a part of life I had never before experienced. This feeling, as well as my extreme exhaustion, and my damaged feet, made me look at civilization as though from a great distance. It took time to readjust; Frank decided to have a holiday, but my desk in Hong Kong called me. From Jakarta I was able to phone Leela and Pandit, and tell them I was on my way home. Pieter Schumaker was in Jakarta; he helped us in our final task before Frank flew to Bali and I back to Hong Kong. On the tapes we had brought out of Buru there were messages from Pramudya and Suprapto to their families. We felt we must deliver them.

Schumaker said, 'Look, it is seven years since these men disappeared. All kinds of things may have happened since then. Suppose the wives have remarried? Their old lives have already been destroyed. If you go and tell them that their first husbands are not dead, you will personally destroy their new lives.' Frank was inclined to agree; but I felt that the wives should know. If, at any time, their husbands were to be released, unlikely though it now seemed, it would come as less of a shock. As it turned out, Mrs Suprapto had left Jakarta, and nobody seemed to know where Pramudya's wife was.

The government would not have helped us, and in any case I didn't ask. I was afraid that Mrs Pramudya would suffer. But there was a café in Jakarta much patronized by young poets, and I went there for assistance. One of them had heard of me and read my poetry, and because of this they were willing to help. Pramudya's wife had not remarried. She had several children, the last of whom had been bom three months after her husband's arrest. Having no money, she now worked in a bakery to support them. The young poets gave me her address, but, as a payment in kind, asked to be allowed to listen to the tapes. All had read Pramudya, some had been influenced by his work, and a few had actually met him. I played them the tapes in my hotel room, and some of them wept as they listened.

Mrs Pramudya did not weep. She was a lady of great dignity. We could not forewarn her, and our sudden visit with her husband's voice must have come as a shock. She gathered her children round her, and they all listened to the tapes. We gave her a copy of them. Apart from the two eldest children, who were adolescent, none of her brood remembered their father.

My two big articles from this trip, 'The Prisoners of Buru,' and 'The People Time Forgot,' about the Dani, each filled an entire issue of the magazine. The Buru piece brought an immense and violent response from the Indonesians. Both Frank Fischbeck and I were placed on the official blacklist, and told we would never again be allowed to enter Indonesia. The article was syndicated in the *Sunday Telegraph* in London, and in other magazines outside Hong Kong. Amnesty International then approached us for affidavits about the camp's conditions. I would have thought that the article and the photographs would have been sufficient proof, but we signed and sent the affidavits, and copies of the photographs and tapes. Some time later, seven thousand of the ten thousand people on Buru were released. This wasn't entirely due to the article, but it had been the first report out of Buru, and played its part. It was the most effective piece I have ever written as a journalist. But I was unable to find out if Pramudya and Suprapto were among the people released, and I still do not know if they were.

'The People Time Forgot' was published as a small book, with Fischbeck's pictures. Often, when I glanced at the text and photographs, it seemed to record the experiences of someone I did not know. I could hardly believe that I had been to West Irian at all. Even now that part of my life is a kind of dream to me. Father Camps was sent a copy of the article, which he mildly criticized for certain commissions and omissions. His letter was some proof to me that my visit had in fact taken place. The more I travelled around Asia after the Indonesian trip, the more anticlimactic my travels became.

Adrian Zecha, whose liquor I had once unwittingly drunk in Bombay, now owned a newspaper called the *Asian*, and a string of glossy magazines. We were, in a sense, rivals, and our staff seldom fraternized with Zecha's editors, except, in my case, with Suman Dubey, a young Indian who was an editor for the *Asian*, and who later became the press secretary to Rajiv Gandhi. It was through Suman that I heard that Tarzie Vittachi wanted to meet me. I didn't see why I couldn't meet Tarzie over drinks and dinner, but Suman said that everything had to be very secret. In Asia, I had become accustomed to the idea of intrigue. As Suman suggested, I went to Tarzie's office on a Sunday, when nobody else was there. He sat at his desk and looked at me very carefully.

Tarzie was perhaps the best journalist Asia had ever produced. Ceylonese by birth, he had edited various papers in his own country, moved into the Far East, and then retreated to Britain to start a kind of Asian news agency. I had first met him there. He had written a classic book, *The Brown Sahib*. This was about the human relics the British Empire had left in Asia. Abdullah Patel had once called me a black Englishman. I wasn't sure that either his own label or Patel's didn't fit Tarzie, who sat at his desk that Sunday like a version of Buddha, or, as it suddenly struck me, a swarthier Father Camps.

Tarzie, in the friendship we later developed, always struck me as a kind of catherine-wheel, spinning on no fixed epicentre, from which ideas burst. Sometimes these ideas fizzled out, sometimes, the catherine-wheel still spinning furiously on its axis, the ideas set fire to a whole train of other ideas, which often continued to spark. Tarzie's approach to me that Sunday was fairly simple. He said, 'You're too big for Hong Kong.' After a short pause, he said, 'So am I. But I have an idea. This is in confidence.'

His idea was, when the sputter of sparks around it had died, not unsimple. The United Nations Fund for Population Activity (UNFPA) had recently asked him to New York. There he had met Rafael Salas, from the Philippines, who was the director-general of the agency. We were now at the end of 1972; 1974 was to be World Population Year. Tarzie had been employed by UNFPA as an ideas man and troubleshooter, only responsible to Salas, and, of course, beyond Salas to Kurt Waldheim, then the secretary general of the United Nations. 'I've proposed that for World Population Year,' Tarzie said, 'the UNFPA should fund a film, which Roberto Rossellini has been commissioned to do.'

After a brief pause, he continued, 'I've also proposed that we should fund a book. I want you to write it.' I said that I knew nothing at all about population problems. 'That's exactly why I thought of you,' Tarzie said. 'You probably know nothing about light bulbs, but I once read an article by you about them. You interested me in light bulbs. Now I want you to interest a world audience in your discoveries about the population problem.' He also tried to explain to me that it was not exactly a problem, but I lost him somewhere along the way. 'No matter,' Tarzie said. 'Do you accept?'

I didn't know what I would be paid, or what was involved in the work. But he said, 'You'll have to travel all round the world, quite intensively. I'm not saying that this is an easy bit of work. But you'll be paid for it, more than Pandit pays you. I don't promise you anything. After you've finished this book, UNFPA may have finished with you. Then you'll have to re-employ yourself.' I said I would have to talk to my wife. 'Talk to her all you want,' Tarzie said. 'But have dinner with me next week, both of you. If she needs convincing, I'll convince her. I'm going to New York after that. I'll send you a return ticket, and you can sign the contract there.'

He also said, 'You're a poet. I've read your poetry. I warn you, this is going to keep you very busy all next year. You won't be able to write anything but this book.'

This didn't seem important to me then; I had resigned myself to the loss of an arm and a leg. The next week Leela and I lunched with Tarzie. Afterwards, she said, 'I know it's not secure, but if you want to do it, do it.' My father's eyes and voice seemed to speak through hers.

16

Mr Salas was small and friendly, with a hair transplant and a heart problem. 'I loff poetry,' he said. 'You will show me some of yours?' It seemed ironic that he wanted to hire me on the basis of what I no longer wrote. I gave him *My Son's Father* instead. It satisfied him. He said, 'Tomorrow your contract will be ready for you to sign.' Almost as an afterthought, he added, 'Tarzie Vittachi will tell you what you have to do. What we expect of you. I am sure you will live up to our expectations.' I had no idea what these expectations were, but the next day, when I signed the contract, I was told.

The UNFPA offices were not in the UN building, which was variously called by its employees 'the glass house' or 'the temple of lies'. They were situated in an office block between Lexington and Park Avenues, and through their high windows one could see the skyscrapers of winter Manhattan, their outlines softened by mist. I was given a crash course in population studies, and told that I would have to travel from country to country, in Asia, Africa, and South America; I would go as a layman, with a rudimentary knowledge of what I was writing about. Obviously, my knowledge of population problems would increase as my travel mileage did; by the end, I would have learnt a lot, and so, hopefully, would the reader with the patience to follow me through the book.

A rough itinerary was drawn up. I flew back to Hong Kong to arrange my affairs there. Pandit called a meeting of the magazine staff, and told them that I now considered myself too good for them. Leela set about reletting the flat, and selling the furniture. Tarzie kept phoning me from America to ask when I would start. Eventually, it was all fixed. The furniture was sold, the flat let to a couple who hired Ah Mui.

Anyone who says the Chinese are inscrutable are not well acquainted with them. When my departure date was announced, the secretaries at the office wept; Ah Mui brought her family to the flat; she wept, they wept. Amidst this shower of tears, we flew away westward, and, in London, met my father, who was not happy there. Everything I had feared for him had come true. He had few friends; he could not accustom himself to a city completely different from the one he had known. Francis, however, was a frequent visitor, and this cheered him up. We saw Francis; he was now about seven, a small boy with a personality of his own. Judy and I had settled down to being friends, and she was also friendly to Leela, perhaps out of sympathy because she had married me.

All these departures and partings had the effect of making me very anxious to start work. I had, meanwhile, come to an arrangement with Salas and Tarzie. Since Leela and I had no settled home, I wanted to take her with me. She could handle my notes and chores; I intended to work on the book as I went along, so that it could be ready for Population Year in 1974. The financial controller of UNFPA, Ed Gregory, helped with the figures for Leela's travel. It turned out that, if we were careful, my *per diem* allowance would be enough to carry us both. We left, ironically, for India.

It seemed I was always returning. We started in Delhi, where I met Mrs Gandhi and was referred by her to people who were concerned with the population control problem. The Indian population then was about 660 million. This did not take unregistered births into account. I had noticed for years the posters that adhered to walls and even to trees, all over the country. These showed the smiling faces of a couple above an inverted red triangle, and said that two or three children were enough. Pupul Jayakar, an eminent cultural historian, told me that, since the literacy rate was so low, the poster, to many people, said the opposite of what it was meant to say. The happy couple were in fact smiling over a traditional tantric fertility symbol: to the illiterate, it would seem that they were pleased because they had had many children.

This, as I found out during my trips to dusty hospitals and family planning centres, inside and outside Delhi, confirmed a peasant belief which I was to find all over the Third World. In a rural economy, the more hands there were to work the land, the better. In this respect, a male child was a benefit. A girl child, however, would eventually be married off, which involved the payment of dowry. Hence a rural couple wanted male children. If a series of daughters were produced, the parents would keep trying to have a son. If they succeeded, they would want another son, in case the first one died. Bearing in mind the high child mortality rates known in the past, this seemed to them possible. So couples tried to have children, and the ubiquitous family planning posters seemed to confirm this was what the government wanted them to do.

Successive health and family planning ministers had produced other publicity measures which were equally unsuccessful. At one point, when the rhythm method was advocated, glass necklaces of red and green beads were distributed to village women. These were supposed to be used as an abacus on which their fertile and infertile periods could be calculated. The women often used them as ornaments. Those who didn't, rapidly lost count. The government had also initiated a programme whereby elephants toured the districts, showering villagers with packets of condoms. One of the officers in charge of the programme told me sadly,

'Sir, this is not a success. Many children come to see the elephant, but all they do is blow up the condoms and use them as balloons.' This was all very funny, but it was also rather serious.

So the government took to more direct methods. Its family planning officers employed motivators who went about trying to persuade people to be sterilized. They offered their listeners a choice of money or transistor radios if they would submit to the operation. Quite often, the motivators either pocketed the money and sold the transistors, or brought in very old men and women and very young children to be sterilized. In Bombay I met a dynamic doctor called Dinesh Pai, a troubleshooter employed by the Maharashtra government when their family planning programme failed. Pai said, 'At first they told me to insert the IUD, the loop, into women. I replied, "Do you want me to walk around lifting the skirts of any young woman I meet?"' He laughed thunderously and said, 'But I had the answer, my friend! I had the answer!'

His answer was in itself rather fantastic. Bombay being horrifyingly overpopulated, hundreds of thousands of commuters pass through the railway terminals every day. Pai set up a stall in each of these places, distributing free condoms. More than that, he requisitioned a small room in each station, to be used as an operating theatre. The motivators went about on the platforms, trying to coax men to be vasectomized. The few who agreed were taken into these rooms. 'One nick, and it is done!' said Pai. He was, for some reason, inordinately anxious that I watch one of these operations. I was squeamish; I refused. One afternoon Pai took me to a railway station, saying that I could meet his motivators. He pushed me into a small room, where a trouserless man had been strapped to a table. He was howling in terror, his cries drowned by the medley of crowd and train noises outside. A man in a dirty white coat approached him as I watched, a steel instrument in his hand. I closed my eyes, and a moment later Pai took me out of the room, saying, 'How simple, eh? How beautiful.'

In Calcutta we had a long interview with Mother Teresa. At that time she was not well-known outside the city. There her reputation for sanctity had already spread. 'Even the Naxalites did not harm her,' Ranjit Gupta told me, 'though she and her nuns went around the city by night, picking up dying people.' Mother Teresa propagated the rhythm method. Her nuns went around with the bead necklaces which the government had long since discarded, but did not seem very convinced about their mission.

Mother Teresa was very small, but in her blue and white sari and wimple, did not seem in the least frail. She had a strong face, angular and deeply lined, and eyes that were a very pale blue. Her English, spoken with a convent accent, still contained the gutturals of her native Albania. A great steadfastness and peace emanated from her. But I didn't agree with much that she said. She felt that contraception was undesirable in whatever form it was practised. It seemed that it was only because of official pressure that her nuns even went so far as to teach the rhythm method. 'Children should be a joy and a pleasure,' she said, speaking, like Hope Cooke, in a kind of whisper. 'Why are people so worried about world population? God is great. There is enough land in India for people to live in. It is so rich a country. God will provide.'

There was absolutely no point in arguing with her; she had the peace that comes with certitude. She took us into her private chapel, and said we should pray with her. Afterwards, she astonished me by suggesting that Leela should stay in Calcutta and work for her while I continued my trip. One could have wished, I suppose, that saints were more of this world. This impression continued when I met her workers. A svelte young socialite took us to visit 'Nirmal Hriday', where dying people taken off the pavements were cared for during their last days. The dying lay in clean cots, murmured over very softly by solicitous nuns. The only voice raised clearly and confidently was that of our pretty guide. 'I bring them sweets,' she said. 'They like sweets.'

Mrs V did not actually work for Mother Teresa. She alleviated her guilt feelings about her husband's wealth by visiting Nirmal Hriday once a week, and bringing comestibles to the nearly dead. But I also met some of the lay workers, among them a Mrs Phyllis Lovejoy. She was Eurasian; her husband had left her or died, and she had to maintain herself and her seven children. She couldn't manage, she said; she could only feed the children once a day. They went to a free school, but transport was very expensive, so they had to walk there and back. We visited her at home. Mrs Lovejoy's home address was 13 Crematorium Street. This was a hut. She spent about five days a week trudging the thoroughfares with a satchelful of bead necklaces and booklets. For this she was paid a bag of grain a month. 'It is not enough,' Mrs Lovejoy said. 'Mother is so good, she does not think of real problems. I am unqualified for any other work, she knows that, but when I tell her about my problems and ask for a little money as well as the rice, she only says that God will provide for us all.'

The experts at UNFPA had planned my trip carefully. They said it was essential to visit India because it was a classic example of overpopulation; that I should then go to Singapore, where the population policy was under control, and to Malaysia, where it wasn't, because of the intransigence of the Muslim population. I could not visit Indonesia, the best example of a Muslim country in Asia, because I was blacklisted there, so Malaysia had been picked as the next best. From there we had to visit the Philippines, the only Catholic country in Asia due to proselytization by the Spanish colonists. I had been to all these places before, so I knew them, though not in terms of their population problems. We cruised through Singapore and Malaysia, which were mainly a series of boring conversations with family planners, and arrived in Manila. Tristram Eastwood was the UNFPA coordinator, and he was very helpful. He organized trips for me, on one of which I was almost attacked by an irate Filipino husband with a bolo, a species of machete. He also organized parties. One of them was given by the resident representative of the UN Development Programme. His wife had recently employed a maid, who had not yet been trained. On the day of the party, this young woman copiously lubricated the stone stairs that led up to the house with wax polish. It was a formal party, the women were in long dresses, and that night four of them slipped and fell on these stairs. Leela, who was in a sari, was the last. She hurt her ankle, and next day it swelled up and turned blue. I had to travel to Baguio, north of Manila for a meeting. It was impossible for me not to go. I phoned Pacita Roces, who was not only all sympathy, but, as usual, very constructive. She told me that she would immediately send a doctor to the hotel. 'He is,' she said, 'the osteopath to our Olympic football team.'

The osteopath arrived, seized Leela's foot, and twisted it violently. Leela turned pale, but said nothing. 'The ankle is not fractured,' he announced, with a gleeful laugh. I asked him how he knew this. 'If it had been fractured,' said the doctor, 'she would have fainted with pain, no?' He was a small, very cheerful man, obviously much impressed that we were friends of the Roces, who arrived shortly after this and said they would take Leela home with them and look after her while I was in Baguio. So I left her with them.

When I returned, two days later, she was still with them. Her ankle was, in fact, fractured, and the doctor advised against travel. Since we were scheduled to fly to Nairobi that day, this was a considerable problem. Pacita told me to go on ahead. Leela would be safe with them, and as soon as she could travel, they would send her on.

Leela had a very pleasant stay; but she was also a little surprised by the household arrangements. At night the whole house was shuttered; guards were on patrol; and Chino kept a rifle by his bed, like a pioneer on the American frontier. 'This,' Pacita said to Leela, 'is because Marcos wants us dead, and we know it. So we take precautions. Don't come out of your bedroom at night, there are fierce dogs in the house.'

This explained something that had puzzled me. When we arrived in Manila, I had called Chino up from our hotel. Shortly after this, I called General Romulo. He sounded very peculiar on the telephone, and said, 'You are in touch with Chino Roces.' This was a statement, not a question. I concluded that there was a tap on our telephone. The general, very embarrassed, went on, 'I am very busy for some days. But I'll be in touch.' He wasn't, until after I left; then, by circuitous means, he sent a message to Leela saying that he could not see her, because she was staying in Chino's house.

I was disappointed in the little general; but I did not know of his message to Leela until I next saw her. By that time I had flown out of Asia into Africa.

After twenty-four hours at airports or in the sky, I came down at Nairobi. I was greeted by a UNDP driver who said his name was Johnston. He enlivened the drive into town by telling me all about his family in Mombasa, how much he was paid, and how much he thought he deserved. There was a reason behind these confidences, he explained. He would be attached to me throughout my stay, and if I put in a good report about him, he might get a raise. An Asian might have provided me with all this unsolicited information, but he wouldn't have told me the reason. Kenyans were far more frank than, say, Indians. This was exemplified by another passenger on my flight, a young Kenyan who told me that family planning was a specific device invented by white men to kill off the coloured races, and that I should be ashamed of doing what I was doing, and for falling into a racist trap. Nothing I said could appease him.

Nairobi was an attractive city. It sprawled round a small, compact centre, and I came to it on a mild blue day of sun and wind. The black people in its streets were mostly in European clothes, but under it moved with the boneless, flowing African stride; at a traffic intersection I saw a Masai tribesman in red robes, his arms bangled, carrying a long staff. It was my first time in black Africa, and he made me feel that I had really arrived there. I had been booked into a hotel called the New Stanley; I had hardly checked in, Johnston at my elbow, when a small man turned up at the other elbow and said, 'I'm Wilfred Maciel. I heard you were coming.' Maciel was of Indian extraction, and one of the senior reporters at the main paper in Nairobi. Within an hour of our meeting, he had given me a great deal of information, much more than the UNFPA office later gave me. Moreover, Maciel arranged interviews for me more or less on the spot, which was more than the UNFPA office did.

One of these interviews was with the assistant minister of home affairs, who was called Shikuku. By this time I had moved to another hotel called Brenner's, which was run colonial style; it had huge suites, verandahs, and a Hemingway sort of atmosphere. The room-boys were ebulliently friendly. Maciel had brought me here. It was after I had moved into Brenner's that Johnston took me to Shikuku. 'That man,' he said to me, 'is a madman, sir. Why associate with such? He's a Kikuyu.'

The President of Kenya, Jomo Kenyatta, was also a Kikuyu; but Johnston did not condemn him for being one. However, when I told him that I had known Tom Mboya, another Kenyan leader, who had been shot down by political opponents in Nairobi, Johnston said, 'He was killed because he was a Luo, sir. I am a Luo.'

Shikuku turned out to be a short man in a three-piece woollen suit, eccentric in the weather Nairobi now had. He saw me in his office, and began to shout, very loudly, from the moment I entered it. He said that before colonialism Kenyans had lived by what he described as 'African socialism', which meant that the chief of a tribe saw that nobody in it starved. He thought African socialism was much better than British socialism.

'Once, in London,' he said, 'I was strolling in Hyde Park with my friend. I saw a man lying down. He was covered with pigeons.

He had pigeons on his head. I thought the man had died. I took away the pigeons from his head and asked, "Are you dead?" The man said no, but that he was Scottish, and because of this no Englishman would employ him. He said he was a Master of Arts, and had not eaten for thirty-six hours. I gave him ten shillings, because we Africans are traditionally generous people. He went off.'

By this time I thought this might be quite a memorable interview, so I let Shikuku roll. He said that after *uhuru,* independence, the money had moved from the hands of Europeans and Asians, and therefore few Kenyans were rich while many were poor. 'All the money should be taken from Asians,' he said, 'as Idi Amin did in Uganda. We should then take over the entire economy. Maybe the economy in Kenya will suffer, but most people are so poor they won't feel the pinch anyway.' We turned to population problems.

'Pills,' he said, 'make a woman very fat. The loop makes a woman bleed to death and have awful pains. Also, with both the pill and the loop, women either lose all interest in sex or they become very sexy. Women in Nairobi are very reckless. Homes break up and divorces increase. This is okay,' he continued scornfully, 'in the UK and USA, but not in our country. We should not copy the UK and USA. They are forcing us to accept family planning, which is why I oppose it.' He added, 'But I am only a silly little politician.'

Meanwhile, there were problems. Leela telephoned me from Bombay. She had flown there from Manila, and was staying with her parents till the doctor said she was fit for a long trip through Africa. The next day she phoned to say she was fit, and coming on the next flight. Johnston and I went to the airport, but she didn't arrive. She cabled to say she had lost all her luggage, but was definitely booked for another flight. Once more Johnston and I went to the airport; she didn't arrive. This happened a third time. It was quite a long way, each time, from the city to the airport and back.

On the third drive back, Johnston, who had been unusually silent, said to me, 'Sir, do you *really* have a wife?' I was beginning to doubt it myself.

But she arrived, in a wheelchair which had to be brought down off the plane. Her ankle had healed well. Her luggage, booked for Nairobi, had been sent to London, and took days to retrieve. Johnston drove us through the Rift Valley to Kisumu. This was a small town on the shores of Lake Victoria, which was full of bilharia. A family planning conference was to have been held in it, but was, for some mysterious Kenyan reason, cancelled. However, a local British official, Malcolm Milne, came to my help; he showed me many of the lakeshore problems; he was not looking forward to returning to Britain on pension, since he had spent his working life in Kenya. He was rather critical of the new regime. With faded blue eyes and a limp, he was vaguely reminiscent of Sanders of the River.

In fact, the British officials who stayed on in Kenya after *uhuru*, to train young people as administrators, were all relics of a colonial past, and they had been deprived of any future by the fact that they were in their old posts by sufferance only, that they would have to return home soon, and their work experience would be of no use to them in Britain. They tended to sit back and watch the Kenyans take over, as though presiding over a lemming rush to disaster. They sipped whisky after the sundown of the empire, and smiled often, but never really with their eyes.

The Kenyans, at least many of those I met, were slightly paranoic. They were not entirely sure of themselves, and talked hysterically about the plots which the whites and the Asians hatched between themselves to bring Kenya to its knees. The UNFPA was regarded by several of these people as an agent of white imperialism, so the reception I got was mixed. The Kenyans would swing back and forth between paranoia and charm, and the impression they gave was of naturally happy people. But the paranoia was present and real. The two main tribes, the Kikuyu and the numerically inferior Luo, weren't friends then; some Luo felt that family planning, which they seemed to assume would wipe them out, was not a European or Asian but a Kikuyu plot.

However, it was a beautiful country. The growth rate of the population was high, and there could clearly be future problems. On the surface there seemed not to be any. It was not like Asia, where the problems were immediately perceptible in underfed and miserable people, in huge populations that crepitated slowly deathward. Around Lake Victoria and other places outside the cities, there were people who were visibly poor. But all of them seemed very cheerful, and whatever ailments or dietetic deficiencies they had were not immediately visible. They also possessed pride, absent in the Asian poor.

The book had taxed me immensely in Asia. It not only involved hard physical work but constant mental abrasions. I had known Asia, previously, as a correspondent; the stories I wrote weren't usually concerned with poverty. But this book brought me very close to it, day by day; the eyes of the dying in Nirmal Hriday reminded me of my own mortality. I had seen the consequences of malnutrition, and met many people who were helpless and felt unwanted. The long talks with officials trying to control population growth, while knowing that their work would fail, had occupied days; a white-clad man or woman in a small room, a fan turning slowly, their voices as they explained the depth of their failure, these images remained with me.

In my first encounter with black Africa, I had been fortunate. I came to Kenya exhausted after Asia, and had recuperated there. It was as well that I didn't know what lay ahead in Gabon, our next destination. Johnston drove us to the airport. I had written a letter praising his work, and he was pleased. Maciel saw me shortly before our departure, and remarked, 'When you next come back, I may not be here.' I asked why not; he was an institution in Nairobi. 'They're starting to get a little tough with Asians,' he replied, 'and, after all, however long I've been here, I am one!'

As we neared Kinshasa, we saw an extraordinarily thick and clotted forest below us, like a mass of broccoli heads. A broad yellow river wound through it. This must be the Congo river, I thought, and the broccoli heads the Congo forest. At this point an electric storm broke out. The Air Afrique plane, which was old and fragile, came down into it to land. It was flung violently up and down, and from side to side; thunder roared deafeningly around us, and electricity seemed to ripple down the wings. It was pitch dark outside, except when the forest was illuminated by lightning; the pilot made three attempts to land, and was successful on the fourth try.

Somewhat shaken, we drove to a hotel which was arguably the most expensive in Africa. Next morning we returned to the airport for the onward flight to Libreville. I had been thinking a lot. We might quite possibly have been killed in last night's landing; I had an assignment to carry out, but was it fair to expose Leela to all this? She had already hurt her ankle, and it was difficult for her to walk. When I said this to her she was rather angry. 'Who would look after you,' she asked, 'if I wasn't there?'

The office in Nairobi had told me it would be better to enter and leave Zaire on my UN *laisser-passer* since my British passport and Leela's Indian one represented nationalities the authorities there didn't approve of. It was very hot and wet that day in Kinshasa; I carried the *laisser-passer* in my hip pocket, not wanting to wear a coat. The national passports were in a suitcase. At Kinshasa immigration, we were encountered by a surly official with a revolver on his hip. He scrutinized the UN passport and said, in French, 'What country do you come from?' I told him.

'Then where are your passports?' he demanded. 'This is not from any country.'

He was sweating; he was angry. I told him that it was a United Nations passport.

'What is the UN?' he shouted. 'I have not heard of it. Is it a country?'

'No,' I said. 'It is an organization. It has a visa to Zaire in it.

It was stamped here last night. Now we wish to leave Zaire.' This appeared to enrage him further.

'After only one night?' he said. 'Is it that you do not like my country?'

I said we were in transit, and would he look at the visa stamped for entry and stamp it for exit?

He said, 'Where are your national passports?' I said they were in our luggage, and our luggage was in the aircraft. He shouted, 'Bring it from the aircraft!'

I was as hot and angry as he was. I turned to Leela and said in English, 'This is going to be difficult. All this fucking bullshit....' I was amazed to see the officer reach for his revolver. His small eyes had reddened, and watered.

'Hah!' he shouted. 'You think I don't know English? Two words I know. One is "fookeen", the other is "boolsheet". You are insulting my country, hah?'

I denied this. He said, 'Then you are insulting me, and that is worse.'

Leela took over. She said, 'M'sieu, my husband was not insulting you or your beautiful country. When he's angry, he always swears at me like this.'

To my amazement, he stamped the *laisser-passer*. He said to me, 'A gracious lady like Madame should not have such a husband. Why do you habitually insult her? Is this the behaviour of a good man? Go, go, take this document and go. If I catch you insulting Madame again, you will have reason to regret it.'

'Do you see what I mean?' Leela said when we had boarded the plane and were safely seated. 'What would you do without me to look after you?'

At Libreville a UN driver met us. His face and neck were covered with huge pink scabs. I was later told this was due to a traffic accident, but, at the time, had the impression that it was some frightful tropical disease. The city itself wore an air of deep depression. Our hotel stood by the shore; great grey breakers swept in through most of the day, and at evening receded, leaving women and seabirds to rummage the weed-covered rocks for shellfish and other survivors of the tides; the coelacanth, perhaps, since the country seemed prehistoric. After the happy, paranoid Kenyans, I was not entirely prepared for Francophone West Africa. When our pink-necked chauffeur first deposited us at the hotel, he had a rapid and instant quarrel with the male receptionist. They shouted at each other for twenty minutes for no perceptible reason, before we were allowed to occupy our room. My farewell to Kinshasa should have warned me of what was to come. A dank smell of forest, seaweed and petrol fumes pervaded the hotel. Every African in it was either sullen or in a ferocious temper.

'The rain comes all the time,' said Georges, our new driver. 'There is only sun for one or two months a year.' The Gabonese had a curious population problem. Their fertility rate was about one per cent, and the population was virtually static. The United Nations said that Gabonese women had a high level of infertility, and the males of sterility. The country's officials denied this, saying that, including pygmies; 400,000 people lived in the forest unbeknownst to anyone else. How the officials knew about these people, they did not say. But the French, when they consolidated their rule, around 1840, reported that the tribes they had found on the shores and in the forest were at that point of extinction. In 1973, the life expectancy in Gabon was about thirty-seven years.

Many French advisers had stayed on after Gabonese independence. They suffered, in the main, from the same gloom, the same unexpected fits of fury, as the natives. The curator of the museum, Pierre Sallee, was an exception. Bailee was a musicologist employed by UNESCO. We met him in the museum, surrounded by masks and musical instruments. He tapped a drum into temporary life: it throbbed with a dark sound, the sound of an old religion, an old art, a sound out of dank forests where few strangers came. White masks with slits for eyes hung on the walls, and Sallee told us that these represented death. There were also long, glaring masks, which looked truly evil, and stared down with an absence of eyes. 'The civilization here was the most purely African in the entire continent,' Sallee said, 'Picasso took much of his inspiration from Gabonese art.' He added that the main characteristic of the Gabonese population was its deep sadness. Their philosophy was fatalistic, and always connected with death.

'Every foreigner who has come here has noticed how addicted the Gabonese are to liquor,' said Sallee. 'They also take a lot of drugs, mainly a root called iboga. This may explain the impotence, the infertility, the sterility. But to really know all these things, you must travel inland, and see how the people live there, or rather, survive.'

We went inland, to a place called N'Toum, where there was a UN horticultural programme. Beyond Libreville we plunged into what was locally called *la brousse;* it had nothing to do with bush country as I knew it. Gigantic trees rose on either side of the deeply cratered road, with a tangle of undergrowth between them. No flowers were to be seen. Nor was there much evidence of human life; the two villages we passed seemed to be deserted. Twenty miles or so inland, there were thunderclaps of tremendous volume, and flashes all over the clouded sky. An endless, solid fall of rain began. Within five minutes the road was entirely flooded, the potholes bubbled like witches' cauldrons, and the thunderclaps seemed to come closer.

As suddenly as it had arrived, the rain eased off. But no sun appeared, and the forest was hermetically sealed into itself by a lid of cloud. We now passed small, ramshackle villages. People cowered inside the huts, the walls of which were hung with grisgris, talismans against evil spirits. Outside some of the huts were wooden platters containing fruit and vegetables. 'They don't eat them,' Georges explained. 'They sell them. Sometimes lorries come down this road.' I did not see how. Even in a Land Rover, the scarred and potholed track was difficult to drive, or even stay, on.

It still drizzled. We passed drenched women holding banana leaves over their heads as umbrellas. Georges turned down a forest trail of slippery red mud. He stopped; a small boy was coming towards us, carrying a dead pygmy antelope. Its four small feet were bunched up in his hand; it was a plump little beast, its grey pelt stained with mud and blood. Georges appeared to be trying to buy it, which seemed a mistake. Eventually, he found the price too high, and we drove on without the antelope. We saw no other people, until we reached a clearing filled with redbrick huts—Gabonese labourers, and French experts. One of them, slapping at his arm, asked me, 'Why have you come so far? There is nothing here except these tsetse flies.' He was quite right; but he told me that further inland was a Fang village, which might be of some interest.

We tried to reach this place; but the rain began once more. Georges could hardly see through the windscreen, now plastered liberally with mud. He almost drove across a bridge which, we suddenly saw, was broken in the middle. In his attempts to reverse the Land Rover, it capsized into a ditch. We got it out; Georges said he could go no further, and we abandoned our efforts to reach the Fangs. Going back to Libreville, we stopped several times at wayside huts for Georges to buy baby aubergines, yams, and manioc. The sellers emerged suddenly from the forest, and, the transaction concluded, returned to it. It was notable that throughout the entire trip we saw no adult male. The people we did see, women and children, had a dazed and withdrawn look. It was no wonder; they lived in the thickest forest on earth under continual heavy rain. Perhaps it was better for them than for their ancestors, who lived in the same situation, but with no contact with the outside world. Their ancestors would have crouched in their huts, among grisgris, and wondered what might not walk up out of the trees.

The plane to Senegal made a number of stops, which was unfortunate. Seated in front of us was a young Senegalese, clad in a bubu, the flowing robe of his country. He was accompanied by an elderly man. At our first stop, in Togo, because Leela's foot still hurt, we stayed on the plane. So did the couple in front. We soon understood why. The young man stood up and said to a white stewardess who was passing, 'I am mad.' Then he said, 'I was supposed to take a sedative before we left Libreville, but my political enemies prevented it. Unless I have it now, I will take off all my clothes and then become very violent.' The white stewardess fled; a black one replaced her. The white stewardess started to have hysterics, quietly, in the pantry, but her replacement stayed calm. The young man's companion, or keeper, produced a boxful of ampoules and syringes. 'Is it to be intramuscular or intravenous?' asked the stewardess.

Neither the patient nor the keeper knew. The stewardess went off and returned with a doctor. The young Senegalese, in a sober and deliberate way, removed all his clothes. The doctor, as unsurprised as the stewardess, administered an intramuscular shot. We took off. The young man now told the stewardess that he needed to visit the lavatory. She took him there. As they passed us, I noticed that his arms were festooned with amulets. 'An enemy has bewitched me,' he told the stewardess. She nodded seriously, but replied, 'With all the grisgris you carry, that should not have happened.'

Her white colleague stayed in the pantry for the remainder of an interminable flight. But she, an intrepid woman, kept offering him napkins and towels to cover his nudity. He accepted them all, but instead of using them as she intended, piled them on his head. Meanwhile Leela and I moved several rows back. The plane was mostly empty; during the rest of it the madman and his keeper formed an isolated island amidst deserted seats, which only the black stewardess dared visit. Shortly before we landed in Dakar, the young man reattired himself, and descended the ramp decorously, saying to his stewardess friend, 'I am sorry to leave the plane. I was very happy here.'

In Dakar the sun shone, there were violent outbursts of flowers in every tree, and lepers strolled around with ivory smiles, or squatted on the pavements asking for alms. These tall, dignified lepers were dressed in bubus, so were the women, equally tall and dignified, and most of the healthy men. The few who didn't wear bubus wore suits. The population of Senegal then was about four million. Most of it seemed to be in the capital, because in the north there was a drought and a hot wind out of Mauritania. Thousands of people were dying in this wind, of heat exhaustion, thirst, or starvation, and so were thousands of cattle. Despite all this, the inhabitants of Dakar seemed cheerful and courteous; a greater contrast with Gabon could hardly be imagined. Not all of them, however, were as happy as they seemed, or as contented.

Senegal had a progressive President, the poet Leopold Senghor. But it suffered from other politicians, who propagated the idea that family planning had been invented by white criminals to wipe out the black races. As a result, the growth rate was too rapid for a country plagued by drought. At one time, the very poor, particularly those who had come in from the desert, had built their shacks and hovels along the road that led from the airport to the city. The government thought this a bad first impression for foreigners to have, and settled the squatters in Pikine, on the outskirts of Dakar. They lived in squalid conditions, were permanently unwell, and bred rapidly. Human bodies find comfort in other human bodies, and the people of Pikine badly needed comfort. The Senegalese authorities, without any fixed policy towards population, did not seem to realize what was happening, and so Pikine was bursting at the seams.

It was quite different from Dakar, a pleasant metropolis with trees, water, and white houses. French-style bistros abounded, and, as in Kenya and Gabon, large numbers of advisers left over from the colonial period were still around. Leela and I met and befriended Jacques Gagnon, who was head of the department of statistics and busy drawing up a new census, and his wife, Constance. He introduced me to another French adviser called Pierre Ferry. 'The resistance to family planning comes from the marabouts, the priests,' Ferry said. 'But it's nothing to do with Islam. Nothing is said in the Quran about contraception. But Islam here is all intermixed with animism and tribal customs. I can see a number of population problems in Senegal, and the main one is political. What finally makes problems is infant mortality and the control of urban migration. The urban migration is uncontrolled,' he sighed, 'and uncontrollable.'

No floods of people oozed down the streets of Dakar, as they did in Indian cities. But there were too many who were poor and ill, flashing brilliant, improbable smiles. It was a place of paradoxes. The Gagnons and their children accompanied us to the offshore island of Goree, where the slave traders had once kept their captives before loading them on to the grim ships bound for America. The implements of slavery were on display; we saw punishment cells where recalcitrant slaves were chained; the tide had come in through gaps in the walls, submerging them to their chins. But Goree was now a picnic resort for the citizens of Dakar. Many of them were on the island that Sunday, eating and drinking under beach umbrellas; giggling girls in bikinis, strapping young men, who, after their picnic, toured the pink buildings of the prison.

17

Flying over Senegal, I had looked down on what seemed to be an old, tired, mangy lion-skin spread out under the sun. Dakar and the Bassin des Arachides looked up from it, with green, unwinking eyes. Driving away from Dakar, across the lion-skin, one rapidly concluded that there was nothing left in the world but heat, sand, and the sun. Once we had left the city, the whole aspect of Senegal changed. The red earth had vast cracks in it, and spread away for miles, to a soiled horizon. Cactus and tamarisk were the only vegetation; the only indication of animal life were the herds of zebu being driven towards Dakar by skinny boys; they were going to the city abattoirs.

Niang, our driver, was a Wolof, and said disapprovingly, 'The Serere do not know how to drive cattle. They are only Serere.' All over Africa, I had noticed, there was not so much a rivalry between tribes, as a hostility. This complicated matters everywhere. We were on a mysterious mission: we had to locate a French adviser called Gerard in Kongoule. 'Kongoule is not a place,' said the Dakar office. 'It is an area, and we do not know precisely where Gerard is. But if you search, you will find him.' Gerard was exploring the possibilities of moving Serere tribespeople from the fertile Bassin des Arachides into the desert; it was like moving Musovites to the Gobi. Niang approved of the idea. 'There are too many Serere,' he said. 'They will die here.' He had disapproved deeply of my decision to drive into the Sahel.

The red earth faded away into tawny sand. Great quantities of it were blown through the car windows. We had to roll them up, which made it unbearably hot inside. The desert wind strengthened as we went on. It pushed against the car, and vibrated it, it pushed the dunes over on either side of us, and then reassembled them. The whole surface of the desert seemed to be on the move; presently we ceased to be able to see it, since clouds of blown sand rose round us. It was exactly like driving in a thick Devonshire mist. 'I told you,' Niang grumbled. 'This is a very bad place.'

The remarkable thing about the wind was that it never seemed to stop, or even falter. A roaring sound accompanied it. My ears were blocked, as though I was on a long flight. Through the haze of sand, one could sometimes dimly make out lurching shapes of men and camels; but these apparitions were few. After a time, the wind dropped, the sand clouds settled; shortly after this, we discerned, some way off the road, a small collection of beehive huts. Niang stopped, and we walked to it. Going through the sand was like wading through scalding water, with the engorged disc of the sun burning overhead. Eventually we reached the village. I was not looking forward to the return trip. It was so hot that I was too dehydrated to sweat any more.

The villagers, like most Senegalese, were Muslims. But the walls of their huts were adorned with grisgris: black and white feathers, knucklebones, and brass amulets. The headman sat with me and pointed to stretch marks on his brown belly. 'I was much fatter once,' he said. Very few people were about; mostly they were lying in their huts (as the headman had been lying in his, before we came) to keep out of the hot wind and the sun. Before the drought, the people had cultivated millet and peanuts, both as cash crops and items of consumption. Now they were dependent on a bakery van that came round once a week selling bread. 'I am the headman. I have bought two loaves for myself and my family. But my people will not go to Dakar yet.'

He would have offered us water, he added, but the whole village was on rations. He walked back to the car with us. 'Not many people come here,' he said. Not only had he never heard of Gerard, he had never heard of Kongoule, where we were supposed to find the French adviser. Neither had Niang, I now gathered. 'But this road,' said Niang, 'has no turnings. If we follow it we may get to this Kongoule. It is also likely that we will come to Mauritania.' He burst into liquid laughter at the idea.

The desert wind restarted. After nightfall we reached another collection of beehive huts, this time centred on a white colonial house. The huts and the house constituted a township called Kaolack, and the house was in fact a hotel: the epitome of a really bad French provincial hotel, set down by a random hand in the midst of the desert. Not for the first time, I regretted putting Leela through all this; but she seemed to like it, and I thought of other wives who had accompanied their explorer husbands. All night the hot wind shook the hotel and the huts around it; and Niang, though Muslim, got very drunk. Next day the car, its windows up, was filled with sand and the fumes of stale alcohol.

The hotel-keepers, however, had been useful in one way: they had told us that Gerard lived in a township about fifty miles down the road. We reached it around lunchtime, and found him in his house. Apart from loneliness, he seemed content with life. His freezer yielded lamb chops and peas for lunch, as well as beer and wine. He said that three hundred families had been moved from Bassin to the desert over the last three years. 'There are interesting agricultural possibilities here,' he said. 'The soil is very suitable to cotton.' Wind roared at the door in denial all through our lunch.

Shortly after this we left for New York. We had been on the road for three very exhausting months, and Leela's ankle hadn't healed. Smog welcomed us back, the first we had seen for some time. I suggested to Salas and Tarzie that I should write a chapter on the population problems of New York. They agreed and I talked to city officials and schoolchildren; I explored the Bowery and Harlem, and used my eyes. What struck me as curious was the poetic diction employed by the harassed officials when they spoke about their city. 'When people come out of the subway,' said one, 'you can see the agony and anguish in their faces.' Another, talking of the violence in New York, remarked, 'It's in their minds. Something has wounded them there.' This was particularly true of Harlem.

Frank Hercules introduced me to a man called Charles Kenyatta, once a disciple of Malcolm X, and now a black leader in his own right. Kenyatta took me around Harlem, where I met a number of people, all of whom seemed apathetic and slightly miserable. When Kenyatta talked to them, he spoke of 'a day to come', and they seemed ignited by this phrase, particularly the younger ones. I asked him to explain what precisely he meant by it. 'I don't know, man,' he said. 'But it sounds good.' I had met James Baldwin in London; he gave me the impression that he was the sole spokesman of black revolution in the US. Kenyatta and others didn't think so: 'He sold out to whitey.' The past leaders of America, black and white, were being discredited, one by one; Kennedy, a hero of the 1960s, was already being denigrated, and there were no replacements. Nixon was at the time in the process of discrediting himself. The population of New York seemed to have even shorter tempers than when I first visited the city. 'It's the absence of leadership,' Frank Hercules said. 'Now people feel there is no leader.'

The stop in New York could hardly be described as a rest, but we were soon on the road once more. We flew to Colombia, and, on arrival at our hotel in Bogota, suffered from altitude sickness.

'The problem in South America,' I was told, 'is machismo.' The family planning authorities blamed everything on that. We flew down to Santa Marta, on the coast, for a conference on population. Most of the delegates to this were Latin American revolutionaries. Like Charles Kenyatta, they spoke of 'the day to come', but in their case they defined the phrase: they meant the day of revolution, but were unclear against whom or what, or who the revolutionaries would be.

'This is another manifestation of machismo,' said an official. 'They want to prove that they are men by being seen as revolting.' It was a splendid sentence, I thought. Machismo and revolution were only two of the stances in Latin America; there was also the religious attitude which was responsible, according to one family planner, for the very high rate of abortion. 'The Catholicism here is mixed up with the old beliefs of the Chibcha Indians. It's a dangerous mixture, very inflammable. Anyway, confession to a priest is very important. Women who take the pill or the loop cannot do it, because these are continuing processes, whereas abortion is a single act. So they can confess to abortion and be absolved. There are only a thousand hospital beds available to every two or three people in Colombia. About a third of them are occupied by women suffering from the results of bad abortions. We are also short of doctors.'

The person who told me this, Dr Guillermo Lopez Escobar, was one of the founders of the family planning movement in Colombia. 'There is one doctor to every ten thousand people,' he said, 'and, what is more, there is only one trained nurse to every three doctors. Half the population is rural. It suffers from malnutrition and tuberculosis, and intestinal infections are very common because of the shortage of potable water. In the next two decades, our population will probably double, and then we shall find ourselves in a real mess.' At this time there was no evidence of drug barons in Colombia. Bogota seemed a peaceful place, where many people had money. But the poverty found outside Bogota was on an Asian scale. I visited a settlement for poor people from Boyaca, in the south. This place was called 'Vista Hermos', that is, 'beautiful view'. There was a certain irony about the name. It was a slum on a hill of red earth outside the city, and we got to it at dawn on a very rainy day. Raul Trejos, who ran the UN Information Centre in Colombia, was with me, a tall and very unemotional man.

The men of this settlement were construction workers. They earned about ten dollars a month. 'This is what they would earn where they come from,' Raul told me. 'But the food here is not so good. All the children suffer from vitamin deficiencies.' A young man, Luis Ortega, whose father owned the land, arrived, carrying a bottle of aguardiente. 'It is cold now, and wet,' he said. 'Besides, you will need a drink to keep your courage. You will see much sadness here.' I saw even more than he predicted. The people in the settlement had been told that a UN officer had come from America to help them. I discovered a long queue of women, waiting to apprise me of their woes.

I remember particularly a withered and wizened woman, who was, Ortega told me, not yet forty. She had a daughter of fifteen, who was very brilliant at school. The teachers said that she should be sent to a university to learn biochemistry. But there was no money with which to send her. The mother kept breaking down into soundless tears. The daughter, she said, was now pregnant. She had to have an abortion, but the mother wanted it done properly. 'Most abortions are not clear,' she said. 'Many women die.' She wanted the United Nations to pay for the abortion, and then send her daughter to a university. I have seldom felt so helpless in my life; and she depended on me for help. It frequently happened in South America that people addressed their appeals to me, thinking of me as the United Nations incarnated, and were disappointed.

Of the many women I met that day, one, Georgina de Torres, had had sixteen children, nine of whom had died at birth or shortly after. She took me to her hut, where the remaining children lay about on the floor, whimpering for food. The youngest, aged two, had tiny deformed legs, like cigarette ends, and would never be able to walk.

Senora de Torres had a truck-driver husband; they had met when she was a waitress in a café. She didn't know how much he earned; he beat her whenever she asked. He also beat her and the children whenever he was drunk, which was often. Raul pointed wordlessly to a row of empty aguardiente bottles. 'They have never spoken at all,' Raul translated, 'since the children were born. She wishes to speak to him, but he does not wish to speak to her.' A pot of maize porridge simmered on a stove. 'She wakes up at five every morning,' Raul said, 'and starts to cook this porridge to feed the children. In the afternoon she adds more maize, which they eat in the evening. She says if she could leave him she would. She would try and get work, to buy clothes for the children and send them to school. She also wants to know if the United Nations can help her. I have told her this is impossible.' As we talked, I noticed that a lean and mangy dog had come into the hut, and now had its snout deep in the porridge.

I called Senora de Torres' attention to this. She drove the dog away. 'What a pity,' I said, and Ortega shook his head. 'It won't be wasted,' he said. 'They will still eat it.' I asked a question, and Raul translated her reply. 'She is thirty-five.'

Brazil was more extrovert than Colombia, at least the cities were. Rio provided gaudy bursts of sunshine between tropical showers. Huge, glassy waves rolled in to the white Copacabana sands, where girls of all colours paraded in bikinis. Young men rode the rollers on surfboards, or played football on the beach, for this was Pele's country. Beyond the kicking waves stood Pan D'Azucar, Sugarloaf Hill, which cable cars ascended to offer tourists a panoramic view of the city. On an adjacent hill stood a great statue of Christ—as in most South American cities—looking down at the faithful. Some of them badly needed him: the little shoeshine boys who infested the beach restaurants and bars, and the inhabitants of the favelas, or slum areas.

Among all the bronzed bodies, speaking mostly in liquid Portuguese, the shoeshine boys seemed an anomaly. Among the thoroughfares and high buildings of the city, the favelas were an eyesore. Brazil, for one reason or another, was the richest country in South America. But inequities of vast proportions existed. In the north-east, and in much of the Amazon basin, the bulk of the population suffered their lives at a subsistence level. The inequities in Rio were more pronounced, because of the evident wealth all around. The Brazilian authorities, when I spoke to them, appeared to see no real population problem. They were proud of a highway system they were building, which would connect most parts of the country. And, they said, they had the Amazon forest to fall back on. If there was population pressure, they could cut down parts of the forest to provide more space. The ecological aspects of all this did not seem to concern them.

The city of Brasilia was a federal capital, which made one think of Dali's painting, except that it was all white. It had wide avenues, punctuated at intervals with inexplicable and futuristic monuments, tall ministries set in impeccably exact lines, and glittering glass houses. Dust devils whirled in the plains beyond, but did not affect the glass and marble of the ministries. Fountains and pools surrounded them, inhabited by stout, happy goldfish. On the far side of a willowed lake was the residential area, where many diplomats lived. At night, their houses, hung with flowering vines, looked out over the lake at a constellation of fallen stars, the lights of Brasilia.

The ministers admitted that the masses did not have a balanced diet, that the literacy rate was low, and that there were many health problems. "People accuse us of killing off the Indians,' one of them said. 'But why? They are dying out anyway. If we open up in Amazon forest, in a few years we will be able to feed the world. The only problem would be the huge technological expertise needed, and the cost.'

But there were already curious flaws in the planning. Brasilia had been designed for a few inhabitants, and already had 600,000. There was a school of thought which recommended the erection of barricades around the capital, through which only those refugees from the rural areas who were deemed suitable would be allowed to pass. The migration of the underprivileged into the cities was perceived as the main problem Brazil faced. It was these people who lived in the favelas. It seemed obvious that more attention should be paid to the rural population if this migration was to be stopped. But most Brazilians saw it the other way round. They felt that migrants should be discouraged because of the damage they did to urban areas, and gave no thought to the millions of faceless people who dwelt outside Rio, Sao Paolo, and Brasilia, in distress.

My assignment had its disadvantages. I would have liked to spend more time than I did in the favelas, and I would have liked to visit the economically backward north-east. I would have liked to meet more average citizens than I did, but I mostly met the policy-makers. My schedules were too tight and circumscribed for me to be able to change this. Nevertheless, I managed to meet a number of poor people, and visit them in their homes; but to do this more or less every day, in country after country, squeezing these visits in between official appointments, was infinitely depressing, since I could only observe them and listen to them, and could not help in any way. It was also very tiring, since, in order to meet the deadline for World Population Year, I had to write my book as I went. One night, after a day full of appointments and interviews, followed by three hours of work, I stepped into my bath fully clad, and was rescued by Leela.

'There's only one country left,' she said. 'You've got to stop pushing yourself. You can finish the book in New York.'

Santiago was plunged into winter; one could see snow on the Andes beyond the city. Salvador Allende was in power, and, for all his excellent intentions, the Chilean economy had collapsed under him. The official rate for a dollar was 150 escudos. The black marketeers (who were patronized, I later discovered, by many UN officials), offered thrice that amount. Many people wanted to leave Chile, especially, I was told, those of European extraction, and they all needed hard currency to do this.

There were queues everywhere in Santiago: for meat, milk, cigarettes, even for matches. Allende, however, remained enormously popular. Considering the nature of most of his predecessors, who had been rogues or tyrants, this was not surprising. Pedro, the UN driver assigned to us, was a great supporter of Allende, though he had had to suffer considerable hardship because of presidential policies. He took us to the hovel in which he and his family lived. He was comparatively well-paid, as a UN driver. But there were huge numbers of less fortunate people, mostly of Indian blood, who lived almost from day to day. One saw them, in particular, at the family planning clinics—exhausted women, sullen men. The greatest resistance against birth control came from the Church. In Chile, as in other Third World countries, some kind of family planning was badly needed. The prelates were bitterly opposed to Allende and his policies. Those I met pointed to the huge statue of the Virgin Mary above Santiago.

'She will save us,' they said. 'She will send another man to lead us.'

If she did, she made an odd choice, for she picked Pinochet.

The presidential palace dominated the large central square of Santiago. Within the huge wooden gateway, a number of sleepy sentries lolled around. We climbed an unevenly carpeted staircase to an anteroom filled with chandeliers and portraits of dead presidents. Most of them looked as though they had already been dead when the painter started work. President Allende came out of his office and shook hands.

He had started out as a doctor, and was dressed like an English country GP in a tweed coat with leather elbow patches, and rather battered trousers. His hair was black, his moustache white, and he had a somewhat distrait air, which, considering the state of his country, was understandable. Through an interpreter, he asked me several questions which seemed to be about architecture. I said, finally, that I was not an architect. Allende frowned and asked what was obviously a pointed question.

'The President inquires,' said the interpreter, 'why you are not an architect, since you are a UN expert on cheap housing?' An aide stepped in, rather fortunately. 'Sir,' he told Allende, '*that* expert is coming later this week. *This* one is a famous consultant on population matters.' I saw no point in denying this. Allende seemed disposed to continue the interview. He kissed Leela's hand and remarked that she would make a better Indian ambassador to Chile than the present incumbent. Then he turned, rather unwillingly, back to me, and answered my questions, without seeming very interested.

'I was a doctor,' he said. 'Family planning interests me as it affects the health of the people. The main population problem in Chile, you must understand, is one of health. Living conditions here are very bad, and we are trying to improve them. The shortage of potable water and waste disposal systems is our worst problem.'

He seemed to become more interested in the conversation as it went on. 'Look at Santiago. It has so many problems, so many tens of thousands of poor people, so many children. The problems are wide and complex, and they vary from area to area. A very primary problem is housing. That is why I was so anxious to meet a housing expert.' Then he kissed Leela's hand once more, shook mine, and departed into his office, where, a very short while after our brief encounter, he was murdered as Pinochet made his coup.

The problems seemed to vary little from country to country. But there were certain specific obstacles in each case: in Asia, mainly, peasant tradition and superstitions connected with fertility; in Africa, the tribal system and the feeling by some fanatics that population control was somehow connected to the extermination of the black race by the white; in South America, machismo and the Catholic Church.

We flew back to New York by way of Buenos Aires. At customs in Kennedy Airport, where no one seemed to be impressed by our diplomatic passports, the officer who examined Leela's suitcase withdrew her hand from it and said 'Yucks!' Her fingers were coated with a sticky yellow substance. It turned out to be orange liqueur. A bottle had broken in another passenger's suitcase, and soaked the ones below. Leela was very upset; all her clothes had been ruined. The customs woman said to me, in a placatory way, 'That's nothing. Some woman on your flight heard from her son that there was a meat shortage in New York, and brought a side of beef in her case. All the luggage under hers was covered in blood. Yucks!' She waved us onward, ruined clothes and all.

There was certainly a meat shortage in New York. In the supermarkets we saw old people buying tins of dog food, murmuring shamefacedly to the cashier that they had several pets. The advertisements for pet food emphasized that it was fit for human consumption. There was also a petrol shortage coming up, and New Yorkers were in a worse temper than ever. I went back to the office and finished the book. Not very much of it was left; on completion I found myself with nothing to do, and a year still to run on my contract. After some thought, I suggested to Rafael Salas that UNFPA produce a book of essays by different people about their views on human life. Salas was the right person to approach for this kind of thing: he read assiduously for pleasure, and was always asking me what I thought about various authors.

He agreed to my proposal and inquired who I would approach for the essays. I replied that I did not feel that demographers or other population experts should contribute; this book should contain unexpected names, at least names unexpected in a volume sponsored by UNFPA. I mentioned some, and Salas agreed. Then he made a suggestion of his own, which was original; he suggested that I should ask Muhammad Ali, the heavyweight boxing champion. I wrote to Muhammad Ali's agent, and never received a reply. Then I sent off a letter to W.H. Auden. A few days later I wrote to Pablo Neruda. Very shortly after the Auden letter went, he died. Soon after this, Neruda also died. I felt sorrow over Auden and Neruda, both of whom I had known in my youth. Tevia Abrams, a colleague of mine, a Canadian playwright whose work had been put on off-Broadway, said I should stop writing to poets, otherwise I would kill off every one of any consequence in the world.

Tevia and his wife, Judy, were good friends to have; once the book was underway, I spent most of the day at the office. My secretary, Sabena Wenzel, opened files for me; she also lined the windows of my office on the twenty-third floor with potted plants, to ease my vertigo. In consultation with Tevia, I prepared my final list and started to send out a steady stream of letters. When the addressees actually replied, I was surprised. I had never expected any answers at all, much less affirmative ones. I felt that the book was now properly started. The population book was to appear for 1974, World Population Year. Praeger, in America, and Andre Deutsch, in London, were the publishers, Periodically, I went to the Praeger office in Washington to confer with the editor of *A Matter of People*, which was the book's final title. Praeger and Deutsch were also to bring out the essays.

My life became office-bound and slightly tedious. The letters written, the answers received, I had very little to do. Tarzie started a UNFPA magazine, *Populi*, the title of which I suggested. I worked on it; I worked on the proofs of *A Matter of People*. Tevia lived in Queen's, a long way from the office; he, Leela, and I would eat lunch together, in a different restaurant each day. Tevia, who was a gourmet, usually found and selected the restaurants. Sometimes Peter Hyun, a Korean poet who worked for a New York publisher, was with us; often there were other people from the office. When it was decided that the book needed another chapter, Tarzie sent me to Costa Rica; Leela returned to India to visit her parents, so this time I went alone, and spent a couple of weeks there.

It rained all the time in Costa Rica; the most famous residents of the capital, San Jose, were Margot Fonteyn and her invalid husband, Roberto Arias, but they were both out of town. Robert Vesco, the fraudulent American financier, also lived there, but the UNFPA representative strongly advised me against a visit to him, which my journalistic instincts urged me to pay. The representative also supplied me with an interpreter, a slim lady from India. She told me that her husband was a financier who had been less fortunate than Vesco; he had been arrested and imprisoned in Delhi for fraud. She, alone with her child in Costa Rica, awaited his release. She showed me around San Jose, though there was not much to see. Travel to other parts of the country was impossible; communications had broken down in the rain. I made one trip to an Indian settlement, and met a number of forest-dwellers who flourished machetes in a very unfriendly fashion. They calmed down quickly when assured that I was not from the government. Otherwise it was an uneventful trip.

Back in New York, there were small problems. Eugene Ionesco had sent me a puzzled reply, saying he did not understand what I wanted. Gunter Grass telephoned me from Berlin saying that he wanted to be interviewed; he didn't want to write anything. He also said, in excellent English, that he wanted to be interviewed in German. Leela was now back, and we flew to Europe to interview Grass, persuade Ionesco, and find a couple of extra contributors. The contributions were found, Ionesco persuaded. The difficulty about Grass was that I knew no German. The New York office found me an interpreter in Hamburg; we had no representative there. We checked into a Hamburg hotel and contacted the interpreter. Grass had a country house at Wewelsflete, outside the city, and the interpreter, a pallid, willowy young man, said he would drive us there.

It happened that the way out of the city went past the Reeperbahn. It was early in the day, but a few prostitutes were visible. The interpreter, who had previously been silent, pointed towards them and said, 'He would not have allowed this.' We spoke about the division of Germany, and he said, 'He would have wept for us today.' It occurred to me that he was capitalizing the 'h' in 'He', and that the 'He' being referred to was not Jesus Christ. I began to feel more and more nervous as we approached Wewelsflete.

Grass, however, made us very welcome; the upstairs of his cottage was a studio, with a number of pen-and-ink sketches of snails arrayed against the walls, and framed lithos of snails hanging on them. While we looked at them, he went and fetched several bottles of white wine and glasses. 'This should be good,' he said. 'My publisher sent it to me.' He was energetic, spry, and cheerful. The interpreter remained silent.

The interview started. Replying to my first question, Grass said, 'It was my misfortune to be born when Hitler was in power....' The interpreter translated this, but, still in English, shouted, 'He should have put you in a labour camp! You are a Jew and a Communist!' Grass was taken aback, but I had anticipated that something like this might happen. I sent the interpreter back to the car to wait, and the rest of a very long interview passed off peaceably. Grass would answer my questions in German, which I taped, then translate the answer. It was in all ways a peculiar sort of encounter. When Grass saw us off, he said, 'Where does the UN find such interpreters?'

On the way back, the interpreter, not unsettled by his brief encounter with Grass, said that his friends had a party on that night. Would we care to come? I was by now inquisitive about his friends. So we went. The group of people we met, about sixty of them, had their party in a kind of office which appeared to be their headquarters, and they sang Hitler Youth songs, very loudly into the small hours.

From Hamburg we flew to London.

Hamburg had been cold and wet. But it was sunny in London. I had no real business here, but we telephoned my father, who asked us to visit him. His house in Connaught Square was large; he lived there with Marilyn, his Apsos, and Sauri, as a kind of housekeeper. But despite the size of the house, he confined himself to a study. It had a desk at which he wrote and a liquor cabinet from which he drank.

He looked terrible; his hair was almost completely white, and he had lost an enormous amount of weight. We arrived at about ten a.m., and left around noon. In that time he drank about a dozen large whiskies. I drank hard, and so did many of my friends, but none of us as hard as this. I watched him in a slight daze. All through my childhood, he had been my protector; ever since then he had been a close friend. I was not now in any position to protect him, and it has usually been my policy to let my friends go to hell in their own way. But I found myself mumbling rather absurdly, 'You know, you oughtn't to drink like this.' He smiled in a faraway fashion, and nodded.

That night Judy and Francis came to his house. It was then that my father, in one of his coherent moments, suggested that we take Francis back to New York for a holiday.

I said that the idea of taking Francis to America for a few weeks was excellent. This seemed to soothe my father. I thought a change of scene might do him good. So I suggested that we all go to Oxford the next day. He seemed pleased with the idea.

But next morning, when we arrived in a hired car, he was extremely drunk. He slept all the way to Oxford; he was in no condition to look at his old college, or at mine. It was difficult to take him into a pub; most were crowded, and he couldn't steer himself. We wound up lunching at the Randolph. On the way back, he fell asleep once more. I went ahead and obtained an American visa for Francis, and got him a return ticket. On the last day, on the way to the airport, we stopped at my father's house to say goodbye. He kissed Leela and Francis, put his hand on my shoulder, and said, in a rather slurred voice, 'Be a good boy.' It was something he'd used to say in my childhood, but I hadn't heard the phrase for years. My eyes filled. I had a strong feeling, indeed a certainty, that I would not see my father again.

In New York, Francis settled down quickly. He was an ardent reader of Spiderman comics. We took him to the Spiderman comics office, where he met the chief illustrator, and had a special Spiderman poster drawn for him. He also said he was much interested in playing the violin. Yehudi Menuhin was in New York. He and I had once been guest speakers together at the Cambridge Union; I had met him off and on for years, and he was also a contributor to the UNFPA book of essays. We visited him at his hotel, where he showed Francis his Stradivarius, and also gave him and Leela tickets for his concert the next day. Francis' interest in music, Leela told me later, was less intense than he professed it was. They were sitting next to Diana Menuhin, and, in the middle of the performance, Francis said to his stepmother, 'Polly, this is boring. Can we go?'

Mrs Menuhin was not tremendously amused. Also in town, was the Indian philosopher Jiddu Krishnamurti. Leela had known him for years, and he was also a contributor to the UNFPA book, one of those who wanted to be interviewed rather than write an essay. When I went for this interview, I took Leela and Francis. Krishnamurti had a beautiful face under silky white hair, and a very soft voice. But there were great difficulties involved in this interview, since, every time I asked a question, he answered by asking it back. This, according to Tarzie later, was an old technique of his; but my own technique as an interviewer faltered in its face. He was attended to by a formidable American lady. To collect my mind, I asked Krishnamurti if I could smoke. He said I could; I lit a cigarette, and he immediately began to cough. 'Put out your cigarette,' growled his attendant. 'This always happens when thoughtless people smoke in his presence.'

The interview finished, I left Leela and Francis behind, since she wanted to talk to Krishnamurti. Francis, in my absence, had a nosebleed, to which he was then prone. According to Leela, Krishnamurti laid a hand on his head, and it stopped. I always thought Krishnamurti a very good person, but not gifted with paranormal powers—though, during the interview, he had remarked that levitation was quite a simple matter.

A Matter of People appeared, received some excellent reviews, but sold very badly. It was distributed to all the delegates at the World Population Year conference in Bucharest, but that was little consolation to the publishers or to me. However, I sent a copy to my father, and then heard from Marilyn, over the phone, that he was very ill, and was being taken to the Middlesex Hospital. Marilyn called every day after that to tell us about his progress, and it seemed that he was improving. I was very glad.

Leela, however, was very worried. The publishers, in a desperate effort to sell *A Matter of People*, arranged for me to appear on radio and television talk shows. I did a television show in Boston, and, when I came out of the studio, was told I should phone Sabena Wenzel at the office. Sabena had become our friend as well as my secretary; when I called, she told me that Marilyn had been on the phone, saying that my father's condition had suddenly become worse. We got back to New York at dusk; Leela took a telephone call from Marilyn. She was at the Middlesex hospital. A few minutes before this, an Atlantic away, my father had died. He was to be cremated the next day, which was also the day that Francis was to fly home to London. *The New York Times* carried a long obituary on Friday morning. Salas and Tarzie called with condolences. Salas said, 'Why don't you fly to London for the funeral?' I said the funeral would take place in a few hours; there was absolutely no point my attempting to attend it. Salas said, 'Don't you want to arrange his affairs?' I said that they would be taken care of by Marilyn. That night Francis flew back, and later Marilyn called.

She told me that for some reason the cremation was postponed till Monday. If I tried hard, I could still come. But I suddenly found that I had no desire to attend this particular funeral. I did not want to see those good hands and eyes go down into the electrical cooker. I thought I would spend Sunday as I wanted to. This was in accordance with something my father had also once told me, which was not to think of whatever other people might assume, so long as one felt one was right. It was not exactly original advice, but I thought myself out, and applied this formula.

Tevia and Judy came to brunch on Sunday. They both had the ability to calm me down, and I began to figure out what hurt me about my father's death. What a child may feel about his parents can vary hugely from case to case. Some remain dependent upon their progenitors for long periods. Some shake off these shackles early. But my father was my friend. Most of my other friends were roughly my own age, and were likely to die at about the same time as me. My father's death was my own intimation of mortality, as well as being the death of a friend, I also felt guilty about my mother. Till the end, he had begged me to write to her. He wrote to her, he said, but it wouldn't be the same as if I did. Leela had written to her constantly, but that wasn't the same either. His guilt and responsibility about my mother had now been entirely transferred to me. That was something else I didn't really want to face, not now at least.

Every time we met in the office corridors, Salas would say, 'My condolences.' After about three weeks, I found this irritatingly repetitive. The change, when it came, was sudden, he summoned me to his office and said, without condolences or any other preamble: 'Where is De Bocquer?' I did not understand what he meant. I knew nobody, either among my colleagues or my outside friends and acquaintances, who was called anything like De Bocquer. Salas went on, 'You and Tarzie and I, we hoff read all the essays, no? But I do not see De Bocquer's. Where is De

Bocquer?' And the mildest of all the Filipinos I had known, except for General Romulo, advanced on me, shaking his fists in my face. 'Hoff you got De Bocquer?' he demanded menacingly.

Tevia's office was next to mine. I took my problem to him. Tevia said, 'De Bocquer? De Bocquer? Is there some French writer of that name?' I shrugged; Tevia said, 'And you say he shook his fists at you? That isn't like Salas. Let me think.' Having thought, he said, 'Salas is a Filipino. He doesn't pronounce words the way you do. Didn't he ask you to get an essay out of Muhammad Ali?' I looked at him without real comprehension. 'When he said De Bocquer,' Tevia explained, 'he shook his fists at you, right? What he meant was, have you got the boxer? Where is the boxer?'

I started to laugh, because he was obviously correct, and this laughter was a kind of exorcism. For the first time in weeks, I forgot my father, and became human again.

18

Up to about this time in New York we had been living at the Gramercy Park Hotel, but Sabena had gone on leave for several months, and below her flat was one occupied by another UN staffer, a Haitian girl who was attending a conference in Caracas and would be absent for some time. These flats were in a small brownstone on West 72nd Street, and for the next few months we shuttled between the two as and when each was vacant. This was the first time Leela had had to maintain a flat in New York. She was delighted, though at intervals we ran into slight difficulties.

The Japanese photographer, Hiroji Kubota, with whom I had often worked in the past, came to stay with us. He had a great quantity of expensive equipment with him. At that time we were in Sabena's flat, but were caretaking the one downstairs; we put Hiroji into it. The Haitian girl had a slab of iron for a front door, for security; Hiroji, feeling secure, left his cameras behind it when he went out. One night, we returned to find someone had blow-torched his way through the iron and taken all the equipment. Nothing else was touched. The janitor had heard nothing. The cameras were insured.

Hiroji, when he left, threw a farewell party. He cooked shabu-shabu in a sort of burner, but forgot to switch it off when the party ended. Consequently it left a large, black, burn mark on a Swedish table of white wood. Leela, horrified, looked up a firm that specialized in this sort of thing, and they removed the mark, but charged us $300. Since we were responsible to the owner, we thought it was worth it. But when the Haitian tenant returned, and Leela explained the episode to her, she shook with laughter. 'It was great of you to do it,' she said. 'But that table only cost fifteen dollars.'

We had other guests. The English playwright Arnold Wesker, who had contributed an essay to my book, arrived in New York on a visit with his wife Dusty, three children, and nowhere to stay. We put him and his family up in one of the flats. My clearest memory of this is of Wesker in a blue undershirt, looking extremely morose as his progeny consumed huge numbers of fried eggs and demanded that he show them around New York. I also recollect his expression of anguish every time he returned from one of these forays. But he was a dutiful father.

Buckminster Fuller sent me an essay of 25,000 words, accompanied by an explanatory letter which seemed nearly as lengthy. Since the maximum length for an essay was three thousand words, I had to explain to him why I would have to cut it. The ensuing correspondence was voluminous, and, towards the end, acrimonious, but in the end we got it down, between us, to about five thousand words, which I used. Slowly the book concretized.

All the essays came in on time, except for Mrs Gandhi's. She was one of the three women contributors, the others being Margaret Mead and Gloria Steinem. Miss Mead was a large, intelligent, talkative lady with white hair, who told me many interesting things, all of which I have forgotten. What I recollect vividly is her leading the way into a restaurant for lunch, holding a huge shepherd's crook obtained somewhere on her travels. She looked like some kind of pilgrim leading a flock of disciples. The other lunchers put down their knives and forks and stared, mouths open, at our progress.

Gloria Steinem was slim and quiet, a contrast; but once we took her to lunch at the Delegate's Lounge, and she talked, throughout, about the equality of women, and how men denigrated them by offering to do things for them. The Delegate's Lounge had massive glass doors; when we left I forebore to open them to let Gloria and Leela pass. Neither said a word, but both looked extremely displeased. Her essay, to my surprise and slight dismay, quoted from *A Matter of People*, and cited me as an authority on world population. It was, however, flattering to be considered an authority on *something.* It was now nearly a decade since I had more or less stopped writing poetry that satisfied me. I remained very conscious of this, and though these days in New York were happy, and now seem to me dreamlike, I moved through them with a perpetual sense of an amputated limb, still in position, but rendered invisible.

In October 1974, my UN contract was extended for three years. At about the same time, I was asked to look at the film which had been commissioned from Roberto Rossellini. I had written the book for Population Year, and he had been asked to make the film. It had cost well over a million dollars. Rossellini arrived in New York for the preview. He was a short, bald, pallid person, accompanied by a nymphetlike secretary who wore expensive furs at night. From time to time, in conversation, Rossellini showed a certain fire and conviction, but this was only when he talked about his past films. He often looked tired and ill. The secretary hardly ever spoke.

An audience from UNFPA, including Salas, watched the film. It had no commentary, though it seemed to have been finally edited. A large part of it was devoted to an Indian village in the Amazon basin. The camera continually cut back to a side of raw meat hanging from a tree. Flies swarmed over it. There was also a sequence of poor people in India. The print was scratched, and the sequence seemed to have been shot years before. As the film continued to run, one could feel increasing dismay in the audience. When the lights went up, I looked at Salas, whose eyes were closed. The film was shown thrice on successive days. After the third showing, Salas summoned me.

'What do you think of de film?' he inquired. 'Rossellini says it is all filled with symbols. You, as a poet, should detect de symbols. Frankly, I cannot.'

I suggested that he should ask Rossellini. 'I hoff tried,' said Salas. 'But I do not wish to seem unintelligent.' With that, we parted. I never knew the eventual fate of the film, for, some days after this meeting, I was told to see the Indian ambassador in Washington. I had known Tiki Kaul for some years, and he informed me that his government had started a scheme whereby 2,400 Indian villages would receive television beamed from a satellite. 'All the hardware is in place,' he said, 'but we need software. We need someone to write scripts on educational subjects, like, for instance, family planning, but not in a direct way. You understand what I mean? We would like UNFPA to lend you to us.' They had already approached Tarzie. Salas asked me what I wanted to do. 'I think,' he said, 'that there is not much you can do here once de book of essays is finished. At least, not in de immediate future. So why don't you do dis?'

It was endearing of Salas that he pronounced his 'th' sounds in this manner. His hair transplant was endearing also, it gave him the slight touch of absurdity which makes many people likeable. Once we had flown together to La Paz. When the plane doors opened, and the thin air of Bolivia flooded the plane, he clutched at his throat and turned pale, and I remembered his heart problem. I felt immediate and spontaneous concern for him. Our relationship was not close, but he seemed to me a good man, and I think he liked me because I was a writer and he longed to be one. He now said, 'It would also be a goodwill gesture if you went. How is de book of essays?' I said the last possible deadline had arrived and I had still not received Mrs Gandhi's essay, but had telexed New Delhi twice to remind her.

'Mrs Gandhi, eh?' said Salas. 'Perhaps she hopes to give it to you in Delhi.'

As it happened, the Indian embassy in Washington received Mrs Gandhi's contribution by telex the day before the deadline, and I was able to get it in. The book consisted of twenty-five essays of about three thousand words apiece, except for those by Buckminster Fuller and Jonas Salk, which were longer for reasons beyond my control. We paid a visit to friends in Washington before we left: Lois O'Neill, my Praeger editor, and her husband Ed, a soldier and diplomat, and a man of great silence and success. The Nixon government had failed and was about to fall; Watergate had passed into the language. On the first evening we stayed with the O'Neills, a kind of celebratory party was held for the imminent fall of Nixon. Woodward and Bernstein, the reporters who had played a great part in this, were the guests of honour. Lois and Ed had got invitations for us, but, though Leela went, I didn't go. It was partly because I wanted to walk around Washington by myself while they were at the party.

I was not very well acquainted with the city; but I knew a number of places where I had been before; after revisiting a couple of places I headed for Rock Creek Park. I watched people pass. There were not many muggers then, and I have never looked like a prospective victim. Something in the air suggested a world I was soon to leave, and in New York it seemed the same. For some reason which I could not analyse then, I felt all this would be my last time in the West as a free person, a part of my known world, a belonger.

Flown to Delhi, I landed at least in cool weather. I contemplated through the UN car's windows the welling of dust from the earth, and the numbers of wretched and starving people. The weather had not benefitted them in any respect. I settled into a place called the India International Centre, and awaited Leela's arrival from Bombay, to where she had once more travelled to visit her parents. I didn't really want to see them. I knew about possessive progenitors: a long childhood with an insane mother had taught me this. But Leela's parents were a good deal more protective and possessive than most. They kept begging her to stay with them in Bombay.

In the meantime, I was not really established in Delhi. The day after I arrived, I went to the information ministry, as instructed by the New York office, to report my arrival. I met Inder Gujral, who was then the minister. Gujral was a slight, smiling, and very pleasant man, with a beard which he has retained through the various vicissitudes of his political life, though it has greyed now, like my hair. He said, 'How nice to see you here. What are you here for?' This dismayed me slightly. I said, 'I'm on loan to you from UNFPA to make satellite films. Tiki Kaul asked for me.'

Gujral said, 'Tiki has no authority to ask for anyone without formal approval from Mrs Gandhi. Let me find out from Tiki.' What was I to do, I inquired, in the meantime? 'Whatever you were supposed to do,' said Gujral cloudily. 'After we know, I will call a meeting of the concerned authorities.' Meanwhile, not knowing what I was supposed to do, I called Salas, who said, 'I do not know this either.'

Six weeks after this, Gujral asked me to come to a meeting which involved everyone connected with the satellite television, or SITE, programming. Having nothing else to do, I had drawn up prototypes of twelve television series, with twelve twenty-minute programmes in each, about education, health, family planning, and so on, as well as the draft proposals for a children's programme. The conference table in Gujral's office was surrounded by sad men. Gujral said to me, 'Now I know who asked for you. Mrs Gandhi.'

His office was two doors down from hers and he might have found out earlier. Besides which, the conclusion of the meeting was that, though I had drawn up, altogether, 144 television programmes of twenty minutes each, the concerned ministry had only enough money to make two. I looked towards Gujral for counsel. He smiled affably. 'You have our go-ahead,' he said. 'Will UNFPA pay for the programmes you make, and provide crews?'

I said, 'I don't think so.' I phoned Salas, who said, 'Stay where you are. You are our gesture of goodwill to India.' It seemed a very peculiar thing to be.

The two films I decided to do were quite separate in theme. One was to do with diet, and was built around my friend, Hari Ahluwalia, the mountaineer and soldier, now a cripple. All through his life he had eaten frugally and simply, but his diet was nutritious, and also inexpensive. The second was about Rajasthani potters in the desert. Here they fettled up their wares, and then took them to the Delhi markets. Some of them had settled in the city, and formed a rather pathetic little colony near the New Delhi railway station. Most of them wanted to go back to their villages. This film, really speaking, was a sermon against urban migration.

The budgets the government offered me for these films was ludicrously low, though it supplied the equipment and crews. I had to find directors, and through Leela met two who offered to work free of charge.

Ram Kumar, who specialized in animation, was one of them, a shy but very efficient person. The other was S. Sukhdev, who had the reputation of being the finest director and cameraman in India. He had made his own documentary films, the most notable of which were a long work called *India 1967* and a study of the 1971 war against Pakistan. He had the reputation of being difficult and temperamental, but I never found him so, at least not with me. Sukhdev was an alcoholic, and was frequently told by doctors that he would die if he continued to drink. Why he consulted them at all was not clear, since he never listened to a word they said. If he obeyed them, it was only for a few days.

He was not a big man, but thickset, very strong and when at work carried his Arriflex like a gun, delighting in his own prowess at handheld shots. He was a shaven and deturbaned Sikh, who came from a Punjabi village. We got on exceptionally well; he called me 'Dom Singh' and I called him 'Sukh Moraes'. Leela and I acquired a flat, which she furnished beautifully. Whenever Sukh was in Delhi, he came there. He had a boisterous and noisy exterior, but was also a gentle and thoughtful person when one knew him. The cook we employed, Kishan Chand, was a favourite of his. They would talk in Punjabi, their mother tongue. When Sukh died suddenly in 1979, we were in London. Kishan Chand, however, went to the funeral. Later, he said, 'When Sukh Sahib visited us it was as though the garden came into the house with him.' Kishan Chand was a peasant, and didn't usually sound so poetic.

It was Sukh who told me that my entire mission was doomed. 'Sure, Mrs G. asked you,' he said. 'But she went over the heads of all the bureaucrats, and the whole film establishment. Every scriptwriter, producer, and director wants to get in on this. They are very angry that Mrs G. has called in a foreigner. Because that's what they see you as, Dom Singh. None of them is going to help you. They'll do exactly the opposite.'

I found this to be true. After the two films were shot, they were sent to Bombay to be processed. There the negatives were inexplicably scratched. When I tried to obtain financing for more films, all kinds of obstacles were placed in my way. Later on, I went to see how the satellite television films worked in the villages they were meant for; I discovered that they didn't. Remote villages had been provided with sets and umbrellas, one to each village. At first, apparently, the villagers turned up in large numbers. The sheer dullness of the educational programmes they were shown put them off. The set and umbrella, when not in use, were locked in a shed, to which a local schoolmaster had the only key. If he was not conscientious—and there was no reason why he should be, since he wasn't paid—there was no television. Often the key was lost and not replaced, and eventually the experiment was a failure. I made no more films. I asked Salas to move me back to headquarters. My presence here was without point.

But Salas said that he had promised me to Mrs Gandhi for two years, and I should wait for them to end. Meanwhile, the tedium was broken when I was sent on brief visits to Singapore and Mauritius, to write country reports. In Mauritius, the prime minister, Sir Seewoosagur Ramgoolam, insisted on my becoming a state guest. More than that, he flew Leela out to be with me. We were given a beach house and a car driven by a Chinese police inspector. Ramgoolam also threw a party, where Leela danced the sega with a man so diminutive that he hardly came up to her chin. Returning to our table, where two Mauritian ministers and Ramgoolam were seated, she whispered to me, 'Who's that absurd little person?' Unluckily, one of the ministers overheard this, and repeated it, with loud chuckles, to his colleagues and the prime minister. All of them went into prolonged convulsions of mirth. When they recovered, Ramgoolam said, 'That is the finance minister.'

Such trips were a relief, but there were only those two. Meanwhile, I was supposed to stay at my post, doing nothing. At first I sent progress reports, but soon there was nothing to report, so I stopped. I could not write poetry, and I was so bored that I surrendered completely, lay in bed for hours, and bestirred myself only to drink.

Leela pulled me out of this by arranging two commissions for books, one on Goa, the other on Karnataka. Mario Miranda, the cartoonist, did the illustrations for both. He was an excellent travelling companion, and a brilliant artist. He proved then, and since, to be very much more than a cartoonist. His drawings and paintings are often beautiful. Besides the pleasure of having something to do, I learnt a great deal about India during these assignments. The UNFPA auditors were quite happy; Salas told them that I had his authority to do what I liked. I think he understood the depth of my boredom.

Occasionally we met Mrs Gandhi. She invited us to a lunch for Prince Charles. This was given in the garden of the presidential palace, which had once been the Viceroy's house. After lunch, the Duke of Gloucester and his wife suddenly disappeared. He had told me that he was going to play polo, but Mrs Gandhi was furious that they had not said goodbye to her. 'Don't they know that I am the prime minister of India?' she demanded. It was hardly a question I could answer. But she sent me in search of them. On this futile errand, I encountered Earl Mountbatten kneeling beside a flowerbed. 'I planted all this,' he said, 'when I was Viceroy. How are you, Frank? I didn't know you were still alive.' I attempted to correct his assumption that I was my father, but without much success. He spoke of the rough times we had been through together in Burma during the Second World War. I never found the Duke and Duchess, and Mrs Gandhi continued to be cross.

Pupul Jayakar, who was very close to the prime minister, was also a disciple of Jiddu Krishnamurti. He stayed with her in Delhi; we lunched with him at her house. He disclosed that his favourite reading was detective stories, 'the bloodier the better'; I kept him supplied while he was in Delhi. Pupul, a large and gentle lady, is one of the great living experts on Indian art, about which she has written several books. She has also produced biographies of Krishnamurti and Mrs Gandhi. Once, Geoffrey Hill, whom I had known in England, came to India to read his poetry for the British Council. He arrived in Delhi feeling ill. The British high commission doctor said that he had laryngitis. It turned out to be appendicitis, and he was in hospital for days. We used to visit him daily; Leela made him his favourite apple pudding, which he guarded fiercely from hungry nurses. When he left hospital, we took him to see Pupul.

Geoffrey, as his friends know, is a taciturn person. He guards his private life as grimly as his apple pudding. After he had talked to Pupul for a few minutes, he suddenly asked Leela and me to leave the room. Since Pupul had invited us all to tea, this seemed rather strange, but we complied, and wandered in the garden till we were summoned back. This was not for some time, because, as we later discovered, he had been telling Pupul all about his life and troubles. She is the kind of person who invites confidences, being both gentle and intelligent. But, knowing Geoffrey, this was one of the most amazing things I have ever seen. Pupul later said, 'He's so sad, he must be a good poet.'

Other friends passed through Delhi. Tevia Abrams stayed with us; so did the Korean poet Peter Hyun. They were like messengers from another world. Tevia observed my lack of occupation, and promised to tell Salas, who sent me a comforting letter and urged me to stay on. I felt like some obscure officer at a remote frontier post, with nobody willing to relieve him. This is not to say that we did not have friends in Delhi: besides Pupul, there were the Beveridges, James and Margaret. James was regarded as one of the best Canadian directors of the documentary; he was a quiet man with a dry sense of humour. One of our neighbours was the painter Jatin Das, who often visited us, and so did Sanjeev Prakash, a young film-maker with a deep social commitment. Most nights the flat was full of people; but I still felt frustrated, powerless to change anything.

In 1975, Mrs Gandhi declared an Emergency situation in India. Opposition politicians were imprisoned or placed under house arrest; some went underground. The prime minister's popularity waned as she adopted these draconian measures. We did not often meet, but when we did she seemed tired and irritable; and Mrs Gandhi's irritation had much the same effect as others people's fury. The Emergency did not much affect us. I was a foreign national and a UN officer. But the mood of the people did not augur well for her Congress party in the next election, and some critics wondered if there would ever be one.

However, the Emergency continued. Meanwhile, I worried from time to time about my mother. It was all very well for my father to entrust her future to my care, but I was in no position to do very much. For one thing, it had become very difficult for me to see her without feeling physical nausea and illness. It was not her fault; no doctor could explain it. It was psychosomatic, an accumulation of the effects of memory. What she had done to my childhood was something I tried to forget; but it expressed itself physically. It even made me ill when I saw her handwriting, and writing to her was a tremendous effort. Objectively, I felt great grief and pity for her; she was so utterly alone. Subjectively, I could not control my physical reaction. I did not travel to Bombay to visit her, as I might well have done; Leela wrote her regular letters, but it was contact with me that my mother wanted, needed, and did not ever receive.

Towards 1976, she suddenly left the 'hotel' which stood on her brother's land. She had lived in this place for something like fifteen years. She now went to stay, uninvited, with her sister. The sister's husband had a nervous breakdown, and my mother was asked to leave. Her brother refused to have her. She would not return to her old hotel since she said the waiters were trying to poison her. Instead, she moved into another, near the earlier one. I learnt about all this through increasingly frantic messages from my uncle. Finally he telephoned to say that the manager of the new hotel had called him. My mother had locked herself in her room, and had not, apparently, eaten or drunk anything for a week. She would not open the door to her relatives, and said that she would never open it unless and until Leela and I came. So we flew to Bombay.

The situation was now impossible. Neither her sister nor her brother could keep her; I could not face the prospect of her continual physical presence in my life. It was very unlikely that any hotel would put up with her. There are no such places as old people's homes in India; even if there had been, they would not have taken people in her condition. The only option was to do what had been forced upon my father many years back: to commit her to a mental home. I approached the National Institute of Mental Health and Neurosciences, NIMHANS, where she had, for some years, lived in a cottage under special care. They agreed to accept her if she was properly certified. I engaged a medical doctor and a lawyer and went to her hotel. I wanted to leave Leela behind, but she insisted that she must come. The hotel was small and, though new, had an aura of decrepitude. The manager handed me an enormous bill. He also said that my mother was in the habit of presenting the waiters with large sums of money. 'This is bad for the morale of the waiters,' he said austerely. 'Also, this development is bad for *my* morale. This is a new hotel. I don't want anyone dying here, even though,' he added in a courteous aside to me, 'it is your mother.'

We knocked on the door, and called through it. There was no reply for a while. Then a feeble voice answered, 'Who are all those other people? I won't let them in.' Leela pleaded, but there was no further reply. I said to the manager, 'Don't you have a pass-key?' Inexplicably, he didn't, but uttered a scream of anguish when we broke the door down. My mother lay on a bed, incredibly emaciated, her face like a death mask in wax. She was too weak to resist the doctor when he injected her with a sedative. We carried her down to the car. She was as light as a dead bird. The manager asked me for the bill back. 'I must put down the cost of the door,' he explained.

My mother was taken to hospital and put on a drip. When she was physically better a psychiatrist came to see her. He came several times, and finally said, 'There seems to be no option but NIMHANS.' Bangalore was a two-hour flight to the south. After some negotiations with Indian Airlines, they agreed to fly her, though it was against their policy to accept mental patients. They stipulated that she would have to travel on a stretcher, accompanied not only by us, but by a qualified doctor. They also stipulated that we would have to buy six seats, to accommodate us and the stretcher.

Leela, it must be said, dealt with nearly all of this. On the day of departure, the doctor who was to accompany us came to the hospital. My mother was injected with pethedine, put on the stretcher, and strapped in. We then drove to the airport, where the Bangalore plane was four hours late. The Indian Airlines officer suggested that we get my mother on board ahead of the other passengers.

When the flight was called, a van took us out to the aircraft. As we carried the stretcher up the ramp, my mother woke up. Once onboard, the doctor gave her a second shot of pethedine. The other passengers came on, eyeing us suspiciously; we waited in the cabin for half an hour. It got stiflingly hot. Sweat ran into my eyes as Leela and I sat by the figure on the stretcher, each patting a limp, cold hand.

The pilot then came back and said that this plane was unfit to fly. Would we therefore change to a standby aircraft? We managed to do this, stretcher and all. My mother woke up again. The doctor said, 'I have given her enough pethedine to put a horse to sleep. I cannot risk any more.' The plane took off; all the way to Bangalore Leela sat on the cabin floor beside the stretcher, soothing my mother. Just before we landed, a violent electrical storm broke out, like the one in Zaire. The whole plane was tossed about, shaken in every seam. 'My God,' said the doctor. 'I will have to risk another shot.'

The only thing that had so far gone according to plan was that an ambulance was waiting on the runway. Efficient nurses carried the stretcher into it. We also got in and drove off to NIMHANS. My mother was deeply asleep, like an exhausted child.

This was not the end of it. The doctor at NIMHANS, smiling like a hotel manager at a cherished guest, said, 'We are preparing the same cottage that she had before. But, alas, it is not yet prepared. Meanwhile, we will put her in a small room near the office.' Down the corridor was a large, barred dormitory full of patients who, according to the hospital doctor, tended to be violent. We left my mother asleep. When we returned at dawn, we found her standing outside the barred cell, apparently lecturing its inmates for having woken her up with their noise. The cottage was shortly ready for occupancy, and she was moved into it. She invited us to come to tea.

I couldn't really understand how she, Leela, or I had survived the past day and night. I myself felt guilty, as usual. I had approached the task of taking my mother to NIMHANS as I would have done a work assignment: something that had to be done as efficiently and as well as I could. Almost everything possible had gone wrong, though even I accepted that this was not my fault. But in the end, I had done very little of the hard work. This had mostly been done by Leela. All through this exercise, I had had my usual feelings of revulsion and nausea. I had also felt angry; my mother had messed up my childhood and adolescence, or so I felt, and was now successfully messing up my adult life. What annoyed me most was not being able to suppress this feeling, which was as irrational as any of my mother's attitudes. Like her, I couldn't help it.

Eventually we left Bangalore for Delhi. On the advice of the doctors, I didn't tell her of our departure. In Delhi a stream of letters from her arrived. She was arranging her cottage, she said, so that it would be ready when we came to live with her. One fortunate point about all this was that she greatly approved of my choice of wife. She had been friendly with Leela's parents, and had known her as my childhood playmate. She also thought that Leela had reputable ancestors; on her French mother's side, my mother declared, she was descended from both Marie Antoinette and Joan of Arc. Later I had to fly back to Bangalore to settle my mother's estate. During these trips, which I undertook with my Bombay lawyer and without Leela, I usually felt very ill. The doctors told me that my mother was a burnt-out case. 'We cannot treat her now,' they said. 'She is already old.'

The next few months in Delhi were full of turmoil. Sanjay Gandhi, the prime minister's younger son, had been put in charge of birth control in the north. Forcible sterilizations, it was alleged, were carried out by his minions. The sterilization vans, which had an inbuilt operating room, were dreaded by the poor people. We were once in a cinema when somebody spread the rumour that the vans were parked outside. Most of the male audience immediately rushed for the exits to escape. A friend of mine, the deaf artist, Satish Gujral—whose brother had been the information minister, but had now resigned from Mrs Gandhi's cabinet and party—told me that the new Janata Party was bound to win the elections, should there be any. In the midst of all this, I flew alone, twice, to New York, to see Salas and Tarzie. I was fairly discontented with Delhi.

But Salas and Tarzie both seemed to feel that I should stay on there, and report on the new developments vis-à-vis the population. Sanjay's exploits were already well-known to the UNFPA, which didn't approve of them. 'Speak to Karan Singh,' Salas said. 'Report his views.' Karan Singh, a poet and writer, and the former ruler of Kashmir, was, at this time, the family planning minister. I knew him, he was a pleasant and civilized man; but the idea of spending weeks filing reports on his reactions was not very challenging. On these trips I made stopovers in London to see Francis, who was growing well and had shown some talent as a child actor. I also met a number of old friends, and drank with them in pubs I had once regarded as second homes. They all said more or less the same thing.

'You're a writer,' they said. 'Write. You're turning into a bloody bureaucrat.' I privately agreed with this assessment, but attempted to defend myself. I had written *A Matter of People,* I said. I had edited *Voices for Life.* They were unimpressed. Several of them suggested that I resign from UNFPA 'before it's too late'. I thought so myself. But, if I was in a rut, it was a financially profitable rut. My friends told me all they did because they were anxious that I preserve myself as a poet. They did not know that there seemed to be no poet left in me to preserve.

I resigned from the UNFPA at the end of 1976. This meant I had no earnings coming. But I had always relied on my luck to see me through whatever hardships faced me and my immediate dependants. If I felt like someone released from a prison, it was my fault that I had gone in when I did, and I had been richly repaid. Frank Norman and Brendan Behan, both writers and ex-convicts, had told me of their feeling when they were released from prison. Someone had looked after them for years, and now they were left on their own. My prison had done more for me than theirs had for them. I was grateful.

It was unnerving to be, in a professional sense, alone in life. In the meanwhile, other things were breaking up all round me: for example, the structure of India, as it had previously been. Mrs Gandhi had released most of the imprisoned opposition leaders, lifted the clamps on the press, and declared elections for February. I met her at about this time, and she seemed less irritable than she had been during the Emergency, and utterly confident that she would win the mandate of the Indian people.

When the elections happened, they happened in silence. They surged soundlessly around one; for two days the telephone was dead. On the third day the newly released press announced the crushing defeat of the prime minister in her own constituency, and later that of her whole party. I had, at least then, very little interest in Indian politics. But I knew Mrs Gandhi as a person. I thought she was a very interesting person. Six years earlier, when it had been suggested that I write a book about her, the whole idea had collapsed because she had had no time to speak to me as a person, only as a politician.

So a couple of days after the election results had been declared, and it was announced that Mrs Gandhi would have to move out of the prime minister's residence at 1 Safdarjung Road, and also that the new Janata government had sworn to bring her and Sanjay to trial for various misdemeanours, I went to see her, taking Leela with me. The intention was to condole with her over the election result, purely as friends: at the back of my mind there was also the idea that I might write a book about her now that she obviously *would* have time. I didn't for a moment believe that the Janata government would actually bring her, so recently a national heroine, and Nehru's daughter as well, to trial. I also remembered that she had once thought of herself as a Joan of Arc, a person meant to be martyred. Perhaps a trial was what she wanted.

But we went to see her. She was alone in her former residence, except for the security people. Her two grandchildren, Rajiv's children, were playing in the garden beyond the house. Their high, clear voices, as they called to each other, floated to us over the Delhi winter air. All the furniture which belonged to her had been removed to the house where she would be living, at 12 Willingdon Crescent. This belonged to a supporter of hers called Mohammed Yunus. Mrs Gandhi explained all this to us, and said, 'I'm sorry there's nowhere for you to sit down.' The absence of furniture, the solitary person, all reminded me of the last time I had seen my father in this city. I had endeavoured, then, to persuade him not to go into exile.

But I could hardly say the same things to Mrs Gandhi. She *was* in exile, not of her own choice. She looked extremely sad, and Leela burst into tears. It was not so much out of sympathy for Mrs Gandhi's political beliefs as for her situation. Mrs Gandhi said, rather absently, 'Don't cry, Leela, don't cry.' I suddenly decided to bring up the idea of a book once more. When I did, she appeared to be slightly cheered, but said, 'If you didn't do it, I'm sure there would be someone else.' I said I was also sure of that, grinding my teeth slightly. 'Well,' she said, 'that will be all right.'

She had never, as long as I had known her, been very explicit in her statements. I said, 'You'll give me time? You'll help me to get whatever documents I might need?' She nodded. 'Yes,' she said. 'I am finished with politics. I want to retire to a cottage in the mountains, within sound of a river.' She spoke in the clear, rather precise accents of her father: it wasn't an accent that could be placed, being partly Oxbridge and partly Indian, the kind of English that children educated by nuns in convents on the subcontinent speak. I said, 'Are you sure about this?' Laughing as she had done in the past, she asked, 'What do you mean? Of course I'm sure.' And so I felt that, as a writer, I had found something to write about. To write about such a person would be a kind of poetry, After we left her, I telephoned my agent in London. I hadn't availed myself of Curtis Brown's services in about a decade. I was put on to Peter Grose, who was then a senior partner, and told him of the book I wanted to write. He said incredulously, 'You've got *Mrs Gandhi?* My God, hold on a minute, can you come to London?'

I had honestly intended to write a kind of literary study of a woman who had been the daughter of a person generally considered to be the liberator of his country. I had wanted to follow this woman through the death of her mother, the death of a husband, from whom she had been separated by the selfishness of her father, and follow her, finally, into her accession to power and how she had felt then. But Peter Grose, who later became a good friend of mine, didn't know what kind of book I had in mind. He said, 'Marvellous, marvellous.... Come to London, I'll be waiting for you with publishers.'

I flew to London. On the first day, Peter, a strongly built, affable Australian, with a moustache and an interest in gliders, said, 'Okay, I'd better come to Delhi with you to confirm all this. Meanwhile, let's call her up.' We called Mrs Gandhi up. We had to wait some time before she came on the line. I could visualize what was happening; there would be the secretary, in the office on the veranda of 12 Willingdon Crescent, calling a peon; there would be the peon, ambling off to convey a message to Mrs Gandhi. There would be Mrs Gandhi, coming irritably to the phone. Then I heard her voice.

She confirmed that she was willing to assist me in whatever way she could to write her biography. She said she would have plenty of time. She said she was not returning to politics. Peter was delighted. He began to plan his visit to Delhi. And I, myself, suddenly found I was out of my depth. There was something in my mask that had slipped; also something had happened to my identity along the way that had brought me to this book.

Everyone wears some kind of mask, which is expressed in the face he or she presents to the world. A mask of this kind is not difficult to invent. For example, my mask was that of a rather casual person, unperturbed by what was happening around me, known as a poet, experienced in the world, a veteran war correspondent. I could respond to the demands of my mask, and offer its smile, with some confidence, to others. Behind this mask, I thought, lay my identity, which was not to be exposed. It was by keeping the identity, not the mask, that I remained alive. The identity contained all the experiences the mask had, but experienced them differently. A great part of my identity lay in my ability to write poetry, and also in knowing exactly what world I belonged to.

Now that I didn't write poetry, I no longer knew which world I belonged to. This had never been my problem before. I had belonged to England, to the West; my sensibility belonged to it. Did I now? I had visualized a world in which Mrs Gandhi came, with great delay, to answer the telephone, and felt I understood it; equally, I belonged to a world of hurry—contracts quickly signed, assignments executed—of which Peter and, for example, James Cameron, were also members. This was a problem which I was first to confront square-on during the writing of my book on Mrs Gandhi. I was not aware that this was to happen. I was glad to be in London, but went back to India, as often before, full of hope, full of anticipation, my mask on and my identity still unconfirmed.

19

Peter was to follow me to Delhi. Meanwhile, I settled down to a daily routine of interviews with Mrs Gandhi. She was always rather morose. The tic at the corner of her left eye worked convulsively. Her mind seemed on something else. She had assured me that she had retired from politics, and I concluded that this absence of mind came from the absence of politics from her life, and was in the nature of a withdrawal symptom.

I was confirmed in this when, about a fortnight after I started these interviews, I arrived at Willingdon Crescent one day to find the verandah full of white-capped Congressmen. Mrs Gandhi took me into her drawing room. Her face, which in the last few days had become very inexpressive, was alight. 'I'm going back into politics,' she said. 'The country needs me.' I had seldom heard a thinner excuse than this for returning to an addiction. She also said, 'I won't be able to see you as often as I have, and I may have to travel a lot. But there's no reason why you shouldn't travel with my people and me.' I was bitterly disappointed, for I knew what this meant.

It meant that I would have to scramble for time, and the book would be much delayed. But that couldn't be helped now. Peter arrived in Delhi and stayed with us. I took him to see Mrs Gandhi. It was sunset. As we left her house, Peter said, 'When she came through the door, with the light on the white streak in her hair, I swear to God that she looked like a queen wearing a tiara.'

He wasn't usually as impressionable. What Mrs Gandhi said to him was actually very little. She affirmed that she was helping me to write the book. She would give me access to her letters and papers. This was no more than what she had told me before his arrival.

But now other things happened. People from her party suggested that any money I earned from the book should be donated to the party. Mrs Gandhi then wrote Peter a letter saying that she might, in the future, write her autobiography, because of which she could not offer me the full cooperation she had promised. The English and American publishers had settled for very large advances; on hearing of this new development, they cut their offers in half. I found myself getting less and less enthusiastic about the book. But I continued with the interviews, which grew further and further apart.

My intention, when I started the book, had not been to write a political biography, but a study of a remarkable woman, revealing how she had become what she was, in terms of personality rather than worldly achievement. In this I was handicapped because Mrs Gandhi was reluctant to reveal herself as a person. She had not one mask, but a series of them behind which her identity lay, quiveringly sensitive, or so I guessed. She was very unwilling to tell me what she had felt about other people.

As an adolescent she had watched her mother, Kamala, die. She later married Feroze Gandhi, a Parsee, who had helped care for the tubercular Kamala. This was a marriage made purely out of love. But when Nehru asked her to be his housekeeper, after he became prime minister, she allowed it to fall apart, though they had had two sons. Feroze Gandhi died of a heart attack. A few years later, her father also died. I once asked her which of all the deaths in her life had most affected her. I was astonished when she said, 'My husband's,' for they had not lived together for several years before Feroze Gandhi's death. Mrs Gandhi elaborated on this a little. 'My whole life changed,' she said, 'my mental outlook, my physical functions, everything.' I was intrigued by this, and asked why she had agreed to look after her father's household, when she must have known it would affect her marriage badly. 'It was necessary,' she said, and then became vague once more. This phrase, 'it is necessary,' ran through much of her conversation. It was as though her life had been conducted in terms of actions which were necessary, in that they had been virtually forced upon her; or at least she seemed to wish one to think they had. This remark about her husband was the most personal revelation she ever offered me. Once she said, of her two sons, 'Rajiv is a thinker, Sanjay a doer. My father was continually betrayed by people he thought of as friends. In politics, it's better to have people around you who can be trusted. What could be better than members of your own family?' Sanjay had been brought into politics before his elder brother. I formed the impression that she would have preferred Rajiv.

Sanjay and his petite wife, Maneka, who later became an ardent conservationist, often visited us. Maneka ran a magazine, *Surya,* in which I wrote. She was a person of great and passionate convictions, and, at that time, was totally engrossed in defending her mother-in-law. The government was threatening to take Mrs Gandhi to court for various misdeeds, most of which were imaginary. Popular opinion seemed curiously divided about this; Mrs Gandhi still had her followers, and their numbers increased as the government continued to press its cases against her. In contrast with Maneka, Sanjay Gandhi seemed a little cold, not so much interested in the accusations brought against his mother as in those brought against him. He had pale eyes behind his spectacles, and spoke rarely.

In this he was similar to his brother. Rajiv was handsome, but had, then, rather a wooden look, due to shyness. His Italian wife, Sonia, and he sometimes came to our flat. Sonia seemed as wordless as he; but what they both radiated was a kind of niceness; in other circumstances they would have been the pleasant young couple next door. He could remember little about his father, except that he used to make fretwork toys for him and Sanjay. As we grew to know him a little better, he sometimes allowed himself little spurts of confession. He was, at that time, an airline pilot by profession. He said, once, 'Living with my mother isn't really good for the children; the house is always full of politicians.' This, his mother apart, was a category of people he seemed to abhor. 'I'd like to move, to live separately,' he continued. 'But on my salary I can't afford to. Besides, my mother's in trouble. If we moved away, it would look as though there was dissension in the family, and we can't have that now.' He seemed a little embittered by this.

One day Mrs Gandhi's secretary rang me and said, 'Madam is making her first public appearance since the elections. There are floods in West Delhi. She invites you to come with her and watch her talk to the flood victims.' This only meant that I was allowed to follow her cavalcade of Land Rovers in a taxi. It was raining hard, and in the low-lying areas of the capital brown water rose above our hubcaps. The cavalcade stopped in a rippled and pocked sea of brown. Mrs Gandhi stood up in her Land Rover while someone held an umbrella over her. As though in response to some unseen signal, thousands of people started to wade from their villages, through the floods, towards her. They all held up umbrellas against the rain; the waste of water became a field crowded with shiny black mushrooms. It was a most extraordinary spectacle.

Leela and I went with her to Kashmir. I followed her on a trip to Rae Bareli, her old constituency. Everywhere she went she collected people in tens of thousands to watch her, listen to her speak, and applaud her. The government which had replaced hers was following no definite policies, and cracks had begun to show in its infrastructure. She had always, politically, had a great gift for timing her moves; she timed her first public appearances to coincide with the first revelations of frailty in her opponents. One could almost watch public opinion change as she addressed the crowds. The Indian electorate is somewhat sentimental. Because she was perceived as a woman alone, persecuted by men, it regretted having voted her out of power. All this while I worked on the book, sometimes without seeing her for days.

She had her own paranoia. She sometimes came to visit us, and the house was always surrounded by her guards. I thought this excessive, but considering what happened to her in her own house in 1984, I don't now. She also seemed to feel isolated from the world, especially as the government would not allow her to travel. More than once she gave me messages to be passed on by telephone. 'Mine is tapped,' she said. When I told her that mine was too, she said irritably, 'Well, at least you can go personally and tell these people. I can't, you see.' The messages were perfectly innocuous, and mainly refusals of invitations. However, she accepted ours. Once she said that she was dying of boredom and yearned for conversation with what she called 'artists and intellectuals'.

On this occasion, I invited the head of the British Council in India, Denis Gunton, and his wife, and a gifted young Indian poet, Arvind Krishna Mehrotra. Mrs Gandhi, when she arrived, rebuffed all attempts at any kind of conversation. Throughout the evening, she talked to Leela and Mrs Gunton about the high price of figs and other commodities in the Delhi market. I did not know how she knew this. Admirers constantly sent her huge quantities of fruit, almonds, and pistachio nuts, and she quite certainly never visited the bazaars; her cook did that for her, and sometimes Sonia Gandhi.

One morning, Mrs Gandhi told me that her cook had been killed. 'He was Mohammed Yunus' cook,' she said. 'He came with the house. They [her opponents] killed him a few minutes ago on his way to market. I've just heard.' I made inquiries with the police, who said the cook had been killed in a perfectly ordinary traffic accident. The driver of the car that had run him over was under arrest. I told Mrs Gandhi this, but she replied, 'Of course they would say that.' Then, coming back to reality, she said, 'Now I have to find another cook. Your Kishan Chand is very good.' What she meant was obvious. I consulted Kishan Chand. He said he was willing to work for Mrs Gandhi till she found someone else. He added gleefully, 'I will also be able to report on her for your book.'

When she was finally arrested, Kishan Chand reported, 'Rajiv sahib and Sanjay sahib knew that the police were coming. They came into the kitchen carrying files. In the kitchen there is a machine for making spaghetti. Sonia memsahib brought it from Italy. It is a very good machine. They put the files in the machine. When they were all cut up, they put them in baskets and took them into the garden. It is the time that leaves fall, and the gardeners had lighted fires to burn the leaves....'

Mrs Gandhi kept the police waiting for a while. By this time reporters and photographers had collected. Holding out her hands, she invited the police officer in charge to manacle her. Highly embarrassed, he refused to do so. The police drove off with her, hotly pursued by the press, and she was finally lodged in Tihar prison, but very briefly. When she came out, I went to see her. She was radiant. As a child, her great heroine had been Joan of Arc; this arrest had been Mrs Gandhi's martyrdom.

I was totally engrossed in the book; the affairs of the rest of the world passed me by. Mrs Gandhi could be maddening, but she was also the most charismatic person I have ever met. When she was charming, she could make the birds come down from the trees. I thought of myself as a hardened professional—another mask—but she could often make me feel that I was a cavalier riding to rescue her from the stake. She could not conceal her faults very well, an endearing quality. James Cameron came to India with a BBC team to do a piece about Indian politics. She refused to let him interview her, because, she said, the BBC hated her, and always had done. James visited us, laughing as usual, the lines on I his known, loved face creasing as he said, 'Will you get that silly old bitch to do it? After all, I knew her father a long time ago.'

I persuaded her, in the sense that I received one of her less charismatic smiles, and was told that she would answer questions in her own way. What actually happened was that she answered all James' questions with strange asides about how the similarities between Indian costumes and foods, from area to area, demonstrated the cohesion of the country. She should have known that this was palpably not true, which James surely did.

That was, in fact, the last time I ever saw James; he had had an accident while covering the East Pakistan war in 1971, and a pacemaker became part of him for the rest of his life. But I acquired some new friends in Delhi, including the great cricketer, Bishen Singh Bedi. Bishen, when I first met him, had recently come back from a brilliant tour of Australia as captain of the Indian team. He was thickset, turbaned, and bearded; he had large, sparkling eyes, often full of mischief, and had got into a great deal of trouble over the years with the cricket selectors and board members; in fact, with anyone in authority.

He had at this time collided sharply with the authorities of the Northamptonshire cricket team, which he had represented for five years. They had terminated his contract, saying he was a liability to the side. Bishen thought this libellous, and sued them, but didn't succeed. He was also having trouble with his marriage to an Australian girl. They had two children, whom she took back to Australia. In addition to this, his captaincy was being competed for by Sunil Gavaskar, a great batsman, who, ironically, later became another of my friends. In 1978 Bishen went to Pakistan as the Indian captain and main strike bowler, and failed in both capacities. The critics were very hard on him, and, in the Indian season that followed, he lost his captaincy.

Gavaskar took over. Later on, in the series against the West Indies, Bishen lost his place in the Indian side. He was like a brave bull, coming up against his tormentors for charge after hopeless charge. His fitness had suffered, he had lost his zip from the pitch, and he was no longer great in his chosen field, a hard thing to accept. But though he was belligerent when it came to his enemies, he was very gentle with his friends. At one point, when Leela had gone to visit her parents, I fell ill with some form of pleurisy. Bishen dropped in every evening to tell Kishan Chand what soup he should make for me. He would, when I was convalescent, take me to concerts of classical Indian music, of which he was a connoisseur. He said, at some time during this period, 'I think I've lost everything else, so I ought to keep up my friendships.'

At some point he expressed a desire to meet Mrs Gandhi, who, he said, was in the same position that he was. I did not think this very true, since Mrs Gandhi seemed very likely to come back in the next elections, and seemed to depend on her agility of mind rather than of body to get back all that she had recently lost. Anyway, she was very pleased to see him, and told him how she hoped to see him lead the Indian cricket team to further triumphs. This was rubbing salt into the wound; I felt that Mrs Gandhi should have read more of the newspapers than just the editorials and political reports. This would have enabled her to know more about Bishen's predicament.

If this episode demonstrated Mrs Gandhi's lack of tact, she, like Bishen, often spoke of how often she had felt herself betrayed by all her colleagues. Like Bishen, she did not seem to know how often her present supporters betrayed her. There were members of Mrs Gandhi's inner council who had extremely scurrilous remarks to make about her; I was supposed to listen to them under the seal of the confessional. Why all these people chose to make a confidant of me, I never knew. But they all had ambitions, and it was possible that they did not want a biography of Mrs Gandhi to appear which would be wholly favourable to her.

Sooner or later, Mrs Gandhi would find them out, hence the continual reshuffles of advisers which took place when she was in power. The considerable mistrust she had of those around her made them distrust her; they never knew when their heads would roll. Many of those who made derogatory remarks about her also warned me that I would sooner or later fall from favour. Since I was not a Congressman, but a biographer, I took no notice of these predictions; when they came true, I was utterly amazed.

This was when the book was virtually finished, midway through 1979. In a week when Mrs Gandhi was not busy, I made an appointment to see her, and came to Willingdon Crescent in the afternoon, as arranged. Her private secretary, usually very friendly, told me that Madam was asleep. Afternoon siestas were not her style, but I said I would telephone her later. At this the secretary asked me for my address, which he knew perfectly well. Madam, he said, had written me a letter. I pointed out that I was here, and he could hand it over to me. He did, and I read it on the way home.

It said that it had come to her attention that I had filled my book with statements which maligned her younger son, Sanjay, and she would not cooperate with me any further. I was astonished. I had had four copies made of each chapter. One went to Peter Grose and another to Jonathan Cape in London, a third to Little Brown in Boston, and the master copy was locked up in my safe. Nobody in India except Leela had read any of it. Many of the Congressmen I had spoken to thought that the party would do better under Sanjay than under his mother. It was possible that they had told Mrs Gandhi that I had attacked her son in the course of my chapters, but it was surprising that she believed them. I had not attacked Sanjay personally, as she seemed to think, but had said that I didn't approve of many of his actions; I felt that it was something I was entitled to say.

The next time I saw her, she had won the 1980 elections. I went to Willingdon Crescent once more, to congratulate her. Large numbers of people had come for the same purpose. She attended to all of them, till eventually I was the only person, except for her, left in the room. Then, giving me an icy stare, she said, 'I don't have a minute to spare,' and went off. It was a deliberate snub; it fitted into her patterns of behaviour. I was very hurt, but now feel I ought not to have been.

Between the ending of the book and this event, Peter Grose told me in London that *Time/Life* wanted me to write a book about Bombay for their 'Cities of the World' series. The biography being over, I took on this book, finished it reasonably fast, and was asked by *Time/Life* to come back to London to edit the manuscript with their people. Leela and I went together, and lived at Dolphin Square while the editing was completed. The changes made in the text were largely done by *Time/Life*, and I was not very satisfied with them. We saw friends in London; we saw Francis. I also became very conscious that whatever reputation I had made in London was now past history. It would be very difficult for me to start over in the West as a freelance writer. Even if the Mrs Gandhi book was a success, it would tend to identify me as someone now exiled from England. So, indeed, would the Bombay book. The bulk of my previous reputation had been based on my poetry, and now I wasn't writing any. It had now become virtually impossible to return. I was past forty; I was no longer resilient.

But, on the other side of the Atlantic, I had burned my bridges. Having once resigned from the UNFPA, it was not very conceivable that Salas would want me to return. There was not much point in our staying on in Delhi now that the biography was over and my relationship with Mrs Gandhi more or less severed. We went back to Bombay. One problem in the city was the extreme difficulty of finding accommodation. Because of this, we had to stay with Leela's parents. I did not much want to, but there was no option. Then I had the idea of restarting a version of the *Asia Magazine*, in India.

It had been nearly a decade since Dozier, Gale, and I had left the magazine, and during this time it had fallen on bad days. In fact, I understood, it was nearly defunct, and nothing had replaced it. I felt that if a version of it could be started from Bombay, it could go into the same Asian papers it had once covered. There was, by this time, quite competent colour printing in India. Regarding the financing for such a magazine, it seemed to me that a prospective proprietor would be tempted by the thought of earning badly needed foreign exchange. I began to scout about for somebody who might take on the responsibility, but I had very little success. Pandit was now back in India; but he didn't want to be involved once more. His interests were now in Indian politics, and he was strongly opposed, as always, to Mrs Gandhi.

He wanted to fight her, which would leave him little time for publishing. Moreover, he may have thought that the magazine had brought bad luck, and that its resurrection might bring worse. While based in New York, I had been told that John Gale had committed suicide in London. Always, behind John's bluff manner, there had been a hint of a great capacity to feel depressed, but the deaths of friends, especially if they kill themselves, come as a shock. Apart from this, John Koffend, another friend after he returned from Hong Kong to Samoa, had gassed himself to death in his garage. His suicide came as more of a surprise than Gale's; Koffend had always seemed able to manage his life.

After a good deal of looking around, I was approached by Ramnath Goenka, who owned and ran the *Indian Express,* my father's old paper. Goenka was now seventy-eight, an ancient maverick, and an avowed foe of Mrs Gandhi. His newspapers had attacked her fiercely during her period out of power. Now that she was back, he needed to be in her good graces. He had heard that I had written a book about her, with her collaboration, and possibly thought that he could come back to being one of her chosen, through me. He said that my magazine idea was excellent, and that he had colour printing machinery. He omitted to tell me that it didn't work. But he did tell me that it might take a while to get the magazine organized. During this time, he suggested that I edit the Sunday edition of the *Indian Express.* He wanted me on his staff, he said, immediately.

My cousin, Darryl D'Monte, was then the Bombay Editor of the daily paper, and it was through him that I first met Goenka. Actually, I had met him before, in London. He had looked then, exactly as he looked now—squat, bald, and powerful, with a small grey moustache that looked like a blister on his upper lip. He dressed, then as now, in a white kurta and dhoti, like most Marwaris, a class noted as industrialists and moneylenders. In London, Goenka had said that he wanted to improve the standard of English in the *Indian Express,* since, apart from my father, nobody wrote it well. So he wanted to employ several young British reporters as Senior Editors. I asked if my father knew about this. Goenka said he did. I gave a lunch party to which a number of candidates had come, as well as James Cameron. James watched as Goenka talked to the young men, promising them much in the way of salary, accommodation, and perks. When lunch was over, all of them, about half a dozen, had been recruited. 'But,' Goenka said to me later, 'that old man who was there,' he meant James, 'I want to hire him. I will pay him three times what I am paying these boys.' James laughed softly when he heard this, and advised me to phone my father to tell him what was happening. 'I wouldn't take that ruffian Goenka's word about anything,' he said. 'If he says he's told Frank, I'd bet anything he hasn't. All Frank's staff will resign when they hear about this.' Goenka, of course, hadn't told my father, who was furious. Only one of the young men selected ever reached India; he returned miserable, but toughened.

I remembered all this two decades later, when Goenka spoke to me in Bombay. But I accepted his proposal, and next day became the Editor of his Sunday paper. The *Indian Express* was published from about a dozen centres. Goenka himself divided his time between Madras, where he had a house, Delhi, and Bombay, where he lived in a penthouse above the office. He used to ask me to lunch in the penthouse, where the food was vegetarian. The first time I went to this place, he eyed me pensively for a while, then suddenly roared, 'Sack Monto!' I looked at him uncomprehendingly, for I didn't know what he meant. 'I am telling you,' he shouted, 'sack Monto!' He thumped his fist on his knee.

'Why should I sack him?' I asked. 'Anyway, who is he?'

'It is enough that I want you to sack him,' Goenka said. 'And what do you mean, who is he? He is Monto, I am telling you! Monto! Your own cousin, and you don't know him?' He meant Darryl D'Monte, whom I promptly told about this new development. I also pointed out to Goenka that I had no authority to sack Darryl, and wouldn't. For days after this he pointed out to me that I should not allow family considerations to come between me and my duty, which was to sack my cousin. 'You think you are being a gentleman,' he would thunder. 'Gentlemen never become rich. I have only seen one bigger bloody fool than your father, and that is you.' I found this amusing, but he meant it.

He made other peculiar demands. He once invited Leela and me to dinner with him. The only other guests were the chief minister of Maharashtra, A.R. Antulay, and his wife. Antulay was a Muslim—a short, affable man, and a fervent supporter of the Congress party and Mrs Gandhi. He had so far, in his short tenure as chief minister, made an excellent impression on most people. He had set up a number of trusts which were intended to alleviate the condition of the poor in Bombay. In addition to this, he had begun to issue cement, of which there was a shortage, to industrialists willing to put up factories which would provide employment to unskilled labourers.

I did not know it at the time, but Goenka needed cement for his Delhi office, to which he was adding a new wing. He encouraged me to befriend Antulay. As a matter of fact, I needed no encouragement. I liked the chief minister. Eventually Goenka asked me if we could help Antulay in any way. Antulay said that he would like to meet some industrialists. I invited J.R.D. Tata and several other industrialists to a party in an expensive hotel. They were anxious to meet the new chief minister. Shortly after this, Goenka asked for a huge amount of cement, and Antulay turned him down. One of the *Express* Editors was then put on to the task of attacking him by alleging that he was corrupt, was mishandling the trusts and profiting from the sale of cement. Antulay was taken to court and his political career ruined. By this time I had ceased to be in Goenka's employment.

This came about by subtle stages. Goenka at first pampered me like a favoured son. The ways in which I started to annoy him then multiplied. Antulay's refusal to supply him with cement enraged him; so did my constant inquiries as to when he proposed to start the promised magazine. I realized, later than I should have, that he had no intention of starting it at all. He had thought at the beginning that, as the biographer of Mrs Gandhi, I would have some pull with her, and with her government; that was why he employed me. When he found he had been mistaken, it angered him. He didn't like being mistaken. Our relations became more and more strained, till, at last, I resigned.

Meanwhile the Mrs Gandhi book had appeared. It was well reviewed, by and large, in the Indian press, which now wanted to be reconciled with her. In England and the USA the critics seemed to feel that the book praised the prime minister too highly. In India they said that I was too critical of her. In Delhi I went to her house to present her with a copy. A large number of Congress MPs stood on the veranda; it was early in the day, and at this time they usually came to her with petitions and complaints. They obviously felt, like Goenka, that I was in her good books; they surrounded me, passing the biography from hand to hand, and saying how pleased she would be with it.

Then she came out on to the verandah. I offered her the book. She said abruptly, 'I don't want to read it.' She went on, 'You have misrepresented me. Many people have told me so.' I replied that this was strange, since the book was not yet on sale; what I had was an advance copy. Whether she wanted to read it or not was beside the point; she might like to have it for reference. She snapped back angrily, 'I don't even want to touch it.' Then she swept into her car and was driven off. I stood with the book in my hand, feeling absurd. The MPs studiously avoided looking at me.

After Goenka and I parted company, I was approached by Sudeep Banerjee, who was at that time the information officer for the state of Madhya Pradesh. This state is the largest in India, and occupies much of the central part of the country. It also has the highest percentage of tribal people in India. My childhood friend, Verrier Elwin, had worked with the tribes, and written several books about them. Verrier was now dead, but I had read his books, and remembered much of what he had told me about his experiences.

When Sudeep Banerjee asked me to write a book about the state, I agreed. Sudeep was of Bengali origins, but his family had been settled in Madhya Pradesh for some years. He wrote poetry in Hindi. He was a quiet man with a dry sense of humour, and we quickly became friends. Leela's mother, at this time, was suspected to be suffering from cancer. So Leela stayed behind in Bombay, and I went to Bhopal, the state capital. Here I was told that a government officer would accompany me through the state. This was P.S. Dhagat.

Dhagat was in his fifties. He had a kindly face and a soft, whispery voice; physically he was sturdy, but slightly clumsy in his movements. This impression was underlined by his attire, which always seemed too large and loose for him. Sudeep had been newly appointed to the information office, and, as he later told me, he did not yet know much about his staff. He had felt that

Dhagat was the one officer who could be spared for me, because he had the impression that Dhagat was incompetent. Dhagat, a photographer, and I set off on a trip which eventually took up something like 30,000 kilometres.

I quickly found out that his incompetence was a kind of mask. He was very gentle and shy. Because he was so excessively unmilitary, I called him the General. He addressed me as Dom Sahib. At first I was slightly irritated by what seemed to be his slowness and his fussiness. One night, in a village, it was too hot to sleep. I went out on the verandah of the circuit house where we were staying, and found him standing, ghostly, dressed in white, under a garden tree. When I approached him, he held up a twig and said, 'Do you see this? Dom Sahib, this is the product of the silkworm.' His stubby fingers delicately parted a bud of silk. 'Is it not beautiful?' he asked. I looked at him with new eyes.

After that he taught me all sorts of things about Madhya Pradesh. He took me around the predominantly tribal area of Bastar, and told me about the habits of the tribals. He had extraordinary friends around the state, and, appeared, at one time or another, to have lived all over it. Once, in some remote area, he led me to an old house in which there was a collection of tribal artefacts. It was a large and varied collection, though in a terrible mess. 'I have not been here for some years,' said the General. But, very impressed with the nature of the museum, I asked him who had founded it.

He was a little reluctant to answer, but finally coughed behind his hand and said, 'I did.' In Gwalior he introduced me to a businessman who spent his spare time travelling through tribal areas and acquiring specimens of tribal sculpture. He had a huge assembly of specimens, which he kept in cartons and boxes all over his house. The General had known him and his hobby for years, but nobody else did. After I had written and published my book, his collection became famous; but it was all due to the General. When I told Sudeep about the range and depth of

Dhagat's knowledge, he was astonished. 'Why didn't he tell me?' Sudeep asked. The General was too shy to promote himself in this way. But he was a man of great perception and even passion.

For example, there were other matters that cropped up during all the months we spent in the state. I had decided to write about Verrier Elwin's activities, and we went to a hilltop in a tribal area called Patangarh, where Verrier and a friend and assistant, Shamrao Hivale, had lived with their wives. Verrier had first married a girl, Kosi, of the Pardhan tribe; they had later divorced. But, while they lived at Patangarh, Verrier and Shamrao had run a school and a dispensary, and tried to protect the tribals from harassment by the police and local moneylenders.

The General had started to show me various aspects of India which I hadn't known of. In my youth, I had felt desperate in India, because of its very obvious limitations; I had felt that I would be happy in England. England had ended badly for me; back in India thirty years later, I had suffered what I considered to be betrayals by Mrs Gandhi and Goenka. I once more felt trapped by the country. But in Madhya Pradesh, which is the Indian heartland, with the General playing the role of Virgil, I had made new discoveries, not only about the country, but myself. When we saw the deserted hilltop at Patangarh, I said to the General that I felt Verrier's work here should be continued.

To my surprise, he took this very seriously. He set about measuring the available area for a school and dispensary, and working out all we might need. From then onward, this was an obsession with him; years after our trip he was still talking about it. In the meantime, in Jabalpur, I wanted to find Verrier's son, Jawaharial, usually known as Kumar; I had been told that he now lived there. When Kumar was a small boy, and Verrier was wifeless, he had been sent to school in Bombay, where I had looked after him. I was only about five years Kumar's senior, but considered myself adult. He was certainly a child—noisy, lively, and fond of sport. After Verrier's death, he had come to Jabalpur to look after his mother. The General found him there; he was in terrible shape. He was now almost forty, emaciated and haggard. He had hardly any money, but had to support his mother, Kosi, his own wife, and two of his wife's relatives. I was horrified; my remembrance of Kumar was of a happy child; and the General was even more affected.

It was he who urged me to write to the state government. Since Verrier Elwin had delivered to the tribal people great services, the General said, the government should give his widow and son a pension. It took a month for the government to do this, and by that time we had moved northward; here we received a telegram saying that Kumar had died in Jabalpur, of malnutrition and a burst ulcer. I was very upset. The General actually wept.

The Chambal Valley in Madhya Pradesh has a long tradition of dacoity. Not only are there family feuds, as in Sicily, but a history of oppression by landlords and moneylenders. The Chambal river is surrounded by deeply cut ravines, which provide ideal cover to the bandits; they are normally protected by the local people, though whether this is due to sympathy or intimidation is not clear. Gwalior is the nearest city to the Chambal Valley. In the courtyard of the police station there, we met a boy of about nineteen, chained in a cell. Small boys pelted him with stones through the window. His name was Lachchi Ram; he was a dacoit, and had surrendered that day.

'He does not know what he is doing,' said the police superintendent we talked to. 'He was with Malkhan Singh's people—they are very ferocious dacoits—and he says that in his own village he had killed a man. For that he will hang. But he does not know that yet. He needs somebody to help him, but nobody will help him.' I caught the General's eye, in which a sudden light of solicitude had kindled. I asked if we could talk to the boy. The SP was a sympathetic man; he had Lachchi brought to us.

A land dispute had taken place in his village. A landlord called Wali Mohammed had swindled Lachchi's father out of some property. The landlord had then, after the father's death, tried to take the remainder of the land. Lachchi had beaten him up severely, left him for dead, and fled, in the traditional manner, to become a professional bandit. After six months with the notorious Malkhan Singh, his mother had sent him a message, urging him to surrender. He had done this. Now he waited for what would come next; he was a big, strong boy, and very frightened by what that would be. After this meeting, I told the General I thought Lachchi rather dumb.

'No matter,' said the General, 'we must help him, Dom Sahib.' He added, defensively, 'I do not think him stupid, only simple. And if he is stupid, what matter of that?'

Some extraordinary months then began. We hired a lawyer to represent Lachchi. We visited his remote and dusty village and met his mother. The village people we talked to all spoke a kind of dialect, which not even the General could fully understand. They said that Lachchi was a good, quiet boy, and had not used violence except under extreme provocation. After this we visited Lachchi in various prisons, when we were anywhere near the Chambal. From time to time I went back to Bombay to see Leela. Her mother's condition had not improved; it was confirmed that she had cancer. Lachchi remained in the Chambal, in chains; when I was in Bombay the General looked after the case.

In the middle of the monsoon we were told that he would come up for trial at a place called Bhind, the next day. We drove through flood and rain for twenty hours from Bhopal. Midway through the trip, our back axle broke; but we got to Bhind an hour before the trial, and were there when he was brought to court in chains. There were a number of defence witnesses, but, rather strangely, none for the prosecution.

The reason for this emerged rather late in the day, when a witness was produced who pointed out that Wali Mohammed, for whose murder Lachchi was being tried, was not dead. He had simply moved to another village, finding himself unpopular in his former abode. The judge discharged Lachchi on the spot. We took him back to Bhopal, where he is now the chief peon with the information office, and happily married.

The General said to me afterwards. 'It was very foolish, Dom Sahib. I think the villagers were telling us Wali Mohammed was not dead, but I could not understand. But I think we have both done a good deal. If we had not fought the case, Lachchi would have been hanged. We have at least saved a human life, is it not so?'

Leela's mother died in hospital. I brought Leela to Bhopal for a rest. Then we flew back to Bombay. The book was finished. We were seen off by Sudeep, the General, and Lachchi, all looking very well.

20

I came back to Bombay from Madhya Pradesh in early 1982, not knowing exactly what I would do next. Leela had been appointed editor of a magazine, and was away most of the day. During this time I wandered around the city. I visited scantily stocked bookshops; I walked by the polluted sea. I did this one afternoon, when the tide was low; there were beached boats on the wet sand, and, across the shimmery, gauzelike water beyond, a single island lay, with a look of solitude. There was nobody about. A peculiar shiver ran down my spine, and at first I thought I must be ill. Then I recognized my own symptoms. I had not felt like this for seventeen years.

Certain words and phrases came to my mind. I went home, sat down, and began to write a poem; it was about what it would be like if everything in the world was dead. As I worked, I felt pure power coming out of me. I was concentrated to such an extent that the world around me did, in fact, seem dead: there was only me left, and my writing hand. It was a sensation I had forgotten, slightly unpleasant, but simultaneously exceptionally exciting. After about four hours, I could not continue any more. I followed an old habit, and put what I had written aside for some days.

During these days I worried; what if, when I went back to the poem, it was no longer there, was no longer as good as I had thought while at work on it? When I returned to my notebook, the two days being up, I found it was still there, and I could see some of what needed to be done. I continued to work on it. It was protean, taking on different shapes as I worked, until at last one strong shape remained.

I typed this out, and called it 'Absences'. It was the first poetry I had written in seventeen years which I felt was poetry. It was like nothing I had previously written, but, partly because of that, I felt once more what Cecil Day Lewis called 'The poet's inward pride. The certainty of power.' This only lasted a day or two; then I began to feel a peculiar uncertainty about my power. Suppose this was a one-off thing, and would not recur? One thing I had learnt in the last seventeen years was not to force it. When I had tried to do so, in those years, the result was dead, so dead that I felt even more grief over it than if I hadn't tried to write at all.

About a week after I finished 'Absences', Leela and I took our dachshund to the racecourse for a walk. It was nearly sunset, and I thought of poets, isolated, studying the onset of darkness. I fell completely silent, and lines started to move in my head. When we went home, I wrote another poem, called 'Visitors'. From then on I was confident. Even when poetry did not present itself to me, I was patient. At these times I dug out bits and pieces of old attempts and worked on them, trying to recapture a mood. After about a year, I had about a dozen pieces of work ready.

At this time I began to meet young people, most of whom worked on Leela's magazine, *Keynote*. One of them was tall, bespectacled, and had literary ambitions. David Davidar suggested that I should bring out a small book, privately printed, simply to see how the poems looked in print. This seemed to me an excellent idea. David introduced me to a typographical expert, Anil Madnani. I felt that, if I was paying for the booklet, it should look as good as possible. Madnani sympathized and advised. Presently the booklet was ready, in an edition of five hundred copies. I called it *Absences*. The title poem, I thought, was the best. Perhaps I should quote it here. I feel a tremendous pride in it still, not because of its quality, but because it was the precursor of a great deal of new poetry in the years to come, a John the Baptist.

Absences

Smear out the last star.
No lights from the islands
Or hills. In the great square
The prolonged vowel of silence
Makes itself plainly heard
Round the ghost of a headland
Clouds, leaves, shreds of bird
Eddy, hindering the wind.

No vigils left to keep.
No enemies left to slaughter.
The rough roofs of the slopes,
Loosely thatched with splayed water,
Only shelter microliths and fossils.
Unwatched, the rainbows build
On the architraves of hills.
No wounds left to be healed.

Nobody left to be beautiful.
No polyp admiral to sip
Blood and whisky from a skull
While fingering his warships.
Terrible relics, by tiderace
Untouched, the stromalites breathe.
Bubbles plop on the surface,
Disturbing the balance of death.

No sound would be heard if
So much silence was not heard.
Clouds scuff like sheep on the cliff.

The echoes of stones are restored.
No longer any foreshore
Or any abyss, this
World only held together
By its variety of absences.

The ability to write poetry once more intoxicated me; even though *Absences* was so small a book, I sent copies out for review to some of the Indian papers, and to friends in England, and the response was remarkable. This emboldened me to write to several people in both England and America, asking about the possibilities of creative writing posts in the West. The universities I formally applied to all turned me down; my friends wrote to say that it was impossible to subsist on the salaries I would be paid as an academic. I wasn't exactly discouraged. I felt the time had come for me to determine my future course of action once for all.

I started to write, occasionally, for the Indian papers. In comparison to what I had once earned in the West, the fees I was paid were ridiculous. But they were the highest in India, and went much further in Bombay than they would have done in London or New York. It also occurred to me that I had travelled, perhaps, as much as I wanted. Not only would it be difficult to return to places once familiar to me, now greatly changed; but after fretting for the best part of twenty years about not being able to write poetry, shifting my abode once more might be a mistake now that the gift had returned. I resolved to try and make the best of where I was.

In 1984, I returned to Bhopal, in order to do another story about the tribals in the Mandla district. Sudeep made arrangements for me to be driven there. The question now arose as to who was to accompany me as an interpreter. The obvious choice was the General; but Sudeep told me that the General, who had always had heart trouble, was now suffering rather badly from it. I went to the General's for dinner, and met Lachchi, who looked, and was doing, well. 'He is like a son to us,' Mrs Dhagat told me.

The General was rather gloomy on this occasion. After dinner he walked back to the circuit house. 'What is this I hear, Dom Sahib?' he said. 'Lachchi has told me that Mr Banerjee is arranging a car for you to visit Mandla, and someone else is to accompany you.' I said that was true. 'Why not myself?' he asked, worried. 'Ah, I know! You have been told I have a cardiac problem, is it not? What matter of that? We have been so many thousands of miles together, we have done so many things together. This may be the last time we travel together. Do you not understand how I feel about being left behind?' I said, cravenly, that it was entirely up to Sudeep to choose who went with me. It was only a short trip, I added, and Sudeep probably couldn't do without him in Bhopal.

'That is not true,' said the General without rancour. 'If you say you want me, he will agree. If I have a small heart problem, what of that? I will feel worse if I am left behind.' I was forced to agree that he should accompany me, and the next day we left. It was a drive of several hours to Mandla, a remote area of thick forests and tribals. In fact, though we started in the early morning, we didn't arrive till well after dark. During the first part of the trip, the General frequently stopped the car so that I could inspect particular aspects of the forest. The second part was on largely unmade roads, and he became rather silent. In pitch darkness, we reached a village called Dindori, which was to be our night stop. There was a small dak bungalow there.

The cook, aroused from sleep, showed us to the only two beds. The General, quite uncharacteristically, threw himself down on one of them. Presently, he said, 'Dom Sahib, please look in the pocket of my briefcase. The top left-hand pocket. There are some pills there. Will you give them to me; also a glass of water?' It was the first time in our entire friendship that he had asked me to do something for him. He was usually busy doing things for me. I was alarmed. I looked for the pills. They were not where he had said they were. I ransacked the briefcase, his only luggage. I could find no pills. The General was breathing stertorously. He wrote down the name of the pills and then collapsed. I awoke the driver. All the village lights were out, and heavily forested hills humped round us in darkness. The driver said in dismay, 'Sahib, where will we find this medicine in this place? There is no doctor here.'

I suggested that I should stay with the General, while he went to the nearest town and found a doctor. 'Sahib,' he replied, 'I am only a small man. How can I deal with such matters?' I agreed that he might find things difficult if he went by himself. But I can't drive, and we seemed at an impasse. I took another look at the General, who appeared now to be in a coma. I decided to telephone Sudeep in Bhopal for advice. But, so far as the dak bungalow cook knew, there was only one telephone in Dindori, and that was with the policeman, who lived down the hillside.

I went to the policeman. By the light of a kerosene lamp, I used his telephone. It took nearly four hours, on this antiquated instrument, to raise Bhopal. The cook and driver were, meanwhile, keeping watch over the General. At about three in the morning, I woke Sudeep. We had a Land Rover with us; I didn't think I could move the General in that.

'No, don't try that,' Sudeep said. 'Jabalpur is the closest town to you. I'll get them to send a proper car for you, with a doctor in it. No ambulance will be able to come uphill to Dindori. Simply wait there till the car reaches you. It might take quite a while.' I brooded over the General in the dak bungalow. He bubbled slightly at the corners of the mouth; his skin was damp to the touch, and bluish. I have seldom felt so utterly helpless in my life; I also felt tremendously guilty.

Dawn came with a trumpet blast of colour and sound, with every bird and beast in the surrounding forest crying out for the day, and red and yellow spread over the green hills. The General, who loved nature, lay in his cot in the dingy room, only half alive. Sometimes his breath seemed to fade away for long seconds. The cook and I took turns at rubbing his chest, which rose and fell very slightly. He made a snoring sound. The driver, meanwhile, showed great initiative. He drove to a nearby village and found a sort of paramedic, whom he brought back with him. 'All I have for heart trouble,' the paramedic said, 'is this pill.' He was a literal man: he had only one pill in his pocket. 'But I do not know,' he said, 'if this is suitable for the present case. If *you* think it is, I will administer it.' I didn't dare allow him to do that; I was guilty enough without permitting him to feed the General a pill whose powers neither of us knew.

Towards noon a government car ploughed up to the bungalow amidst clouds of yellow dust. A doctor emerged and took charge, first handing me a bottle of brandy. 'Mr Banerjee,' he said, 'thought you might need this.' Then, having had a look at the General, he said with some alarm, 'We must get him to Jabalpur at the earliest.'

Jabalpur was about four hours away, down an awful, potholed road. At last we were able to put the General, now semiconscious, into a hospital. It had been some twenty hours since his attack. The doctors assured me there was nothing I could do. I went to the circuit house and opened the brandy. Sudeep phoned me up. 'Mrs Dhagat and the children are on their way to Jabalpur,' he said. 'As soon as they arrive, come back to Bhopal.' Next day I was back in the state capital, and Sudeep put me into a government guest house, with a garden full of flowers and dragonflies, by a lake over which birds flew. In the afternoon Sudeep phoned and said, 'Dom, I am very sorry. The General died an hour ago.' I could not believe it; then I remembered how he had looked when I last saw him. I consoled myself by looking at the living things around the lake. It was only after I had flown back to Bombay and Leela that I shed any tears for my friend.

The General, strange to say, was my deepest connection to Indian life. He had introduced me to an India I had not known, and in death as in life he made me understand the country. I was somewhat reconciled, through him, to living in it. I now turned my attention to earning a living. The Indian press employs a huge number of columnists. I began to write columns in five different newspapers every week. They paid very well by Indian standards; Leela and I were able to live fairly well. She had not acted in a film since our marriage; she now took the main part in a film called *Trikal*, produced and directed by Shyam Benegal, a well-known Indian cineaste. The magazine she had edited was defunct, largely due to the aberrations of its proprietor. The film was shot in Goa; I went there to be with her. I was glad that both she and I had returned to our original vocations. I wrote a good deal of poetry during the shooting of the film; I suddenly realized that I had nearly enough for another book. But I had no publisher in view. If I approached anyone, it would have to be as if with a first book; I was not humble enough to do that. I had a desultory correspondence with Michael Schmidt of Carcanet Press; he said I had far too few poems. This was either an indication that he did not want to publish them, or that I was far behind the times. In the 1950s and 1960s, the number of poems I now had would have been enough for a book. I enveloped myself in depression. I was not as resilient as I had once been. Once I recognized this, a further depression descended, like a cloak of cobwebs and dust.

Meanwhile, the great Indian batsman, Sunil Gavaskar, and his wife, Pammi, approached me. I had known them on and off for some years, and they wanted me to write a biography of Sunil. This involved a great deal of research, and a number of meetings with Gavaskar. He was much easier to deal with than Mrs Gandhi; like her, he had heavy calls on his time, but he did his best, whenever he was in Bombay, to come to our flat and talk. He is a very civilized and intelligent man, and, strangely enough, far more able to express himself than the late prime minister. Once he said that he had to practise at the nets at the Brabourne Stadium, and wouldn't be able to come to the flat. Why didn't I come to the nets? So I went. I suggested to Gavaskar that I should stand behind him as he practised. 'If I miss one,' he said, alarmed, 'you might be badly damaged.'

'Then don't miss any,' I said, and, for the next hour, he didn't.

I was at work on the Gavaskar book, late in 1984, when somebody phoned me up and said, 'Mrs Gandhi is dead. Her guards shot her. Now there are riots all over Delhi.' She had seemed to me born for martyrdom; she had desired it, the bitter chalice which her heroine Joan of Arc had drunk in the Rouen flames. My memories of her were varied, but I was stunned by her death. By this time Sanjay had died in an air crash in Delhi, and Rajiv had been dragged into politics. Mrs Gandhi had been through many deaths before her own. I had urgent matters to attend to; Leela was in Delhi the day Mrs Gandhi died.

I didn't know where she was, exactly. The telephone lines to the capital, on the evening of the assassination, were mostly down. Flights to and from it had been cancelled. However, I managed to book a seat on one of the few surviving flights, but before I could take it she returned, looking very harrowed. She had seen a Sikh rickshaw-driver beaten to death by a Hindu mob, and part of the city on fire. It was at this time that I first realized how potentially dangerous a country India was. Its people were already, to some extent, disaffected, particularly in the Punjab and in Assam, and they were exposed, day by day, to shock after shock. Nehru, the founder of the country, died in bed; but his grandson had died violently, and so had his daughter. The only surviving members of the dynasty were Rajiv and his two children. Soon Rajiv, like his mother, was to be murdered. I felt my own mortality, and, more sharply, that of Leela's. In my mind's third eye, images formed of destitution and desolation. I did not feel that I should expose my wife to what I saw coming; but I seemed to have no options left.

Some months after the assassination, I went to the Punjab. I had made an extensive trip there a few years before, and then it had been disturbed, certainly, but it was nothing like as turbulent as it now was. A friend of mine, Julio Ribeiro, had been put in charge of the police force there. He had recently been wounded in a terrorist attack. His house, in Chandigarh, had tall sandbagged walls around it, barbed wire emplacements, and sentry towers. From this fortress Julio issued his directives; when, as frequently happened, he went into the field, a cloud of guards surrounded him. 'These people, the terrorists, never forgive,' he said. 'Wherever I go now, I'll be in danger.' In 1991, when he was the Indian ambassador to Romania, he was fired upon and wounded by a Sikh terrorist squad. I admired Julio for his stoicism in the Punjab itself, when he was even more naked to his enemies than he was to be in Bucharest.

On this trip, I also interviewed Bimal Kaur. She was the widow of Beant Singh, one of the two security men who actually shot Mrs Gandhi. Nobody seemed to have thought of interviewing her before. I was rather surprised to find her in a spacious new house, attended by servants. She served me tea from expensive china, and was expansive when she told me of how the conspirators had met at their government flat in Delhi to plan Mrs Gandhi's murder. Security policemen in India are not highly paid; when I asked Bimal Kaur how she found herself in this house, she evaded the issue.

It was an interesting interview, but I was taken aback by what happened when it was published. Two plainclothes officers arrived from Delhi. They were employed by the government Research and Analysis Wing, the notorious RAW. They wanted to know why I had visited Bimal Kaur. I said that it should be obvious; she represented a good story, and I wrote for the press. 'But why her?' asked one of the officers. 'Nobody else has interviewed her.' I said this was precisely why. 'There are many other ladies in India,' the officer said. 'Those are respectable ladies. Why not one of them?' His companion asked, 'Did she make any remarks you didn't publish?'

She had made one such remark, I said. But I did not think the government would receive it well. This excited my interrogators greatly. 'You must tell us what it was,' they said. I replied, 'She said that Beant Singh had been in government service,' I told them. 'She asked whether she ought to apply for a government pension.' They did not think this funny; they wanted to see the original of the article, and to search my desk for any notes I might have made at the time of the interview.

The Komic Kops element was very notable at first, but when they kept coming back to ask the same questions, their charm palled. I began to find this insistence that I should meet them every day, rather tiring, and also, in an indefinable way, rather scary. It added to the images of desolation I had about India.

Gradually, over the years, small impressions and fears had collected in my mind, and had formed a picture. This picture reflected itself in some of the poetry I was writing. An Indian critic said I had a nihilistic vision; but it seemed to me that my new situation was nihilistic, not me. It was through David Davidar that the poems were finally published. He had now become publisher of the new Penguin branch in Delhi. David said to me, very sensibly, that it was pointless to try and negotiate with publishers seven thousand miles away. Penguin India would publish my *Collected Poems*, which would not only include bits of the old books, but the fifty-odd new poems I had. This book, anyway, would be distributed in England, and reviewed. So in 1987 my *Collected Poems 1957–1987* appeared.

This was, up to a point, reviewed in England. Stephen Spender and Peter Levi wrote about it in a very flattering way. Apart from a mention in the *Times Literary Supplement*, it otherwise sank without trace. I had expected to be like the kind of poet who Auden described as 'exploding like bombs', on my return to the Western literary scene. When this didn't happen, I got to be somewhat resigned. Then I thought, I should be fairly grateful.

At least I was writing poetry once more, and, I also thought that this was good.

In the same year as the *Collected Poems*, my Gavaskar biography appeared with Macmillan. This was Macmillan India, who didn't distribute it at all in the West; so this book, too, could hardly be called a spectacular success. I wished deeply that John Arlott, for example, could have read it. I had known Arlott fairly well in the 1960s. News from English visitors was that he was very unwell; and also that James Cameron was dead. He had meant a great deal to me; he had started me as a journalist. I did not connect him with death, any more than I connected Stephen Spender, who had helped me as a young poet, with age. Spender and his wife Natasha visited Bombay; he was about to celebrate his eightieth birthday. He told me about the British literary scene, as did other visitors, like Brian Patten, Alan Brownjohn, and Anthony Thwaite.

They acted as bridges to my former life, somewhat necessary bridges, since I had burnt the old ones many years before. What was now happening to me was that young Indian poets came to our flat, apparently to seek my advice about their work. When I had been young, and in London, most of my friends had been older than myself. In fact, I do not think any of the people I knew, except for girlfriends, were ever younger than I was, until I was about twenty-five. Until then, even the girlfriends had been older.

My friends—I mean the male ones—had taught me more about poetry by talking about painting, women, and cricket than I would ever have got had I constantly conversed with them about the art or craft in which we were all involved. I felt that whatever I taught all these young men was more through conversation than from actual criticism. By doing this, I was partly healing myself from not having, for many years, a son of my own. I was also confirming to myself that I was ageing fairly rapidly. I was now in the position, towards these young people, that my mentors of the past had been in to me.

There was also the point of recovering a lost youth, seeing through their eyes. I was able to get David Davidar to publish a book which contained the poems of two of them, Jeet Thayil and Vijay Nambisan. This was a great compensation for lost parts of my life. My general tiredness seemed to vanish in the presence of these various young men, and I was glad that at various points they used to confide in Leela and me their problems with their families, drugs, alcohol, and young women they desired.

Once, during my travels in Madhya Pradesh, the General took me to a place called Amarkantak, which is above a gorge from which the Narmada, one of the sacred rivers of Hinduism, issues rather reluctantly from a moss-walled hole in the rock. From then on the Narmada picks up pace and drops into the plains, coiling away like a soiled snake towards its eventual conclusion in the sea. On top of the gorge there was a small cement hut, where a maharishi lived with several dogs and puppies. They all seemed very attached to one another, happy in their hilltop solitude.

This maharishi was not like the one who influenced the Beatles, or the richer people in the world. He looked exactly like Santa Claus. He was swathed in a woollen robe against the chill of the winter hilltop, he had a white beard, and a very soft, hypnotic voice. He brought me a chair on which to sit, with a 4,000-foot drop to the valley behind me. I felt a great surge of my usual vertigo, though I couldn't see the drop. He said, 'Don't be afraid.' At this moment a smell of English apples came to my nostrils. He murmured on, behind this odour of apples, and caressed the dogs which sat at his feet.

My fear of what I might fall into, were my chair to tip backward a bit, abandoned me. I sat and listened to what he was saying, which was being translated, in the same whispers as the holy man used, by the General. He said that, since he was young, about fifteen, he had started to walk around India, sometimes to as far north as Nepal, sometimes to Kanyakumari, the southernmost tip of the subcontinent. He was now seventy-eight. 'No matter where he travelled,' the General whispered in translation, 'he couldn't find himself. Now that he has settled here, he thinks he has found something else, which is to be desireless. He says to you, do not look for yourself. If you become desireless, nothing will trouble you.' I have seldom heard such a fatuous piece of advice in my life, nor one that influenced me more. I interpreted what he said as something quite different from what he probably meant. If someone could become desireless, I thought this could only be by acquiring enough money in life, so as not to be distressed by the absence of it.

But the smell of apples and spices that surrounded the sadhu, the scuffling of the dogs around his and my feet, the cold darkness around, and the sense, still remaining, of the drop behind me, still conduced to a feeling of myself, somewhere within me, that resisted the effect that all these factors, and also his large, luminous eyes, had. My darkness fought his, but when eventually he went away, I remembered him for years.

Deaths, absences, memories; to be continually reminded by my own responses of my past life, and, because of being in a country of ephemeral sages, being told of my future existence: all of these confused me. I decided to follow my own path, which was possibly, as the supposedly holy men I met told me, predestined: to carry on earning as much as was possible, and to wait for any poetry that there might be around in the air, sometimes full of dust and heat, sometimes of thick polluted rain, and, very infrequently, of winter winds out of the Himalayas. I am now doing this, to the best of my ability.

But to forget the past is impossible, and to have apprehensions of the future—on the whole—undesirable. I had a letter from Francis, whose name was now Heff, a derivative of the Heffalump nickname of his childhood. I do not now have this letter—for I have thrown away most of the letters I have received in my lifetime, and have a certain dread of writing any of my own, for no very good reason—but what it said was something that impressed me deeply. Perhaps 'impressed' is the wrong word; what he wrote, in effect, said that he had seldom met Leela and me since he was a child, and, that, though he knew some of my books, he didn't know about me really, or his history on my side of the family. I didn't know what to say in reply. I wrote a poem about this, which started with the title, the word 'Key'. This key could have been the key to myself; I don't know:

Key

Ground in the Victorian lock, stiff,
With difficulty screwed open,
To admit me to the seven mossed stairs
And the badly kept garden.

Who runs to me in memory
Through flowers destroyed by no love
But the child with brown hair and eyes,
Smudged all over with toffee?

I lick his cheeks;
I bounce him in air.
Two bounces, he disappears.

Fifteen years later, he redescends,
Not as a postponed child, but a letter
Asking me for his father who now possesses
No garden, no house, not even any key.

I sent him this, and a vague kind of letter; I told him about my parents, his grandparents, now dead, whom he had briefly met in his childhood; about as much of the family history as I knew; about as much of myself as I was aware of, at least consciously. Not to my surprise, he didn't reply.

It wasn't a key, either for him or for me, to our pasts. That key, I thought, was lost forever; till he came to spend Christmas with us, in 1991, with his fiancée Nadia. Perhaps this is a key which will turn in the future; at any rate I hope so.

Perhaps I have become desireless, at any rate in so far as determining my desired point of location in the world is concerned. India, after my long presence, punctuated by occasional travel, still seems a foreign country. But England, after a long absence, punctuated by occasional visits, seems equally so. The best thing to do is to preserve some form of balance on the constantly ground tectonic plates of this planet.

While finishing this book, some weeks ago, I gave instructions to the household that I was not to be disturbed. Anyone who telephoned, any visitor, was to be told that I was out, and that nobody knew when I would return. I finished the book, rescinded the orders, and immediately had a telephone call from a friend who had had urgent business to discuss with me over the past few days.

'Where in hell have you been?' he asked. 'I've been phoning you all day for a week. I've even phoned you at night, and they say you're somewhere else, they don't know where. Are you never at home?' This question answered a question in my mind, and gave me the title for this book.

I am waiting to be at home; where, I don't know yet. Sometime in 1976 (it must have been June or July, since it was raining heavily in the southern state of Karnataka), I went to meet a famous local writer called Karanth. He was small, with a white moustache, and very old, but exceptionally lively for his years. In the front room of his house, he awaited me with tea, sweetmeats of many sorts, including Mars bars, and a chalkboard on which various numbers and mathematical equations had been scrawled. 'It is surprising for you that I wanted to meet you,' he said, 'is it not? But apart from being a great writer, I am a student of numerology.' He pointed to the board, and intoned four words once familiar on British television, 'This is your life.'

I expected everyone I had ever known to emerge one by one from the wings: that is, from the kitchen that opened off the room we were in. Nobody did. 'Look at the board,' said Dr Karanth. 'You were born on 19 July 1938. Do you understand what that means? Nineteen, think hard of that number. It is the number with which your whole life is involved. Think of the year 1938. That is a number divisible by nineteen, is it not?' Outside, a small rain was falling, scented by the flowers on which it fell.

This deflected my attention from him for a moment. But, schoolmasterlike, he produced a cane, with the tip of which he rapped the chalkboard. 'In 1957,' he said, 'you won the Hawthornden Prize in Britain. Now tell me, what is 1957 divisible by? By nineteen. And, at that time, you were nineteen years old. Is that not proof enough of your affinity with this number? It is. It is. My good boy, I tell you, it is *proof!*'

I had made some mathematical calculations, and said, 'Dr Karanth, this is 1976, which is also divisible by nineteen. Nothing very remarkable has happened to me this year,' He replied, 'Oh, my dear, my darling boy, but it has. You have met *me*.'